THE
ROYAL AIR FORCE
MANUAL

THE ROYAL AIR FORCE MANUAL

The Aircraft, Equipment and Organization of the RAF

TIM LAMING

ARMS AND ARMOUR

Arms & Armour Press
A Cassell imprint
Villiers House, 41–47 Strand, London WC2N 5JE

Distributed in the USA by Sterling Publishing Co. Inc., 387 Park Avenue South, New York, NY 10016-8810

Distributed in Australia by Capricorn Link (Australia) Pty Ltd, 2/13 Carrington Road, Castle Hill, New South Wales 2154

© Tim Laming, 1994
All rights reserved. No part of this book may be reproduced or transmitted in any form or by any means electronic or mechanical including photocopying recording or any information storage and retrieval system without permission in writing from the Publisher.

British Library Cataloguing-in-Publication data: A catalogue record for this book is available from the British Library.

ISBN 1 85409 190 5

Edited and designed by Roger Chesneau/DAG Publications Ltd

Squadron and station badges by Mike Keep
Aircraft elevations by Terence Wong-Lane
Photographs by the author (except where credited otherwise)

Printed and bound in Great Britain

Title page photograph: A Panavia Tornado GR.1 from No 15(R) Squadron climbs vertically for the camera. (BAe)

CONTENTS

Introduction, 7
Colours and Camouflage, 13

Squadron Directory, 15

No 1 Squadron, 16
No 2 Squadron, 17
No 3 Squadron, 19
No 4 Squadron, 20
No 5 Squadron, 21
No 6 Squadron, 22
No 7 Squadron, 24
No 8 Squadron, 25
No 9 Squadron, 26
No 10 Squadron, 27
No 11 Squadron, 28
No 12 Squadron, 30
No 13 Squadron, 31
No 14 Squadron, 32
Mo 15 Squadron, 33
No 16 Squadron, 34
No 17 Squadron, 35
No 18 Squadron, 37
No 19 Squadron, 38
No 20 Squadron, 39
No 22 Squadron, 40
No 24 Squadron, 41
No 25 Squadron, 43
No 27 Squadron, 43
No 28 Squadron, 44
No 29 Squadron, 45
No 30 Squadron, 46
No 31 Squadron, 47
No 32 Squadron, 48
No 33 Squadron, 49
No 39 Squadron, 50
No 41 Squadron, 51
No 42 Squadron, 52
No 43 Squadron, 53
No 45 Squadron, 54
No 47 Squadron, 55
No 51 Squadron, 56
No 54 Squadron, 57
No 55 Squadron, 58
No 56 Squadron, 59
No 57 Squadron, 61
No 60 Squadron, 61
No 70 Squadron, 62
No 72 Squadron, 63
No 74 Squadron, 63
No 78 Squadron, 64
No 84 Squadron, 65
No 92 Squadron, 66
No 100 Squadron, 67
No 101 Squadron, 68
No 111 Squadron, 69
No 120 Squadron, 70
No 201 Squadron, 70
No 202 Squadron, 71
No 206 Squadron, 72
No 208 Squadron, 73
No 216 Squadron, 74
No 230 Squadron, 74
No 360 Squadron, 75
No 617 Squadron, 76
No 1312 Flight, 77
No 1435 Flight, 77
No 1563 Flight, 77
The Queen's Flight, 78
Northolt Station Flight, 78
Gatow Station Flight, 78
St Athan Station Flight, 79
Sentry Training Squadron, 79
Trinational Tornado Training Establishment, 79
Electronic Warfare & Avionic Unit, 79
Strike/Attack Operational Evaluation Unit, 80
Tornado F.3 Operational Evaluation Unit, 80
Institute of Aviation Medicine, 80
Empire Test Pilots' School, 80
Battle of Britain Memorial Flight, 80
Central Flying School, 81
No 1 Flying Training School, 81
No 2 Flying Training School, 82
No 3 Flying Training School, 82
No 4 Flying Training School, 82
No 6 Flying Training School, 83
No 7 Flying Training School, 83
Joint Elementary Flying Training Squadron, 83
University Air Squadrons, 83
Air Experience Flights, 84
Volunteer Gliding Schools, 85
Non-Flying Units, 86
Non-Aviation-Equipped Units, 87
Royal Air Force Regiment, 89
Royal Auxiliary Air Force, 90
Royal Auxiliary Air Force Regiment, 90
Royal Air Force Volunteer Reserve, 90
Other units, 90

Airfield Directory, 91

RAF Akrotiri, 92
RAF Aldergrove, 92
RAF Barkston Heath, 94
RAF Benson, 94
RAF Brize Norton, 95
RAF Bruggen, 97
RAF Catterick, 98
RAF Chivenor, 98
RAF Church Fenton, 100
RAF Colerne, 100
RAF Coltishall, 100
RAF Coningsby, 101
RAF Cosford, 103
RAF Cottesmore, 104
RAF Cranwell, 105
RAF Finningley, 107
RAF Gibraltar, 108
RAF Halton, 109
RAF Henlow, 109
RAF Honington, 109
RAF Kinloss, 110
RAF Kirknewton, 112
RAF Laarbruch, 112

CONTENTS

RAF Leeming, 113
RAF Leuchars, 115
RAF Linton-on-Ouse, 117
RAF Little Rissington, 118
RAF Lossiemouth, 118
RAF Lyneham, 119
RAF Machrahanish, 121
RAF Manston, 121
RAF Marham, 121
RAF Mount Pleasant, 123
RAF Newton, 123
RAF Northolt, 123
RAF Odiham, 125
RAF St Athan, 126
RAF St Mawgan, 127
RAF Scampton, 128
RAF Sealand, 130
RAF Shawbury, 130
RAF Swanton Morley, 132
RAF Syerston, 132
RAF Ternhill, 132
RAF Topcliffe, 132
RAF Turnhouse, 132
RAF Valley, 132
RAF Waddington, 134
RAF Wattisham, 135
RAF West Raynham, 135
RAF Wethersfield, 135
RAF Wittering, 135
RAF Woodvale, 137
RAF Wyton, 137

Aircraft Directory, 139

BAe 125/Dominie, 140
BAe 146, 142
BAe Andover, 142
BAe Bulldog, 144
BAe Canberra, 145
BAe Harrier, 147
BAe Hawk, 150
BAe Jetstream, 152
BAe Nimrod, 154
BAe VC10, 156
Boeing Chinook, 158
Boeing Sentry, 159
De Havilland Chipmunk, 160
Lockheed Hercules, 161
Lockheed TriStar, 163
Panavia Tornado, 164
Pilatus Britten-Norman Islander, 170
SEPECAT Jaguar, 170
Shorts Tucano, 173
Westland Gazelle, 176
Westland Puma, 176
Westland Sea King, 178
Westland Wessex, 180

Operations Profiles, 183

Tornado F.3, 184
Helicopter Operations, 188
Hercules, 190
Nimrod, 194
Sentry, 197
VC10, TriStar, 199
Jaguar, 203
Tornado GR.1, 209
Harrier, 217
Hawk, 223

Weapons Directory, 229

500lb GP Bomb, 230
1,000lb GP Bomb, 230
ADEN 25mm Cannon, 231
ADEN 30mm Cannon, 231
ALARM, 231
BL.755 Cluster Bomb, 233
Mk 11 Depth Charge, 233
Hades, 233
Harpoon, 233
HB.876, 234
JP.233, 234
Matra 155 SNEB Rocket Pod, 234
Mauser 27mm Cannon, 234
Paveway, 236
Rapier, 236
Sea Eagle, 236
SG.357, 237
AIM-9L Sidewinder, 237
Sky Flash, 237
Stingray, 238
TIALD, 238

Equipment Gallery, 239

RAF Trade Groups, 243

Avionics, 244
Ground Electronic Engineering, 245
General Engineering, 245
Mechanical Transport, 246
Air Traffic Control, 246
Aerospace Systems, 247
Telecommunications, 247
Aircraft Engineering, 248
Photography, 249
Accounting and Secretarial, 250
Supply, 251
Safety and Surface, 251
RAF Police, 252
Gunner, 253
Catering, 253
Medical Trades, 254
Dental, 255
Musician, 256
Fireman, 256
General Service, 256
Movements, 256

INTRODUCTION

It has been but an instant in the history of warfare since the Wright Brothers demonstrated man's mastery of the air in 1903, yet in the succeeding years of the twentieth century the importance of that mastery to a nation's security has grown enormously. For thousands of years, military power had been constrained to operate on the surface of the earth or on the sea, but, released from these bonds, air power has given new freedom and brought new dangers.

Air power is in essence quite different from other forms of military force. It brings an ability to react to any threat at short notice, over enormous distances, and can concentrate firepower in time and space whenever it may be required. Before the beginning of the present century, military forces would take weeks to mobilize and to deploy to a potential trouble area. Once there, the forces could only attack the enemy where they were in contact, and then to a depth of just a few miles using their artillery. Aircraft can react in minutes, cover hundreds of miles over land and sea in a single hour, and deliver destructive power to any part of the enemy's territory. Using the Gulf War as an example, the grave and apparently imminent threat to Saudi Arabia following the Iraqi invasion of Kuwait demanded an immediate response from the rest of the world. The build-up of air power was particularly rapid and proved decisive in deterring further Iraqi aggression and containing the crisis in its early critical stages. Within fifty hours of the British Government's decision to deploy forces, a Tornado F.3 squadron was flying operational sorties from Saudi Arabia, and forty-eight hours later a balanced air force with offensive, defensive and combat support capabilities had been deployed over 3,000 miles from its main bases and brought up to full operational strength. Similar responses from the Allies brought the total number of aircraft in the theatre to

Below: A Hawk and a Hunter from the Empire Test Pilots' School.

INTRODUCTION

Above: A BAe VC10 refuelling a Nimrod MR.2P over the North Sea.

301 by Day 5, 1,220 by Day 35 and 2,430 by the start of the air campaign.

Even from the time of the earliest primitive military aircraft, no nation could feel safe from attack. Aircraft were used to find targets, military or civilian, which could then be attacked from any direction, with massed force concentrated to devastating effect. They could be used to move troops at short notice to wherever they might be needed. Such power carried with it new dangers, however, for what one nation could do to its enemy from the air, so could the enemy reply in kind. Protection from this threat is crucial to the success of any military operation. The force which fails to control its own airspace is the force which is defeated. How can the threat from the air be countered? Primarily by forces which can react quickly wherever and whenever that threat materializes—that is, through air forces. Air power is the essential counter to enemy air power: this is a lesson the Iraqi Air Force learned very much to its cost.

Today, some make the mistake of assuming that, in the age of the nuclear missile, all other forms of weaponry are obsolete. Yet the fear of nuclear war has meant that conventional non-nuclear weapons have continued to be a crucial factor in any nation's military strength. Wars that have been fought since 1945 have employed non-nuclear weapons systems and air power has, time and time again, proved crucial to success.

In NATO, air power has a critical contribution to make to its members' security. Although it may be said that, as a result of the ending of the Cold War, East and West are no longer adversaries, the two sides are not yet partners. Dramatic events have transformed the European security environment over the last few years, but not all the developments have been favourable. We have witnessed the use of force by Soviet military units in the Baltic republics, we have experienced problems with the Soviet Union over the implementation of the Conventional Armed Forces in Europe Treaty, and we have seen the outbreak of war in Yugoslavia and in new republics such as Georgia. The remnants of the Soviet Union retain substantial and sophisticated military capabilities that could pose a formidable challenge at short notice, and, within the framework of the NATO alliance, air power therefore has a vital role to play in deterring unwanted aggression. Air power can provide the timely intelligence to determine a potential aggressor's intentions; it can deploy friendly forces where they are needed; it can defend airspace and bring concentrated force to bear wherever the enemy may have decided to fight the battle; and it can provide rapid resupply and reinforcement. By having a demonstrated capability in all these areas, NATO can continue its strategy of

INTRODUCTION

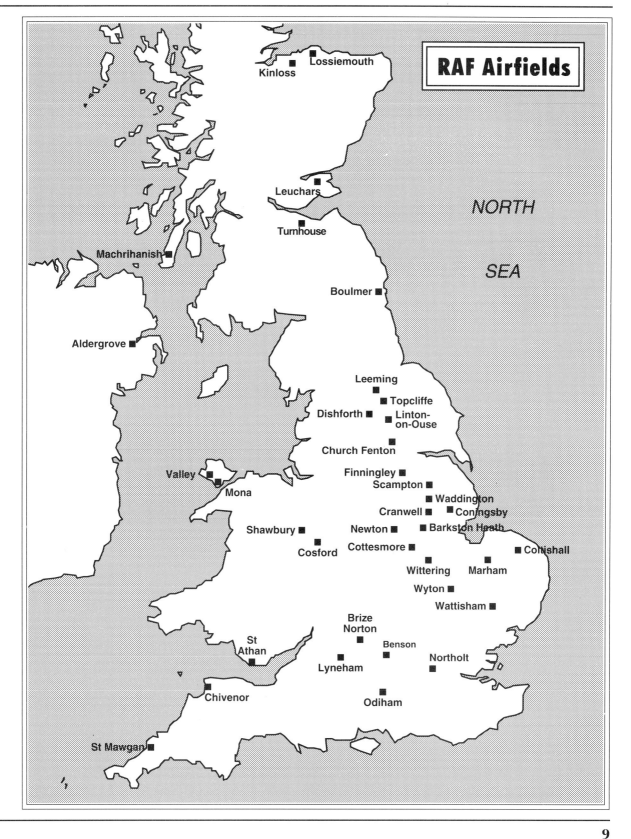

ROYAL AIR FORCE STRENGTH, APRIL 1994

STRIKE/ATTACK
9 Squadron	Bruggen	13 Tornado GR.1
12 Squadron	Lossiemouth	13 Tornado GR.1B
14 Squadron	Bruggen	13 Tornado GR.1
17 Squadron	Bruggen	13 Tornado GR.1
31 Squadron	Bruggen	13 Tornado GR.1
617 Squadron	Lossiemouth	13 Tornado GR.1B

OFFENSIVE SUPPORT
1 Squadron	Wittering	14 Harrier GR.7/T.4
3 Squadron	Laarbruch	13 Harrier GR.7/T.4
4 Squadron	Laarbruch	13 Harrier GR.7/T.4
6 Squadron	Coltishall	14 Jaguar GR.1A/T.2A
54 Squadron	Coltishall	15 Jaguar GR.1A/T.2A

RECONNAISSANCE
2 Squadron	Marham	13 Tornado GR.1A
13 Squadron	Marham	13 Tornado GR.1A
39 Squadron	Marham	7 Canberra PR.9, 3 Canberra T.4, 2 Canberra PR.7
41 Squadron	Coltishall	14 Jaguar GR.1A/T.2A
51 Squadron	Waddington	3 Nimrod R.1/R.1P

MARITIME PATROL
120 Squadron	Kinloss	
201 Squadron	Kinloss	30 Nimrod MR.2P
206 Squadron	Kinloss	

AIR DEFENCE
5 Squadron	Coningsby	13 Tornado F.3
11 Squadron	Leeming	13 Tornado F.3
25 Squadron	Leeming	13 Tornado F.3
29 Squadron	Coningsby	13 Tornado F.3
43 Squadron	Leuchars	16 Tornado F.3
111 Squadron	Leuchars	16 Tornado F.3
1435 Flight	Mount Pleasant	4 Tornado F.3

AIR DEFENCE (RAF REGIMENT)
15 Squadron	Leeming	Rapier
16 Squadron	Honington	Rapier
19 Squadron	Honington	Rapier
20 Squadron	Honington	Rapier
26 Squadron	Laarbruch	Rapier
27 Squadron	Leuchars	Rapier
37 Squadron	Bruggen	Rapier
48 Squadron	Lossiemouth	Rapier
66 Squadron	Honington	Rapier

AIR DEFENCE (ROYAL AUXILIARY AIR FORCE REGIMENT)
1339 Wing	Waddington	Skyguard/Oerlikon
2729 Wing	Waddington	Skyguard/Oerlikon
2890 Wing	Waddington	Skyguard/Oerlikon

AIRBORNE EARLY WARNING
8 Squadron	Waddington	7 Sentry AEW.1

AIRBORNE REFUELLING
10 Squadron	Brize Norton	10 VC10 C.1K
101 Squadron	Brize Norton	9 VC10 K.2/K.3
216 Squadron	Brize Norton	8 TriStar K.1/KC.1/C.2

TARGET FACILITIES
100 Squadron	Finningley	12 Hawk T.1

AIR TRANSPORT
7 Squadron	Odiham	18 Chinook HC.1, 1 Gazelle HT.3
10 Squadron	Brize Norton	10 VC10 C.1K
18 Squadron	Laarbruch	5 Chinook HC.1, 5 Puma HC.1
24 Squadron	Lyneham	13 Hercules C.1P/C.3P
28 Squadron	Sek Kong	Wessex HC.2
30 Squadron	Lyneham	13 Hercules C.1P/C.3P
32 Squadron	Northolt	12 BAe 125, 8 Andover, 4 Gazelle
33 Squadron	Odiham	12 Puma HC.1
47 Squadron	Lyneham	11 Hercules C.1P/C.3P
60 Squadron	Benson	9 Wessex HC.2
70 Squadron	Lyneham	12 Hercules C.1P/C.3P
72 Squadron	Aldergrove	15 Wessex HC.2
78 Squadron	Mount Pleasant	Sea King, Chinook
84 Squadron	Akrotiri	5 Wessex HU.5C
216 Squadron	Brize Norton	8 TriStar K.1/KC.1/C.2
The Queen's Flight	Benson	3 BAe 146 CC.2, 2 Wessex HCC.4
1312 Flight	Mount Pleasant	Hercules C.1P
1563 Flight	Belize Airport	Puma HC.1

SEARCH AND RESCUE
22 Squadron:	St Mawgan	
'A' Flight	Chivenor	2 Sea King HAR.3
'B' Flight	Wattisham	2 Sea King HAR.3
'C' Flight	Valley	2 Wessex HC.2
202 Squadron:		
'A' Flight	Boulmer	2 Sea King HAR.3
'D' Flight	Lossiemouth	2 Sea King HAR.3
'E' Flight	Leconfield	2 Sea King HAR.3

BASIC FLYING TRAINING
1 Flying Training School	Linton-on-Ouse	Tucano T.1
2 Flying Training School	Shawbury	Wessex HC.2, Gazelle HT.3
3 Flying Training School	Cranwell	Tucano T.1

ADVANCED FLYING TRAINING
4 Flying Training School:		
74(R), 208(R) Sqns	Valley	Hawk T.1/T.1A
7 Flying Training School:		
19(R), 92(R) Sqns	Chivenor	Hawk T.1/T.1A
Central Flying School	Scampton	Tucano T.1, Bulldog T.1
	Valley	Hawk T.1/T.1A
	Shawbury	Gazelle HT.3
SAR Training Unit	Valley	Wessex HC.2
Sea King Training Unit	St Mawgan	Sea King HAR.3
RAF Aerobatic Team	Scampton	Hawk T.1A

OPERATIONAL CONVERSION UNITS
15(R) Squadron	Lossiemouth	25 Tornado GR.1
16(R) Squadron	Lossiemouth	10 Jaguar GR.1A/T.2A
20(R) Squadron	Wittering	20 Harrier GR.7/T.4
27(R) Squadron	Odiham	6 Chinook HC.1, 8 Puma HC.1
42(R) Squadron	Kinloss	Nimrod MR.2P
55(R) Squadron	Brize Norton	VC10 C.1K
56(R) Squadron	Coningsby	24 Tornado F.3
57(R) Squadron	Lyneham	Hercules C.1P/C.3P
TTTE	Cottesmore	17 Tornado GR.1

INTRODUCTION

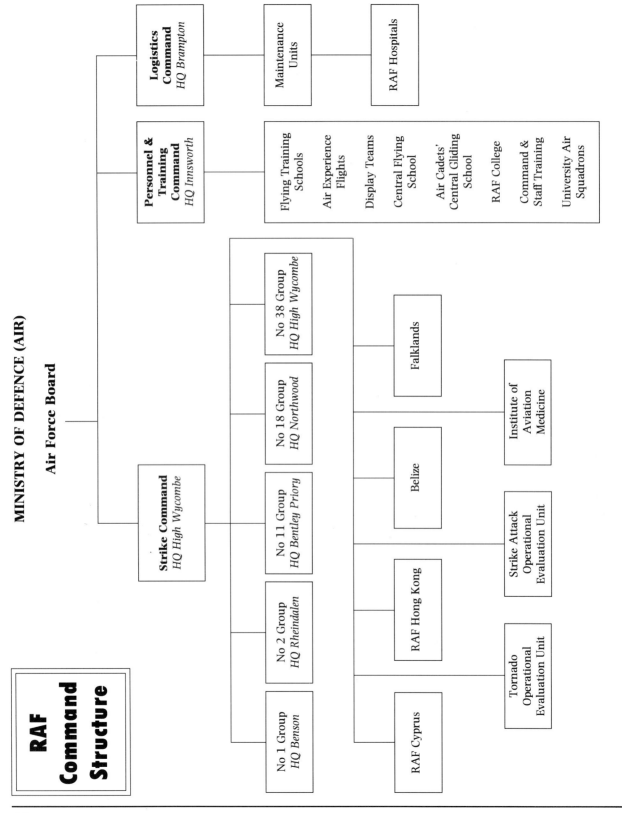

COLOURS AND CAMOUFLAGE

Above: A Tornado F.3 from No 56(R) Squadron departs on a training mission.

keeping the peace. Fortunately, in the United Kingdom, this need is understood, and the Royal Air Force continues in its tradition of excellence—excellence of resolve and excellence of equipment and doctrine but, above all else, excellence in its men and women and in their total commitment. All contribute to that ingredient so crucial to the security of the nation—air power.

In this book the present-day RAF is described in some detail. Each individual squadron is explored, with a basic background history, details of the current aircraft type or types operational with that unit, and the serial numbers and codes of aircraft that are currently allocated to it. Each operational RAF airfield is also explored, with descriptive maps and background histories. The Royal Air Force's current range of aircraft types is described, together with the main weapons that each may carry. Attempts to reduce Government expenditure have led to a series of severe cuts in the amounts of money allocated to the defence of the United Kingdom, and, like the other Services, the RAF has been forced to implement closures and withdrawals in order to meet a decreasing budget. Despite this, the RAF continues to maintain an effective fighting force, albeit a constantly changing one.

Producing a book which describes the present-day RAF effectively means that a particular time period has to be applied to the information which is included within its pages. The details presented are therefore generally specific to 1994, though in some areas are subject to change as the RAF continues to adapt to the financial constraints applied by Government.

Colours and Camouflage

Tornado GR.1, Jaguar GR.1A/T.2A, Harrier T.4, Chinook HC.1, Puma HC.1, Hercules C.1P/C.3P, Wessex HC.5C

Overall two-colour disruptive camouflage of Dark Sea Grey (BS.381C:638/FS.36173) and Dark Green (BS.381C:641/FS.34079). Chinooks, Pumas and some Hercules have Night (BS.381C:642/FS.37038) undersides and some Tornado GR.1s and Jaguar GR.1As carry a temporary (removable) overall camouflage (FS.33531) for operations in the Gulf region. National insignia are Post Office Red (BS.381C:538/FS.11136) and Roundel Blue (BS.381C:110/FS.15044).

VC10 C.1K, TriStar K.1/KC.1/C.2, Andover CC.2, Gazelle HT.3

Gloss White upper surfaces and Light Aircraft Grey (BS.381C:627/FS.16440) lower surfaces, separated

Above: A Shorts Tucano T.1. (Shorts)

by an Aircraft Blue (BS.381C:108/FS.15056) cheat line. National insignia are Post Office Red, white and Roundel Blue.

Harrier GR.7
Upper surfaces NATO Dark Green (BS.381C: 285), lower surfaces Lichen Green (BS.4800:12B21). National insignia are Post Office Red and Roundel Blue.

Hawk T.1/T.1A
Upper surfaces Medium Sea Grey (BS.381C:637/FS.36270), lower surfaces Barley Grey (BS.4800: 18B21/FS.36314). National insignia are Pale Red (RDM.28A/FS.32356) and Pale Blue (RDM.28A/FS.15299). Some Hawks are finished in high-visibility colours of Signal Red (BS.381C:537/FS.11350) and Oxford Blue (BS.381C:105/FS.15050), divided by Gloss White. National Insignia are Post Office Red, white and Roundel Blue. *Red Arrows* Hawks are Signal Red overall, with Gloss White trim.

Tucano T.1, Jetstream T.1, Bulldog T.1, Dominie T.1, Chipmunk T.10, Andover E.3
High-visibility trainer colours of Signal Red undersides and outer wings, with Gloss Light Aircraft Grey wings (upper and lower surfaces) and Gloss White upper fuselage. National insignia are Post Office Red, white and Roundel Blue.

Canberra PR.9/T.17, Nimrod R.1P/MR.2P, VC10 K.2/K.3/K.4
Low-visibility camouflage comprising Hemp (BS.2660:4-049/FS.30450) upper surfaces and Light Aircraft Grey undersides. National insignia are Pale Blue and Pale Red.

Tornado F.3
Upper surfaces Barley Grey (BS.4800:18B21/FS.36314), undersurfaces Light Aircraft Grey (BS.381C.627/FS.36440). National insignia are Pale Red and Pale Blue.

Wessex HC.2, Sea King HAR.3
Standard Search and Rescue colours of Golden Yellow (BS.381C:356/FS.13538) overall with Post Office Red, white and Roundel Blue national insignia. No 78 Squadron's Sea Kings carry low-visibility colours of overall Dark Sea Grey with red/blue national insignia.

Individual squadron markings are generally applied in full colour but may be toned down (mixed with white, or confined to white/black outline) on aircraft featuring Hemp or grey camouflage schemes. Serials are usually white on the latter types but black on high-visibility colour schemes and on aircraft painted in 'tactical' camouflage.

SQUADRON DIRECTORY

WESTLAND

No 1 Squadron

Current base: Wittering.
Aircraft types: Harrier GR.7, Harrier T.4.
Role: Ground attack, reconnaissance.
Squadron badge: Winged numeral '1'.
Squadron motto: 'In Omnibus Princeps' ('First in All Things').
Markings: Badge on white disc on nose, flanked by white diamond edged in red. Yellow code outlined in red on tail.

Formed on 13 May 1912, No 1(F) was one of the first four squadrons of the Royal Flying Corps, taking over the operation of balloons and airships from No 1 Airship Company, Royal Engineers. Airships became the responsibility of the Navy on 1 January 1914, but the Squadron remained at Farnborough and on 1 May that year was re-formed at Brooklands.

The outbreak of the First World War resulted in many of the unit's aircraft being re-assigned to the British Expeditionary Force and sent to France, and training resumed with a variety of aircraft types. No 1 Squadron itself moved to France in March 1915 as a reconnaissance unit, flying Scouts and Nieuport 17s from 1916 and becoming a fighter squadron in January 1917. S.E.5as were delivered to the unit (based at Ste Marie Cappel) in January 1918, and fighter patrol and ground attack operations continued for the remainder of the war before the unit returned to the United Kingdom and, on 20 January 1920, disbanded.

Just one day later No 1 Squadron re-formed at Risalpur in India, equipped with Sopwith Snipes. It moved to Hinaidi in Iraq during May 1921 to join the RAF policing force in that area, and it continued to operate in Iraq until 1 November 1926. Re-forming at Tangmere on 1 February 1927, the unit was now equipped with Siskins as a United Kingdom air defence fighter squadron, and it re-equipped with Hawker Furys during 1932. The legendary Hurricane was delivered to No 1 Squadron in October 1938, and following the outbreak of the Second World War the unit again returned to France with the RAF's Advanced Striking Force. The withdrawal from France saw the Squadron providing fighter cover for the Biscay ports, and, after the evacuation of Allied forces had been completed, it returned to Britain.

Following early participation in the Battle of Britain, No 1 Squadron moved to Wittering. It remained there until December 1940, when a move was made to Northolt, followed by further moves to Kenley, Croydon and Redhill. Night fighter operations began during 1941 and lasted until the beginning of 1942, when intruder missions to German bomber bases in France were initiated; these continued until July, when the Squadron transferred to Acklington, for conversion on to Hawker Typhoons.

After a fairly lengthy transition and training period, the Squadron moved to Biggin Hill, ready to commence operations early in 1943. However, a year later, the Typhoons were replaced by Spitfires, for a period of fighter-bomber operations over the Brittany area from home base at North Weald. Activities were directed towards the defence of South-East England when V-1 attacks commenced, and these fighter missions continued until the V-1 launch sites in France had been captured and destroyed. No 1 Squadron was then redesignated a long-range escort unit and it operated with Lancasters and Halifaxes on daylight raids over Germany, flying from a number of airfields, including Detling, Manston, Hawkinge, Lympne and Coltishall.

Spitfire F.21s were delivered to the Squadron as the Second World War ended, and the first jet aircraft, in the shape of Meteor F.3s, arrived in

Below: No 1 Squadron nose markings.

1946. During August 1947 the Meteors were replaced by Oxfords and Harvards when the Squadron was re-tasked as No 11 Group's instrument training unit, in which role it continued until June 1948, when it received Meteor F.4s at Tangmere. Conversion to the Hawker Hunter was completed in October 1955, and the Squadron disbanded at Tangmere on 23 June 1958, re-forming (as a renumbered 263 Squadron) at Stradishall on 1 July. The fighter-dedicated Hunter F.6s were replaced by ground attack Hunter FGA.9s during March 1960, and the Squadron moved to Waterbeach in November 1961, followed by a further move to West Raynham during August 1963.

The unit's association with the Hunter ended in 1969, when No 1 Squadron moved to Wittering to re-equip with the Harrier GR.1. The first of these VTOL ground attack fighters arrived in July that year, beginning another long association with a classic Hawker aircraft. The GR.1s (later converted to GR.3 standard) were replaced by GR.5s during 1988, and deliveries of GR.7s began in 1992. One Harrier T.4 is used for continuation training.

AIRCRAFT
Harrier GR.7: ZD470/01, ZD431/02, ZD483/03, ZD435/04, ZD437/05, ZD380/06, ZD462/07, ZD469/08, ZD463/09, ZD464/10, ZD465/11, ZD468/12.
Harrier T.4: XZ145/14.

Below, left and right: No 2 Squadron markings.

No 2 Squadron

Current base: Marham.
Aircraft types: Tornado GR.1, Tornado GR.1A.
Role: Reconnaissance, strike.
Squadron badge: A Wake Knot over three concentric circles.
Squadron motto: 'Hereward'.
Markings: Badge on white disc flanked by white triangles, on a black rectangle, on aircraft nose. Code letter in black, on a black-edged white triangle, on tail.

Formed as one of the original Royal Flying Corps units on 13 May 1912, No II(AC) Squadron operated various types from its base at Farnborough, including the B.E.1, Farman and Blériot. Following the outbreak of the First World War it moved to Amiens in France as part of the BEF, flying several types of aircraft on reconnaissance duties. Tactical reconnaissance and artillery-spotting became the Squadron's main tasks, and, as the B.E.2c became the standard aircraft type within the Squadron during 1915, operations were expanded to include bombing missions. During April 1917 the B.E.2cs were replaced by F.K.8s, and operations continued until 20 January, when the Squadron, having returned to Great Britain, disbanded. It re-formed on 1 February as an army co-operation unit at Oranmore, equipped with Bristol Fighters.

After a brief period at Digby in 1922, the unit returned to Ireland, operating from Aldergrove until

September; that month it moved back to Farnborough, retaining only a detachment in Ireland (which stayed until February 1923). The Squadron moved to Shanghai Racecourse in April 1927 in response to disturbances in China, but in September it returned to Manston. It re-equipped with Atlases in 1929. For the next ten years the Squadron operated in conjunction with the Army, moving to Hawkinge in 1935.

As the Second World War began, No 2 Squadron moved to France, equipped with Lysanders operating from Abbeville/Drucat. However, the operating base was quickly overrun by German forces and the Squadron returned to Britain. Missions consisted largely of bombing and supply dropping, together with early morning patrols, looking for signs of enemy landings which might have taken place under cover of darkness. In August 1941 Tomahawks were delivered for low-level tactical reconnaissance, and these aircraft operated alongside the Lysanders until April 1942, when the first Mustangs arrived. Based at Sawbridgeworth, and briefly at Bottisham, Fowlmere, Odiham, North Weald, Dundonald and Gravesend, the Squadron photographed French coastal defences in preparation for the Allied invasion, and on D-Day it provided spotter aircraft for the naval bombardment force. In July 1944 a move was made to Normandy, where the Squadron operated with the 21st Army Group during its steady advance into the Netherlands. Spitfires began to replace the Mustangs during November 1944, the last Mustang mission taking place in January 1945.

When the war ended the Squadron remained overseas, based at Celle, Wunstorf and Bückeburg. In December 1950 the Spitfires were replaced by Meteor FR.9s (which were in turn later replaced by FR.10s), and in May 1952 the Squadron moved to Gütersloh. The Supermarine Swift arrived during March 1956, the short career of this aircraft ending in March 1961 when Hunters were delivered to the Squadron at Jever. The Squadron moved back to Gütersloh in September.

Hunter FR.10s remained in service until 7 December 1970, when No 2 re-formed at Bruggen with new Phantom FGR.2s, although the Squadron's Hunter operations at Gütersloh continued for another four months. On 1 April 1971 the Phantoms were transferred to Laarbruch, and they remained in service until 1976, when conversion to Jaguar GR.1s began. The Squadron became fully operational on the type in September of that year, but after a long and successful association the Jaguar was replaced by the Tornado GR.1A during 1988. Following the end of the Cold War, No 2 Squadron

Below: A Tornado GR.1A of No 2 Squadron touches down at home base—RAF Marham in Norfolk.

returned to the United Kingdom in 1991, establishing an operating base at Marham as a reconnaissance/strike unit within Strike Command.

AIRCRAFT
Tornado GR.1: ZA411/Z, ZA551.
Tornado GR.1A: ZA370/A, ZA371/C, ZA372/E, ZA373/H, ZD996/I, ZA395/N, ZA397/O, ZA401/R, ZA398/S, ZA400/T, ZA404/W, ZA405/Y, ZA369/II.

No 3 Squadron

Current base: Laarbruch.
Aircraft types: Harrier GR.7, Harrier T.4A.
Role: Ground attack, reconnaissance.
Squadron badge: A cockatrice on a monolith.
Squadron motto: 'Tertius Primus Erit' ('The Third shall be First').
Markings: Badge on white disc on nose, flanked by green rectangle edged in yellow. Code in yellow on tail.

Formed on 13 May 1912 at Larkhill, No 3 Squadron at first operated a variety of trainer aircraft. It moved to Netheravon in 1913, and to Amiens in France as the First World War began, operating its aircraft in the reconnaissance role for the British Expeditionary Force. The mixed fleet of aircraft was eventually rationalized, and the Morane Parasol became the standard type until 1917, when Sopwith Camels were delivered and the Squadron began operations as a fighter unit. For the rest of the war No 3 Squadron remained active in the fighter and ground attack roles, until it disbanded at Dover on 27 December 1919.

Re-formation took place on 1 April 1920 at Bangalore in India, where Sopwith Snipes were operated for eighteen months. After again disbanding, No 3 Squadron re-formed on 1 October 1921 at Leuchars, where D.H.9As were operated on Fleet co-operation duties; Westland Walruses were delivered in 1922. During 1923 the Squadron was divided into two Flights, each of which became independent units.

On 1 April 1924 No 3 Squadron re-formed at Manston, again operating Snipes, before moving to Upavon, where fighter operations continued for ten years with Snipes, Woodcocks, Gamecocks and Bulldogs. The Bulldogs were deployed to the Sudan in October 1935 during the Abyssinian Crisis and they returned to Britain in August 1936. The first Hawker Hurricanes were delivered to the Squad-

Below: A Harrier GR.5 with No 3 Squadron's markings on the engine intake and tail unit.

SQUADRON DIRECTORY

Above: No 3 Squadron fuselage markings.

ron—now based at Kenley—in March 1938, but a change in RAF policy led to the unit's being re-equipped with Gladiator biplanes just three months later; Hurricanes were delivered again in May 1939, when the Squadron moved to Biggin Hill.

As the Second World War began, No 3 Squadron was tasked with the air defence of South-East England, and in May 1940 a brief deployment to Merville in France was made in support of the British Expeditionary Force following the German attack on the Low Countries. However, the stay in France lasted for only ten days, as German forces progressively occupied more RAF-manned airfields. Upon returning to the United Kingdom, the Squadron moved to Wick, while re-equipment took place and new pilots were trained. 'B' Flight was detached from the Squadron on 21 July 1940 (forming No 232 Squadron), while the remainder of the unit continued to operate from Castletown, Turnhouse, Sumburgh and Skeabrae in succession, defending the Scapa Flow area, flying convoy patrols and eventually concentrating on night fighter operations in co-operation with Turbinlite crews. The Squadron moved south in early 1941. Hawker Typhoons were delivered in May 1943, and intruder operations over Northern France were also conducted.

Fighter-bomber missions, directed against shipping and enemy targets in France, began in June 1943, the Squadron now being based at Manston. When German V-1 raids began during June 1944, No 3 Squadron was one of the first units to fly its aircraft (Tempests) on interception sorties against the weapons, and when the V-1 launch sites were captured and dismantled it resumed armed reconnaissance duties, moving to Grimbergen.

At the end of the Second World War No 3 Squadron remained in Germany, re-equipping with Vampires (at Gütersloh) in 1948. Five years later Sabres replaced the Vampires, the Squadron now being based at Geilenkirchen, and in 1956 Hunters replaced the Sabres. The Squadron disbanded on 15 June 1957. Re-formation took place on 21 January 1959 at Geilenkirchen when No 96 Squadron was renumbered. Javelin all-weather fighters were operated until 31 December 1960, when No 3 again disbanded, only to re-form one day later as a renumbered 59 Squadron, flying Canberra B(I).8 interdictors.

The unit moved to Laarbruch during 1968, and moved again four years later to Wildenrath, where the Canberras were replaced by Harrier GR.1 ground attack/reconnaissance aircraft. In 1977 the Squadron moved to Gütersloh, and with the closure of that base in 1992 it moved back to Laarbruch, equipped with the Harrier GR.7 and one Harrier T.4A.

AIRCRAFT
Harrier GR.7: ZG861/AA, ZG471/AB, ZG504/AC, ZD430/AD, ZG503/AG, ZG857/AH, ZG479/AI, ZG505/AJ, ZG502/AM, ZD433/AS, ZD467/AV, ZG858/CB.

No 4 Squadron

Current base: Laarbruch.
Aircraft type: Harrier GR.7.
Role: Ground attack, reconnaissance.
Squadron badge: A sun in splendour, divided by a lightning flash.
Squadron motto: 'In Futurum Videre' ('To See Into the Future').
Markings: Nose marking comprising a red '4' divided by a yellow lightning flash, flanked by red/black rectangles, each divided diagonally by a yellow lightning flash, edged in yellow. Code in black on tail.

During August 1912 No 2 Flight of No 2 Squadron RFC, based at Farnborough, was re-formed as No IV Squadron, flying a variety of trainer aircraft types. In June 1913 the unit moved to Netheravon. When the First World War broke out the Squadron flew patrols

Above: No 4 Squadron fuselage markings.

over the Straits of Dover and the Thames Estuary before moving to Maubeuge in France on 16 August 1914, selecting the best aircraft available for reconnaissance missions to take with it as part of the British Expeditionary Force. Towards the end of 1914 the Squadron began artillery observation and photography flights, and during 1916 it standardized on B.E.2cs. These were replaced by R.E.8s during May 1917, and 'A' Flight became No 4A Squadron for two months in 1919 while attached to the Portuguese Corps.

Having returned to the United Kingdom, the Squadron re-equipped with Bristol Fighters at Farnborough during April 1920. From November 1920 'A' Flight was deployed to Aldergrove and Baldonnel in support of security forces based in Ireland, and during September 1922 the Squadron moved to Kilid-el-Bahr in Turkey for operational duty during the Chanak Crisis. Returning to Britain in 1929, the unit re-equipped with Atlases, which were replaced by Audaxes in 1931; after the Squadron had moved to Odiham in 1937, the Audaxes were in turn replaced by Hectors.

Equipped with Westland Lysanders, No 4 Squadron moved to France after the outbreak of the Second World War and flew sorties in support of the British Expeditionary Force. In May 1940 the Squadron was forced to abandon its base at Clairmarais in the face of the German advance, and after its return to Britain the unit employed its Lysanders on coastal patrol and air/sea rescue duties. In 1942 the Lysanders were replaced by Tomahawks and Mustangs; the Squadron later standardized on the latter, flying tactical reconnaissance missions from Clifton. In January 1944 the Mustangs were replaced by Spitfires and Mosquitos, which were used for reconnaissance missions over occupied France. The Mosquito was only briefly employed, however, and the Spitfires were later supplemented by Typhoons. No 4 Squadron continued flying reconnaissance missions until 31 August 1945, when it disbanded at Celle; it re-formed the next day as a renumbered 605 Squadron, equipped with Mosquitos.

The first Vampire fighter-bombers arrived in 1950, and these were replaced by Sabres three years later at Jever. As a day fighter unit, the Squadron relinquished its Sabres in favour of Hunters in 1955. It remained at Jever until the end of 1960, after which it re-formed at Gütersloh. No 4 Squadron returned to the United Kingdom (West Raynham) during September 1969, and it was stationed for a brief period at Wittering in 1970 before it returned to Wildenrath in Germany in June of that year, equipped with the Harrier GR.1 ground attack/reconnaissance aircraft. In March 1977 the Squadron moved to Gütersloh, and after re-equipping with the Harrier GR.7 it moved to Laarbruch during 1992 when Gütersloh was closed.

AIRCRAFT
Harrier GR.7: *ZG507/CA, ZG532/CC, ZG511/CD, ZG510/CE, ZG533/CF, ZG508/CG, ZG509/CH, ZG512/CI, ZG856/CJ, ZG530/CL, ZG506/CM, ZG531/CN, ZG862/CO, ZD407/AQ.*

No 5 Squadron

Current base: *Coningsby.*
Role: *Air defence.*
Aircraft type: *Tornado F.3.*
Squadron badge: *A maple leaf.*
Squadron motto: *'Frangas non Flectas' ('Thou Mayst Break but Shall Not Bend').*
Markings: *A yellow 'V' over a green maple leaf flanked by red bars on tail. Code letters on tail in white.*

Formed from part of No 3 Squadron at Farnborough on 26 July 1913, No 5 Squadron operated a wide variety of aircraft on training duties until the outbreak of the First World War, including the Avro 504, Bristol Scout, Vickers F.B.5 and Caudron G.III.

In September 1914 the Squadron moved to Fère-en-Tardenois in France, flying reconnaissance missions for the British Expeditionary Force. During the spring of 1917 the Squadron standardized on the R.E.8 and continued its reconnaissance role for the remainder of the war. In December 1918 it moved to Elsenborn in Germany, returning to the United Kingdom for disbandment on 20 January 1920.

The Squadron re-formed two months later when No 48 Squadron was renumbered at Quetta, and the unit—now equipped with Bristol F.2Bs—began a stay of more than two years, flying patrols in the North-West Frontier region of India and in Baluchistan. During May 1931 the Bristol Fighters were replaced by Westland Wapitis, which remained in use until June 1940. Now redesignated a bomber squadron, the unit received Hawker Harts at Lahore, changing to fighter duties in February 1941 when the Harts were replaced by Audaxes at Risalpur.

Following the outbreak of war with Japan, No 5 Squadron moved to Calcutta to fly air defence sorties in the area, and towards the end of 1941 the first Mohawks were delivered, the last Audaxes being replaced in September 1942. Two months later the Squadron moved to Assam, escorting Blenheims on attacks over northern Burma and attacking Japanese river vessels and camps. Re-equipment with Hurricanes took place during June 1943, and operations continued until June 1944, when No 5 withdrew from the area and converted to P-47 Thunderbolts. Ground attack and escort operations with the Thunderbolt began in December 1944, and these continued until May 1945, when the Squadron ceased operations in preparation for the invasion of Malaya. The Japanese surrender caused a change of plan, however, and No 5 remained in India, converting to Tempests in March 1946 and returning to the North-West Frontier during November for a final period of operations before disbandment took place on 1 August 1947.

On 11 February 1949 the Squadron re-formed at Pembrey as a renumbered 595 Squadron, equipped with Spitfires, Martinets, Oxfords and, later, Beaufighters on anti-aircraft co-operation duties, over weapons ranges in Wales and the South-West. Disbandment in September 1951 was followed by re-formation on 1 March 1952 with Vampire fighters at Wunstorf in Germany. The Vampires were replaced by Venoms in December 1952, and the unit again disbanded in October 1957.

Above: No 5 Squadron tail markings.

No 5 re-formed at Laarbruch in January 1959 when No 68 Squadron was renumbered and the latter's Meteors were transferred prior to their replacement by Javelins in 1960. All-weather fighter operations with the Javelin continued until 7 October 1965, when the Squadron disbanded at Laarbruch, to be re-formed the next day at Binbrook as a Lightning F.3/F.6 unit. A long association with the Lightning and Binbrook continued until 1987, when operations ceased and No 5 Squadron stood down prior to its re-equipment with Tornado F.3s at Coningsby.

AIRCRAFT
Tornado F.3: ZG757/CA, ZE761/CB, ZG730/CC, ZG731/CG, ZG753/CH, ZG728/CI, ZG772/CN, ZG735/CO, ZG798/CS, ZE768/CT, ZE792/CU, ZH555/CV, ZG751/CW, ZE734/CX, ZE793/CY

No 6 Squadron

Current base: Coltishall.
Aircraft types: Jaguar GR.1A, Jaguar T.2A.
Role: Ground attack.
Squadron badge: An eagle preying on a serpent.
Squadron motto: 'Oculi Exercitus' ('The Eyes of the Army').
Markings: Red zig-zag over blue band on tail, red 'flying can-opener' motif on intake. Code in black outlined in white on tail.

Formed at Farnborough on 31 January 1914, No 6 Squadron was, like its fellow RFC squadrons, equipped with a mix of trainer types. During August 1914 its aircraft were largely transferred to the British Expeditionary Force, and the unit eventually moved to Belgium on 7 October though was sent to France one week later as the trench lines were formed in Flanders. Throughout the war No 6 Squadron carried out tactical reconnaissance and artillery-spotting over the Western Front, occasionally flying bombing missions as required.

The Squadron was transferred to Iraq in July 1919, flying patrols over the north of the country against Turkish-backed rebels; it remained in Iraq until October 1929, when it moved to Egypt, changing its title in 1931 from 'Army Co-operation Squadron' to 'Bomber Squadron' and exchanging its Bristol Fighters for Gordons. The latter were replaced by Harts late in 1935, and a small number of Demons were also used for a short period. In 1938 the Harts were replaced by Hawker Hardys, later supplemented by Gloster Gauntlets and Westland Lysanders, and the Squadron now flew many of its missions in co-operation with the local police and Army, in response to increasing tension between Arabs and Jews in Palestine.

The Squadron remained in Palestine following the outbreak of the Second World War and its first operational missions were flown during September 1940 against Italian forces in the Western Desert. By the end of 1940 it was equipped exclusively with Lysanders, flying tactical reconnaissance missions in support of the Army, but the Lysander was unsuitable for sorties which often encountered enemy fighters and so one Flight was re-equipped with Hurricanes. The remainder of the Squadron exchanged its Lysanders for Hurricanes in June 1941. However the Squadron's aircraft were re-distributed to other units just a few weeks later, and No 6 was withdrawn from the area. It was re-equipped with Lysanders, Gladiators, Blenheims and Hurricanes during August 1941 for a further period of service (at Kufra), but in January 1942 it was re-assigned to maintenance duties for three months until more Hurricanes were allocated. These aircraft, equipped with anti-tank cannon, were employed against the *Afrika Korps* during June 1942, and following a two-month transfer to Egypt for shipping protection duties the Squadron returned to the desert as an anti-tank attack unit. After a spell in Tunisia, it returned to Egypt to re-equip with rocket-armed Hurricanes, which were deployed to Grottaglie in Italy during February 1944 for operations over the

Below: A Jaguar GR.1A from No 6 Squadron, with a mixed load of bombs, an external fuel tank, a Phimat chaff dispenser and an AN/ALQ-101 ECM (electronic countermeasures) pod. (BAe)

Adriatic and Balkans. These ground attack missions (and some anti-shipping sorties) continued until the end of the war, and in July 1945 the Squadron returned to Palestine.

The first Spitfires were received during December 1945, although another year was to pass before the last Hurricanes were withdrawn. After the Squadron moved to Nicosia in Cyprus during 1946, the Spitfires were replaced by Tempests. A move to the Sudan in November 1947 was followed by a return to Egypt in May 1948, the Squadron re-equipping with Vampires in October 1949 and with Venoms in February 1954. No 6 moved to Akrotiri in April 1956, where the Venoms were replaced by Canberras, and these aircraft remained in service until January 1969 and disbandment.

Re-forming on 7 May 1969, No 6 Squadron returned to the United Kingdom and re-equipped with the Phantom FGR.2 at Coningsby for ground attack and reconnaissance operations. After disbanding again on 1 October 1974, the Squadron re-formed the next day at Lossiemouth with a fleet of Jaguar GR.1 ground attack bombers, and after working up in Scotland the unit moved to Coltishall in November 1974.

AIRCRAFT

Jaguar GR.1A: *XX766/EA, XZ377/EB, XZ381/EC, XZ732/ED, XX719/EE, XZ369/EF, XZ400/EG, XX970/EH, XX741/EJ, XX962/EK, XZ111/EL, XZ396/EM, XX720/EN, XZ356/EP, XX752/EQ, XX733/ER*
Jaguar T.2A: *XX841/ES, XX829/ET*

No 7 Squadron

Current base: Odiham.
Aircraft types: Chinook HC.1, Gazelle HT.2.
Role: Helicopter medium and heavy lift transport.
Squadron badge: Seven mullets forming a representation of the constellation Ursa Major.
Squadron motto: 'Per Diem Per Noctem' ('By Day and By Night').
Markings: Ursa Major motif on a blue disc, on tail rotor housing. Code letters in black, on tail rotor housing.

No 7 Squadron was formed on 1 May 1914—the last to be so before the outbreak of the First World War—and until April 1915 it flew training and experimental sorties, equipped with various types of aircraft, including the Farman, B.E.8 and Bristol Scout. Moving to France on 8 April 1915, the Squadron was allocated reconnaissance and artillery-spotting duties, in which roles it standardized on the B.E.2c during 1916 and re-equipped with R.E.8s in July 1917. For the remainder of the war it operated as a corps reconnaissance unit, flying tactical reconnaissance missions and directing artillery fire over the Western Front. It returned to the United Kingdom in September 1919 and disbanded three months later.

Re-formation took place on 1 June 1923 at Bircham Newton, with Vickers Vimy bombers. Four years later the Vimys were replaced by Virginias at Worthy Down and in 1935 the Virginias were replaced by Handley Page Heyfords, the Squadron moving to Finningley in September the following year. In April 1937 a number of Wellesleys were delivered to re-equip 'B' Flight, and in November 1938 conversion to Whitleys began. Five months later the Squadron changed aircraft again, to Hampdens, but by June 1939 it was allotted training duties, and it eventually merged with No 76 Squadron to form No 16 Operational Training Unit.

On 30 April 1940 No 7 Squadron was re-formed once more (again at Finningley), but it disbanded just two months later. It re-formed yet again on 1 August 1940 at Leeming as the first RAF Stirling bomber squadron and in October moved to Oakington. After being transferred to the Pathfinder

Below: No 7 Squadron markings.

Force, it flew its last Stirling missions in June 1943, after which it converted to Lancasters, and it continued to fly night bombing missions for the rest of the war.

After the war No 7 Squadron remained active, re-equipping with Avro Lincolns in August 1949. Detachments were sent to Malaya during 1954 to take part in attacks on terrorist camps in the jungle. The Squadron disbanded on 1 January 1956. Re-formation took place at Honington on 1 November 1956 with a fleet of Vickers Valiant V-bombers, and the Squadron moved to Wittering during September 1960. The unit's association with the Valiant continued until 1 September 1962 when the Squadron disbanded, to begin an eight-year period of inactivity. No 7 returned to the RAF inventory on 1 May 1970 as a target facilities squadron based at St Mawgan and equipped with Canberra TT.18 target tugs and B.2, T.4 and T.19 trainers. After transferring most of its Canberras to No 100 Squadron, No 7 disbanded, re-forming again at Odiham in September 1982 as the first RAF Chinook heavy lift helicopter squadron.

AIRCRAFT
Chinook HC.1: *ZD574/EE, ZD983/EF, ZD574/EH, ZA704/EJ, ZA709/EK, ZA684/EL, ZA682/EM, ZA713/EN, ZA671/EO, ZA720/EP, ZA712/ER, ZA681/ES, ZA677/EU, ZA707/EV, ZA683/EW, ZA714/EX, ZA710/EY, ZA679/EZ*
Gazelle HT.2: *ZB627/A*

No 8 Squadron

Current base: *Waddington.*
Aircraft type: *Sentry AEW.1.*
Role: *Airborne early warning.*
Squadron badge: *An Arabian dagger, sheathed.*
Squadron motto: *'Uspiam et Passim' ('Everywhere Unbounded').*
Markings: *Squadron motif in grey and white on tail, City of Lincoln coat of arms on port nose. Yellow, blue and red horizontal bars either side of fuselage roundel. Code in white on tail.*

Formed at Brooklands on 1 January 1915, No 8 Squadron, equipped with B.E.2cs, moved to France in April that year, flying reconnaissance missions and bombing sorties over the Western Front and eventually being designated a corps reconnaissance unit. R.E.8s were delivered during 1917, and these aircraft were employed on artillery-spotting and reconnaissance duties for the remainder of the First World War.

The Squadron returned to the United Kingdom (Duxford) in July 1919 with Bristol Fighters, disbanding in January 1920. It re-formed in October 1920 at Helwan and was deployed from Egypt to Iraq in February 1921, its D.H.9As being used for patrol duties in the area. In February 1927 the Squadron was relocated to Aden to undertake similar patrol duties in that area, where it remained until the end of the Second World War.

Having operated Fairey IIIFs and Vincents, the Squadron re-equipped from the latter with Blenheims in April 1939 and flew bombing missions against bases in Italian East Africa. A Free French Maryland unit was attached in August 1940 for reconnaissance duties, but this left for the Middle East in January 1941. Following the capture of the Italian colonies in East Africa, No 8 Squadron became responsible for both internal security and anti-submarine patrols. Hudsons were delivered to one of the Squadron's Flights during 1943 but Wellingtons arrived early in 1944 and these continued in service with the Squadron until it disbanded on 1 May 1945.

No 8 re-formed on 15 May 1945 as a renumbered 200 Squadron, now based at Jessore and equipped with Liberators, which were quickly moved to Ceylon and assigned various duties including supply drops in support of guerrilla forces in Malaya. Following the Japanese surrender, the Squadron disbanded in November 1945, but it re-formed again on 1 September 1946 when No 114 Squadron at Aden was renumbered. Mosquitos were replaced by Tempests, followed by Bristol Brigands in 1949. The first jet aircraft arrived during 1952 in the shape of Vampires, and these were later replaced by Venoms, Meteors and Hunters. No 8 Squadron remained at Aden until the base closed.

Having converted to Hunter FGA.9s in January 1960 (with Hunter FR.10 reconnaissance aircraft also being allocated), the Squadron was regularly employed to deal with incursions across the Aden frontier. It moved to Muharraq in Bahrain in September 1967 and to Sharjah in September 1971, disbanding three months later. It re-formed at Kinloss on 8 January 1972, equipped with Shackleton MR.2s, which were operated on training duties pending the arrival of Shackleton AEW.2 airborne early warning aircraft. After moving to Lossiemouth the Squadron began a long and successful association with the venerable Shackleton, finally re-equipping with the Boeing Sentry AEW.1 at Waddington during 1991.

AIRCRAFT
Sentry AEW.1: ZH101/01, ZH102/02, ZH103/03, ZH104/04, ZH105/05, ZH106/06, ZH107/07

No 9 Squadron

Current base: Bruggen.
Aircraft type: Tornado GR.1.
Role: Strike, ground attack.
Squadron badge: A bat.
Squadron motto: 'Per Noctum Volamus' ('Through the Night We Fly').
Markings: Green bat edged in yellow on tail. Green chevron outlined in yellow astride nose roundel. Black code outlined in white on tail.

No IX Squadron was formed on 8 December 1914 at St Omer from the Headquarters Wireless Unit, becoming the Royal Flying Corps' first operational squadron equipped with radio for artillery-spotting. The success of radio communications led to the decision to disperse the Squadron, 'A' Flight being transferred to No 6 Squadron, 'B' Flight going to No 2 Squadron and 'C' Flight being divided into two, half going to No 5 Squadron and half to No 16; No 9 Squadron itself disbanded on 22 March 1915.

Re-forming a few days later at Brooklands, however, No 9 was assigned radio training duties, equipped with B.E.2s, B.E.8s, Farmans and Blériots. It moved to Dover in July to undertake coastal patrols in addition to its training functions. After moving to France the Squadron began operational bombing and reconnaissance flights during December 1915, re-equipping with R.E.8s in May 1917 as part of a concentration on the corps reconnaissance role. The unit remained active in artillery-spotting, tactical reconnaissance and bombing duties until the end of the war, participating in the Allied counter-offensive which directly led to the termination of hostilities. Having re-equipped with Bristol Fighters, the unit returned home and disbanded at Castle Bromwich on 31 December 1919.

No 9 Squadron re-formed on 1 April 1924 at Upavon, equipped with Vimys for night bombing. After moving to Manston, the Squadron's Vimys were replaced by Virginias, and in 1936 the Virginias were replaced by Heyfords. No 9 then moved to Scampton, and in March 1938 to Stradishall, where it re-equipped with Vickers Wellingtons. At the beginning of the Second World War it began anti-shipping sweeps over the North Sea, and following the German invasion of Norway it formed a detachment at Lossiemouth in order to carry out anti-shipping operations and night bombing missions against captured airfields.

Conversion to Lancasters took place during 1942, and the Squadron continued to operate this type on

Below, left and right: No 9 Squadron markings.

Above: No 10 Squadron tail markings.

long-range bombing missions until the end of the war, including in its sorties a famous attack upon the battleship *Tirpitz* with 12,000lb bombs on 12 November 1944.

Following the end of the war in Europe, No 9 Squadron was allocated to the Tiger Force, in anticipation of bombing raids against Japan, but the Japanese surrender led to a change in role for the Squadron, and after arriving in India during January 1946 it flew photographic survey missions in the area until April of that year, when it returned to the United Kingdom and converted to Lincolns.

The Avro Lincoln was operated by No 9 at Binbrook until May 1952, when the Canberra jet bomber was first delivered, and in March 1956 the unit's aircraft were deployed to Butterworth to fly bombing missions against terrorist camps in Malaya. In October 1956 the Squadron deployed to Hal Far in Malta, to fly attack sorties against Egyptian airfields as part of the Suez operation. It returned home in November and disbanded in July 1961.

The Squadron re-formed on 1 March 1962 at Coningsby, where it received the Vulcan B.2 V-bomber, and in January 1969 it became part of the Near East Air Force, moving to Cyprus where it joined the Akrotiri Strike Wing. Returning to the United Kingdom early in 1975, No 9 Squadron continued operating the Vulcan as part of the Waddington Wing. After disbanding at Waddington, it re-formed at Honington on 1 June 1982 as the RAF's first Tornado GR.1 squadron. During 1986 it moved to Bruggen in Germany, from which station it continues to operate.

AIRCRAFT
Tornado GR.1: *ZD810/AA, ZD746/AB, ZD739/AC, ZD719/AD, ZD890/AE, ZD845/AF, ZD720/AG, ZD851/AJ, ZD748/AK, ZD747/AL, ZD789/AM, ZD714/AP, ZG754/AU, ZG756/AX, ZG769/AY*

No 10 Squadron
Current base: *Brize Norton.*
Aircraft types: *VC10 C.1, VC10 C.1K.*
Role: *Strategic transport, aerial re-fuelling.*
Squadron badge: *A winged arrow.*
Squadron motto: *'Rem Acu Tangere' ('To Hit the Mark').*
Markings: *Squadron badge on nose, Squadron emblem on tails of some aircraft. Code in black on tail.*

No 10 Squadron was formed at Farnborough on 1 January 1915 from a nucleus supplied by No 1 Reserve Squadron RFC. It employed a variety of aircraft types on training duties, including the B.E.2, Farman and Blériot. Moving to France on 25 July 1915, the Squadron was employed throughout the First World War as a reconnaissance, bomber and artillery-spotting unit equipped with B.E.2s and B.E.12s. These aircraft were replaced by Armstrong Whitworth F.K.8s in 1917, which continued in service until the unit disbanded on 31 December 1919.

Re-forming at Upper Heyford on 3 January 1928, No 10 Squadron was equipped with Hyderabads for night bombing operations and from early 1931 with Hinaidis before it moved to Boscombe Down in April of that year. In September 1932 the first Virginias were delivered to the unit, these being supplanted by Heyfords two years later. After moving to Dishforth in January 1937, the unit began to receive Whitley bombers. As part of the Royal Air Force's expansion, No 10 Squadron's 'B' Flight was detached to become No 97 Squadron in September 1935 and was detached again to form No 78 Squadron in November 1936.

From September 1939 the Squadron's Whitleys were used to drop leaflets over Germany, these sorties continuing until the following spring. Halifaxes replaced Whitleys in December 1941, and a detachment was sent to the Middle East in June 1942 to form the basis of a heavy bomber force in the area, the remainder of No 10 Squadron being brought back to full strength to continue bombing operations for the duration of the Second World War.

As the war ended, the Squadron was transferred to Transport Command, converting to Dakotas in August 1945, moving to Bilaspur in India two months later and redeploying to Poona in May 1947. It disbanded on 20 December 1947. No 238 Squadron at Oakington was renumbered 10 Squadron on 5 November 1948, the unit's Dakotas taking part in the Berlin Airlift before disbandment in February 1950.

The Squadron re-formed again at Scampton on 15 January 1953, equipped with Canberra bombers, which were deployed to Cyprus in October 1956 as part of the Suez operation. Disbandment three months later was followed by re-formation on 15 April 1958, when the Squadron received Victor V-bombers at Cottesmore to begin a six-year period of operations with this aircraft.

After disbanding on 1 March 1964, No 10 re-formed at Brize Norton as a VC10 strategic transport unit on 1 July 1966, although early operations were conducted from nearby Fairford until handling facilities were completed at No 10's new home base. The VC10 fleet is now being upgraded to C.1K standard with a two-point air-to-air refuelling capability, effectively giving the Squadron a combined transport/tanker role.

AIRCRAFT
VC10 C.1: *XR806/806, XR807/807, XR808/808, XR810/810, XV102/102, XV104/104, XV105/105, XV106/106, XV107/107, XV109/108*
VC10 C.1K: *XV101/101, XV103/103, XV109/109*

No 11 Squadron

Current base: Leeming.
Aircraft type: Tornado F.3.
Role: Air defence.
Squadron badge: Two eagles.
Squadron motto: 'Ociores Acrioresque Aquilis' ('Swifter and Keener than Eagles').
Markings: Eagle emblem on tail, yellow and black rectangles either side of nose roundel. Codes in black on tail.

Below: A Tornado F.3 from No 11 Squadron about to 'hook up' for fuel.

Above, left and right: No 11 Squadron markings.

Formed on 14 February 1915 at Netheravon, No XI Squadron was built around a nucleus of aircraft and personnel supplied by No 7 Squadron. Equipped with Vickers Gunbuses, it moved to France in July 1915, flying fighter patrols over the Western Front. It re-equipped with F.E.2b twin-seat fighters in June 1916, though these were used primarily for reconnaissance missions behind German lines. Bristol Fighters replaced the F.E.s in 1917, returning the Squadron to fighter operations. No 11 came back to the United Kingdom in September 1919 and disbanded three months later.

The Squadron re-formed on 13 January 1923 at Andover—where its personnel, drawn from the resident Air Pilotage School, flew aircraft belonging to the Group Communications Flight—before moving to Bircham Newton and receiving D.H.9As. Following the formation of a second Flight equipped with Fawns, it moved to Netheravon, where Horsleys were received in November 1926. No 11 was deployed to India during November 1928, with Westland Wapitis, becoming fully equipped in March 1929 at Risalpur. Reconnaissance patrols and army co-operation flights were supplemented by occasional bombing raids against tribesmen in the North-West Frontier region. Hawker Harts replaced the Wapitis in 1932. Reinforcement Flight detachments were made to Singapore in 1935 and 1937, and to Egypt during 1938, and Blenheims replaced the Harts in 1939.

In May 1940 the Squadron moved to Egypt, then deployed to Aden to mount bombing raids on Italian bases in Eritrea and Ethiopia Returning to Egypt in June, the Squadron deployed to Greece in January 1941 to conduct reconnaissance and bombing sorties over Albania. A move back to Egypt in April was followed by a further deployment to Palestine one month later as part of the occupation of Syria. In August another move was made, this time to Iraq in support of the occupation of Iran.

No 11 Squadron transferred to Ceylon during March 1942, attacking the Japanese carrier force which arrived in the area a month later. It remained in Ceylon until January 1943, then moved to the Burma Front, where further bombing raids on Japanese bases were made. Hurricanes were delivered in August 1943, and the Squadron reverted to army support duties four months later. In March 1944 it moved to the Imphal area for close air support duties.

At the end of the Burma offensive No 11 Squadron moved to India, where the Hurricanes were replaced by Spitfires, in preparation for the Allied invasion of Malaya, although the Japanese surrender brought about a change of plan and the unit was flown off HMS *Trumpeter* to Kelanang. It remained in Malaya until May 1946 as a fighter and reconnaissance unit, transferring to Japan as part of the Commonwealth occupation force. Disbandment took place at Miho on 23 February 1948.

No 11 Squadron re-formed in October 1948 when No 107 Squadron, equipped with Mosquitos at Wahn, was renumbered. Conversion to Vampires took place in August 1950, with a further change to Venoms in August 1952. The Squadron disbanded again on 15 November 1957. No 256 Squadron at Geilenkirchen was renumbered 11 Squadron on 21 January 1959 and its Meteor night fighters were replaced by Javelin all-weather fighters later that year. Javelin operations continued until 12 January

1966, when the Squadron disbanded, to re-form at Leuchars on 1 April 1967 with Lightning interceptors. No 11 Squadron moved south to Binbrook during 1972 and continued to operate the Lightning until 1988, when it moved to Leeming and re-equipped with the Panavia Tornado F.3 interceptor.

AIRCRAFT
Tornado F.3: ZE164/DA, ZE200/DB, ZE204/DD, ZE251/DE, ZE788/DF, ZE764/DH, ZE887/DJ, ZE942/DK, ZE982/DM, ZE934/DX, ZE941/DY, ZE966/DZ

No 12 Squadron

Current base: *Lossiemouth.*
Aircraft type: *Tornado GR.1B.*
Role: *Maritime strike.*
Squadron badge: *A fox's mask.*
Squadron motto: *'Leads the Field'.*
Markings: *Green arrowhead outlined in white, surrounding nose roundel. White tail band outlined in green and black, featuring a fox's head on a white circle. Tail code in black, outlined in white.*

No 12 Squadron was formed at Netheravon on 14 February 1915. It moved to France seven months later, equipped with a variety of training aircraft, including the Avro 504. The Squadron's main tasks were bombing and reconnaissance over the Western Front, and early in 1916 it became a corps reconnaissance unit and standardized on the B.E.2. Re-equipping with R.E.8s in August 1917, it continued to fly artillery-spotting and reconnaissance missions until the end of the First World War, when it moved to Germany, remaining with the occupying forces until its disbandment on 27 July 1922.

No 12 Squadron re-formed at Northolt in April 1923, equipped with D.H.9As. These were replaced by Fawns in March 1924, and in June 1926 the Squadron became the only RAF unit to operate Foxes. Hawker Harts arrived in 1931, and the Squadron moved to Aden during the Abyssinian Crisis in October 1935, returning to the United Kingdom in August 1936.

Having re-equipped with Hawker Hinds in October 1936 and with Fairey Battles in February 1938, the Squadron moved to France on the outbreak of the Second World War, and after having lost most of its aircraft to the German offensive the unit returned to the United Kingdom to re-arm during 1940. Conversion to Vickers Wellingtons took place in October 1940, and this type was used successfully on night bombing missions until November 1942, when Lancasters were delivered. No 12 Squadron continued as a major component of Bomber Command until the end of the war.

In August 1946 the Lancasters were replaced by Avro Lincolns, which remained in use until the Canberra was introduced during April 1952. As

Below: A No 12 Squadron Tornado GR.1B.

part of the Suez operation, No 12 Squadron deployed from its base at Binbrook to Hal Far in Malta in September 1956, its Canberras taking part in bombing missions over Egypt. After returning to the UK the Squadron disbanded on 13 July 1961. It reformed on 1 July 1962 as part of the Coningsby V-bomber Wing, equipped with Vulcan B.2s, and transferred to the Cottesmore Wing during November 1964. Disbandment followed on 31 December 1967. The Squadron re-formed as a Buccaneer maritime strike unit on 1 October 1969 at Honington. The Buccaneers moved to Lossiemouth in July 1980 and were replaced by Tornado GR.1Bs during 1993.

AIRCRAFT
Tornado GR.1B: *Tail codes in the range FA–FZ. Serial numbers not available at time of writing.*

No 13 Squadron

Current base: Marham.
Aircraft types: Tornado GR.1, Tornado GR.1A.
Role: Tactical reconnaissance, strike.
Squadron badge: *In front of a dagger, a lynx's head.*
Squadron motto: 'Adjuvamus Tuendo' ('We Assist by Watching').
Markings: Green and blue rectangle outlined in yellow, with yellow lightning flash running through two halves, either side of nose roundel. Blue tail band edged in yellow, featuring Squadron badge on white background. Tail code in blue outlined in yellow.

Formed at Gosport on 10 January 1915, No 13 Squadron was initially equipped with Avro 504s, but it moved to France in October of that year as a corps reconnaissance unit flying B.E.2cs. Throughout the First World War it flew artillery-spotting and photographic reconnaissance missions, the B.E.s being replaced by R.E.8s in April 1917. The Squadron returned to the United Kingdom in March 1919 and disbanded eight months later.

No 13 re-formed at Kenley on 1 April 1924 as an army co-operation unit equipped with Bristol Fighters; Atlases and Audaxes were introduced in August 1927 and July 1932 respectively, with Hectors following in May 1937 and Lysanders in January 1939. Following the outbreak of the Second World War it moved to France as part of the British Expeditionary Force, flying tactical reconnaissance missions during the German invasion of 1940. After suffering severe losses, the Squadron returned to the United Kingdom in June 1940 to re-equip and to fly patrols along the Lancashire and North Wales coasts from airfields at Speke and Hooton Park.

Blenheims were delivered during 1941, and in addition to bomber training the unit also practised gas-laying and smokescreen-laying techniques before resuming operational bomber sorties. After taking part in the first 'Thousand Bomber Raid' in May 1942, No 13 Squadron laid smokescreens for Allied landing craft during the Dieppe raid in August that year. After the Allied landings in Algeria the Squadron moved to Blida, flying both day and night bomber raids over Tunisia but later restricting its operations to night missions following No 18 Squadron's heavy daylight losses. Conversion to Venturas took place in November 1943.

In early 1944 the Squadron moved to Egypt, re-equipping with Baltimores, then transferred to Italy in February to become part of No 3 (SAAF) Wing. Attacks on enemy communications sites were followed by night interdictor operations, the Baltimores being replaced by Bostons in October 1944. No 13 Squadron moved to Hassani in Greece during September 1945 and disbanded on 19 April 1946.

No 680 Squadron was renumbered 13 Squadron on 1 September 1946, and moved from Palestine to Egypt two months later, the Squadron's Mosquitos being replaced by Meteor PR.10s in January 1952. No 13 was transferred to Akrotiri in 1956, converting to Canberra PR.7s then being relocated to Luqa in November of that year. The Canberra PR.7s were replaced by high-altitude PR.9s in August 1961, although the Squadron reverted to PR.7s before its return to the United Kingdom in October 1978, when British forces withdrew from Malta. After a brief period of operations at Wyton, the Squadron disbanded. It re-formed at Honington as a reconnaissance/strike unit equipped with Tornado GR.1As and later moved to Marham.

AIRCRAFT
Tornado GR.1: *ZG750/Y, ZG752/Z*
Tornado GR.1A: *ZG705/A, ZG707/B, ZG708/C, ZG710/D, ZG711/E, ZG712/F, ZG713/G, ZG714/H, ZG709/I, ZG725/J, ZG726/K, ZG727/L, ZG729/M*

No 14 Squadron

Current base: Bruggen.
Aircraft type: Tornado GR.1.
Role: Strike, attack.
Squadron badge: A winged plate with a cross, and shoulder pieces of a suit of armour.
Squadron motto: 'I Spread My Wings and Keep My Promise' (in Arabic script).
Markings: Squadron badge flanked by blue diamonds on a white rectangle, outlined in blue, on nose. Blue diamonds edged in white on tail. Black tail codes outlined in white.

Formed at Shoreham on 3 February 1915, No 14 Squadron was initially equipped with Maurice Farmans, flying training missions until November, when it left for the Middle East. From main operating bases in Egypt the Squadron supported detachments of B.E.2s on army co-operation duties in Egypt, Palestine and Arabia throughout the First World War. After receiving various aircraft types during 1917, including the F.B.19, Scout, Nieuport 17 and R.E.8, for fighter protection, the Squadron carried out bombing and reconnaissance duties until August 1917, when No 111 Squadron was formed, allowing No 14 Squadron to concentrate on army co-operation.

The Squadron was transferred to Greece in October 1918, returning to the United Kingdom and disbanding on 4 February 1919. One year later No 111 Squadron was renumbered 14 Squadron, based at Ramleh with Bristol F.2Bs and flying fighter patrols in Palestine and Transjordan. The Squadron was divided between Ramleh and Amman, the Bristol Fighters being replaced in 1932 by Gordons, which were supplanted in 1938 by Wellesleys.

When the Second World War began the Squadron moved to Egypt, but it returned to Amman a few months later, transferring to the Sudan during 1940 to begin bombing missions against Italian bases in Eritrea during June. Three months later a Flight of Gladiators was attached to the Squadron before conversion to Blenheims began.

No 14 began bombing operations over the Western Desert early in 1941 after moving to Egypt, and these were followed by periods of activity in Palestine and Iraq. After returning to the desert in November 1941 to continue bombing operations, the Blenheims were replaced by Marauders in August 1942. Bombing, reconnaissance and mine-laying continued until March 1943, when the Squadron was transferred to Algeria to begin anti-submarine patrols, with detachments in Sardinia and Italy.

No 14 returned to the United Kingdom at the end of 1944, re-forming at Chivenor and receiving Wellingtons during November of that year. It continued to operate the Wellington until the end of the war. Disbandment took place on 1 June 1945, but No 143 Squadron at Banff was renumbered 14 Squadron on the same day, its Mosquito aircraft being operated by the unit until March 1946, when it disbanded.

No 128 Squadron at Wahn was renumbered 14 Squadron on 1 April 1946, the unit's Mosquitos being replaced by Vampires early in 1951. Venoms arrived two years later, and Hunters were delivered in summer 1955, at which time the Squadron was

Below, left and right: No 14 Squadron markings.

Above: A No 14 Squadron Tornado GR.1.

redesignated a day fighter unit. On 17 December 1962, as No 14 Squadron disbanded at Gütersloh, No 88 Squadron was renumbered at Wildenrath, equipped with Canberra interdictors. The Canberras were replaced by Phantoms in July 1970, and ground attack/reconnaissance missions were flown from Wildenrath until November 1975. After moving to Bruggen, No 14 re-equipped with Jaguars, continuing its ground attack role until 1985, when the Jaguars were replaced by Tornado GR.1 strike/attack bombers.

AIRCRAFT
Tornado GR.1: ZD809/BA, ZD848/BC, ZD744/BD, ZD895/BF, ZG792/BH, ZD892/BJ, ZD707/BK, ZD846/BL, ZD745/BM, ZA452/BP, ZD709/BR, ZD713/BX, ZD712/BY, ZA410/BZ

Below: No 15 Squadron tail markings.

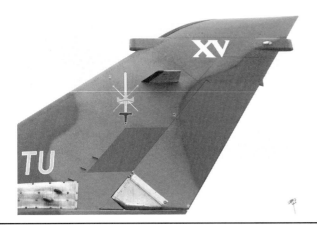

No 15 Squadron

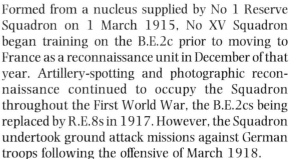

Current base: Lossiemouth.
Aircraft type: Tornado GR.1.
Role: Tornado Weapons Conversion Unit.
Squadron badge: A hind's head between wings.
Squadron motto: 'Aim Sure'.
Markings: Numerals 'XV' in black, with TWCU emblem on tail.

Formed from a nucleus supplied by No 1 Reserve Squadron on 1 March 1915, No XV Squadron began training on the B.E.2c prior to moving to France as a reconnaissance unit in December of that year. Artillery-spotting and photographic reconnaissance continued to occupy the Squadron throughout the First World War, the B.E.2cs being replaced by R.E.8s in 1917. However, the Squadron undertook ground attack missions against German troops following the offensive of March 1918.

After returning to the United Kingdom, No 15 Squadron disbanded on 31 December 1919 but it re-formed on 24 March 1924 at Martlesham Heath as an armament testing unit within the Aeroplane and Armament Experimental Establishment, for which task it was equipped with a variety of aircraft. After transferring its aircraft to the A&AEE, the Squadron re-formed at Abingdon on 1 June 1934 as a bomber unit equipped with Hawker Harts. The

Harts were replaced by Fairey Battles during 1938, and the Squadron moved to France in September 1939 as part of the Air Striking Force, returning to the United Kingdom to re-equip with Blenheims three months later.

Now based at Wyton, No 15 conducted bombing missions over the Low Countries and mounted night raids on enemy airfields and barges in the Channel ports. In November 1940 the Blenheims were replaced by Wellingtons, and in April 1941 the Wellingtons were replaced by Short Stirlings. Attacks on northern France were flown with heavy fighter escort, in an effort to draw enemy fighters into the air, but the Stirling's bulk made the aircraft susceptible to attack and during 1942 the Squadron began to concentrate on minelaying activities. Lancasters replaced the Stirlings towards the end of 1943, and the Squadron began to take part in strategic bombing raids over Germany, which it continued for the remainder of the Second World War.

The Lancasters were replaced by Avro Lincolns in February 1947, Boeing Washingtons being delivered to the Squadron at Coningsby from January 1951. Canberra bombers replaced the Washingtons during 1953, a detachment being sent to Akrotiri in October 1956 as part of the Suez operation. The Squadron disbanded on 15 April 1957, re-forming on 1 September 1958 as a Victor V-bomber unit at Cottesmore. It disbanded again in October 1964 but re-formed at Honington on 1 October 1970 as a Buccaneer strike unit, moving to Laarbruch in January 1971. In 1983 the Buccaneers were replaced by Tornado GR.1s.

Following disbandment at Laarbruch during 1992 the Tornado Weapons Conversion Unit at Honington was redesignated No 15 (Reserve) Squadron, and this moved to Lossiemouth during 1993.

AIRCRAFT
Tornado GR.1: *ZA556/TA, ZA559/TB, ZA563/TC, ZA587/TD, ZA589/TE, ZA600/TH, ZA601/TI, ZA607/TJ, ZA608/TK, ZA541/TO, ZA544/TP, ZA548/TQ, ZA549/TR, ZA552/TS, ZA562/TT, ZA594/TU, ZA595/TV, ZA599/TW, ZA602/TX, ZA604/TY, ZA612/TZ*

No 16 Squadron

Current base: *Lossiemouth.*
Aircraft types: *Jaguar GR.1A, Jaguar T.2A.*
Role: *Jaguar Operational Conversion Unit.*
Squadron badge: *Two keys.*
Squadron motto: *'Operta Aperta' ('Hidden Things are Revealed').*
Markings: *Squadron badge on black circle outlined in yellow, on tail. Tartan band across fin top, tail code in black outlined with white.*

Below: A specially marked Jaguar GR.1A from No 16 Squadron. The 'Saint' marking reflects the fact that the unit was formed at St Omer in France, while the crossed keys refer to the unit's reconnaissance role—unlocking the enemy's secrets.

No 16 Squadron was formed on 10 February 1915 at St Omer from a combination of detached Flights from Nos 2, 5 and 6 Squadrons. Equipped with various types including Blériots, Scouts and Gunbuses, the unit standardized on B.E.2s in 1916, flying tactical reconnaissance, artillery-spotting and photographic reconnaissance missions throughout the First World War.

The Squadron disbanded in the United Kingdom on 31 December 1919. It re-formed at Old Sarum as an army co-operation unit on 1 April 1924 with Bristol Fighters, re-equipping with Atlases in January 1931 and with Audaxes in December 1933. For ten years the Squadron was attached to the School of Army Co-operation, becoming an independent unit again in 1934.

Westland Lysanders were introduced in June 1938. Trials to find a Lysander army co-operation replacement were conducted by the Squadron, but in comparison with the Anson, Battle and Oxford the Lysander was still regarded as the best machine. The Squadron took its Lysanders to France in April 1940 for training, but after the German attack in May that year the unit flew operational missions for only a few days before returning to Lympne to fly reconnaissance and supply-dropping sorties. Coastal patrols were also undertaken off East Anglia and over the coats of Devon and Cornwall, and these continued until March 1941. Although Lysanders remained with the unit until May 1943, Mustang reconnaissance fighters were delivered in April 1942, assigned the interception of German fighter-bombers attacking coastal towns. Spitfires replaced the Mustangs in September 1943, and these were used primarily for photographic reconnaissance in anticipation of the invasion of Europe.

No 16 Squadron joined the 2nd TAF in Europe during September 1944, remaining under that Command for the rest of the war and operating a high-speed mail service for the occupation forces during 1945. On 17 September of that year the Squadron was divided into three Flights (which became Nos 2, 26 and 268 Squadrons) and after returning to the United Kingdom it disbanded on 20 October 1945.

However, during September 1945 No 487 Squadron was renumbered 16 Squadron; so was No 268 Squadron, and the confusion was clarified only when No 487 was officially redesignated No 268 and the latter No 16 on 20 October 1945. No 16 remained at Celle with fighter-reconnaissance Spitfires until its disbandment on 31 March 1946. The following day No 56 Squadron was renumbered 16 Squadron at Fassberg, equipped with Tempests, which were replaced by Vampires during December 1948. Venoms arrived five years later, and disbandment followed in June 1957.

No 16 Squadron re-formed at Laarbruch with Canberra interdictors on 1 March 1958 and continued to operate these until 6 June 1972, when they were replaced by Buccaneer strike/attack bombers. The Squadron became operational on the Tornado GR.1 on 1 March 1984, remaining at Laarbruch until disbandment in 1992. The Jaguar Operational Conversion Unit (No 226 OCU) at Lossiemouth was then renumbered 16 (Reserve) Squadron.

AIRCRAFT
Jaguar GR.1A: *XX119/01, XX116/02, XZ399/03, XX745/04, XZ391/05, XX117/06, XX965/07*
Jaguar T.2A: *XX846/A, XX139/C, XX144/I, XX146/J, XX150/W, XX838/X, XX839/Y, XX141/Z*

No 17 Squadron

Current base: *Bruggen.*
Aircraft type: *Tornado GR.1.*
Role: *Strike, attack.*
Squadron badge: *A gauntlet.*
Squadron motto: *'Excellere Contende' ('Strive to Excel').*
Markings: *White arrowhead with black zig-zags astride nose roundel. Squadron badge on tail. Black tail codes outlined in white.*

Formed at Gosport on 1 February 1915, No 17 Squadron was initially equipped with B.E.2 series aircraft. It was transferred to Egypt in November 1915 and operations began the following month, supporting the Army in the Western Desert and reconnoitring Turkish lines in Sinai. Detachments were also sent to Arabia until July 1916, when the Squadron moved to Salonika with B.E.2s, D.H.2s and Scouts.

After transferring its fighter aircraft to No 150 Squadron, the unit spent the remainder of the First World War on reconnaissance and artillery-spotting duties over the Bulgarian border. Re-equipment

Above, left and right: No 17 Squadron markings.

with D.H.9s and Camels took place in December 1918, with 'A' Flight moving to Batum to support White Russian forces while 'B' and 'C' Flights transferred to Constantinople in January 1919. Disbandment followed on 14 November that year.

After re-forming at Hawkinge with Snipes on 1 April 1924, the Squadron became part of the United Kingdom's air defence force, Woodcocks being delivered in 1926, followed by Gamecocks, Siskins, Bulldogs and, in August 1938, Gauntlets. Although the Squadron remained in the United Kingdom during the Abyssinian Crisis, its Bulldogs were transferred to squadrons assigned to the Middle East, and Hawker Harts were operated as replacements for six months beginning in October 1935.

Hawker Hurricanes were received in June 1939, and these flew air defence patrols until the German attack on France in May 1940, when operations switched to fighter sweeps over Holland and Belgium and over French airfields which were being used to cover the retreat of Allied troops. During June the Squadron moved to Brittany, before transferring to the Channel Islands and, finally, the British mainland.

Below: A Tornado navigator's eye view of a No 17 Squadron aircraft during a low-level 'attack' mission. (RAFG)

No 18 Squadron was formed on 11 May 1915 at Northolt from a nucleus supplied by No 4 Reserve Squadron. Moving to France in November the same year, the unit was deployed in the fighter and reconnaissance role, equipped with Vickers Gunbuses, which were replaced by F.E.2bs during April 1916. The Squadron flew tactical reconnaissance missions during the Battle of the Somme on behalf of the Cavalry. It re-equipped with D.H.4 bombers in May 1917, remaining active in the day bombing role until the end of the First World War and receiving D.H.9As shortly before the Armistice.

Returning to the United Kingdom in September 1919, the Squadron disbanded on 31 December that year. It re-formed at Upper Heyford on 20 October 1931, equipped with Hawker Hart light bombers, and these it retained until April 1936 when Hinds were delivered. 'C' Flight was detached from the Squadron during February 1936 to form the nucleus of No 49 Squadron. Conversion to Bristol Blenheims took place during May 1939, and the Squadron moved to France after the outbreak of the Second World War.

In May 1940 No 18 Squadron flew bombing and reconnaissance missions against the advancing German forces, subsequently directing its attention to coastal shipping and to barges in the Channel ports. Inland targets were selected towards the end of 1940, sorties being flown with fighter escort. In October 1941 the Squadron's aircraft deployed to Malta to begin a period of attack missions against shipping in the Mediterranean. In January 1941 they withdrew to Egypt, where the detachment was disbanded on 21 March 1942.

Back in the United Kingdom, the remaining ground element of No 18 Squadron began to re-build into a full-strength unit, resuming bombing missions on 26 April. Still equipped with Blenheims, it next moved to Algeria in November 1942, mounting daylight raids on German targets in Tunisia. However, during December the Squadron suffered heavy losses against strong fighter opposition and, as a result, switched to flying night missions. Douglas Bostons were delivered to the unit in March 1943, before a move was made to Sicily in August and a further move to Italy in October. For the remainder of the war the Squadron flew interdiction and bombing missions over northern Italy and the Balkans. It moved to Greece in September 1945, disbanding on 31 March 1946.

After participating in the Battle of Britain, No 17 Squadron moved to Scotland in April 1941 but within a year it had been redeployed to the Far East, arriving in Burma during January 1942. Here defensive patrols were flown until the Rangoon airfields were overrun by enemy troops. Following re-assembly in Calcutta, the unit resumed ground attack missions in February 1943. It received Spitfires in March 1944 after having moved to Ceylon. The aircraft were deployed back to Burma in November to resume attacks in the area before withdrawing in June 1945. The Squadron was transferred to Japan as part of the Commonwealth occupation force in April 1946, and it disbanded on 23 February 1948.

On 11 February 1949 No 691 Squadron was renumbered 17 Squadron at Chivenor. Equipped with Beaufighters, the unit was engaged on anti-aircraft co-operation duties until 13 March 1951, when it disbanded, re-forming again on 1 June 1956, at Wahn, as a Canberra photographic reconnaissance squadron. It moved to Wildenrath and remained active until 12 June 1969, re-forming again on 16 October 1970 at Bruggen with Phantom ground attack fighters. Phantoms were replaced by Jaguars during December 1975, by which time the Squadron had moved to Bruggen. The Jaguars were in turn replaced by Tornado GR.1s in 1984.

AIRCRAFT
Tornado GR.1: ZD793/CA, ZD788/CB, ZG775/CC, ZA465/CD, ZA457/CE, ZD792/CF, ZD847/CH, ZG777/CK, ZD850/CL, ZG779/CM, ZA374/CN, ZD743/CX, ZD842/CY, ZD742/CZ

No 18 Squadron

Current base: *Laarbruch.*
Aircraft types: *Chinook HC.1, Puma HC.1.*
Role: *Medium and heavy lift helicopter support.*
Squadron badge: *A Pegasus rampant.*
Squadron motto: *'Animo et Fide' ('With Courage and Faith').*
Markings: *Blue Pegasus marking on red disc, on tail rotor housing, with black codes.*

On 1 September 1946 No 621 Squadron, flying Lancaster maritime reconnaissance aircraft, was renumbered 18 Squadron but disbanded on the 15th of the month. No 18 re-formed again on 15 March 1947 at Butterworth as a meteorological unit, disbanding eight months later. On 8 December 1947 the Squadron re-formed once more at Waterbeach, equipped with Dakotas, and later became involved in the Berlin Airlift.

After disbanding on 20 February 1950 the Squadron re-formed yet again on 1 August 1953 at Scampton, where it was equipped with Canberra bombers. After four years of Canberra operations it disbanded, but it re-formed on 16 December 1958 as a Valiant V-bomber unit at Finningley, remaining operational until 31 March 1963. The Wessex Trials Unit at Odiham was renumbered 18 Squadron on 27 January the following year and, after a brief period of working-up in the United Kingdom, the unit moved to Gütersloh, where it re-equipped with Chinook heavy lift helicopters. Following the withdrawal of No 230 Squadron from Germany, No 18 Squadron partially re-equipped with Pumas, and it now operates a mixed fleet of Chinooks and Pumas from Laarbruch, at which airfield it has been based since 1992.

AIRCRAFT
Chinook HC.1: *ZA674/BA, ZA675/BB, ZD576/BC, ZD981/BD, ZA670/BG, ZD982/BI, ZD575/BL, ZA711/BT*
Puma HC.1: *XW218/BW, XW222/BX, XW226/BY, XW236/BZ*

Below: No 19(R) Squadron markings.

No 19 Squadron

Current base: *Chivenor.*
Aircraft types: *Hawk T.1, Hawk T.1A.*
Role: *Advanced flying training, tactical weapons training.*
Squadron badge: *A dolphin's head between wings.*
Squadron motto: *'Possunt quia Posse Videntur' ('They Can Because They Think They Can').*
Markings: *Blue and white checks either side of fuselage roundel. Squadron emblem on tail.*

No 19 Squadron, the nucleus of which was provided by No 5 Squadron, was formed on 1 September 1915 at Castle Bromwich. It was equipped with various types, including Avro 504s and Farmans, before it received R.E.7s in December 1915. A move to France was at first postponed, but the Squadron finally arrived in July 1916, equipped with B.E.12s for fighter duties. It flew patrols over the Western Front for five months until Spads were delivered. The latter were used for fighter and ground attack operations until January 1918, when Dolphins were received; these remained in use until the Armistice. The Squadron returned home in February 1919 and disbanded on 31 December that year.

On 1 April 1923 No 19 Squadron re-formed at Duxford, equipped with Snipes which were drawn from a flight of trainers used by No 2 Flying Training School at the same airfield. At the end of June No 2 FTS moved out and No 19 became an independent fighter squadron, receiving Gloster Grebes during December. The Grebes were replaced by Siskins, which were followed by Bristol Bulldogs and Gloster Gauntlets, and in August 1938 No 19 became the first fighter squadron to receive Spitfires.

At Duxford as the Second World War broke out, the Squadron participated in the evacuation of the BEF from Dunkirk and played a major part in the Battle of Britain, during the course of which it was equipped temporarily with twin 20mm cannon-armed Spitfires (which were withdrawn from service owing to technical problems). In March 1941 the Squadron began flying fighter sweeps over northern France and also mounted night patrol missions. It joined the 2nd TAF upon its formation and continued operations in preparation for the invasion of Europe, providing bomber escorts.

Above: No 20(R) Squadron fuselage markings.

No 20 Squadron

Current base: Wittering.
Aircraft types: Harrier GR.5, Harrier GR.7, Harrier T.4.
Role: Harrier Operational Conversion Unit.
Squadron badge: An eagle perched on a sword in front of a rising sun.
Squadron motto: 'Facta non Verba' ('Deeds not Words').
Markings: Squadron badge flanked by red, blue and red bars, on intakes. OCU emblem on a blue circle on tail, OCU red, black and yellow wedges edged with blue stripes on fin cap. White code on tail.

Mustangs replaced the Spitfires during February 1944, and following D-Day the Squadron's aircraft provided close support for the Army, attacking enemy communications. In September 1944 No 19 Squadron reverted to long-range escort missions, moving to Scotland in February 1945 in support of strike Wings operating off the Norwegian coast. It continued these duties until the end of the war.

During March 1946 the Mustangs were replaced by Spitfire 16s for a brief period until Hornets were delivered in October that year. Meteors replaced the Hornets during January 1951, and the Meteors were in turn replaced by Hunters in October 1956. The English Electric Lightning was delivered to the Squadron (at Leconfield) in November 1962, and in September 1965 No 19 moved to Gütersloh to begin a long stay in Germany. Phantom FGR.2s began to replace the Lightnings in July 1976, and the Squadron became operational on the type at the end of that year.

Phantom operations continued until January 1992, when the last aircraft was retired and the Squadron, now at Wildenrath, was disbanded. However, No 19 reappeared during September 1992 as a Reserve Squadron, part of No 7 Flying Training School at Chivenor and equipped with Hawks. It is due to disband again late in 1994 when No 7 FTS closes, but it is expected eventually to re-form as a Eurofighter unit.

AIRCRAFT
Hawk T.1: XX174, XX175, XX185, XX225, XX231, XX245, XX313
Hawk T.1A: XX158, XX217, XX219, XX230, XX246, XX254, XX256, XX263, XX278, XX282, XX289, XX320, XX321, XX326, XX338, XX345, XX346, XX352

Formed at Netheravon on 1 September 1915, No 20 Squadron was equipped with various aircraft types until it moved to France in January 1916 with F.E.2bs as a fighter and reconnaissance unit. The F.E.2bs were replaced by Bristol Fighters, and the Squadron continued to operate these until the end of the First World War. On 6 June 1919 No 20 Squadron arrived in India to begin patrols along the North-West Frontier. Westland Wapitis were received in 1932, and at the end of 1935 Hawker Audaxes, these latter being replaced by Westland Lysanders upon the outbreak of war in the Far East.

During July 1942 No 20 Squadron began operations against the Japanese, flying tactical reconnaissance missions and liaison sorties in support of Chinese ground forces. After moving to the Arakan in October 1942, the Lysanders were flown on army co-operation duties until Hurricanes were received in February 1943. After completing re-equipment with the Hurricane, the Squadron began operations again on 23 December, although a shortage of ammunition and a lack of appropriate targets restricted operations; as a result, tactical reconnaissance was added to the unit's duties.

The Squadron moved to India following the termination of its operations on 10 August 1944, some of its rocket-armed Hurricanes being used for anti-mosquito spraying. Ground attack operations resumed in December 1944, and these continued until May 1945, when the unit was withdrawn for re-equipment with Spitfires. Moving to Thailand after the Japanese surrender, the Squadron converted to Hawker Tempests in 1946 but disbanded on 1 August the following year.

Above: A Wessex HC.2 from No 22 Squadron.

On 11 February 1949 No 631 Squadron was renumbered 20 Squadron at Llanbedr, and various aircraft types were operated on anti-aircraft co-operation duties until disbandment on 16 October 1951. Re-forming at Jever on 1 July 1952, the Squadron was again assigned fighter-bomber duties, its Vampires being replaced by Sabres in 1953. Hunters replaced the Sabres towards the end of 1955, and the unit continued to operate as a daytime fighter squadron until 30 December 1960, when it again disbanded.

Re-formation took place on 3 July 1961 at Tengah in Singapore, where Hunter aircraft were used for ground attack duties in the Far East. The Squadron maintained a detachment in Thailand from May to November 1962 as part of a counter-communist force in the Thai/Laotian border area. Scottish Aviation Pioneers joined the Hunters as a FAC (forward air control) Flight following the disbandment of No 209 Squadron, but No 20 itself disbanded on 13 February 1970.

After re-forming at Wildenrath on 1 December 1970 as a Harrier ground attack and reconnaissance unit, the Squadron re-equipped with Jaguars at Bruggen in March 1977. Conversion to the Tornado GR.1 took place in 1984, this aircraft remaining in use until 1992, when the Squadron disbanded at Bruggen. Late in 1992 No 233 Operational Conversion Unit was renumbered 20 (Reserve) Squadron, flying Harriers at Wittering.

AIRCRAFT
Harrier GR.5: ZD354/5C, ZD378/5D, ZD346/5E
Harrier GR.7: ZD350/A, ZD409/B, ZD376/F, ZD348/G, ZD466/I, ZD345/J, ZD347/K, ZD327/L, ZD329/M, ZD405/N, ZD401/AA, ZD406/AB, ZD377/AE, ZD411/AG
Harrier T.4: ZD990/Q, ZB602/R, XZ146/S, XW270/T, ZD993/U, ZD991/V, XW265/W, XW271/X, XW934/Y, ZB600/Z

No 22 Squadron

Current base: St Mawgan.
Detached Flights: 'A' at Chivenor, 'B' at Wattisham, 'C' at Valley; SAR Training Unit at Valley.
Aircraft types: Wessex HC.2 ('C' Flight), Sea King HAR.3 ('A' and 'B' Flights).
Role: Helicopter search and rescue.
Squadron badge: A Maltese cross on a torteau, over all a 'pi' symbol.
Squadron motto: 'Preux et Audacieux' ('Valiant and Brave').
Markings: Maltese cross and 'pi' character on a white circle, on tail rotor housing.

Following its formation at Gosport on 1 September 1915 and a subsequent period of training, No 22 Squadron moved to France on 1 April 1916. Equipped with F.E.2bs, the unit was assigned to the reconnaissance role, flying surveillance sorties over enemy camps and railheads behind the Western Front. Considerable opposition was encountered during these operations, resulting in heavy losses, and during July 1917 the Squadron re-equipped with Bristol Fighters. These aircraft were used for reconnaissance and fighter missions, but for the rest of the First World War the unit was engaged predominantly in fighter operations. After the Armistice the Squadron briefly moved to Germany before returning to the United Kingdom in September 1919, disbanding on the 30th of that month.

No 22 Squadron re-formed four years later, on 24 July 1923, as part of the Aeroplane and Armament Experimental Establishment, engaged in a variety of trials programmes. It disbanded on 1 May 1934 but re-formed the same day at Donibristle, equipped with Vildebeest torpedo bombers. During October the following year the unit deployed to Malta during the Abyssinian Crisis, returning to the United Kingdom in August 1938.

The Squadron was still equipped with Vildebeests at the outbreak of the Second World War but they were replaced by Beauforts from November 1939, the last Vildebeest leaving in February 1940. The first operational missions by the Beauforts were flown on 15 April 1940, mainly in the form of minelaying sorties although anti-shipping strikes were made against German Navy units out at sea as well. During August 1940 the Squadron's 'C' Flight re-equipped with Marylands and, after a period of crew training, moved to Malta to form No 431 Flight. No 22 Squadron meanwhile flew attack missions against enemy-occupied ports on the French and Belgian coasts until a variety of technical problems with the Beaufort had been overcome, allowing the Squadron to fulfil its proper role as a torpedo bomber unit.

The Squadron's aircraft began to deploy to the Far East via Gibraltar, Malta and Egypt on 18 March 1942, arriving in Ceylon on 28 April. Although attacks from carrier-based Japanese aircraft were expected, none was made and the Squadron flew convoy escort and anti-submarine patrols until June 1944, when it re-equipped with Beaufighters. Although the Beaufighter retained a torpedo bombing capability, rockets now became the principal means of attack, and after moving to the Burma Front in December 1944 the Squadron flew ground attack and air/sea rescue missions until 1945, disbanding on 30 September that year. On 1 May 1946 No 89 Squadron at Seletar was renumbered 22 Squadron, and after a few months of operations with Mosquito fighter-bombers the unit disbanded on 15 August 1946.

No 22 Squadron re-formed at Thorney Island on 15 February 1955 as a search and rescue unit, equipped with Whirlwind helicopters. The Whirlwinds were replaced by Wessexes during May 1976 and the latter type remains in service pending further deliveries of Sea Kings. Having moved to St Mawgan from Finningley during 1992, the Squadron supports three search and rescue detachments, at Chivenor, Wattisham and Valley.

AIRCRAFT
Sea King HAR.3: *For serial numbers see No 202 Squadron.*
Wessex HC.2: *XR501, XR504, XR507, XR518, XR520, XR524, XR588, XS675, XT601, XT602, XT604, XT670, XT680, XV720, XV724, XV729, XV730*

No 24 Squadron

Current base: *Lyneham.*
Aircraft types: *Hercules C.1P, Hercules C.3P.*
Role: *Tactical transport.*
Squadron badge: *A blackcock.*
Squadron motto: *'In Omnia Parati' ('Ready in All Things').*
Markings: *None.*

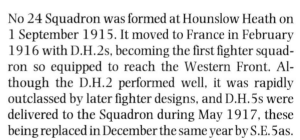

No 24 Squadron was formed at Hounslow Heath on 1 September 1915. It moved to France in February 1916 with D.H.2s, becoming the first fighter squadron so equipped to reach the Western Front. Although the D.H.2 performed well, it was rapidly outclassed by later fighter designs, and D.H.5s were delivered to the Squadron during May 1917, these being replaced in December the same year by S.E.5as.

No 24 Squadron continued to fly fighter and ground attack missions until the end of the First World War, returning to the United Kingdom in

February 1919 to become part of No 41 Training Depot Station at London Colney until disbandment on 1 February 1920. Re-formation took place at Kenley on 1 April 1920 with Bristol Fighters for communications and training duties.

For the next twenty-four years the unit operated in the communications role, providing transport for Government officials and both Air Ministry and RAF personnel; additionally, a small Flight of aircraft was retained to enable Air Ministry-employed pilots to remain in practice. A huge variety of aircraft types served with the Squadron, including the Tomtit, Tutor, Anson, Oxford, Hudson, Wellington and Dakota. The Squadron moved from Kenley to Northolt in January 1927, and to Hendon in July 1933. Many of its aircraft were civil machines impressed into RAF service, especially during the Second World War.

Until the German occupation of France, the Squadron flew regular communications and mail flights to that country. During April 1942 it was transferred to Ferry Command and began flights to Malta with mail and passengers. Avro Yorks equipped for VIP flights were delivered during May 1943, after which the Squadron began to concentrate on long-range VIP flights while No 512 Squadron handled most of the shorter-range operations. The Squadron standardized on Dakotas and Ansons during October 1944 and in February 1946 it moved to Bassingbourn, where it was joined by No 1359(VIP) Flight's Yorks and Lancasters. The York then became the standard equipment, and in April 1947 the unit became No 24 (Commonwealth) Squadron, receiving Hastings transports in December 1950.

Following the introduction of the latter, general transport flights became an increasingly important part of the Squadron's duties. In January 1957 the Squadron moved to Colerne, becoming part of a Transport Wing. Operations with the Hastings continued from Colerne until January 1968, when the Lockheed Hercules was introduced. The Squadron moved to Lyneham on 9 February 1968, becoming part of the Lyneham Transport Wing. The LTW Hercules fleet is 'pooled', and aircraft are used as required by each component squadron.

AIRCRAFT
Hercules C.1P: *(Drawn from Lyneham Transport Wing)* XV178, XV179, XV181, XV182, XV185, XV186, XV187, XV191, XV192, XV195, XV196, XV200, XV201, XV203, XV205, XV206, XV210, XV211, XV215, XV218, XV291, XV292, XV293, XV295, XV297, XV298, XV300, XV306

Hercules C.3P: *(Drawn from Lyneham Transport Wing)* XV176, XV177, XV183, XV184, XV188, XV189, XV190, XV193, XV197, XV199, XV202, XV207, XV209, XV212, XV214, XV217, XV219, XV220, XV221, XV222, XV223, XV290, XV294, XV299, XV301, XV302, XV303, XV304, XV305, XV307

Below: Commemorative markings on a Lyneham Transport Wing Hercules, illustrating the badges of each component LTW squadron, Nos 70, 57(R), 47, 30 and 24.

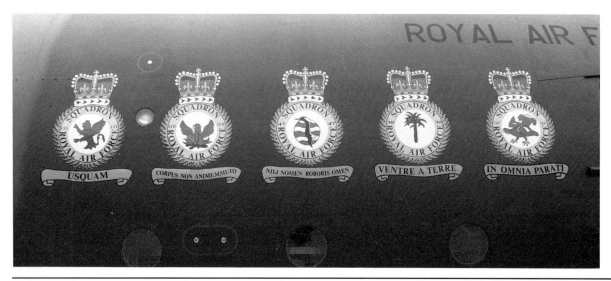

No 25 Squadron

Current base: Leeming.
Aircraft type: Tornado F.3.
Role: Air defence.
Squadron badge: A hawk upon a gauntlet.
Squadron motto: 'Feriens Tego' ('Striking I Defend').
Markings: Squadron hawk and gauntlet emblem on tail. Silver tail band edged in black. White tail codes.

Above: No 25 Squadron tail markings.

No 25 Squadron was formed from a nucleus supplied by No 6 Reserve Squadron at Montrose on 25 September 1915. It moved to France in February 1916, equipped with F.E.2bs, and was allocated fighter and reconnaissance duties over the Western Front.

D.H.4 bombers replaced the F.E.2bs during June 1917 and remained in use with the Squadron for the rest of the First World War. Conversion to D.H.9As was planned, but instead the Squadron retained its D.H.4s and moved to Scopwick, where it disbanded on 31 January 1920. It re-formed at Hawkinge with Sopwith Snipes the following day as one of the few active RAF fighter squadrons at that time.

During September 1922 the Squadron deployed to Turkey, returning in October 1923. A year later it converted on to Grebes, and in May 1929 to Siskins. Hawker Furys replaced the Siskins during February 1932, and in October 1937 the Hawker Demon twin-seat fighter was delivered. Bristol Blenheims arrived in December 1938, and the Squadron began flying night patrols when the Second World War began.

After moving to Northolt, then Filton, Northolt again, North Weald, Martlesham Heath and Debden, the Squadron converted to Beaufighters at Wittering in January 1941. De Havilland Mosquito fighter-bombers replaced the Beaufighters during October 1942, and the Squadron flew intruder missions as well as defensive fighter patrols and bomber support sorties, engaging enemy night fighters over Germany on many occasions.

When the war ended No 25 Squadron continued to operate as a fighter unit, replacing its Mosquitos with Vampires in 1951. Meteor NF.12 night fighters replaced the Vampires in March 1952, and the Squadron disbanded on 23 June 1958. It re-formed at Waterbeach on 1 July 1958 when No 135 Squadron was renumbered. The unit was now equipped with Meteors, but conversion to Javelins took place in March 1959; operations continued from Waterbeach until October 1961, when a move was made to Leuchars. The Squadron disbanded again on 30 November 1962, re-forming on 1 October 1963 at North Coates with Bloodhound surface-to-air missiles.

After having served in Germany from 1971 with Flights at Bruggen, Laarbruch and Wildenrath, No 25 Squadron moved to Wyton, with Flights at Barkston Heath and Wattisham. After nearly twenty-seven years as a Bloodhound squadron, the unit re-formed at Leeming on 29 September 1989 to fly Tornado F.3 interceptors.

AIRCRAFT
Tornado F.3: ZE808/FA, ZE210/FB, ZE908/FC, ZE961/FD, ZE737/FF, ZE161/FG, ZE203/FI, ZE962/FJ, ZE162/FK, ZE199/FL, ZE339/FO

No 27 Squadron

Current base: Odiham.
Aircraft types: Chinook HC.1, Puma HC.1.
Role: Chinook and Puma Operational Conversion Unit.
Squadron badge: An elephant.
Squadron motto: 'Quam Celerrime ad Astra' ('With All Speed to the Stars').
Markings: Squadron emblem under cockpit glazing.

Formed at Hounslow Heath on 5 November 1915, No 27 Squadron was initially equipped with Martinsyde Elephants for to the scouting role, but after it moved to France during March 1916 the less than agile Elephants were employed as bombers and reconnaissance aircraft. They were replaced by D.H.4s towards the end of 1917.

From May 1918 the Squadron received D.H.9s, and bomber-reconnaissance operations continued until the end of the First World War, when No 27 returned to the United Kingdom, disbanding on 22 January 1920. No 99 Squadron at Mianwali was renumbered 27 Squadron on 1 April 1920 and the unit's D.H.9As were replaced by Wapitis during May 1930, continuing patrols over the North-West Frontier. On the outbreak of the Second World War the Squadron was redesignated a training unit and equipped with Harts and Tiger Moths.

After being returned to operational status with Bristol Blenheims on 21 October 1940, the Squadron moved to Malaya in February 1941, only to have most of its aircraft destroyed during the Japanese invasion. It withdrew to Sumatra in January 1942 and dispersed to various locations in response to the continuing Japanese invasion, effectively disbanding one month later. The Squadron re-formed with Beaufighters on 19 September 1942 at Amarda Road and began attacks on targets in Burma on 25 December the same year.

Conversion to Mosquitos began late in 1943, although further deliveries of rocket-equipped Beaufighters were made when the Squadron became part of a Strike Wing with No 47 Squadron. A shortage of suitable maritime targets resulted in the resumption of ground attack operations over Burma in November 1944; five months later No 27 Squadron was reorganized as an air and jungle rescue unit, flying search and rescue missions over South-East Asia until 1 February 1946 and disbandment.

Re-forming as a transport unit equipped with Dakotas on 24 November 1947 at Oakington, No 27 participated in the Berlin Airlift but disbanded again on 10 November 1950. It reappeared on 15 June 1953 as a Canberra bomber unit at Scampton, from where the Squadron deployed to Cyprus during the Suez Campaign. Disbandment came once more on 31 December 1956, but on 1 April 1961 the Squadron re-formed again, this time at Scampton as a Vulcan V-bomber unit equipped with Blue Steel stand-off nuclear missiles.

Vulcan operations continued until 29 March 1972, when the Squadron disbanded, only to re-form at Scampton on 1 November 1973 with Vulcan B.2(MRR) maritime radar reconnaissance aircraft. Following the withdrawal of the Vulcan from operational service, No 27 Squadron became a Tornado GR.1 strike unit at Marham early in 1983. A ten-year association with the Tornado ended when the Squadron moved to Lossiemouth towards the end of 1993 to form No 12 (Designate) Squadron following the retirement of the latter's Buccaneers; No 240 Operational Conversion Unit at Odiham, equipped with Pumas and Chinooks, then became No 27 (Reserve) Squadron.

AIRCRAFT
Puma HC.1: *XW200/FA, XW225/FE, XW220/CZ*
Chinook HC.1: *Drawn from No 7 Squadron as required.*

No 28 Squadron

Current base: *Sek Kong.*
Aircraft type: *Wessex HC.2.*
Role: *Helicopter army support.*
Squadron badge: *In front of a demi-pegasus, a fasces.*
Squadron motto: *'Quicquid Agas Age' ('Whatsoever You May Do, Do').*
Markings: *Squadron Pegasus marking in yellow on a green circle, outlined in yellow, on tail rotor housing. White stripes on nose and rear fuselage.*

No 28 Squadron began life as a training unit, forming at Gosport on 7 November 1915. It moved to France during October 1917, equipped with Sopwith Camels and now designated a fighter unit. However, before operations could begin, the Squadron was sent to Italy as part of an Anglo-French force following the Battle of Caporetto. The Squadron patrolled the north-east Italian front until the collapse of the Austro-Hungarian Empire, returned to the United Kingdom in February 1919 and disbanded on 20 January 1920.

On 1 February 1920 No 114 Squadron, flying Bristol Fighters from Ambala on internal security patrols over the North-West Frontier, was renumbered 28 Squadron, and it continued in this role until the outbreak of the Second World War. After receiving Westland Wapitis in September 1931 and Hawker Audaxes in June 1936, the Squadron re-equipped with Westland Lysanders during September 1941, moving to Burma in December of that year following the Japanese attack. Bombing raids and army co-operation flights were carried out until Burma was eventually overrun.

No 28 re-formed at Lahore during March 1942, and after a period of army exercise support it received Hurricanes and took up tactical reconnaissance duties, resuming operations in January 1943 which continued until the Japanese surrender. Spitfires replaced the Hurricanes in July 1945 and the Squadron moved to Malaya four months later.

No 28 Squadron moved to Hong Kong during May 1949 in response to the civil war in China, receiving Vampire fighters in January 1951 and Venoms in February 1956. Hawker Hunters replaced the Venoms in July 1962, and these remained in use until 2 January 1967, when the unit disbanded.

The Squadron re-formed at Kai Tak in Hong Kong on 1 April 1968 from a detachment of Whirlwind helicopters provided by No 103 Squadron. Assigned transport and search and rescue duties, the Whirlwinds were replaced by Wessex helicopters in January 1972, and following a move to Sek Kong in 1978 the Squadron is active in Hong Kong and will remain until the official hand-over of the colony to China in 1997.

AIRCRAFT
Wessex HC.2: XR522/A, XR515/B, XT675/C, XR508/D, XT605/E, XT667/F, XT673/G, XT678/H

No 29 Squadron

Current base: Coningsby.
Aircraft type: Tornado F.3.
Role: Air defence.
Squadron badge: An eagle preying on a buzzard.
Squadron motto: 'Impiger et Acer' ('Energetic and Keen').
Markings: Squadron emblem on tail in red and yellow. A line of three red crosses, outlined in yellow, on engine intake lips. Tail code in red.

Formed at Gosport from a nucleus supplied by No 23 Squadron on 7 November 1915, No 29 Squadron moved to France during March 1916 after a period of working up in the United Kingdom. Equipped with D.H.2s, it flew fighter escort missions in support of reconnaissance aircraft operating over the Western Front. During March 1917 the D.H.2s were replaced by Nieuport Scouts, and these were in turn replaced by S.E.5as in April 1918. The last remained in use with the Squadron as fighter and ground attack aircraft for the remainder of the First World War.

Returning to Britain in August 1919 after a short period of operations in Germany, No 29 Squadron disbanded on 31 December 1919. It re-formed at Duxford on 1 April 1923 with Sopwith Snipe fighters, which were replaced by Gloster Grebes in January 1925; Armstrong-Whitworth Siskins replaced the Snipes during March 1928, and Bulldogs replaced the Siskins during June 1932. Hawker Demons were delivered in March 1935, and seven

Below, left and right: No 29 Squadron markings.

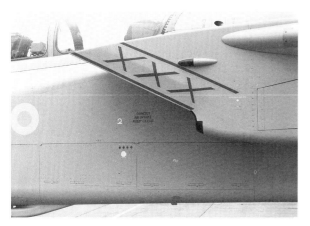

months later the unit deployed to Egypt during the Abyssinian Crisis, the Demons being accompanied by Gordons which were used for night patrols.

After returning to the United Kingdom the Squadron re-equipped with Bristol Blenheims during December 1938 and flew shipping defence patrols with these aircraft until after the outbreak of the Second World War. Early trials with airborne radar equipment were also undertaken by No 29 Squadron, and from June 1940, when German forces began major night bombing operations, the unit concentrated on night fighter duties, re-equipping with Beaufighters by February 1941. Mosquito fighters arrived during May 1943, and No 29 switched to intruder operations in May 1944, continuing in this role until October 1945 when it moved to West Malling to become a night fighter unit.

Meteor fighters replaced the Mosquitos during August 1951, by which time the Squadron had moved to Tangmere; it later moved to Acklington and then to Leuchars. Javelins replaced the Meteors in November 1957, and during February 1963 the Squadron moved to Nicosia and then, a year later, to Akrotiri. A nine-month detachment to Ndola in Zambia during 1966 was followed by a return to the United Kingdom, where the Squadron re-equipped with Lightnings at Wattisham. The Lightnings were operated until 19 July 1974, when No 29 disbanded. The Squadron re-formed on 31 December 1974 at Coningsby, equipped with Phantoms, and it became the first operational Tornado F.3 squadron in April 1987.

AIRCRAFT
Tornado F.3: ZE763/BA, ZG755/BB, ZG732/BC, ZG776/BD, ZE911/BE, ZE729/BF, ZG734/BG, ZG780/BH, ZE165/BJ, ZG733/BK, ZH553/BY, ZE965/BZ

No 30 Squadron

Current base: Lyneham.
Aircraft types: Hercules C.1P, Hercules C.3P.
Role: Tactical transport.
Squadron badge: A date palm.
Squadron motto: 'Ventre à Terre' ('All Out'—i.e. 'At Full Speed')
Markings: None.

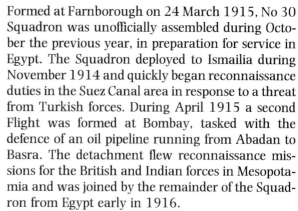

Formed at Farnborough on 24 March 1915, No 30 Squadron was unofficially assembled during October the previous year, in preparation for service in Egypt. The Squadron deployed to Ismailia during November 1914 and quickly began reconnaissance duties in the Suez Canal area in response to a threat from Turkish forces. During April 1915 a second Flight was formed at Bombay, tasked with the defence of an oil pipeline running from Abadan to Basra. The detachment flew reconnaissance missions for the British and Indian forces in Mesopotamia and was joined by the remainder of the Squadron from Egypt early in 1916.

The Squadron's normal reconnaissance and bombing operations continued until the end of the First World War, although during April 1916 it flew one of the first air-drop sorties when supplies were delivered to the besieged garrison at Kut-el-Amara.

In April 1919 the Squadron was reduced in strength at Baghdad, but following the decision to give the RAF responsibility for security in Mesopotamia (now the Kingdom of Iraq), it was brought up to full strength on 1 February 1920. Westland Wapitis replaced D.H.9As in 1929 and Hawker Hardys re-equipped the Squadron in April 1935. Bristol Blenheims were delivered in January 1938, and shortly before the outbreak of the Second World War these aircraft were deployed to Egypt.

Following the entry of Italy into the war, No 30 Squadron's Blenheims began flying fighter escort missions over the Western Desert, providing air defence for Alexandria. When Italian forces invaded Greece, the Squadron moved to the latter and flew attack missions over enemy bases in Albania, officially becoming a fighter squadron during March 1941. After a short stay in Crete during April, the Squadron returned to Egypt and replaced its Blenheims with Hurricanes, flying air defence sorties in the Alexandria area until Western Desert operations began in December 1941. In March 1942 it was deployed to Ceylon, having embarked in the carrier HMS *Indomitable*.

The Squadron remained in Ceylon as an air defence unit until February 1944, when it redeployed to the Burma Front, flying ground attack and escort sorties until May 1944, when re-equipment with P-47 Thunderbolts began. Operational missions began again on 15 October, continuing until 13 May 1945. Following the Japanese surrender the Squadron remained in India, converting to Tempests in June 1946 and finally disbanding on 1 December 1946.

No 30 re-formed at Oakington on 24 November 1947 with Dakotas and took part in the Berlin Airlift. Valettas replaced the Dakotas during November 1950, and Beverleys replaced the Valettas in April 1956. The Squadron deployed to Kenya in November 1959 and to Muharraq in September 1964. It disbanded in Bahrain on 6 September 1967 but re-formed at Fairford with Lockheed Hercules transports on 10 June 1968, moving to Lyneham to become part of the Lyneham Transport Wing in September 1971.

AIRCRAFT

Hercules C.1P: *Aircraft drawn from Lyneham Transport Wing. For serial numbers see No 24 Squadron.*
Hercules C.3P: *Drawn from Lyneham Transport Wing Hercules fleet as above.*

No 31 Squadron

Current base: *Bruggen.*
Aircraft type: *Tornado GR.1.*
Role: *Strike, attack.*
Squadron badge: *In front of a laurel wreath, a mullet.*
Squadron motto: *'In Caelum Indicum Primus' ('First into Indian Skies').*
Markings: *Yellow mullet on tail. Yellow and green chevron outlined in black, astride nose roundel. Black tail code outlined in white.*

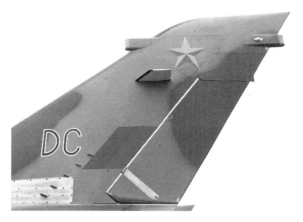

Above: No 31 Squadron tail markings.

Formed at Farnborough on 11 October 1915, No 31 Squadron was originally created for service in India, and on 27 November 'A' Flight departed for Risalpur, equipped with B.E.2cs. Two more Flights were formed at Gosport during January and April the following year, reaching full strength in May.

The Squadron remained in India for the rest of the First World War, engaged in army co-operation duties on India's North-West Frontier. Bristol Fighters were delivered to the Squadron during 1919, and these remained until 1931 when Wapitis were received. Vincents replaced the Wapitis during 1935.

No 31's role was changed to bomber and transport duties on 1 April 1939 when the Bomber Transport Flight in India was absorbed into the Squadron. After re-equipping with Valentias the

Below: A Tornado GR.1 from No 31 Squadron.

unit received DC-2s in 1941. During April 1942 the DC-2s began to be replaced by DC-3 Dakotas, and the Squadron was fully re-equipped with the latter by May 1943, flying supply-drop missions for the 14th Army in Burma until the end of the Second World War. However, during the summer of 1944 the unit was allocated glider-towing training duties.

Following the Japanese surrender the Squadron transferred to Singapore, before moving to Java in support of Allied forces there. It disbanded on 30 September 1946 but re-formed on 1 November that year when No 77 Squadron was renumbered at Mauripur. Still assigned transport duties, No 31 Squadron continued to operate until 31 December 1947, when the unit again disbanded.

On 19 July 1948 the Metropolitan Communications Squadron at Hendon was redesignated No 31 Squadron, although the original title was re-acquired on 1 March 1955. On the same day No 31 Squadron re-formed at Laarbruch with Canberra photographic reconnaissance aircraft, and operations continued here until 31 March 1971, when the unit again disbanded, only to re-form again on 7 October that year with Phantoms at Bruggen. Jaguars were delivered during 1976, the Squadron becoming operational on its new equipment on 1 July. Tornado GR.1s replaced the Jaguars during 1984, and the Squadron continues to operate from Bruggen in the strike/attack role.

Below: A BAe 125 CC.1 from No 32 Squadron.

AIRCRAFT
Tornado GR.1: ZD740/DA, ZD715/DB, ZG791/DC, ZD844/DE, ZD811/DF, ZE116/DG, ZD843/DH, ZA492/DJ, ZA461/DK, ZD790/DL, ZA554/DM, ZA455/DP, ZG771/DW, ZD812/DX, ZD711/DY, ZD741/DZ

No 32 Squadron

Current base: Northolt.
Aircraft types: Andover CC.2, BAe 125 CC.1, BAe 125 CC.2, BAe 125 C.3, Gazelle HT.3.
Squadron badge: A hunting horn, stringed.
Squadron motto: 'Adeste Comites' ('Rally Round, Comrades').
Markings: Squadron emblem on tail.

No 32 Squadron was first formed at Netheravon on 12 January 1916, equipped with D.H.2s. After moving to France during May 1916 the Squadron flew patrols over the Western Front, and the following year the D.H.2s were replaced by D.H.5s, which were in turn replaced by S.E.5as in December 1917. The S.E.5as remained for the rest of the First World War, employed on fighter and ground attack duties. The Squadron returned to the United Kingdom in March 1919 and disbanded on 29 December that year.

No 32 re-formed at Kenley on 1 April 1923 with a Flight of Sopwith Snipe fighters, a second Flight forming on 10 December and a third on 1 June 1924. Gloster Grebes were delivered towards the end of 1924, Gamecocks replacing the Grebes at the end of 1926. Siskins arrived in 1928, followed by Bulldogs in September 1930 and Gauntlets in July 1938. Hurricanes began to equip the Squadron in October 1938, and these were employed in air defence patrols when the Second World War began.

In May 1940 No 32 Squadron was tasked with defensive patrol duties in Northern France. During the Battle of Britain it took part in the defence of South-East England before moving north to Acklington during August 1940. After returning to the south of England in December, it continued flying defensive missions until May 1942, when night training began. Operational intruder sorties began in July, and these continued for two months until the Squadron was declared non-operational in preparation for the invasion of North Africa.

Deployed to Algeria in December 1942, the Squadron flew patrols over convoys and ports, and this work continued until the end of the campaign. Spitfires arrived during 1943, and these were briefly deployed to Italy in October that year before the Squadron returned to North Africa. Moving back to Italy in January 1944, No 32 flew fighter and bomber missions until October, when a move to Greece was made. During February 1945 the Squadron was re-located to Palestine and it remained in the Middle East until the end of the war.

Moving to Cyprus in May 1948, the Squadron re-equipped with Vampires in March 1949. It returned to Egypt in January 1951, Venoms replacing the Vampires in January 1955 when the Squadron moved to the Persian Gulf region. Towards the end of 1955 No 32 moved to Malta, and then to Jordan, before returning to the United Kingdom. The Squadron received Canberra bombers at Weston Zoyland in January 1957, and it continued to operate these aircraft from Cyprus until 3 February 1969, when it disbanded. On the same day the Metropolitan Communications Squadron at Northolt was re-designated No 32 Squadron, and the unit continues to operate from here, dedicated to VIP transport and communications work.

AIRCRAFT
Andover CC.2: *XS789, XS791, XS792, XS794*
Andover E.3A: *XS639, XS643, XS644*
Gazelle HT.3: *XW582, XW855, XZ935, ZB629*
BAe 125 CC.1: *XW788, XW789, XW790, XW791*
BAe 125 CC.2: *XX507, XX508*
BAe 125 CC.3: *ZD620, ZD621, ZD703, ZD704, ZE395, ZE396*

No 33 Squadron

Current base: *Odiham.*
Aircraft type: *Puma HC.1*
Role: *Helicopter support.*
Squadron badge: *A hart's head.*
Squadron motto: *'Loyalty'.*
Markings: *Squadron emblem, flanked by blue and red bars, under cockpit glazing.*

Following the transfer of No 12 Squadron to France, a nucleus was left behind at Filton which became No 33 Squadron on 12 January 1916, equipped with B.E.2cs. During March the Squadron moved to Sheffield, allocated to the defence of the North Midlands industrial area against airship attacks. Although initially tasked with training, the Squadron transferred this responsibility to No 57 Squadron and remained active as a night patrol unit for the

Below: No 33 Squadron markings.

rest of the First World War. It flew F.E.2bs, but these were replaced by Bristol Fighters in June 1918, followed by Avro 504s two months later. The Squadron disbanded on 13 June 1919.

Re-formation took place at Netheravon on 1 March 1929 with Horsley bombers. Hawker Harts replaced the Horsleys in February 1930, and in October 1935 the unit moved to the Middle East during the Abyssinian Crisis, remaining in the area after other units returned to the United Kingdom. Gladiator fighters arrived in March 1938 and in 1938–39 the unit was engaged in policing flights over Palestine.

Following Italy's entry into the Second World War, No 33 Squadron was tasked with desert air defence patrols until Hurricanes arrived in September 1940. Ground attack operations then began, and these continued until January 1941, when the unit moved to Greece. During the following month the unit began flying bomber escort missions, until German attacks prompted its evacuation from the area. The last Hurricanes left Greece in April 1941, amalgamating with No 80 Squadron's aircraft in Crete to form a fighter defence unit, but German attacks quickly forced the unit to abandon the island and the No 33 Squadron's one remaining Hurricane was flown to Egypt, where its ground crew were captured (though they later escaped).

The Squadron became operational again in June 1941, flying missions over the Western Desert. It converted to Curtiss Tomahawks in February 1942 but re-equipped with Hurricanes again shortly afterwards. Spitfires were first received early in 1943, although the Hurricane was not completely replaced until December. In April the following year the Squadron returned to the United Kingdom to participate in the invasion of Europe. Fighter operations began from North Weald during May 1944, and the Squadron moved to Normandy during August. After flying ground attack missions in support of the Army, it returned to the United Kingdom in December and converted to Tempests.

In February 1945 No 33 Squadron was transferred to Germany, remaining there until July 1949, when a move was made to Malaya to fly ground attack missions against communist troops. After re-equipping with Hornets, the unit merged with No 45 Squadron, re-forming again on 15 October 1955 at Driffield with Venoms, which were used until disbandment on 3 June 1957.

On 30 September 1957 No 264 Squadron was renumbered 33 Squadron, flying Meteor night fighters from Leeming. Conversion to Javelins took place during 1958, and the Squadron disbanded on 17 November 1962. It re-formed as a Bloodhound guided missile unit on 1 March 1965 in Malaysia, disbanding again on 30 January 1970. Re-forming again on 14 June 1971 at Odiham, it was equipped with Puma support helicopters, which currently remain in service.

AIRCRAFT

Puma HC.1: *XW204/CA, XW223/CB, XW202/CE, XW209/CF, XW211/CH, XW213/CJ, XW234/CO, XW217/CS, ZA937/CV, ZA938/CW*

No 39 Squadron

Current base: Marham.
Aircraft type: Canberra PR.9.
Role: Photographic reconnaissance.
Squadron badge: A winged bomb.
Squadron motto: 'Die Noctuque' ('By Day and By Night').
Markings: Winged bomb emblem on tail. White tail codes.

No 39 Squadron formed at Hounslow, Middlesex, on 15 April 1916 as a home defence unit, equipped with B.E.2cs and with Flights detached to Sutton's Farm (Hornchurch) and Hainault Farm in Essex. The Squadron moved to nearby Woodford during August, an additional detachment being formed at North Weald. The B.E.2cs were replaced by Bristol Fighters in response to the Germans' replacement of Zeppelins by Gotha bombers. During November 1918 the unit moved to France, but following the Armistice a few days later it disbanded on 16 November 1918.

No 37 Squadron at Biggin Hill was renumbered 39 Squadron on 1 July 1919 and the unit moved to Spittlegate in February 1923 equipped with D.H.9A bombers. The Squadron deployed to India during December 1928, beginning patrols over the North-West Frontier with Westland Wapitis two months later. Hawker Harts replaced the Wapitis in November 1931 and Bristol Blenheims re-equipped the Squadron in 1939, shortly before it moved to Singapore.

No 41 Squadron

Current base: *Coltishall.*
Aircraft types: *Jaguar GR.1A, Jaguar T.2A.*
Role: *Tactical reconnaissance, attack.*
Squadron badge: *A double armed cross.*
Squadron motto: *'Seek and Destroy'.*
Markings: *Red cross surmounted by a yellow crown, outlined in white, on tail. Emblem repeated on intakes, flanked by red and white bars. Black tail code outlined in white.*

Although the nucleus of No 41 Squadron was first formed during June 1916, this unit was re-designated No 27 Reserve Squadron and No 41 Squadron was officially formed at Gosport on 14 July 1916, equipped with F.E.8 fighters. Moving to France in October 1916, the Squadron was employed on patrols over the Western Front, and despite the F.E.8's deficiencies the type remained in use until July 1917, when S.E.5as were received. These remained in use until the end of the First World War, primarily on fighter duties but also flying ground attack sorties. The Squadron returned to the United Kingdom in January 1919 and disbanded on 31 December that year.

No 41 Squadron re-formed at Northolt on 1 April 1923 with Snipes, which were replaced by Siskins a year later. Bulldogs were delivered to the unit during October 1931, and Hawker Demons replaced the Bulldogs in July 1934. The Squadron deployed to Aden in October 1935 during the Abyssinian Crisis. After returning home in August 1936 it received Hawker Furys, which remained in use until January 1939 when the first Spitfires arrived.

The Squadron flew defensive fighter patrols from Catterick and Wick for the first months of the Second World War, but at the end of May 1940 it moved south to fly fighter cover over the Dunkirk beaches. During the Battle of Britain it flew alternately from Catterick and Hornchurch.

In July 1941 it began fighter sweeps over France. These continued until August 1942, when the unit moved north to conduct patrols over the Irish Sea. After re-equipping with later-mark Spitfires, the Squadron returned south, flying fighter-bomber missions against coastal targets and also reconnais-

During April 1940 the Squadron moved to India en route for the Middle East, but it became diverted to Aden following Italy's entry into the Second World War. After flying bombing missions over Italian East Africa, the Squadron moved to Egypt during November 1940, converting to Marylands two months later. Strategic reconnaissance missions began during April 1941.

Beauforts were received in August 1941 for anti-shipping duties; these began in September, although Maryland reconnaissance flights continued until January 1942. Torpedo bomber missions against enemy convoys were mounted from forward bases in Egypt and Libya, with a detachment in Malta. The detachment joined Nos 86 and 217 Squadrons on 20 August 1942 to form a new No 39 Squadron, the remaining elements of the original unit in Egypt being absorbed by No 47 Squadron. Beaufighters were received in June 1943, and the Squadron deployed to Italy during July 1944, re-equipping with Marauders in December of that year. A move to Sudan in October 1945 saw Mosquitos replacing the Marauders, and the Squadron disbanded on 8 September 1946.

No 39 Squadron re-formed at Nairobi on 1 April 1948 with Tempests but disbanded less than a year later, re-forming again at Fayid with Mosquito night fighters on 1 March 1949, tasked with the defence of the Suez Canal. After re-equipping with Meteor night fighters, the unit returned to Malta in January 1955, disbanding on 30 June 1958. No 69 Squadron, with Canberra photo-reconnaissance jets, was renumbered 39 Squadron on 1 July 1958 and operations from Malta continued until September 1970, when the unit returned to the United Kingdom.

In 1982 the Squadron, now based at Wyton, was reduced in size and became No 1 Photographic Reconnaissance Unit, but ten years later the title was changed to No 39 (1 PRU) Squadron. The unit's Canberra PR.9s moved to Marham in 1994 and these aircraft were later joined by three Canberra T.4 dual-control trainers and a pair of Canberra PR.7s for radar-calibration duties.

AIRCRAFT
Canberra T.4: *WJ866/BL, WT480/BC*
Canberra PR.7: *WJ874/BM, WH779/BP*
Canberra PR.9: *XH134/AA, XH168/AB, XH169/AC, XH131/AF, XH135/AG*

Above: A No 41 Squadron Jaguar GR.1A wearing special 75th Anniversary markings.

sance bomber escort sorties. From April 1944 the Squadron was employed on fighter sweeps over Brittany, but it returned to defensive operations when V-1 attacks over the Kent coast began.

No 41 Squadron moved to Belgium in December 1944, flying armed reconnaissance missions over Germany and eventually becoming a renumbered 26 Squadron at Wunstorf. On the same day, 1 April 1946, No 122 Squadron at Dalcross was renumbered 41 Squadron and two weeks later moved to Wittering with Spitfires. The latter were replaced by Oxfords and Harvards when the Squadron became an instrument flying training unit.

In June 1948 No 41 re-equipped with Hornets, converting to Meteors in 1951 before moving to Biggin Hill. The Squadron flew Hunters from 1955 to 1958 but in January that year it disbanded, re-emerging as a renumbered 141 Squadron at Coltishall the same day. Now equipped with Javelins, it operated from Coltishall until 6 December 1963, when disbandment was followed by re-formation at West Raynham as a Bloodhound missile unit.

After disbanding again on 18 September 1970, the Squadron re-formed at Coningsby on 1 April 1972 with Phantom fighter-reconnaissance/ground attack jets. During August 1976 it began converting to Jaguars, and following the disbandment of the Phantom element at Coningsby it re-formed at Coltishall with Jaguars on 1 April 1977. It flies from here today in the reconnaissance and ground attack role.

AIRCRAFT
Jaguar GR.1A: *XZ398/A, XZ114/B, XZ115/C, XZ113/D, XZ362/E, XZ118/F, XZ119/G, XZ107/H, XZ355/J, XZ357/K, XZ358/L, XZ104/M, XZ360/N, XZ363/O, XZ103/P, XZ101/Q, XZ106/R, XZ366/S*
Jaguar T.2A: *XX847/X, XX146/Y*

No 42 Squadron

Current base: *Kinloss.*
Aircraft type: *Nimrod MR.2P.*
Role: *Nimrod Operational Conversion Unit.*
Squadron badge: *On a terrestrial globe, a figure of Perseus.*
Squadron motto: *'Fortiter in Re' ('Bravely in Action').*
Markings: *Normally none.*

Formed at Filton on 1 April 1916, No 42 Squadron moved to France four months later after a period of working-up, equipped with B.E.2es for artillery spotting and reconnaissance duties over the Western Front. In November 1917 the unit transferred to Italy, having replaced its B.E.2es with R.E.8s in April 1917. The latter were operated over the Austro-Italian Front for three months before the Squadron returned to France in March 1918 in response to the German offensive. After returning to the United Kingdom after the Armistice, the Squadron disbanded on 26 June 1919.

On 14 December 1936 No 42 Squadron re-formed at Donibristle with Vildebeest torpedo bombers, and as one of only two torpedo bomber units based in the United Kingdom it retained its Vildebeests until April 1940, when Beauforts were received as replacements. Anti-shipping and minelaying missions over the coasts of Northern Europe continued until June 1942, when the unit departed for the Far East. The Squadron's aircraft deployed via the Mediterranean, and en route they were attached to No 47 Squadron to carry out attacks on enemy shipping both before and after the Battle of El Alamein. The Squadron was established in Ceylon in December 1942, converting to Blenheims two months later, and these aircraft were used operationally over Burma during March 1943. Hurricanes replaced the Blenheims from August 1943, and ground attack missions began on 22 December 1943, continuing until May 1945.

No 42 Squadron disbanded on 30 June 1945 but re-formed the following day when No 146 Squadron was renumbered. P-47 Thunderbolts were operated until 30 December 1945, when the unit again disbanded. No 254 Squadron at Thorney Island was renumbered 42 Squadron on 1 October 1946, and Beaufighters were operated on strike duties until 15 October 1947 when the unit disbanded once more.

The Squadron re-formed at St Eval on 28 June 1952, equipped with Shackleton maritime reconnaissance aircraft. It moved to the larger airfield at nearby St Mawgan during October 1958, supporting detachments in the Persian Gulf and Madagascar. The Shackletons were replaced by Nimrods during April 1971. Operations from St Mawgan continued until 1992, when the Nimrod Operational Conversion Unit (No 236 OCU) was renumbered 42(R) Squadron at Kinloss.

AIRCRAFT
Nimrod MR.2P: *(Drawn from Kinloss Wing)*
XV226, XV227, XV228, XV229, XV230,
XV231, XV232, XV233, XV235, XV236,
XV237, XV238, XV239, XV240, XV241,
XV243, XV244, XV245, XV246, XV248,
XV250, XV251, XV252, XV254, XV255,
XV258, XV260, XZ284

No 43 Squadron

Current base: *Leuchars.*
Aircraft type: *Tornado F.3.*
Role: *Air defence.*
Squadron badge: *A game cock.*
Squadron motto: *'Gloria Finis' ('Glory is the End').*
Markings: *Fighting cock emblem on tail, black and white checks either side of nose roundel. White tail code.*

Equipped with Sopwith 1½-Strutters, No 43 Squadron moved to France in January 1917, having formed at Stirling on 15 April 1916. It was tasked with fighter and reconnaissance duties, though some bombing raids were also flown behind German lines, before the unit converted to Sopwith Camels during September 1917. It remained active in the fighter and reconnaissance roles until the end of the First World War, taking delivery of Sopwith Snipes shortly before the Armistice.

The Squadron then moved to Germany for a brief period before returning to the United Kingdom and disbanding on 31 December 1919. It re-formed at Hendon, again with Snipes, on 1 July 1923, replac-

Below: No 42 Squadron tail markings.

Above: No 43 Squadron tail markings.

ing these aircraft with Gloster Gamecocks during 1926. Armstrong-Whitworth Siskins were received in 1928, followed by Hawker Furys in 1931 and Hawker Hurricanes towards the end of 1938.

On the outbreak of the Second World War the Squadron moved north to fly defensive missions, before returning south to Tangmere in May 1940 to fly patrols over the Dunkirk beaches. Following participation in the early part of the Battle of Britain, the Squadron moved north again to re-equip, and then moved to Scotland as a training unit, still tasked with a defensive role. In June 1942 the unit moved south to fly fighter sweeps over France and night intruder missions. It withdrew from operations in September 1942 to begin training in anticipation of a move to Gibraltar, which took place in November.

Following the Allied landings in North Africa, No 43 moved to newly captured airfields in Algeria, providing fighter cover for the Army. Hurricanes were replaced by Spitfires in February 1943, and the Squadron moved to Malta in June to cover the landings in Sicily. It moved to Italy three months later, transferring to Corsica in July 1944 to cover landings in southern France and returning to Italy six weeks later to fly fighter-bomber missions until the end of the Second World War. Disbandment came on 16 May 1947.

No 266 Squadron, equipped with Meteors at Tangmere, was renumbered 43 Squadron on 11 February 1949. The Squadron moved to Leuchars in October 1950, and the Meteors were replaced by Hunters in 1954. It was transferred to Nicosia in June 1961 as a ground attack unit, moving to Aden in March 1963 to fly missions in support of the Army. After disbanding on 14 October 1967, it re-formed at Leuchars on 1 September 1969 as one of only two RAF squadrons to fly the 'navalized' Phantom FG.1. During 1990 No 43 Squadron converted to Tornado F.3 interceptors, which it continues to fly from Leuchars.

AIRCRAFT
Tornado F.3: ZE755/GB, ZE207/GC, ZE380/GD, ZE733/GE, ZE757/GF, ZE288/GG, ZE838/GH, ZE732/GI, ZG554/GJ, ZE731/GK, ZG774/GN, ZE760/GP

No 45 Squadron

Current base: Finningley.
Aircraft type: Jetstream T.1.
Role: Multi Engine Training Squadron (part of No 6 FTS).
Squadron badge: A winged camel.
Squadron motto: 'Per Ardue Surge' ('Through Difficulties I Arise').
Markings: Pegasus emblem surrounded by titles, on a white circle on forward fuselage. Blue bars incorporating red diamonds on tail.

Formed at Gosport on 1 March 1916, No 45 Squadron moved to France in October of the same year following a period of training. Equipped with Sopwith 1½-Strutters, the unit flew fighter patrols over the Western Front, re-equipping with Sopwith Camels before moving to northern Italy in November 1917 to begin operations on the Austrian Front as part of an Anglo-French force sent to reinforce the Italian lines. In September 1918 the Squadron returned to France, joining the Independent Force to fly bomber escort missions for the remainder of the First World War. After returning to the United Kingdom in February 1919, the unit disbanded on 31 December that year.

Re-forming on 1 April 1921 at Helwan with Vickers Vimys, the Squadron helped to open up air routes in the Middle East, re-equipping with Vernons in March 1922 and moving to Iraq at the same time to begin bomber and transport operations. It was absorbed by No 47 Squadron on 17 January 1927 and re-formed at Heliopolis on 25 April that year, equipped with D.H.9As for fighter patrols in Egypt and Palestine. Fairey IIIFs arrived in 1929, followed by Hawker Harts in 1935, although the one Flight which was so equipped was transferred to No 6 Squadron in January 1936; Vincents replaced the IIIFs in December 1935. 'B' Flight was detached to Nairobi in September 1935, receiving Gordons in January 1936 before being redesignated No 223 Squadron on 15 December that year. During November 1937 Wellesleys were delivered to the Squadron, followed by Bristol Blenheims in June 1939.

When Italy entered the Second World War the Squadron began bombing operations, having sent a detachment to the Sudan in July 1940 to fly attack missions over Italian East Africa. The entire Squadron moved there for three months beginning in September, before returning to Egypt to participate in the Syrian Campaign in June 1941. The Squadron moved to Burma in February 1942, but it arrived as the Allied forces were withdrawing and so it re-assembled in India during March 1942.

After re-equipping with Vengeance dive-bombers, the Squadron continued to mount attacks on Japanese targets, with Mosquitos eventually replacing the Vengeances. After flying its last operational mission of the Second World War on 12 May 1945, the unit transferred to India, and then in May 1946 to Ceylon. Bristol Beaufighters arrived during December 1945, supplemented by Brigands for meteorological duties until the latter aircraft were transferred to No 1301 Flight. After moving to Malaya in August 1948, the Squadron re-equipped with Brigands in 1949, followed by Hornets in 1952. Vampire jets arrived in May 1955, followed by Venoms seven months later. Conversion to Canberra bombers took place at Coningsby in November 1957, and these aircraft remained in use until 13 January 1970 when the Squadron disbanded.

No 45 Squadron re-formed at West Raynham on 1 August 1972 with Hunter ground attack aircraft, transferring to Wittering in September the same year. The unit disbanded again on 4 June 1976, reappearing as a 'shadow' squadron for the Tornado Weapons Conversion Unit at Honington on 1 December 1986. Following the redesignation of the TWCU as No 15(R) Squadron, the Multi Engine Training Squadron—part of No 6 FTS at Finningley—was renumbered 45(R) Squadron during 1992.

AIRCRAFT
Jetstream T.1: *XX492/A, XX494/B, XX495/C, XX496/D, XX497/E, XX498/F, XX499/G, XX500/H, XX482/J, XX491/K, XX493/L*

Below : No 45(R) Squadron fuselage markings.

No 47 Squadron

Current base: *Lyneham.*
Aircraft types: *Hercules C.1P, Hercules C.3P.*
Role: *Tactical transport.*
Squadron badge: *In front of a fountain, a crane's head.*
Squadron motto: *'Nili Nomen Roboris Omen' ('The Name of the Nile is an Omen of Our Strength').*
Markings: *None.*

No 47 Squadron was first formed at Beverley on 1 March 1916. It departed for Greece six months later, arriving at Salonika to join a British, French and Serbian force which was defending an area of Macedonia against Bulgarian and Austro-Hungarian forces. Two Flights were equipped with reconnaissance-configured B.E.2s and a third flight flew fighters until April 1918, when it became part of No 150 Squadron.

No 47 Squadron operated a variety of aircraft types in addition to the B.E.2 and was engaged primarily in bombing operations against the Bulgarian Army following its retreat. During April 1919 the Squadron moved to Russia in support of White Russian forces. No 206 Squadron at Helwan was renumbered 47 Squadron on 1 February 1920, equipped with D.H.9s and with a detachment at Khartoum. The detachment was joined by the remainder of the Squadron in October 1927, and cooperative flights with the Sudan Defence Force continued until Italy entered the Second World War in June 1940, a floatplane Flight being operated from the Nile for ten years from February 1929. Wellesleys were delivered to the Squadron in June 1939, replacing Gordons and Vincents.

Following the outbreak of war in East Africa, No 47 Squadron began bombing missions over Italian airfields in Eritrea and Ethiopia but it was transferred to Asmara when the Italian forces in Eritrea surrendered. During December 1941 it deployed to the Middle East to begin anti-submarine patrols along the Egyptian coast. Beauforts replaced the Wellesleys during 1942, and the Squadron moved to Tunisia in June 1943, re-equipping with Beaufighters. After moving to Libya in October 1943, it went to India in March 1944, converting to Mosquitos seven months later. However, problems with the Mosquito led to the reintroduction of the Beaufighter during November. Mosquitos returned in February the following year, and operations continued until 21 March 1946 and disbandment.

No 644 Squadron at Qastina was renumbered 47 Squadron on 1 September 1946 and its Halifax transports were returned to Fairford a few weeks later. After moving to Dishforth in September 1948, No 47 became the first Hastings squadron, flying these aircraft during the Berlin Airlift, and in March 1956 it became the first to operate Blackburn Beverleys, which it flew until 31 October 1967, when it disbanded. Re-formation took place on 25 February 1968 at Fairford when Hercules transports were introduced. After moving to Lyneham during September 1971, the Squadron became part of the Lyneham Transport Wing, and it remains operational today with Hercules.

AIRCRAFT
Hercules C.1P: *Aircraft drawn from Lyneham Transport Wing. For serial numbers see No 24 Squadron.*
Hercules C.3P: *As above.*

No 51 Squadron

Current base: *Wyton.*
Aircraft type: *Nimrod R.1P.*
Role: *Electronic intelligence-gathering*
Squadron badge: *A goose.*
Squadron motto: *'Swift and Sure'.*
Markings: *Squadron emblem in red on tail.*

Formed at Thetford on 15 May 1916, No 51 Squadron was initially tasked with home defence, with detachments at Marham, Mattishall, Tydd St Mary and Sutton's Farm. Equipped with B.E.2s, the unit flew anti-Zeppelin patrols, defending London and the Midlands against enemy attacks routed over The Wash. The Squadron moved to the London area in May 1919 and disbanded on 13 June that year.

On 5 March 1937 'B' Flight of No 58 Squadron was renumbered 51 Squadron at Driffield, flying Virginias and Ansons until Whitleys were delivered in February 1938. When the Second World War began the unit flew leaflet-dropping missions, but the German invasion of France led to the commencement of bombing operations. In February 1942 the Squadron flew paratroops on their first raid on France, and three months later it was transferred to Coastal Command to begin patrols over the Bay of Biscay.

No 51 Squadron returned to Bomber Command in October 1942, re-equipping with Halifaxes, which it continued to operate until May 1945 when it received Stirlings configured for transport duties. Trooping flights to India and the Middle East continued until the end of 1945, and during February 1946 the unit converted to Yorks, using these aircraft during the Berlin Airlift. Disbandment followed on 30 October 1950.

On 21 August 1958 No 192 Squadron at Watton was renumbered 51 Squadron, with a mixed fleet of Canberras and Comets for electronic intelligence-gathering and reconnaissance. After moving to Wyton in 1961 the Squadron replaced the Comets with Nimrods during 1971 and gradually retired the Canberras. No 51 Squadron moved to Waddington in 1994.

AIRCRAFT
Nimrod R.1P: *XW664, XW665, XW666*

Above: A BAe Nimrod R.1 from No 51 Squadron.

No 54 Squadron

Current base: Coltishall.
Aircraft types: Jaguar GR.1A, Jaguar T.2A.
Role: Ground attack.
Squadron badge: A lion rampant semée de lys.
Squadron motto: 'Audax Omnia Perpeti' ('Boldness to Endure Anything').
Markings: Blue lion on a yellow shield on nose, blue and yellow checks on intake fairings and on tail RWR fairing. Black tail codes outlined in white.

No 54 Squadron formed at Castle Bromwich on 16 May 1916, moving to France in December. Its Sopwith Pups were replaced by Camels a year later. In addition to fighter and escort missions, the Squadron flew low-level attack sorties on troops and transports behind enemy lines, roles it continued until the end of the First World War. It handed its aircraft over to No 151 Squadron during January 1919 and returned to the United Kingdom, where it disbanded on 25 October that year.

Re-formation took place on 15 January 1930 at Hornchurch, where the Squadron was equipped with Siskin fighters, which were replaced by Bulldogs that summer. Gauntlets replaced the Bulldogs during September 1936, and Gladiators arrived in May 1937. Supermarine Spitfires replaced the Gladiators in March 1939, and after the outbreak of the Second World War the aircraft were used for defensive patrols.

During the Dunkirk evacuation the Squadron flew patrols over the Belgian coast, and following active participation in the first half of the Battle of Britain the unit moved to Yorkshire in September, returning south in February 1941 to begin fighter sweeps over France. It continued in this role until November, when it moved to Scotland.

No 54 Squadron moved to Australia as part of a Spitfire Wing during June 1942, tasked with the air defence of north-west of the country. However, because of commitments in the Middle East, aircraft were not available until January 1943, and Japanese attacks in the area ceased by the end of July. With little activity to occupy the Squadron for the rest of the war, it lost most of its aircraft to other units and it disbanded on 31 October 1945.

No 183 Squadron at Chilbolton was renumbered 54 Squadron on 15 November 1945 and, equipped with Tempests, the unit moved to Odiham during June 1946, converting to Vampires the following month. Meteors replaced the Vampires during April 1952, and Hunters replaced the Meteors during March 1955.

The Squadron moved to Stradishall in July 1959 and converted to ground attack Hunters during March 1960. A further move was made in August 1963, this time to West Raynham, where the unit

Above: A No 54 Squadron Jaguar GR.1A. (G. Ashley)

joined No 1 Squadron. Like the latter, No 54 Squadron was scheduled to convert to Harriers, but on 1 September 1969 it disbanded, re-forming on the same day at Coningsby as a Phantom ground attack squadron.

Phantom operations ceased on 23 April 1974, and the Squadron transferred to Lossiemouth, to take over a Jaguar-equipped unit which had formed on 29 March previously. It moved to Coltishall on 8 August 1974 and continues to operate the Jaguar from this station.

AIRCRAFT
Jaguar GR.1A: XZ112/GA, XZ362/GC, XZ108/GD, XX767/GE, XZ373/GF, XZ117/GG, XX974/GH, XZ364/GJ, XX478/GK, XZ109/GL, XZ385/GM, XZ394/GN, XZ367/GP, XX723/GQ, XZ375/GS, XX725/GU
Jaguar T.2A: XX143/GS

No 55 Squadron

Current base: Brize Norton.
Aircraft types: VC10 C.1/C.1K/K.2/K.3/K.4, TriStar K.1/KC.1/C.2.
Role: VC10 and TriStar Operational Conversion Unit.
Squadron badge: A cubit arm grasping a spear.
Squadron motto: 'Nil Nos Tremefacit' ('Nothing Shakes Us').
Markings: None.

Equipped with D.H.4s, No 55 Squadron was formed at Castle Bromwich on 27 April 1916 and took its aircraft to France in March 1917, having trained on a variety of aircraft types during its first year of service. The Squadron flew reconnaissance and bombing missions behind the Western Front, and following the formation of the Independent Force in June 1918 it was attached to No 41 Wing, mounting strategic raids on German targets. The Squadron also delivered mail to occupation forces before returning to the United Kingdom and disbanding on 22 January 1920.

The following 1 February No 142 Squadron at Suez was renumbered 55 Squadron, and having replaced D.H.9s with D.H.9As it moved to Turkey in July, returning in September to take up residence in Iraq. Westland Wapitis were delivered in February 1930, and Vincents arrived in February 1937. The Squadron formed part of a peace-keeping force in Iraq, flying a variety of missions against tribesmen. Blenheims were delivered in March 1939, and during August that year they were deployed to Egypt. Italy's entry into the Second World War led to the commencement of bombing raids by No 55 Squadron, and by March 1941 No 55 was the only day bomber squadron remaining in the Western Desert, the rest having moved to Greece.

In May 1942 the unit converted to Baltimores, and after flying offensive missions at El Alamein it moved forward to remain within bombing range of the enemy, eventually reaching Tunisia, where attacks continued until the Axis forces surrendered. Attacks on bases in Sicily were launched from Tunisia, and when airfields in Sicily were secured the Squadron moved there during August 1943. The Squadron moved in to captured bases in southern Italy towards the end of September and it remained in the theatre until the end of the war, flying in support of the Army. In September 1945 it moved on to Greece and in June 1946 it re-equipped with Mosquitos, which it operated until 1 November 1946 and disbandment.

No 55 Squadron re-formed at Honington on 1 September 1960 as a Victor V-bomber unit, moving to Marham in May 1965 to take up refuelling tanker operations with the Victor. It remained active in this role until October 1993, having continuously operated a single aircraft type for a longer period than any other RAF squadron. On 15 October 1993 the Squadron disbanded, but it re-formed as No 55(R) Squadron at Brize Norton, flying VC10s and TriStars previously operated by No 241 OCU.

AIRCRAFT

VC10: *Aircraft drawn from Nos 10 and 101 Squadrons (q.v.) as required.*
TriStar: *Aircraft drawn from No 216 Squadron (q.v.).*

No 56 Squadron

Current base: *Coningsby.*
Aircraft type: *Tornado F.3.*
Role: *Tornado F.3 Operational Conversion Unit.*
Squadron badge: *A phoenix.*
Motto: *'Quid si Cœlum Ruat' ('What if Heaven Falls?').*
Markings: *Phoenix emblem on tail, red and white checks either side of nose roundel. White tail codes.*

No 56 Squadron was formed on 9 June 1916 from a nucleus supplied by No 28 Squadron. Based at Gosport and equipped with various training aircraft, the unit moved to London Colney in July, receiving S.E.5s in March 1917 and moving to France in April. Apart from a two-week return to the United Kingdom to fly air defence sorties, the unit remained active in France throughout the First World War.

During the final German withdrawal the Squadron flew ground attack missions against enemy troops and transport, returning to the United Kingdom in February 1919 and disbanding on 22 January 1920. No 80 Squadron at Aboukir was renumbered 56 Squadron on 1 February 1920, and the unit operated Sopwith Snipes until disbandment on 23 September 1922.

The Squadron number remained in use at Constantinople, where a detachment was attached to No 208 Squadron, but No 56 officially re-formed at Hawkinge on 1 November 1922 with Sopwith Snipes. Gloster Grebes replaced the Snipes in September 1924 and Siskins arrived in September 1927, followed by Bulldogs in October 1932, Gauntlets in May 1936 and Gladiators in July 1937. Hurricanes were delivered to the Squadron in May

Below: No 56(R) Squadron nose and tail markings. No 43 Squadron's black and white chequerboard nose markings are carried in a similar position to No 56's.

Above: A No 56(R) Squadron Tornado F.3 specially painted for air display appearances in a scheme similar to that worn by the Squadron's Lightning F.1 Firebirds *aerobatic team during the 1960s.*

1938, and following the outbreak of the Second World War these were flown on defensive patrols until fighter cover was required for the Dunkirk evacuation.

The Squadron operated from various French airfields during the Battle of France, and it was active throughout the Battle of Britain. It re-equipped with Typhoons in September 1941. Ground attack and anti-shipping operations were now the Squadron's main tasks, rocket firing sorties beginning in February 1944. Conversion to Spitfires took place in April 1944, but replacements in the shape of Tempests were received at the end of June and these were used against V-1 flying bombs. Towards the end of September the Squadron moved to the Low Countries, flying armed reconnaissance missions over Germany.

No 56 was renumbered 16 Squadron on 31 March 1946, and the following day No 124 Squadron, equipped with Meteors at Bentwaters, was renumbered 56 Squadron. The unit received Swifts in February 1954, followed by Hunters in May 1955. English Electric Lightnings were delivered during January 1961, and the Squadron moved to Cyprus in 1967 as part of the Near East Air Force.

Following its return to the United Kingdom No 56 was based at Wattisham until 29 June 1976, when the unit became a Phantom interceptor squadron, at first based at Coningsby but later moving back to Wattisham. Phantom operations ended in June 1992, and No 229 OCU at Coningsby was renumbered 56(R) Squadron, equipped with Tornado F.3 interceptors.

AIRCRAFT
Tornado F.3: *ZE163/AA, ZE157/AB, ZE253/AC, ZE290/AD, ZE340/AE, ZE166/AF, ZE202/AG, ZE287/AH, ZE343/AI, ZE258/AJ, ZH556/AK, ZE735/AL, ZE205/AM, ZE208/AN, ZE785/AO, ZG770/AP, ZG799/AQ, ZE295/AR, ZE836/AS, ZG797/AU, ZG796/AV, ZE789/AW, ZG768/AX, ZG795/AY, ZH552/AZ, ZE839/A6, ZE832/A7, ZE791/A9*

No 57 Squadron

Current base: Lyneham.
Aircraft types: Hercules C.1P, Hercules C.3P.
Role: Hercules Operational Conversion Unit.
Squadron badge: Issuant from two logs, a phoenix.
Squadron motto: 'Corpus Non Animum Muto' ('I Change My Body, Not My Spirit').
Markings: None.

No 57 Squadron was formed at Copmanthorpe on 8 June 1916 from a nucleus supplied by No 33 Squadron, and the first months of its existence were occupied with training, on a variety of aircraft types. Moving to France in December 1916 with F.E.2ds and D.H.4s, the Squadron operated initially as a fighter unit, before changing to the bomber and reconnaissance roles, in which it continued to operate until the end of the First World War. It then received D.H.9As for mail carrying, before returning to the United Kingdom in August and disbanding on 31 December 1919.

Re-formation took place at Netheravon on 20 October 1931 as a light bomber squadron equipped with Hawker Harts. The latter were replaced by Hinds in May 1936, and Blenheims were delivered to the unit in March 1938. The Squadron deployed to France during September 1939 to begin strategic reconnaissance missions, and during May 1940 it was tasked with the location and destruction of enemy columns which were invading Belgium and France.

After being evacuated to England, the Squadron continued to fly reconnaissance missions until June. One month later it moved to Scotland to begin anti-shipping operations over the North Sea, returning south to convert to Wellingtons in November 1940. Night bombing missions began two months later and continued until the end of the Second World War. Lancasters replaced the Wellingtons during September 1942, and although a small number of Avro Lincolns were delivered to the Squadron in August 1945 the unit disbanded on 25 November the same year.

The following day No 103 Squadron's Lincoln Flight at Elsham Wolds was redesignated No 57 Squadron. Boeing Washingtons replaced the Lincolns in May 1951, and Canberra bombers replaced the Washingtons in May 1953. Operations with the Canberra continued until 9 December 1957, when the Squadron disbanded. It re-formed on 1 January 1959 as a Victor V-bomber unit based at Honington and it moved to Marham in June 1966 to begin in-flight refuelling tanker operations with the Victor, remaining active in this role until June 1986, when it disbanded. During 1992 the Hercules Operational Conversion Unit (No 242 OCU) was renumbered 57(R) Squadron. It continues to operate from Lyneham, with aircraft drawn from the Lyneham Transport Wing as required.

AIRCRAFT

Hercules C.1P: Aircraft drawn from Lyneham Transport Wing. For serial numbers see No 24 Squadron
Hercules C.3P: As above.

No 60 Squadron

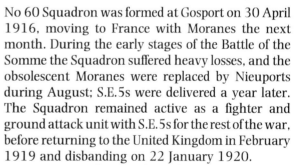

Current base: Benson.
Aircraft type: Wessex HC.2.
Role: Helicopter support.
Squadron badge: A markhor's head.
Squadron motto: 'Per Ardua ad Aethera Tendo' ('I Strive through Difficulties to the Sky').
Markings: Squadron emblem in black and white, on the tail rotor housing, flanked by black rectangles featuring white lightning strikes.

No 60 Squadron was formed at Gosport on 30 April 1916, moving to France with Moranes the next month. During the early stages of the Battle of the Somme the Squadron suffered heavy losses, and the obsolescent Moranes were replaced by Nieuports during August; S.E.5s were delivered a year later. The Squadron remained active as a fighter and ground attack unit with S.E.5s for the rest of the war, before returning to the United Kingdom in February 1919 and disbanding on 22 January 1920.

No 60 Squadron re-formed on 1 April 1920 when No 97 Squadron at Lahore was renumbered. Equipped with D.H.10s, it moved to Risalpur in support of the Army on the North-West Frontier of India. D.H.9s were received in 1923, and these were replaced by Westland Wapitis in 1930.

The Squadron converted to Blenheims shortly before the outbreak of the Second World War and began flying coastal patrol missions, with detachments at Karachi, Bombay, Madras and Calcutta. It moved to Burma in February 1941 and received Buffalo fighters in July, although these were transferred to No 67 Squadron three months later. When Malaya was invaded by Japanese forces in December 1941 most of No 60 Squadron's aircraft were in Singapore, and enemy shipping and airfields were attacked while the remainder of the unit was evacuated to India, re-forming at Asansol with Blenheims.

Bombing raids on the Japanese in Burma continued until May 1943, when the Squadron moved to India and converted to Hurricanes. Thunderbolts replaced the Hurricanes in 1945, and the Squadron moved to Malaya in September of that year and to Java one month later, in support of Allied forces.

Conversion to Spitfires began in December 1946, and during the Malayan Emergency the Squadron mounted attacks on guerrilla camps and flew reconnaissance missions over the jungle. Vampires replaced the Spitfires early in 1951, and Venoms replaced the Vampires in April 1955. Meteor night fighters arrived in October 1959 and Javelins in 1961. The Squadron disbanded on 30 April 1968.

The RAF Germany Communications Squadron was redesignated No 60 Squadron on 3 February 1969, and the unit remained active in Germany, flying Pembrokes and Andovers from Wildenrath until the RAF withdrew from the base in 1992. The Squadron re-formed at Benson during June 1992 as a Wessex tactical support helicopter unit.

AIRCRAFT
Wessex HC.2: *XV725/C, XT761/D, XR525/G, XT676/I, XV726/J, XR511/L, XR523/M, XR517/N, XS674/R*

No 70 Squadron

Current base: *Lyneham.*
Aircraft types: *Hercules C.1P, Hercules C.3P.*
Role: *Tactical transport.*
Squadron badge: *A winged lion.*
Squadron motto: *'Usquam' ('Anywhere').*
Markings: *None.*

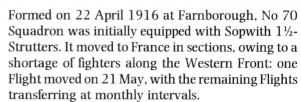

Formed on 22 April 1916 at Farnborough, No 70 Squadron was initially equipped with Sopwith 1½-Strutters. It moved to France in sections, owing to a shortage of fighters along the Western Front: one Flight moved on 21 May, with the remaining Flights transferring at monthly intervals.

Although primarily tasked with fighter operations, the unit also flew reconnaissance and bombing missions as required. Sopwith Camels replaced the 1½-Strutters in July 1917, and No 70 Squadron was the first unit to receive the Camel, retaining this type for fighter and ground attack operations for the remainder of the First World War. After returning to the United Kingdom in February 1919, the Squadron disbanded on 22 January 1920.

No 58 Squadron at Heliopolis was renumbered 70 Squadron on 1 February 1920. This was a combined bomber and transport unit equipped with Vimys, which were operated until transport-configured Vernons were delivered during November 1922. In December 1921 the Squadron deployed to Iraq, and it remained there until the outbreak of the Second World War, flying transport missions on behalf of Iraqi and British forces and evacuating more than 500 British citizens who were caught in a civil war in Afghanistan during 1928. In August 1926 the first Victorias were delivered to the Squadron, followed by Valentias; the latter were used until the Squadron moved to Egypt in 1939.

Following the entry of Italy into the Second World War, the requirement for bombers in the Middle East led to the delivery of Wellingtons to No 70 Squadron, and attacks were made on bases in Libya, Italy and Greece. Further missions were flown over Iraq and Syria during 1941, and as the front line moved westwards the Squadron was redeployed to bases in Libya and Tunisia. It was relocated in the Foggia area during December 1943, remaining there for the rest of the war.

Liberators replaced the Wellingtons during 1945, and after returning to the Middle East the unit disbanded on 31 March 1946. Two weeks later No 178 Squadron at Fayid was renumbered 70 Squadron and began Lancaster operations in Egypt, which continued until disbandment on 1 April 1947. Thirteen months later No 215 Squadron at Kabrit was renumbered 70 Squadron, flying Dakota transports, which were replaced by Valettas in January 1950.

During December 1955 the unit moved to Cyprus, where the Valettas were replaced by Hastings;

Argosys replaced the Hastings during November 1967. Conversion to the Hercules began in November 1970, although Argosys remained in use for a further three years. The Squadron was transferred to Lyneham on 1 February 1975.

AIRCRAFT
Hercules C.1P: *Aircraft drawn from Lyneham Transport Wing. For serial numbers see No 24 Squadron.*
Hercules C.3P: *As above.*

No 72 Squadron

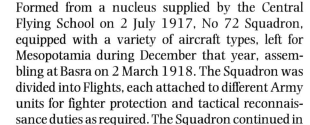

Current base: *Aldergrove.*
Aircraft type: *Wessex HC.2.*
Role: *Helicopter support.*
Squadron badge: *A swift.*
Squadron motto: *'Swift'.*
Markings: *Squadron emblem flanked by blue rectangles edged in red, on tail rotor housing.*

Formed from a nucleus supplied by the Central Flying School on 2 July 1917, No 72 Squadron, equipped with a variety of aircraft types, left for Mesopotamia during December that year, assembling at Basra on 2 March 1918. The Squadron was divided into Flights, each attached to different Army units for fighter protection and tactical reconnaissance duties as required. The Squadron continued in this role with Spads, S.E.5as and other fighter types until the end of the First World War, at which point the units re-assembled in Baghdad before returning to England and disbanding on 22 September 1919.

The Squadron re-formed with Gloster Gladiators at Tang-mere from a No 1 Squadron Flight on 22 February 1937, converting to Spitfires during April 1939. After operating these aircraft on fighter patrols until June 1940, the unit moved south to cover the Dunkirk beaches before moving to Biggin Hill, where it participated in the Battle of Britain. In November that year it moved north to Leuchars but later returned south, beginning fighter sweeps over France during July 1941.

After becoming non-operational in September 1942 the Squadron prepared for deployment overseas and moved to Gibraltar until airfields were captured and readied in Algeria. It then flew fighter patrols and bomber escort missions throughout the Tunisian campaign, moving to Malta during June 1943 to begin fighter sweeps over Sicily. The capture of airfields in Sicily enabled the Squadron to move there, and to the Italian mainland during September 1943. The following July the Squadron joined other Spitfire units in Corsica for six weeks to cover Allied landings in southern France. Returning to the Italian Front, it continued to fly fighter and ground attack missions until the end of the Second World War, and after periods of activity in northern Italy and Austria it disbanded on 30 December 1946.

No 130 Squadron at Odiham was renumbered 72 Squadron on 1 February 1947, flying Vampires until July 1952 when Meteors were received. These day fighters were replaced by Meteor night fighters four years later, and Javelins were operated from 1959 until the Squadron disbanded on 30 June 1961. Re-forming on 15 November 1961, No 72 was now equipped with Belvedere helicopter transports. Based at Odiham, the Belvederes were replaced by Wessexes in August 1964. On 12 November 1981 the Squadron moved to Aldergrove, a pair of Chinooks being attached in August 1988.

AIRCRAFT
Wessex HC.2: *XV728/A, XV719/B, XR529/E, XR497/F, XV721/H, XR527/K, XT607/P, XV723/Q, XT668/S, XR528/T, XT681/U, XR506/V, XR499/W, XR498/X, XV731/Y, XR502/Z*

No 74 Squadron

Current base: *Valley.*
Aircraft types: *Hawk T.1, Hawk T.1A.*
Role: *Advanced flying training, tactical weapons training.*
Squadron badge: *A tiger's face.*
Squadron motto: *'I Fear No Man'.*
Markings: *Tiger's head on a black circle on tail. Black and yellow Squadron colours on horizontal bars either side of fuselage roundel. White tail codes.*

Equipped with S.E.5as, No 74 Squadron moved to France during March 1918, having formed on 1 July 1917 at Northolt. Operations began the follow-

Above: No 74(R) Squadron markings.

ing month and continued until the end of the First World War, fighter patrols being accompanied by ground attack missions as enemy troops began to retreat.

After returning to the United Kingdom in February 1919, the Squadron disbanded on the following 3 July. Re-formation took place on board the transport ship *Neuralia* at Southampton en route to Malta on 3 September 1935. The unit was initially known as 'Demon Flight', the designation '74 Squadron' not being made official until 14 November because of security restrictions brought about by the Abyssinian Crisis. The Squadron's Demons were returned to the United Kingdom during 1936, re-assembling at Hornchurch on 21 September. Gauntlets replaced the Demons during April 1937, and Spitfires were delivered during February 1939.

As the Second World War began, the Squadron flew defensive patrols before helping to provide air cover for the Dunkirk evacuation. Following participation in the early stages of the Battle of Britain, the unit was temporarily withdrawn, but it returned during mid-October. Fighter sweeps over France began in January 1941 and continued until July, when the Squadron was transferred to Acklington to fly defensive patrols. Further transfers were made to Llanbedr and Long Kesh.

The Squadron deployed to the Middle East early in 1942, arriving in Egypt in June. After operating as a maintenance unit (owing to a shortage of aircraft), it received Hurricanes in December 1942. Conversion to Spitfires took place in September 1943, and the Squadron operated over the Aegean during the following month as part of a campaign to occupy some of the smaller islands. No 74 remained in the Eastern Mediterranean until April 1944, when the unit returned to the United Kingdom, re-assembling at North Weald on 24 April 1944.

After flying further fighter sweeps over France, the Squadron flew fighter and bomber missions from Normandy, supporting the Army during its advance into the Netherlands. It began operations in Germany in April 1945 but returned to the United Kingdom to convert to Meteors. It re-equipped with Hunters at Horsham St Faith in March 1957, Lightnings replacing the Hunters in July 1960.

After having moved to Coltishall, the Squadron transferred to Leuchars in February 1964, remaining there until June 1967 when it deployed to Tengah as part of the Far East Air Force. Disbanding on 31 August 1971, the Squadron re-formed during 1984 as an F-4J(UK) Phantom unit at Wattisham, later re-equipping with Phantom FGR.2s. Following the withdrawal of the Phantom, No 4 Flying Training School/3 Squadron was renumbered 74(R) Squadron in October 1992, equipped with Hawks.

AIRCRAFT

Hawk T.1: XX171/TK, XX349/TL, XX165/TM, XX310/TN, XX314/TP, XX926/TR
Hawk T.1A: XX190/TA, XX189/TB, XX350/TC, XX323/TD, XX255/TE, XX319/TF, XX199/TG, XX194/TI, XX222/TJ, XX316/TQ, XX339/TS, XX193/TT, XX302/TV

No 78 Squadron

Current base: Mount Pleasant.
Aircraft types: Chinook HC.1, Sea King HAR.3.
Role: Helicopter support, search and rescue.
Squadron badge: A heraldic tiger rampant.
Squadron motto: 'Nemo non Paratus' ('Nobody Unprepared').
Markings: Yellow lion on a black disc, on tail rotor housing.

Formed at Harrietsham on 1 November 1916, No 78 Squadron was initially equipped with B.E.2s as a home defence unit, moving its headquarters to Hove a month after its formation. From there it controlled three Flights based at Telscombe Cliffs, Gosport and Chiddingstone. After flying anti-Zeppelin patrols, the Squadron moved to Suttons Farm in September 1917, re-equipping with Sopwith 1½-Strutters. The latter were poorly suited to the interception of German Gotha bombers, and Camels were delivered to the unit in April 1918. Sopwith Snipes had also started to arrive when the Armistice was signed, but the Squadron disbanded on 31 December 1919.

The Squadron re-formed at Boscombe Down on 1 November 1936, drawn from 'B' Flight of No 10 Squadron and equipped with Heyford bombers. It moved to Dishforth in February 1937 and the Heyfords were replaced by Whitleys five months later. Following the outbreak of the Second World War the unit was designated a reserve training squadron but began night bombing operations in July 1940. Conversion to Halifaxes took place during March 1942, and these aircraft remained with the Squadron until the end of the war in Europe.

During May 1945 No 78 Squadron was transferred to Transport Command, converting to Dakotas for operations in the Middle East. Re-equipment with Valettas took place in April 1950, and operations continued until 30 September 1954 and disbandment. Re-formation took place on 24 April 1956 in Aden, where the Squadron was equipped with Scottish Aviation Pioneers, tasked with supporting the Army in the Aden Protectorate. The larger Twin Pioneer was introduced during October 1958, and in June 1965 the Squadron converted to Wessex tactical support helicopters, the Twin Pioneers being passed to No 21 Squadron.

During October 1967 No 78 Squadron transferred to Sharjah, in support of the Army based in the Trucial States, before disbanding on 1 December 1971. It re-formed in 1986 at Mount Pleasant in the Falkland Islands as a combined Chinook and Sea King unit, tasked with search and rescue, army support and transport duties.

AIRCRAFT
Chinook HC.1: *ZA705/A, ZA709/B*
Sea King HAR.3: *XZ591/S, XZ599/S*

No 84 Squadron

Current base: *Akrotiri.*
Aircraft type: *Wessex HC.5C.*
Role: *Helicopter support, search and rescue.*
Squadron badge: *A scorpion.*
Squadron motto: *'Scorpiones Pungunt' ('Scorpions Sting').*
Markings: *Playing card emblems on tail rotor housing (each aircraft different). Scorpion motif in black on nose.*

No 84 Squadron was formed at Beaulieu during January 1917, moving to France in September of the same year, equipped with S.E.5a fighters. Throughout the First World War the Squadron flew fighter patrols and ground attack missions before returning to the United Kingdom in August 1919 and disbanding on 30 January 1920. On 13 August that year the Squadron re-formed at Baghdad, moving to Shaibah one month later with D.H.9As to begin policing southern Iraq. Wapitis were delivered to the unit in July 1928, followed by Vincents in 1935 and Bristol Blenheims in February 1939.

The Squadron moved to Egypt during September 1940 and to Greece two months later, flying attack missions against Italian forces in Albania. After being forced to retreat by the Germans during April 1941, the Squadron returned to Iraq and began bombing operations in the Western Desert the following November. It was transferred to the Far East during January 1942, joining Malayan-based units, although Japanese landings in Sumatra led to the Squadron's ground element being evacuated to India during February and the remaining elements the following month. Re-equipment with Blenheims was then halted in anticipation of the arrival of Vengeances, which appeared in December 1942.

Below: No 84 Squadron nose markings. (John Hale)

After a long period of working-up, operations began again in February 1944, although five months later the Squadron was withdrawn for conversion to Mosquitos. It was still training on the Mosquito when the Japanese surrendered, and the unit was now transferred to Singapore, providing support for Allied forces in Java during November 1945.

After returning to Singapore the Squadron received Beaufighters in place of the Mosquitos, and in November 1948 it moved to Iraq, re-equipping with Brigands. It was transferred back to Singapore in 1950 to support security forces in the Malayan jungle, and operations continued here until 20 February 1953, when the unit disbanded. It re-formed the same day with Valetta transports at Fayid when No 204 Squadron was renumbered. It moved to Aden, was re-equipped with Blackburn Beverleys in June 1958 and was transferred in August 1967 to Sharjah, where the Beverleys were replaced by Andovers; the latter remained in service until the Squadron disbanded on 31 October 1971.

No 84 re-formed at Akrotiri on 17 January 1972 when No 1563 Flight and a No 230 Squadron detachment were combined to form a single unit. Equipped initially with Whirlwinds, and now Wessexes, the Squadron is tasked with the support of locally based Army and UN units and also provides a search and rescue service for the area.

AIRCRAFT
Wessex HC.5C: *XS485 (Hearts), XS498 (Joker), XS517 (Diamonds), XT463 (Clubs), XT479 (Spades)*

Below: No 92(R) Squadron markings.

No 92 Squadron

Current base: *Chivenor.*
Aircraft types: *Hawk T.1, Hawk T.1A.*
Role: *Advanced flying training, tactical weapons training.*
Squadron badge: *A cobra entwining a sprig of maple.*
Squadron motto: *'Aut Pugna aut Morere' ('Either Fight or Die').*
Markings: *Squadron emblem on white disc on tail. Red and yellow checks either side of fuselage roundel. White tail codes.*

Having formed at London Colney on 1 September 1917, No 92 Squadron moved to France during July 1918 to fly fighter patrols and ground attack missions over the Western Front with Spads, Pups, Avro 504s and S.E.5as. The Squadron remained active in the area throughout the First World War, returning to the United Kingdom and disbanding on 7 August 1919.

No 92 Squadron re-formed at Tangmere on 10 October 1939, equipped with Bristol Blenheims; these were replaced by Supermarine Spitfires during March 1940, the new aircraft becoming operational the following 9 May. The Squadron flew fighter patrols over France during May and June before being transferred to Pembrey to fly defensive patrols.

During September the unit was transferred to No 11 Group and, after moving to Biggin Hill, participated in the later stages of the Battle of Britain. In October 1941 it moved to Digby and in February 1942 it was transferred to the Middle East, although a shortage of aircraft resulted in its being designated a maintenance unit. Spitfires were delivered to the Squadron during August, however, and the aircraft were flown on fighter sweeps and bomber escort missions over the desert during the Battle of El Alamein and the subsequent withdrawal of the Axis forces. As the Squadron moved with the 8th Army, it eventually reached Tunisia. It was transferred to Malta in June 1943 to cover the Allied landings in Sicily and then to Italy in September, re-assigned fighter-bomber duties in the area. Disbandment took place in Austria on 30 December 1946.

No 92 Squadron re-formed on 31 January 1947 when No 91 Squadron, equipped with Meteor fighters at Acklington, was renumbered. F-86 Sabres were delivered to the unit in February 1954, followed by Hunters in April 1956. English Electric Lightnings re-equipped the Squadron at Leconfield during April 1963, and in 1968 No 92 was transferred to Germany, becoming part of the 2nd ATAF.

Lightning operations ceased in March 1977 and the Squadron disbanded on the 31st of the month at Gütersloh, only to re-form the following day at Wildenrath with Phantoms. It continued to operate these aircraft until September 1991, when it again disbanded. A year later No 92 Squadron became one of two reserve squadron designations (the other being No 19) applied to No 7 Flying Training School, flying Hawks at Chivenor until late 1994, when the FTS closed. No 92 Squadron is expected to reappear eventually as a Eurofighter unit.

AIRCRAFT

Hawk T.1: *XX179/E, XX299/J, XX178/M, XX167/Q, XX292/R, XX311/T, XX311/T*
Hawk T.1A: *XX157/B, XX329/C, XX330/D, XX332/F, XX204/H, XX335/I, XX242/Y, XX337/K, XX301/L, XX201/N, XX281/O, XX202/P, XX287/S, XX265/U, XX205/V, XX322/W*

No 100 Squadron

Current base: *Finningley*
Aircraft types: *Hawk T.1, Hawk T.1A*
Role: *Target facilities*
Squadron badge: *A skull in front of crossed bones*
Squadron motto: *'Sarang Tebuan Jangan Dijolok' ('Never Stir Up a Hornet's Nest')*
Markings: *Blue and yellow checks on tail, blue and yellow chequered diamond featuring skull and crossbones on nose. White tail codes*

Formed at Higham on 23 February 1917, No 100 Squadron was initially equipped with F.E.2bs and B.E.2ds. It moved to France the following month as a night bomber unit, flying missions against German bases until May 1918, when it moved to Nancy to begin strategic bombing operations, equipped with Handley Page O/400s. As part of the Independent Force, the Squadron mounted bombing attacks on German industrial targets until the end of the First World War.

During September 1919 the Squadron returned to the United Kingdom and combined with Nos 117 and 141 Squadrons, becoming operational at Baldonnel on 31 January 1920 as an army co-operation unit. Following the formation of the Irish Free State, the Squadron returned to Britain and was reinstated as a day bomber unit. It re-equipped with Fawns during May 1924 and Horsleys were received in 1926.

The Squadron moved to Donibristle in November 1930 and began torpedo bomber operations with Vildebeests two years later. Following a requirement for torpedo bombers in Singapore, No 100 Squadron deployed to the Far East in December 1933. It was scheduled to re-equip with Beauforts, but the Japanese attack on Malaya began in December 1941, before these aircraft were delivered. The Squadron

Below: No 100 Squadron markings.

flew attack missions against Japanese columns and ships, and in February 1942 its remaining aircraft were absorbed into No 36 Squadron.

On 15 December 1942 the Squadron re-formed at Grimsby. Equipped with Lancaster heavy bombers, it became part of Bomber Command's strategic force employed against Germany until the end of the Second World War. It remained active after the end of the war and in May 1946 the Lancasters were replaced by Avro Lincolns, the latter being transferred to Malaya in June 1950 when the Squadron was tasked with attacking terrorist camps in the Malayan jungle. In January 1954 the Squadron moved to Kenya during the Mau Mau uprising, and in April the same year the Lincolns were replaced by Canberra jet bombers at Wittering. Operations continued until 1 September 1959, when the Squadron disbanded.

No 100 re-formed again on 1 May 1962 as a Victor V-bomber unit at Wittering. Strategic bomber operations from Wittering ended on 30 September 1968 with disbandment, but the Squadron re-formed again on 1 February 1972 as a target facilities unit at West Raynham, equipped with Canberras, and subsequently moved to Wyton. The Canberras were replaced by Hawks during September 1991 and the Squadron moved to Finningley in September 1993.

AIRCRAFT
Hawk T.1: XX195/CA, XX181/CB, XX228/CC, XX283/CD, XX325/CE, XX312/CF, XX290/CI, XX164/CN, XX176/CO, XX177/CP
Hawk T.1A: XX188/CG, XX285/CH, XX248/CJ, XX331/CK, XX284/CL, XX247/CM

No 101 Squadron

Current base: Brize Norton.
Aircraft types: VC10 K.2, VC10 K.3, VC10 K.4.
Role: Aerial refuelling.
Squadron badge: Issuant from the battlements of a tower, a demi-lion rampant.
Squadron motto: 'Mens Agitat Molem' ('Mind over Matter').
Markings: Squadron emblem incorporated within a red '101' motif on tail. White tail code.

Formed at Farnborough on 12 July 1917, No 101 Squadron was initially equipped with F.E.2b and F.E.2d aircraft for night bombing operations. It moved to France at the end of the month and remained active throughout the First World War, mounting night bombing missions against enemy camps, communications centres and airfields in northern France and Belgium. After returning to the United Kingdom in March 1919, the unit disbanded on 31 December of the same year.

The Squadron re-formed at Bircham Newton on 21 March 1928, initially equipped with D.H.9As but receiving Sidestrands a year later; the latter remained in use until 1935, when Overstrands were delivered as replacements. Conversion to Bristol Blenheims took place during June 1938, the transition being completed by the end of August. When the Second World War began the Squadron was occupied with training duties and it did not fly an operational mission until July 1940. During April 1941 it received Vickers Wellingtons and participated in night bombing raids on targets in Germany. Avro Lancasters were received in October 1942. The Squadron was also tasked with electronic countermeasures duties, and its aircraft were equipped with radio-jamming gear, known as 'ABC' or 'Airborne Cigar', with German-speaking operators attached to each crew. On D-Day a total of twenty-one of the Squadron's aircraft were flown on radio-jamming missions during the airborne assault.

Conversion to Avro Lincolns took place in August 1946, and these aircraft remained in use until May 1951, when No 101 became the first RAF Canberra jet bomber squadron, based at Binbrook. Canberra operations continued until 1 February 1957 and disbandment. The Squadron re-formed on 15 October 1957 at Finningley, deliveries of Vulcan V-bombers beginning the following January.

The Squadron moved to Waddington on 26 June 1961 and remained active at that base until 1982 when, as part of the run-down of the RAF Vulcan bomber force, it disbanded. It re-formed on 1 May 1984 at Brize Norton with BAe VC10s equipped for air-to-air refuelling.

AIRCRAFT
VC10 K.2: ZA140/A, ZA141/B, ZA142/C, ZA143/D, ZA144/E
VC10 K.3: ZA147/F, ZA148/G, ZA149/H, ZA150/J

VC10 K.4: ZD230/K, ZD235/L, ZD240/M, ZD241/N, ZD242/O

No 111 Squadron

Current base: Leuchars.
Aircraft type: Tornado F.3.
Role: Air defence.
Squadron badge: *In front of two swords in saltire, a cross potent quadrat, charged with three seaxes fessewise in pale.*
Squadron motto: *'Adstantes' ('Standing By').*
Markings: *Squadron emblem on a black disc, flanked by a black tail band, edged in yellow. Black lightning flash edged in yellow on forward fuselage. White tail code.*

Formed at Deir-el-Belah in Palestine on 1 August 1917, No 111(F) Squadron was equipped with a variety of trainer types until standardization was achieved on the Nieuport and S.E.5a early in 1918. Tasked with the support of Army units in Palestine and Syria, the Squadron flew fighter missions during the offensive against Turk forces until the campaign ended, at which time it was transferred to Egypt and re-equipped with Bristol Fighters. It was renumbered 14 Squadron on 1 February 1920.

No 111 re-formed at Duxford on 1 October 1923 with a Flight of Gloster Grebes; a second Flight equipped with Snipes was added on 1 April 1924 and a third with Siskins in January 1925. The Siskin was later adopted by the whole Squadron until January 1931, when Bristol Bulldogs were received. Gloster Gauntlets replaced the Bulldogs in May 1936 and the unit became the RAF's first Hurricane squadron during January 1938.

In the early months of the Second World War No 111 was engaged in defensive patrols. In May 1940, when the German invasion of France began, the Squadron operated across the Channel, using French airfields, and during the Dunkirk evacuation it provided air cover for the operation. It was active as a fighter defence squadron in the early stages of the Battle of Britain but withdrew to Drem during September to re-equip, moving south again the following July to fly fighter sweeps over France.

In November 1942 the Squadron was transferred to Algeria, accompanying the Allied forces destined to occupy French North Africa; after the capitulation of enemy forces in Tunisia it moved to Malta. It covered the Allied landings in Sicily, moving in as airfields were secured. Further moves to mainland Italy were made, and then to Corsica. In October 1944 it returned to Italy, where it remained as a fighter-bomber unit until the end of the war, disbanding on 12 May 1947.

The Squadron re-formed once more on 2 December 1953 at North Weald, equipped with Meteors. Hunters arrived in June 1955, and No 111 operated the aircraft as the RAF's aerobatic display team, the *Black Arrows*, before converting to Lightnings in April 1961 at Wattisham. It disbanded on 30 September 1974, re-forming the following day at Coningsby as a Phantom unit and moving to Leuchars one year later. Conversion to Tornado F.3s took place late in 1989.

AIRCRAFT
Tornado F.3: ZE376/HA, ZE811/HB, ZG778/HC, ZE341/HD, ZE289/HF, ZE338/HG, ZE252/HH, ZE255/HI, ZE831/HJ, ZE835/HK, ZE167/HM, ZE809/HP, ZE837/HY, ZE250/HZ

Below: No 111 Squadron markings.

No 120 Squadron

Current base: Kinloss.
Aircraft type: Nimrod MR.2P.
Role: Anti-submarine warfare, search and rescue.
Squadron badge: A falcon on a terrestrial globe.
Squadron motto: 'Endurance'.
Markings: None.

Formed at Lympne on 1 January 1918, No 120 Squadron was initially equipped with D.H.9s but then received D.H.9As for day bomber missions with the Independent Force. The Squadron was preparing to move to France when the Armistice was signed, but a change of plan resulted in a move to Hawkinge, from where it flew mail delivery sorties between France and the United Kingdom until August 1919. Disbandment followed on 21 October of the same year.

No 120 Squadron re-formed on 2 June 1941 at Nutts Corner, designated a maritime reconnaissance and anti-submarine unit and equipped with Liberators. Patrols began on 20 September 1941, and during April 1943 the Squadron moved to Reykjavik in Iceland, flying long-range sorties out across the Atlantic between Britain and Canada and destroying or damaging large numbers of U-boats. The Squadron moved to Ballykelly in Ireland during March 1944 and continued to fly the Liberator until 4 June 1945, when it disbanded.

Below: No 201 Squadron tail markings.

Re-formed on 1 October 1946 at Leuchars, the Squadron operated Lancasters until April 1951, when the first Shackletons were delivered. Having moved to Kinloss in December 1949, the Squadron transferred its Shackletons to Aldergrove during 1952 before re-equipping with Nimrods in February 1971. Based at Kinloss, the Squadron remains active in the maritime reconnaissance, anti-submarine warfare and search and rescue roles.

AIRCRAFT
Nimrod MR.2P: Aircraft drawn from Kinloss Wing. For serial numbers see No 42 Squadron.

No 201 Squadron

Current base: Kinloss.
Aircraft type: Nimrod MR.2P.
Role: Anti-submarine warfare, search and rescue.
Squadron badge: Standing on a demi-terrestrial globe, a falcon.
Squadron motto: 'Endurance'.
Markings: None.

No 201 Squadron was formed from No 1 Squadron, Royal Naval Air Service, at Fienvillers in France on 1 April 1918, the day on which the Royal Air Force was created. As with other RNAS units absorbed into the new RAF, the original squadron number was simply added to '200'. Equipped with Sopwith Camels, the unit was engaged on fighter patrols over the Western Front until the Armistice, after which it returned to the United Kingdom. It disbanded on 31 December 1919.

No 480 (Coastal Reconnaissance) Flight at Calshot was renumbered 201 Squadron on 1 January 1929. It was at first equipped with Supermarine Southampton flying boats, but Londons were received as replacements during April 1936 and these were still in service when the Second World War broke out.

Now based in Scotland, the Squadron was tasked with maritime patrols over the North Sea, towards the Norwegian coast where Atlantic-bound surface vessels and U-boats were to be found. The Squadron converted to Short Sunderlands, and during October 1941 a move was made to Castle Archdale in Northern Ireland, from where North Atlantic anti-submarine patrols were conducted. The Squadron moved to Pembroke Dock in April 1944, from where the unit flew patrols over the approaches to the English Channel during the landings in Normandy. It then returned to Ireland and continued to operate from Castle Archdale until the end of the Second World War.

During August 1945 the Squadron was transferred to Pembroke Dock, but it moved to Calshot in March 1946, participating in the 1948 Berlin Airlift before moving back to Pembroke Dock in January 1949. Short Sunderlands were operated until disbandment on 28 February 1957.

Re-formation took place on 1 October 1958 when No 220 Squadron at St Mawgan was renumbered. Equipped with Shackletons, No 201 remained active at St Mawgan until March 1965, when the unit moved north to Kinloss, Nimrods replacing the Shackletons during October 1970. The Squadron remains active at Kinloss with Nimrods, tasked with search and rescue, maritime reconnaissance and anti-submarine warfare duties.

AIRCRAFT
Nimrod MR.2P: *Aircraft drawn from Kinloss Wing. For serial numbers see No 42 Squadron.*

No 202 Squadron

Current base: *Boulmer.*
Detached Flights: *'A' at Boulmer, 'D' at Lossiemouth, 'E' at Leconfield, Sea King Training Unit (SKTU) at St Mawgan.*
Aircraft type: *Sea King HAR.3.*
Role: *Search and rescue.*
Squadron badge: *A mallard.*
Squadron motto: *'Semper Vigilate' ('Be Always Vigilant').*
Markings: *Squadron emblem, on white disc, on forward fuselage.*

Formed at Berugues from No 2 Squadron, RNAS, on 1 April 1918, No 202 Squadron was at first equipped with D.H.4s, tasked with bombing and reconnaissance over France and Belgium. It continued in this role until the Armistice, after which it was recalled and disbanded on 22 January 1920.

Below: Sea King starboard fuselage detail, showing the No 202 Squadron markings stencilled in black.

The Squadron re-formed on 1 January 1929 at Kalafrana in Malta when No 481 Flight was redesignated. It operated with Fairey IIID seaplanes but re-equipped with Fairey IIIFs during 1930. Scapas arrived in May 1935, followed by Londons towards the end of 1937, the latter being used to protect shipping in the area from attacks by Italian submarines during the Spanish Civil War.

The Squadron moved to Alexandria during the Munich Crisis, and to Gibraltar on the outbreak of the Second World War began. During September 1940 the Squadron took control of the Fairey Swordfish floatplanes which were operated by No 3 AACU and in April 1941 acquired Consolidated Catalinas, enabling the aged Londons to be retired. Short Sunderlands started to arrive in December 1941, and during September 1944 the Squadron transferred to Castle Archdale, where it remained until the end of the war. It disbanded on 12 June 1945.

On 1 October 1946 No 512 Squadron at Aldergrove, equipped with Halifaxes for meteorological reconnaissance flights over the Atlantic, was renumbered 202 Squadron. Handley Page Hastings were delivered to the unit in October 1950, replacing the Halifaxes. The Squadron continued to operate from Aldergrove until 31 July 1964 when it disbanded. No 228 Squadron at Leconfield was renumbered 202 Squadron on 1 September 1964. Equipped with Whirlwinds, it was tasked with search and rescue duties, with detachments around the United Kingdom.

In 1978 the Squadron began to convert to Westland Sea Kings, and it continues to operate in the SAR role, with its headquarters at Boulmer and detached Flights at Lossiemouth and Leconfield.

AIRCRAFT
Sea King HAR.3: *XZ586, XZ587, XZ588, XZ589, XZ590, XZ592, XZ594, XZ595, XZ596, XZ597, XZ598, ZA105, ZE368, ZE369, ZE370*

No 206 Squadron

Current base: *Kinloss.*
Aircraft type: *Nimrod MR.2P*
Role: *Anti-submarine warfare, search and rescue.*
Squadron badge: *An octopus.*
Squadron motto: *'Nihil Nos Effugit' ('Naught Escapes Us').*
Markings: *None.*

No 206 Squadron was formed on 1 April 1918, when No 6 (Naval) Squadron, based at Ste Marie Cappel, was renumbered as part of the transfer of naval units to the newly created Royal Air Force. Equipped with D.H.9s, it was assigned bombing and reconnaissance duties over the Western Front and remained active in this role until the end of the First World War. After the war the Squadron remained with the Army of Occupation in the Rhineland, but it moved to the Middle East during June 1919, where it was renumbered 47 Squadron on 1 February 1920.

On 15 June 1936 'C' Flight of No 48 Squadron was redesignated No 206 Squadron, based at Manston and equipped with Avro Ansons engaged on anti-submarine patrol duties. In March 1940 the Squadron re-equipped with Hudsons, and the latter remained in use for patrols off the German coast and Frisian Islands until May 1941, when the Squadron was transferred to St Eval to resume maritime reconnaissance missions in the South-Western Approaches.

During August 1941 the Squadron moved to Aldergrove, and in June 1942 it was transferred to Benbecula, converting to Boeing Fortresses in August that year. It moved to the Azores during October 1943, flying patrols over the Atlantic until March 1944, when it returned to the United Kingdom and converted to Liberators. After a period of operations at St Eval, a move was made to Leuchars, where the

Below: No 206 Squadron tail markings.

Squadron remained until the end of the Second World War, flying patrols off the coasts of Norway and Denmark.

No 206 Squadron was transferred to Transport Command on 10 June 1945, tasked with trooping flights until disbandment on 25 April 1946. It re-formed at Lyneham on 17 November 1947, again as a transport unit, equipped with Avro Yorks. It participated in the Berlin Airlift before disbanding again on 20 February 1950.

Re-forming at St Eval on 27 September 1952, No 206 Squadron now operated Avro Shackletons, tasked with maritime reconnaissance duties. A move to nearby St Mawgan was made during January 1958, and in July 1965 the Squadron was transferred to Kinloss, where conversion to Nimrods took place during November 1970. The unit remains active at Kinloss as a maritime reconnaissance squadron.

AIRCRAFT
Nimrod MR.2P: *Aircraft drawn from Kinloss Wing. For serial numbers see No 42 Squadron.*

No 208 Squadron

Current base: *Valley.*
Aircraft types: *Hawk T.1, Hawk T.1A.*
Role: *Advanced flying training, tactical weapons training.*
Squadron badge: *A sphinx.*
Squadron motto: *'Vigilant'.*
Markings: *Information not available at the time of writing.*

No 208 Squadron was formed at Teteghem on 1 April 1918 from No 8 Squadron, Royal Naval Air Service, a fighter unit which had been active on the Western Front since its formation on 25 October 1916. Equipped with Sopwith Camels, the Squadron was tasked with fighter and ground attack duties and it remained active in this role until the end of the First World War. It was beginning to re-equip with Sopwith Snipes when the Armistice was signed. Following a short period with the Army of Occupation in Germany, the Squadron returned to the United Kingdom and disbanded on 7 November 1919.

No 113 Squadron at Ismailia was renumbered 208 Squadron on 1 February 1920. Initially equipped with R.E.8s, the unit received Bristol Fighters in November 1920 for army co-operation duties. The Squadron was deployed to Turkey for one year beginning in September 1922 in response to the Chanak Crisis, before returning to Egypt, where army co-operation flying continued. The Bristol Fighters were replaced by Armstrong Whitworth Atlases in May 1930, with Audaxes arriving during August 1935. The Squadron's 'D' Flight operated Demons during 1935–36 until it was redesignated No 64 Squadron.

Conversion to Westland Lysanders took place in January 1939, and operations in the Western Desert began in June 1940. Hurricanes arrived some five months later. Following the German invasion the Squadron was evacuated, but it resumed its reconnaissance role in the Western Desert in October 1941, continuing until December of the following year when it was transferred to Iraq. Spitfires replaced the Hurricanes in December 1943, and the unit moved to Italy in March 1944, where ground attack sorties were flown until the end of the Second World War.

In July 1945 the Squadron returned to Palestine, equipping with reconnaissance-configured Meteors in March 1951. The Hunters of No 34 Squadron joined No 208 before the latter moved to Cyprus, and operations continued until 30 March 1959 when the Squadron disbanded. No 142 Squadron, at Eastleigh in Kenya, was renumbered 208 Squadron on 1 April 1959. Equipped with Venoms, the unit received Hunter ground-attack fighters during March 1960, and after moving to Aden in December 1961 it transferred to Muharraq in June 1964, remaining active there until 10 September 1971 and disbandment.

Re-formation came on 1 March 1974 at Honington with Buccaneer strike aircraft as the unit's new equipment, and a move to Lossiemouth was made during 1983. Following the arrival of No 617 Squadron at Lossiemouth, No 208 Squadron disbanded in April 1994, but the unit reappeared as a component squadron of No 4 FTS at Valley, where it replaced No 234(R) Squadron.

AIRCRAFT
Hawk T.1: *Serial numbers not available.*
Hawk T.1A: *Serial numbers not available.*

SQUADRON DIRECTORY

No 216 Squadron

Current base: Brize Norton.
Aircraft types: TriStar K.1, TriStar KC.1, TriStar C.2.
Role: Strategic transport, aerial refuelling.
Squadron badge: An eagle holding a bomb in its claws.
Squadron motto: 'CCXVI Dona Ferens' ('216 Bearing Gifts').
Markings: Eagle and bomb motif on tail.

Formed from No 16 Squadron, Royal Naval Air Service, on 1 April 1918, No 216 Squadron was initially based at Villeseneux, equipped with Handley Page O/400 night bombers. One month after its formation, the unit joined the Independent Force, tasked with strategic bombing duties.

In July 1919 the Squadron was transferred to Egypt as a combined bomber and transport unit, and it remained active in this role until the outbreak of war in the Middle East. The O/400s were replaced by D.H.10s in 1921, and these were succeeded in turn by Vimys in 1922, Victorias in 1926, Valentias in 1935 and Bombays in October 1939.

Although the Valentias were retained for transport flights, the Bombays were tasked with night bombing missions from June 1940; they were replaced by Wellingtons towards the end of 1940, by which time the Squadron was devoted entirely to transport operations across the Middle East, Greece, Africa and beyond. During July 1942 the Squadron re-equipped with Lockheed Hudsons, which were used for supply drops and casualty evacuation flights. Dakotas arrived in March 1943, the last Bombay being retired three months later. The Squadron continued to operate transport services around the Middle East, dropping airborne forces on the Aegean islands as well as supporting a large detachment of the 14th Army in Burma in April 1944.

Vickers Valettas replaced the Dakotas in November 1949, and the Squadron returned to the United Kingdom in November 1955, re-assembling at Lyneham. During June 1956 the unit became the world's first jet transport squadron when De Havilland Comets were delivered at Lyneham. Comet operations continued until 30 June 1975, when the Squadron disbanded. However, it re-formed in July 1979 with Buccaneers at Honington, moving to Lossiemouth the following year. Shortly after this the Squadron again disbanded, following the discovery of metal fatigue in many Buccaneers and the consequent reduction in numbers of aircraft available. No 216 re-formed in November 1984 at Brize Norton, equipped with TriStar strategic transports.

AIRCRAFT
TriStar K.1: ZD949, ZD951
TriStar KC.1: ZD948, ZD950, ZD952, ZD953
TriStar C.2: ZE704, ZE705

No 230 Squadron

Current base: Aldergrove.
Aircraft types: Puma HC.1.
Role: Helicopter support.
Squadron badge: A tiger in front of a palm tree.
Squadron motto: 'Kita Chari Jauh' ('We Seek Far').
Markings: Squadron's tiger motif on a black disc, under cockpit glazing.

Formed at Felixstowe in August 1918, No 230 Squadron was the result of the amalgamation of Nos 327 and 328 Naval War Flights. Equipped with Felixstowe F.2As, it helped to prove the flexibility of flying boats in a campaign against German Zeppelins, surface vessels and U-boats during the latter stages of the First World War and for a period after the Armistice. The post-war cut-backs resulted in the Squadron's being disbanded on 1 April 1922 to become No 480 Flight.

No 230 Squadron re-formed at Pembroke Dock on 1 December 1934 as a flying boat unit once more, equipped with Singapores. It was transferred to Egypt in October 1935 during the Abyssinian Crisis, returning to the United Kingdom in August 1936 but redeploying to Singapore two months later. Short Sunderlands were delivered in June 1938, and following the outbreak of the Second World War, these flew patrols over the Indian Ocean and over the approaches to Malaya and Singapore, with a detachment based in Ceylon.

In February 1940 the Singapore-based personnel were transferred to No 205 Squadron and No 230 Squadron was officially re-located to Ceylon for three months, after which it moved to the Mediterranean, where it flew anti-submarine and reconnaissance missions in support of the Mediterranean Fleet. In June 1941 it was tasked with the administration of No 2 (Yugoslav) Squadron which had escaped from Yugoslavia during the German invasion. In January 1943 the Squadron moved to Tanganyika, with detachments in Madagascar and, from June, in the Mediterranean region. The Squadron was transferred to Ceylon again in February 1944, moving to Burma two months later to begin attacks on Japanese coastal shipping. After being transferred to Singapore in December 1945, it returned to the United Kingdom in April 1946.

From February 1949 No 230 Squadron was stationed at Pembroke Dock, from where the unit participated in the Berlin Airlift. It disbanded on 28 February 1957. No 215 Squadron at Dishforth was renumbered 230 Squadron on 1 September 1958, equipped with Pioneer light transports. Twin Pioneers arrived in January 1960, and both aircraft types remained in use until June 1962, when Whirlwind helicopters were taken on charge at Odiham.

After moving to Gütersloh in Germany early in 1963, the Squadron continued its helicopter support role until January 1965, when it moved to Borneo for two years. After returning to the United Kingdom, it re-equipped with Pumas in November 1971 and moved back to Germany. In May 1992 it was transferred to Aldergrove in Northern Ireland, from where it continues to undertake a wide variety of tasks in support of the Army.

AIRCRAFT
Puma HC.1: *XW208/CJ, XW214/CK, XW221/CM, XW233/CN, XW235/CP, ZA935/CT, ZA940/CY, XW224/DH, XW198/DL, XW227/DN*

No 360 Squadron

Current base: *Wyton.*
Aircraft types: *Canberra T.4, Canberra T.17, Canberra T.17A, Canberra PR.7.*
Role: *Electronic countermeasures training.*
Squadron badge: *A moth in front of a trident.*
Squadron motto: *'Confundemus' ('We Shall Throw into Confusion').*
Markings: *Squadron emblem on tail. Red bars featuring yellow lightning flashes either side of roundel. White tail codes.*

Below: A Canberra T.17A from No 360 Squadron. The responsibility for the unit's ECM training role is being transferred to a civilian contractor at the end of 1994.

SQUADRON DIRECTORY

No 360 Squadron was formed at Watton on 1 April 1966 as a joint Royal Navy and Royal Air Force unit, tasked with electronic countermeasures training. The '360' number was applied provisionally until 23 September, when it was officially confirmed. Equipped at first with Canberra T.4s, the unit absorbed 'B' Flight of No 97 Squadron and operated Canberra T.4s, B.2s and B.6s until specialized Canberra T.17 ECM aircraft were delivered in December 1966. Naval personnel were drawn from 831 Naval Air Squadron, also located at Watton. A second ECM unit, No 361 Squadron, was formed on 2 January 1967 for deployment to the Far East, but this disbanded on 14 July that year.

No 360 moved to Cottesmore in April 1967 and to Wyton in 1975. Operations are to continue until the end of 1994, when the RAF's ECM training is being placed in the hands of a civilian contractor.

AIRCRAFT
Canberra T.4: WT480/BC, WJ866/BL
Canberra T.17: WK111/EA, WJ630/ED, WH902/EK, WF916/EL, WJ986/EP
Canberra T.17A: WJ607/EB, WJ633/EF, WH646/EG, WD955/EM, WJ981/EN
Canberra PR.7: WJ874/BM, WH779/BP

Above: Nose and tail markings of a No 617 Squadron Tornado.

No 617 Squadron

Current base: Lossiemouth.
Aircraft type: Tornado GR.1B.
Role: Maritime strike.
Squadron badge: *A wall in fesse, fracted by three lightning flashes in pile, and issuant from the breach water proper.*
Squadron motto: 'Après Moi le Déluge' ('After Me, the Flood').
Markings: *Black bars edged in red, featuring red lightning flashes, either side of nose roundel. Red lightning flash on black fin-tip marking. Black tail codes outlined in red.*

Formed on 21 March 1943, No 617 Squadron was created specifically to carry out one highly specialized mission—the famous 'Dambusters' attack on the Möhne, Eder and Sorpe Dams in Germany. Equipped with specially converted Lancasters, each capable of carrying one of Barnes Wallis's 'bouncing bombs', the Squadron made its successful and historic attack on 16 May the same year. It was subsequently tasked with other specialized missions, including 12,000lb-bomb and 22,000lb-bomb attacks against V-1 and V-2 bases, and against the German battleship *Tirpitz*. The Squadron also flew conventional strategic missions as part of Bomber Command's Lancaster force.

After the end of the Second World War the Squadron joined the 'Tiger Force' and transferred to the Far East, arriving in India during January 1946. It returned to the United Kingdom four months later, re-assembling at Binbrook. It converted to Avro Lincolns during September 1946 and acquired Canberras in January 1952 as the RAF's second jet bomber squadron. Apart from a four-month deployment to Malaya, where the Squadron flew missions against guerrillas, No 617 remained active at Binbrook until 15 December 1955 and disbandment.

It re-formed on 1 May 1958 at Scampton as a V-bomber squadron equipped with Vulcans. No 617 Squadron's association with the Vulcan ended in December 1981 when it disbanded at Scampton, re-forming at Marham with Tornado bombers. It remained at Marham until April 1994, when it was assigned the maritime strike role and moved to Lossiemouth, replacing No 208 Squadron's Buccaneers.

AIRCRAFT
Tornado GR.1B: Serial numbers unavailable at the time of writing.

No 1312 Flight

Current base: Mount Pleasant.
Aircraft type: Hercules C.1K.
Role: Tactical transport, aerial refuelling.
Markings: None.

First formed during April 1944, No 1312 Flight is currently based at Mount Pleasant in the Falkland Islands, equipped with a pair of Hercules C.1Ks, tasked with tactical transport and aerial refuelling. The Hercules tankers are to be restored to 'standard' transport configuration, and No 1312 Flight will probably receive a VC10 tanker from No 101 Squadron.

AIRCRAFT
Hercules C.1K: XV204, XV213

No 1435 Flight

Current base: Mount Pleasant.
Aircraft type: Tornado F.3.
Role: Air defence.
Markings: Red Maltese cross on tail, Falkland Islands badge on nose. White tail code.

First formed in Malta during the Second World War, No 1435 Flight re-formed on 1 November 1988 at Mount Pleasant with four Phantom interceptors, charged with the defence of the Falkland Islands. Tornado F.3s replaced the Phantoms during 1992.

AIRCRAFT
Tornado F.3: ZE758/C, ZE790/D, ZE812/F, ZE209/H

No 1563 Flight

Current base: Belize International Airport.
Aircraft types: Puma HC.1.
Role: Helicopter support.
Markings: Red cobra emblem on blue disc, carried under cockpit glazing.

First formed at Belize International Airport during 1984, No 1563 Flight is equipped with a small number of Puma HC.1 helicopters, drawn from

Below, left and right: No 1435 Flight markings. (Via John Hale)

Above: A Westland Puma HC.1 from No 1563 Flight, based at Belize International Airport. (J. Webber)

Odiham's Puma fleet and transported to Belize by Hercules. The helicopters are flown in support of locally based Army units.

AIRCRAFT
Puma HC.1: *Serial numbers unknown at the time of writing.*

The Queen's Flight

Current base: *Benson.*
Aircraft types: *BAe 146 CC.2, Wessex HCC.4.*
Role: *VIP transport.*
Markings: *'ER' badge carried on nose.*

First formed on 1 April 1936 (as The King's Flight), this unit is currently based at Benson, equipped with BAe 146 CC.2s and Wessex HCC.4s for the transport of members of the Royal Family and other VIPs.

AIRCRAFT
BAe 146 CC.2: ZE700, ZE701, ZE702
Wessex HCC.4: XV732, XV733

Northolt Station Flight

Aircraft type: *Islander CC.2.*
Role: *Communications, transport.*
Markings: *None.*

Formed in April 1993.

AIRCRAFT
Islander CC.2: ZF573, ZH536

Gatow Station Flight

Aircraft type: *Chipmunk T.10.*
Role: *Communications.*
Markings: *None.*

AIRCRAFT
Chipmunk T.10: WG466, WG486

St Athan Station Flight

Aircraft type: Hawk T.1.
Role: Communications, transport.
Markings: One aircraft carriess a large dragon motif.

AIRCRAFT
Hawk T.1: XX172, XX184

Sentry Training Squadron

Current base: Waddington.
Aircraft type: Sentry AEW.1.
Role: Sentry Operational Conversion Unit.
Markings: No 8 Squadron badge on tail, No 8 Squadron colours either side of fuselage roundel.

AIRCRAFT
Sentry AEW.1: Aircraft drawn from No 8 Squadron (q.v.).

Trinational Tornado Training Establishment

Current base: Cottesmore.
Aircraft type: Tornado GR.1.
Role: Tornado GR.1 Trinational Operational Conversion Unit.
Markings: Black arrowhead outlined in red, containing 'TTTE' initials in white, on tail. Black tail codes outlined in white. Component squadron motifs on tail ('A', 'B', 'C' and 'S').

AIRCRAFT
Tornado GR.1: (Drawn from trinational 'pool' as required) Britain—ZA320/B-01, ZA324/B-02, ZA325/B-03, ZA352/B-04, ZA357/B-05, ZA358/B-06, ZA356/B-07, ZA330/B-08, ZA362/B-09, ZA319/B-11, ZA323/B-14, ZA322/B-50, ZA327/B-51, ZA353/B-53, ZA355/B-54, ZA359/B-55, ZA360/B-56, ZA361/B-57, ZA321/B-58; Germany—43+01/G-20, 43+02/G-21, 43+03/G-22, 43+04/G-23, 43+05/G-24, 43+06/G-25, 43+07/G-26, 43+08/G-27, 43+09/G-28, 43+10/G-29, 43+11/G-30, 43+15/G-31, 43+16/G-32, 43+17/G-33, 43+12/G-70, 43+13/G-71, 43+14/G-72, 43+32/G-73, 43+25/G-75; Italy—MM55001/I-40, MM55002/I-41, MM55000/I-42, MM55003/I-43, MM55005/I-45, MM7002/I-92

Electronic Warfare & Avionic Unit

Current base: Wyton.
Aircraft types: Drawn from other units as required.

Below: A Wessex HCC.4 of The Queen's Flight.

Role: Electronic warfare development, avionics development.
Markings: None.

Strike/Attack Operational Evaluation Unit

Current base: Boscombe Down.
Aircraft types: Tornado GR.1, Tornado GR.1A, Harrier GR.7, Harrier T.4, Jaguar T.2A.
Role: Evaluation of equipment and tactics.
Markings: Emblem consisting of a blue circle containing three swords.

AIRCRAFT
Tornado GR.1: ZD716/O, ZD749/U
Tornado GR.1A: ZG706/E
Harrier GR.7: ZG501/E, ZG472/O, ZG860/T, ZG475/U
Harrier T.4: XW267/SA, XW269/SB
Jaguar T.2A: XX833/N2

Tornado F.3 Operational Evaluation Unit

Current base: Coningsby.
Aircraft types: Tornado F.3.
Role: Tornado F.3 equipment and tactics evaluation.
Markings: Tail marking consisting of a blue circle containing three swords.

AIRCRAFT
Tornado F.3: ZE756, ZE862, ZE889, ZE968

Institute of Aviation Medicine

Current base: Farnborough.
Aircraft types: Hunter T.7, Jaguar T.2, Hawk T.1.
Role: Aviation medicine research and treatment.
Markings: Various (primarily Defence Research Agency 'raspberry ripple' high-visibility colour schemes).

AIRCRAFT
Hunter T.7: XL563
Jaguar T.2: ZB615
Hawk T.1: XX327

Empire Test Pilots' School

Current base: Boscombe Down.
Aircraft types: Andover C.1, BAC-111, Gazelle, Hawk T.1, Hunter T.7, Jaguar T.2, Jet Provost T.5P, Lynx, Scout AH.1, Tornado F.2.
Role: Test pilot training.
Markings: Various (Defence Research Agency 'raspberry ripple' high-visibility colour schemes).

AIRCRAFT
Andover C.1: XS606
BAC-111: ZE432
Gazelle: XZ936, XZ939/Z
Hawk T.1: XX341/1, XX342/2, XX343/3
Hunter T.7: XL564, XL612
Jaguar T.2: XX145, XX830
Jet Provost T.5P: XS230
Lynx: ZD560
Scout AH.1: XP849
Tornado F.2: ZD935

Battle of Britain Memorial Flight

Current base: Coningsby.
Aircraft types: Spitfire, Hurricane IIC, Lancaster B.I, Chipmunk T.10, Devon C.2, Dakota C.4.
Role: Display flying.
Markings: Various (changed regularly).

AIRCRAFT
Spitfire: P7350 (Mk IIA), AB910 (Mk VB), PM631 (Mk XIX), PS853 (Mk XIX), PS915 (Mk XIX)
Hurricane IIC: PZ865
Lancaster B.I: PA474
Chipmunk T.10: WK518
Devon C.2: VP981
Dakota C.4: ZA947

CENTRAL FLYING SCHOOL

Above: A rare glimpse of virtually the entire Battle of Britain Memorial Flight Spitfire and Hurricane fleet. One of these Hurricanes subsequently crash-landed and was written off.
Above right: Nine Hawk T.1As form the familiar shape of the famous *Red Arrows* aerobatic team.

Central Flying School

Current bases: *Scampton, Valley, Shawbury.*
Aircraft types: *Bulldog T.1, Hawk T.1, Tucano T.1, Gazelle HT.3.*
Role: *Flying instructor training.*
Markings: *CFS badge on fuselage.*

AIRCRAFT

Bulldog T.1: *XX539/1, XX520/2, XX689/3, XX693/4, XX692/5, XX614/6, XX714/7, XX696/8, XX698/9, XX555/10*
Hawk T.1: *(Based at Valley) XX159/PA, XX187/PB, XX203/PC, XX220/PD, XX258/PE, XX303/PF, XX318/PG, XX163/PH, XX235/PJ, XX236/PK, XX239/PL*
Tucano T.1: *ZF166, ZF169, ZF172, ZF204, ZF205, ZF206, ZF209, ZF245, ZF265, ZF266, ZF268, ZF269, ZF286, ZF288, ZF318, ZF343, ZF345, ZF372, ZF378, ZF380, ZF406*
Gazelle HT.3: *(Based at Shawbury) Aircraft drawn from No 2 FTS fleet (q.v.)*
The Red Arrows: *Hawk T.1—XX233, XX237, XX294, XX307, XX308; Hawk T.1A—XX227, XX252, XX253, XX260, XX264, XX266, XX306*

No 1 Flying Training School

Current base: *Linton-on-Ouse.*
Aircraft type: *Tucano T.1.*
Role: *Basic flying training.*
Markings: *No 1 FTS emblem and badge.*

AIRCRAFT

Tucano T.1: *ZF145, ZF163, ZF170, ZF211, ZF243, ZF346, ZF376, ZF407, ZF408, ZF410, ZF411, ZF412, ZF416, ZF449, ZF450, ZF483, ZF486, ZF487, ZF488, ZF491, ZF492*

Below: Central Flying School tail markings.

No 2 Flying Training School

Current base: Shawbury.
Aircraft types: Gazelle HT.3, Wessex HC.2.
Role: Helicopter basic and advanced flying training.
Markings: Black fuselage codes outlined in white on Gazelle; white fuselage codes on Wessex.

AIRCRAFT
Gazelle HT.3: XZ941/B, XW858/C, XW862/D, XW866/E, XW870/F, XW898/G, XW902/H, ZA804/I, XW906/J, XW910/K, ZB626/L, XX382/M, ZB625/N, XZ940/O, XX406/P, XZ930/Q, XZ931/R, XZ932/S, XZ933/T, XZ934/U, ZB628/V, ZA802/W, ZA803/X, XZ937/Y
Wessex HC.2: XR505/WA, XR516/WB, XR519/WC, XR521/WD, XT672/WE, XT603/WF, XS679/WG, XV722/WH, XS676/WJ, XS677/WK, XT606/WL

No 3 Flying Training School

Current base: Cranwell.
Aircraft types: Bulldog T.1, Tucano T.1.
Role: Basic flying training.
Markings: Blue fuselage band.

AIRCRAFT
Bulldog T.1: XX515, XX519, XX535, XX632, XX667
Tucano T.1: ZF140, ZF141, ZF143, ZF144, ZF160, ZF164, ZF165, ZF167, ZF171, ZF200, ZF201, ZF202, ZF207, ZF210, ZF212, ZF239, ZF240, ZF241, ZF263, ZF264, ZF267, ZF270, ZF284, ZF285, ZF287, ZF289, ZF290, ZF291, ZF292, ZF293, ZF295, ZF315, ZF317, ZF319, ZF320, ZF338, ZF339, ZF340, ZF341, ZF342, ZF344, ZF347, ZF348, ZF349, ZF350, ZF373, ZF374, ZF375, ZF377, ZF409, ZF414, ZF415, ZF417, ZF447, ZF485, ZF489, ZF512, ZF513, ZF514, ZF515

No 4 Flying Training School

Current base: Valley.
Aircraft types: Hawk T.1, Hawk T.1A.
Role: Advanced flying training, tactical weapons training.
Markings: Component squadron markings (Nos 74 and 208 Squadrons and Central Flying School).

AIRCRAFT
For serial numbers see entries for individual component squadrons.

Left, upper: No 3 FTS tail markings.
Left, lower: No 234(R) Squadron was until 1994 one of the two component Squadrons of No 4 Flying Training School.

No 6 Flying Training School

Current base: Finningley.
Aircraft types: Bulldog T.1, Dominie T.1, Jetstream T.1, Tucano T.1, Hawk T.1.
Role: Navigator training, Air Engineer training, Air Electronics Operator training, Multi Engine training.
Markings: No 6 FTS badge on fuselage.

AIRCRAFT
Bulldog T.1: XX529/W, XX621/X, XX624/Y, XX713/Z
Dominie T.1: XS712/A, XS713/C, XS727/D, XS728/E, XS729/G, XS731/J, XS737/K, XS711/L, XS709/M, XS734/N, XS710/O, XS714/P, XS733/Q, XS735/R, XS736/S, XS726/T, XS738/U
Jetstream T.1: Aircraft drawn from No 45(R) Squadron (q.v.).
Tucano T.1: ZF161, ZF162, ZF242, ZF379, ZF405, ZF413, ZF418, ZF445, ZF446, ZF448
Hawk T.1: XX168, XX169, XX173, XX232, XX240, XX250, XX295, XX309

No 7 Flying Training School

Current base: Chivenor.
Aircraft type: Hawk T.1, Hawk T.1A.
Role: Advanced flying training, tactical weapons training.
Markings: Component squadron markings (Nos 19 and 92 Squadrons)

AIRCRAFT
For serial numbers see entries for individual component squadrons.

Joint Elementary Flying Training Squadron

Current base: Topcliffe.
Aircraft types: Slingsby Firefly.
Role: Joint RAF/RN elementary flying training.
Markings: JEFTS emblem (civilian contract operation).

University Air Squadrons

Role: University student basic flying training.
Aircraft type: Bulldog T.1.

Aberdeen & St Andrews UAS
Current base: Leuchars
Aircraft: XX561/A, XX663/B, XX709/C, XX665/E

Birmingham UAS
Current base: Cosford
Aircraft: XX558/A, XX534/B, XX670/C, XX671/D, XX672/E

Bristol UAS
Current base: Colerne
Aircraft: XX654/A, XX655/B, XX656/C, XX653/E

Below: No 6 FTS fuselage markings.

SQUADRON DIRECTORY

Cambridge UAS
Current base: Teversham
Aircraft: XX658/A, XX634/C, XX659/S, XX657/U, XX518/Z

East Lowlands UAS
Current base: Turnhouse
Aircraft: XX521/01, XX537/02, XX525/03, XX664/04

East Midlands UAS
Current base: Newton
Aircraft: XX687/A, XX694/E, XX623/M, XX556/S, XX704/U

Glasgow & Strathclyde UAS
Current base: Abbotsinch
Aircraft: XX559, XX560, XX611, XX702

Liverpool UAS
Current base: Woodvale
Aircraft: XX630/A, XX685/L, XX688/S, XX686/U

London UAS
Current base: Benson
Aircraft: XX544/01, XX639/02, XX546/03, XX524/04, XX547/05, XX548/06, XX553/07, XX552/08, XX554/09

Manchester UAS
Current base: Woodvale
Aircraft: XX668/1, XX615/2, XX616/3, XX617/4, XX710/5

Northumbrian UAS
Current base: Leeming
Aircraft: XX629/V, XX631/W, XX633/X, XX636/Y

Oxford UAS
Current base: Benson
Aircraft: XX695/A, XX661/B, XX526/C, XX528/D

Queen's UAS
Current base: Aldergrove
Aircraft: XX640/B, XX697/C, XX711/D, XX562/E

Southampton UAS
Current base: Lee-on-Solent
Aircraft: XX706/01, XX701/02, XX708/03, XX707/04, XX705/05

Wales UAS
Current base: St Athan
Aircraft: XX625/01, XX626/02, XX627/03, XX628/04, XX612/05

Yorkshire UAS
Current base: Finningley
Aircraft: XX690/A, XX619/B, XX620/C, XX532/D, XX622/E, XX543/F, XX691/G, XX550/Z

Air Experience Flights

Role: Air experience flying for Air Training Corps and Combined Cadet Force cadets.
Aircraft type: Chipmunk T.10.

No 1 AEF
Current base: Manston
Aircraft: WB569/2, WG430/3, WK544/4, WP855/5, WZ845/6

No 2 AEF
Current base: Hurn
Aircraft: WP480/9, WP920/10, WK630/11, WD373/12

No 3 AEF
Current base: Colerne
Aircraft: WK639/L, WP896/M, WK624/N, WB654/T, WP900/V

No 4 AEF
Current base: Exeter
Aircraft: WB560, WG458, WP803, WP833

No 5 AEF
Current base: Teversham
Aircraft: WP981/D, WZ872/E, WP837/L, WB627/N, WP970/T, WB652/V

No 6 AEF
Current base: Benson
Aircraft: WB586/A, WP901/B, WK589/C, WP805/D, WP914/E, WZ847/F, WP786/G

No 7 AEF
Current base: Newton
Aircraft: WG308/71, WG469/72, WP984/73, WZ856/74, WZ877/75

No 8 AEF
Current base: Shawbury
Aircraft: WB739/8, WP839/A, WP859/E, WP929/F

No 9 AEF
Current base: Finningley
Aircraft: WG407/67, WD390/68, WK590/69

No 10 AEF
Current base: Woodvale
Aircraft: WB697/90, WK562/91, WK572/92, WK609/93, WK642/94, WP692/95

No 11 AEF
Current base: Leeming
Aircraft: WK517/84, WK638/83, WP844/85, WZ878/86

No 12 AEF
Current base: Turnhouse
Aircraft: WB567, WK585, WP872, WP890, WP967

No 13 AEF
Current base: Sydenham
Aircraft: Drawn from Queens UAS (q.v.) as required

Volunteer Gliding Schools

Role: Air experience flying for Air Training Corps and Combined Cadet Force cadets.
Aircraft types: Kestrel TX.1, Valiant TX.1, Vigilant TX.1, Viking TX.1.

Central Gliding School
Current base: Syerston
Aircraft: ZD974, ZD975 (Kestrel); ZD658, ZD659, ZD660 (Valiant); ZH129, ZH185, ZH187, ZH188, ZH189, ZH190, ZH194, ZH195, ZH207, ZH265, ZH266, ZH268, ZH271 (Vigilant); ZE499, ZE501, ZE502, ZE552, ZE554, ZE605, ZE607, ZE626, ZE627, ZE630, ZE635, ZE652 (Viking)

No 611 VGS
Current base: Swanton Morley
Aircraft: ZE551, ZE553, ZE560, ZE587, ZE659 (Viking)

No 612 VGS
Current base: Halton
Aircraft: ZH128, ZH270 (Vigilant)

No 613 VGS
Current base: Halton
Aircraft: ZH208, ZH209 (Vigilant)

No 614 VGS
Current base: Wethersfield
Aircraft: ZE585, ZE653, ZE654 (Viking)

No 615 VGS
Current base: Kenley
Aircraft: ZE496, ZE498, ZE610, ZE633, ZE677 (Viking); ZD657 (Valiant)

No 616 VGS
Current base: Henlow
Aircraft: ZH119, ZH120, ZH122, ZH248 (Vigilant)

No 617 VGS
Current base: Manston
Aircraft: ZE602, ZE603, ZE656, ZE680, ZE681 (Viking)

No 618 VGS
Current base: West Malling
Aircraft: ZE522, ZE528, ZE532, ZE584, ZE600, ZE613, ZE632, ZE657, ZE658 (Viking)

No 621 VGS
Current base: Weston-super-Mare
Aircraft: ZE561, ZE594, ZE678, ZE683 (Viking)

No 622 VGS
Current base: Upavon
Aircraft: ZE495, ZE520, ZE533, ZE550, ZE557, ZE636 (Viking)

No 624 VGS
Current base: Chivenor
Aircraft: ZH197, ZH205, ZH206 (Vigilant)

No 625 VGS
Current base: South Cerney
Aircraft: ZE503, ZE586, ZE592, ZE601, ZE608 (Viking)

No 626 VGS
Current base: Predennack
Aircraft: ZE524, ZE531, ZE555, ZE628, ZE629 (Viking)

No 631 VGS
Current base: Sealand
Aircraft: ZE562, ZE591, ZE593, ZE604, ZE606, ZE609, ZE679 (Viking)

No 632 VGS
Current base: Ternhill
Aircraft: ZH116, ZH117, ZH118, ZH145, ZH269 (Vigilant)

No 633 VGS
Current base: Cosford
Aircraft: ZH125, ZH184, ZH186, ZH196 (Vigilant)

No 634 VGS
Current base: St Athan
Aircraft: ZE521, ZE526, ZE558, ZE563, ZE625 (Viking)

No 635 VGS
Current base: Samlesbury
Aircraft: ZH115, ZH121, ZH247, ZH265, ZH267 (Vigilant)

No 636 VGS
Current base: Fairwood Common
Aircraft: ZE529, ZE651, ZE682 (Viking)

No 637 VGS
Current base: Little Rissington
Aircraft: ZH144, ZH146, ZH147, ZH148, ZH263 (Vigilant)

No 642 VGS
Current base: Linton-on-Ouse
Aircraft: ZH123, ZH124, ZH126, ZH249, ZH264 (Vigilant)

No 643 VGS
Current base: Syerston
Aircraft: Drawn from CGS (q.v.) as required

No 644 VGS
Current base: Syerston
Aircraft: Drawn from CGS (q.v.) as required

No 645 VGS
Current base: Catterick
Aircraft: ZE504, ZE527, ZE530, ZE559, ZE590 (Viking)

No 661 VGS
Current base: Kirknewton
Aircraft: ZE556, ZE564, ZE614, ZE684, ZE685 (Viking)

No 662 VGS
Current base: Arbroath
Aircraft: ZE534, ZE595, ZE631, ZE650 (Viking)

No 663 VGS
Current base: Kinloss
Aircraft: ZH192, ZH193, ZH211 (Vigilant)

Non-Flying Units

No 1 School of Technical Training
Current Base: Halton
Aircraft types: Gnat T.1, Harrier GR.3, Hunter F.6, Jaguar GR.1, Jaguar T.2, Jet Provost T.3, Jet Provost T.4, Wessex HAS.3, Wessex HU.5, Whirlwind HAR.10
Role: Technical instruction

No 2 School of Technical Training
Current base: Cosford
Aircraft types: Buccaneer S.2A, Canberra PR.9, Harrier GR.3, Jaguar GR.1, Jaguar T.2, Jet Provost T.3, Jet Provost T.4, Jet Provost T.5A, Tornado, Victor K.1A, Wessex HU.5
Role: Technical instruction

Non-Aviation-Equipped Units

No 4 School of Technical Training
Current base: St Athan
Aircraft types: Bulldog T.1, Gnat T.1, Jaguar GR.1, Jet Provost T.3, Jet Provost T.5A
Role: Technical instruction

Department of Special Ground Training
Current base: Cranwell
Aircraft types: Harrier GR.3, Hunter F.6A, Hunter T.7, Jaguar GR.1
Role: Technical instruction

Trade Management Training School
Current base: Scampton
Aircraft types: Hunter F.6A, Hunter T.7
Role: Technical instruction

Aircraft Maintenance Unit
Current Base: St Athan
Aircraft types: Various

Non-Aviation-Equipped Units

No 7 Maintenance Unit
Current base: Quedgeley

No 11 Maintenance Unit
Current base: Chilmark

No 14 Maintenance Unit
Current base: Carlisle

No 16 Maintenance Unit
Current base: Stafford

No 30 Maintenance Unit
Current base: Sealand

No 217 Maintenance Unit
Current base: Cardington

Aerial Erector School
Current base: Digby

Airmen's Command School
Current base: Hereford

Balloon Operations Squadron
Current base: Hullavington

Central Servicing Development Establishment
Current base: Swanton Morley

Communications Site
Current base: Edelsborough

Below: The RAF Trade Management Training School at Scampton uses a fleet of Hunter aircraft, some of which have been repainted in the markings Hunters carried when they equipped No 111 Squadron's famous *Black Arrows* formation aerobatics team.

SQUADRON DIRECTORY

Electronics Battle Damage Repair & Prevention Development Centre
Current base: North Luffenham

Ground Radio Servicing Centre
Current base: North Luffenham

Guided Weapons School
Current base: Newton

Headquarters P&SS(UK)
Current base: Rudloe Manor

Joint Services Air Trooping Centre
Current base: Stanbridge

No 1 Aeromedical Evacuation Squadron
Current base: Brize Norton

No 1 Parachute Training School
Current base: Brize Norton

No 1 Radio School
Current base: Locking

No 6 Signals Unit
Current base: Rudloe Manor

No 7 Signals Unit
Current base: Byron Heights

No 12 Signals Unit
Current base: Aylos Nikolaos

No 26 Signals Unit
Current base: Berlin

No 144 Signals Unit
Current base: Ty Croes

No 280 Signals Unit
Current base: Akrotiri

No 303 Signals Unit
Current base: Mount Kent

Below: The Officers & Aircrew Selection Centre at Cranwell. (RAF)

No 339 Signals Unit
Current base: Digby

No 591 Signals Unit
Current base: Digby

No 751 Signals Unit
Current base: Mount Alice

No 840 Signals Unit
Current base: Lindholme

No 1001 Signals Unit
Current base: Oakhangar

Officers & Aircrew Selection Centre
Current base: Cranwell

RAF Hospital Halton
Current base: Halton

RAF Hospital Nocton Hall
Current base: Nocton Hall

RAF Hospital Wroughton
Current base: Wroughton

RAF Music Services
Current base: Uxbridge

RAF Staff College
Current base: Bracknell

RAF Communications Centre
Current base: Rudloe Manor

RAF Mountain Rescue Service
Current bases: Kinloss, Leuchars, Leeming, St Athan, Stafford, Valley

RAF Police School
Current base: Newton

School of Education
Current base: Newton

School of Management Training
Current base: Newton

Signals Engineering Establishment
Current base: Henlow

Supply Control Centre
Current base: Stanbridge

UK Mobile Air Movements Squadron
Current base: Lyneham

Royal Air Force Regiment

No 1 GROUP:

No 2 Squadron
Current base: Catterick
Field Squadron

No 3 Squadron
Current base: Aldergrove
Field Squadron

No 2 GROUP:

No 1 Squadron
Current base: Laarbruch
Field Squadron

No 26 Squadron
Current base: Laarbruch
Rapier Squadron

No 37 Squadron
Current base: Bruggen
Rapier Squadron

No 11 GROUP:

No 15 Squadron
Current base: Leeming
Rapier Squadron

No 27 Squadron
Current base: Leuchars
Rapier Squadron

No 48 Squadron
Current base: Lossiemouth
Rapier Squadron

No 6 WING:

No 19 Squadron
Current base: Brize Norton
Rapier Squadron

SQUADRON DIRECTORY

No 20 Squadron
Current base: Honington
Rapier Squadron

No 66 Squadron
Current base: West Raynham
Rapier Squadron

BRITISH FORCES CYPRUS:

No 34 Squadron
Current base: Akrotiri
Light Armour Squadron

Royal Auxiliary Air Force

No 1 Maritime Headquarters 'City of Hertford'
Current base: Northwood

No 2 Maritime Headquarters 'City of Edinburgh'
Current base: Pitreavie Castle

No 3 Maritime Headquarters 'County of Devon'
Current base: St Mawgan

No 4 Maritime Headquarters 'County of Wiltshire'
Current base: Hullavington

Royal Auxiliary Air Force Regiment

No 1310 Wing
Current base: Catterick

No 1339 Wing
Current Base: Waddington

No 2503 'County of Lincoln' Field Squadron
Current base: Waddington

No 2620 'County of Norfolk' Field Squadron
Current base: Marham

No 2622 'Highland' Field Squadron
Current base: Lossiemouth

No 2623 'East Anglian' Field Squadron
Current base: Honington

No 2624 'County of Oxford' Field Squadron
Current base: Brize Norton

No 2625 'County of Cornwall' Field Squadron
Current base: St Mawgan

No 2729 'City of Lincoln' Squadron
Current base: Waddington

No 2890 Squadron
Current base: Waddington

Royal Air Force Volunteer Reserve

No 7006 Flight
Current base: High Wycombe

No 7010 Flight
Current base: Wyton

No 7630 Flight
Current base: Ashford

No 7644 Flight
Current base: Uxbridge

Other Units

No 63(QCS) Squadron
Current base: Uxbridge.
Ceremonial/Field Squadron

RAF FIRE SERVICE:

Fire Services Central Training Establishment
Current base: Manston

AIRFIELD DIRECTORY

RAF Akrotiri

Resident units: *No 84 Squadron (Wessex); No 34 Squadron RAF Regiment.*

First established in 1955, RAF Akrotiri began its existence as a collection of prefabricated houses and old caravans, but by the end of the year a 1,500yd runway had been laid and the station was able to accept the first transport aircraft. The first Handley Page Hastings arrived on 16 January 1956 and began a series of flights bringing personnel and equipment from the Canal Zone.

The first jet aircraft to arrive at Akrotiri were Gloster Meteors of No 13 Squadron, employed on reconnaissance duties. No 208 Squadron was the next unit to arrive—also with Meteors—followed by No 6 Squadron with Venoms. In August 1956 Nos 1 and 34 Squadrons brought their Hunters to Cyprus. After No 13 Squadron had re-equipped with Canberras in mid-1956, two further squadrons converted on to Canberra bombers in 1956–57 and by 1960 the station's permanent facilities were completed.

Missile-armed Javelin fighters moved to Akrotiri in 1964, followed by Lightning interceptors. No 1563 Flight, equipped with Whirlwind search and rescue helicopters, also arrived at this time, and the station became the Cyprus trooping flight air terminal, in preference to Nicosia. In December 1964 the station replaced El Adam as the Royal Air Force's main staging post in the Mediterranean region.

Some ten years after it had first opened, RAF Akrotiri was temporarily closed while the runway was reconstructed, the resident aircraft moving to Nicosia. After the base reopened, No 70 Squadron joined these units with Hastings transports, making Akrotiri the Royal Air Force's biggest station. More Lightnings arrived in 1967, followed by Argosy transports as replacements for the Hastings. Regular trooping and transport flights by the Argosys were augmented by visits by Britannias, Comets, Belfasts and Hercules, which were joined by a steady stream of combat aircraft deploying to Cyprus for exercises.

During January 1969 the Canberra bombers were phased out and the four squadrons based at Akrotiri were disbanded. To replace them, two squadrons of Vulcan B.2 V-bombers arrived from the United Kingdom, and Nos 9 and 35 Squadrons shared Akrotiri's facilities with No 56 Squadron's Lightnings, No 70 Squadron's Hercules and Argosy transports and the recently arrived Whirlwind helicopters of No 84 Squadron.

The British presence in Cyprus began to be run down in 1975 and all the fixed-wing assets based at Akrotiri were returned to the United Kingdom. The SAR helicopters of No 84 Squadron stayed, together with No 34 Squadron RAF Regiment, the Joint Services Support Unit and the Near East Joint Services Hygiene Unit.

In the 1990s the station remains active as a staging post for long-range RAF flights and plays host to regular deployments of combat aircraft from the UK, taking advantage of the excellent weather conditions. Regular Armament Practice Camps (APCs) are held at the base, and the *Red Arrows* make an annual visit to the station for a concentrated period of pre-season aerobatic training.

RAF Aldergrove

Resident units: *No 72 Squadron (Wessex); No 230 Squadron (Puma, Chinook); No 3 Squadron RAF Regiment; No 13 Air Experience Flight (Bulldog); Queen's University Air Squadron (Bulldog).*

The year 1993 marked the 75th anniversary not only of the formation of the Royal Air Force itself but also of RAF Aldergrove, the first RAF station to be established in Northern Ireland and the last in that province to remain active. Military aviation has had a presence in Northern Ireland since the days of the Royal Flying Corps.

In November 1917 the Air Ministry, looking for suitable airfields for the rapidly expanding RFC, purchased 200 acres of land at Aldergrove. By the time the airfield opened in November the following year, the RFC had been absorbed into the RAF and the First World War was coming to an end, but No 16 Aircraft Acceptance Park (as RAF Aldergrove was originally known) was little more than a collection of wooden huts on a grass airfield, used as a final assembly area for Handley Page bombers built at Harland & Wolff's Belfast factory.

With the signing of the Armistice, activity at Aldergrove diminished, and although the field was

RAF ALDERGROVE

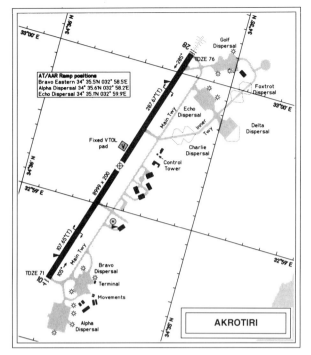

AKROTIRI

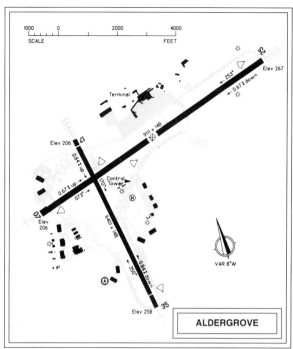

ALDERGROVE

used intermittently by visiting squadrons during the early 1920s, it was not until the formation of No 502 (Ulster) Squadron in 1925 that Aldergrove saw regular use again. No 502 Squadron, equipped with Vickers Vimy bombers, was the first of five special reserve squadrons to be formed, to provide flying practice for pilots of the RAF Volunteer Reserve, and was the first to honour its birthplace by incorporating it into the Squadron's official name.

For the next ten years No 502 Squadron was synonymous with the RAF in Northern Ireland. During this time the boom in civil air transport saw the introduction of civil flights into Aldergrove and the construction of civil airfields at Newtownards and Sydenham. In 1936 Aldergrove became an Armament Training Station, using bombing ranges established on Lough Neagh. Many Battle of Britain pilots from units based all around the British Isles learned their gunnery skills in the skies over the province.

When the Second World War began, all three airfields in Northern Ireland came under Air Ministry control, and by 1944 Ulster hosted some 26 operational airfields and seaplane bases. The protection of North Atlantic convoys formed a large part of the province's contribution to the air effort. RAF Castle Archdale was the most westerly Coastal Command unit in the United Kingdom, and its Catalina and Sunderland flying boats, together with Liberators from Ballykelly, claimed many U-boat kills. Aircraft from Aghanloo flew more operational hours than those from any other Coastal Command station during the war.

Northern Ireland's geographical situation made it an obvious staging base for aircraft ferried from factories in America, as well as those produced in the province's own factories. Aldergrove received the first transatlantic delivery of the war when seven Hudsons arrived in November 1940 from their Lockheed factory in California. No 23 Maintenance Unit was formed at Aldergrove to equip and modify many types of aircraft before operational deployment. The unit handled vast numbers of aircraft and at one time had more than 500 on charge: storage space was at such a premium that they had to be dispersed in surrounding fields and at satellite airfields built at Langford Lodge, Ballywater, Murlough, Maydown and St Angelo.

After the end of the war many units disbanded and the majority of the airfields closed, but the RAF presence continued and No 23 MU became a centre for scrapping redundant bombers. It later became a major servicing depot for aircraft such as the Shackleton, Canberra, Javelin, Argosy and Phantom. RAF Ballykelly meanwhile continued its maritime role, finally operating Shackletons until its closure in 1971. RAF Bishops Court ceased operations as a flying station but formed a part of the United Kingdom's air defence radar system until 1990.

Aldergrove is today the only Royal Air Force station in Northern Ireland, and its personnel and aircraft are active throughout the province in support of the security forces' fight against terrorism. The Wessex, Puma and Chinook helicopters of Nos 72 and 230 Squadrons share the airfield with Army Air Corps aircraft, and the station is the major airhead for all troop movements to the province. No 3 Squadron RAF Regiment is also based at Aldergrove to provide airfield security.

RAF Barkston Heath

Resident units: None.

Relief landing ground for Cranwell (q.v.).

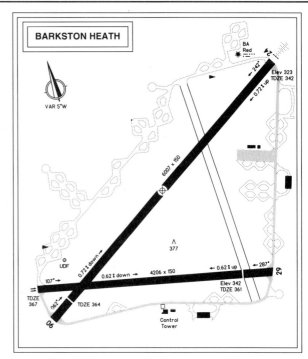

RAF Benson

Resident units: *The Queen's Flight (BAe 146); No 60 Squadron (Wessex).*

Building work on what was to become RAF Benson began during 1937, when the Royal Air Force was expanding in order to meet the ever-increasing Nazi threat. The first unit to arrive at the airfield was No 150 Squadron from Boscombe Down, followed by No 103 Squadron from Abingdon, both units being equipped with Fairey Battles.

When the Second World War began, Benson became the centre of activity for No 12 Operational Training Unit, responsible for the training of pilots, observers and air gunners. The Fairey Battles and Avro Ansons used by the unit were replaced by Wellingtons during 1940, and training operations continued despite a number of *Luftwaffe* bombing raids, which caused some damage although, fortunately, only one fatalilty.

In 1941 the Station became the home of No 1 Photographic Reconnaissance Unit, with Spitfires, and during May the same year a No 1 PRU Spitfire located *Bismarck* near Bergen, leading to the German battleship's eventual demise. Concrete runways were laid in 1941–42, and No 1 PRU was expanded into Nos 540, 541, 542, 543 and 544 Squadrons, RAF Benson being transferred to Coastal Command. The Spitfires were joined by Mosquitos, and photographic reconnaissance work continued. Post-strike images of the Möhne and Eder dams were gathered, and in 1943 one of Benson's pilots managed to gather an almost complete photographic mosaic of Berlin after remaining over the city for nearly 45 minutes. The battleship *Tirpitz* was also photographed, and one of Benson's Mosquitos became the first Allied aircraft to encounter an Me 262, engaging the jet fighter for twenty minutes.

PRU Mosquitos continued to operate from Benson until 1951, in company with Nos 540 and 58 Squadrons, together with the King's Flight, which re-formed in 1946. In 1953 the Station joined Transport Command and Nos 147 and 167 Squadrons arrived, responsible for the ferrying of various aircraft types, mostly to the Middle East; these units had already successfully ferried 400 F-86 Sabres across the Atlantic for the RAF.

The Ferry Wing (as the Station became known) disbanded in 1960 and Benson became the base for the RAF's medium-range tactical air transport force, the first Argosy arriving in November 1961 and becoming one of six belonging to the Argosy Operational Conversion Unit. The first Argosy squadron was No 105, which later moved to Aden; a second

RAF BRIZE NORTON

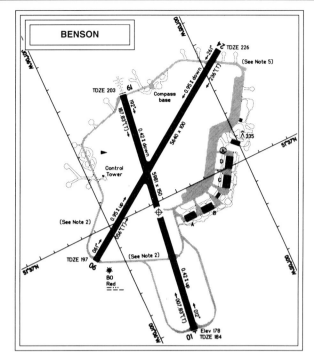

Aldergrove towards the end of 1981 and the Wessex Training Flight disbanded in April 1982. No 115 Squadron moved to Benson in January 1983, and three years later a trio of BAe 146s were delivered to the Queen's Flight, replacing the Andovers which had previously been used by the unit. No 60 Squadron arrived at Benson with Wessex support helicopters during May 1992 and No 115 Squadron disbanded in October 1993, having transferred its Andovers to a civilian contractor at Castle Donington. The Queen's Flight remains at Benson with a fleet of BAe 146s and Wessexes, together with the Wessex helicopters of No 60 Squadron.

unit, No 215 Squadron, also formed at Benson before moving to the Far East. Nos 114 and 267 Squadrons remained at Benson with Argosys, together with the Queens Flight. The Wessex Training Flight arrived from Odiham during 1980, together with No 72 Squadron. The latter unit transferred to

RAF Brize Norton

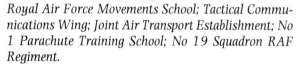

Resident units: *No 10 Squadron (VC10); No 101 Squadron (VC10); No 216 Squadron (TriStar); No 2624 (County of Oxford) Squadron RAuxAF; No 4624 (County of Oxford) Movements Squadron RAuxAF; No 244 Signal Squadron; Royal Air Force Movements School; Tactical Communications Wing; Joint Air Transport Establishment; No 1 Parachute Training School; No 19 Squadron RAF Regiment.*

The history of RAF Brize Norton dates back to 7 September 1937 when No 2 Flying Training School arrived at the station before the initial building programme had been completed. The airfield was used for various types of flying training until July 1942, when it became the home of the Heavy Glider Conversion Unit (later renamed No 21 HGU). This unit remained at Brize Norton until January 1946.

Between March and October 1944 the station was used as a base for parachute and glider operations by Nos 296 and 297 Squadrons, equipped with Albemarles. These squadrons took part in the D-Day landings, launching Airspeed Horsa gliders which dropped paratroops to capture bridges over the River Orne and the Caen Canal and placing two gliders directly on a coastal battery controlling the estuary of the Orne and in a position to oppose the seaborne landings. The squadrons were involved in the airborne landings at Arnhem in September 1944 and also in dropping personnel and supplies to the resistance movements in Europe.

95

Above: A VC10 C.1 from RAF Brize Norton turns at low level.

On 31 December 1945 Brize Norton was transferred from Flying Training Command to Transport Command and became the home of the Transport Command Development Unit and the School of Flight Efficiency. These units were joined in May 1946 by the Army Airborne Transport Development Unit. Flying training activities returned to the airfield briefly in August 1949 when No 204 Advanced Flying School arrived, but the unit left again in June 1950, when the first American forces began to arrive at the station.

The United States Air Force formally accepted control of Brize Norton in April 1951. US Army engineers worked until early 1952 to extend the runway and build taxiways, hardstandings and accommodation. In June 1952 some 21 Convair B-36 bombers became the first American aircraft to arrive at the station; the first jet bombers, in the form of Boeing B-47s, arrived in September 1953.

A rotation of bomber Wings and refuelling squadrons continued until April 1958 except for the period between October 1955 and January 1957 when the runway was reconstructed. In April 1958 the Reflex alert concept came into force, with Strategic Air Command units arriving from the United States for ninety-day rotational tours of duty. A total of seven USAF bomber Wings provided B-47 aircraft for Reflex duty, the last one returning to the United States in December 1964.

In 1965 the station was returned to RAF Transport Command (renamed Air Support Command in August 1967). A steady build-up of personnel and facilities developed the station into the Royal Air Force's strategic transport base, and in June 1970 two Britannia squadrons, Nos 99 and 511, joined the VC10s of No 10 Squadron and the Belfasts of No 53 Squadron to bring the station up to full strength. Early in 1972 the station became part of Strike Command, initially as part of No 46 Group, which was incorporated into No 38 Group in October 1975.

Following a series of defence expenditure announcements in 1974, the two Britannia squadrons, together with the Belfast-equipped No 53 Squadron, were disbanded, leaving No 10 Squadron to provide the RAF with a worldwide air transport capability, concentrated within the NATO area. No 115 Squadron, equipped with Argosy radar and radio calibration aircraft, arrived at Brize Norton in 1979 for a three-year stay before moving to Benson. The Joint Air Transport Establishment, Tactical Communications Wing, No 1 Parachute Training School and the RAF Movements School all moved to Brize Norton during 1976 and were joined by Nos 2624 and 4624 Squadrons RAuxAF in 1983. During the same year a pair of BAe 146 transports were temporarily based at Brize Norton for evaluation as potential replacements for the Andovers of the Queen's Flight. No 101 Squadron re-formed at Brize Norton in May 1984, equipped with VC10 tankers. No 19 Squadron RAF Regiment re-formed at the base in July 1984, and No 216 Squadron, equipped with TriStar tanker/transports, re-formed in November the same year.

The station currently supports three flying squadrons in the strategic transport and aerial refuelling roles. It also supports the training of parachutists, trials associated with the air-dropping of men and equipment, the training of personnel in the movements specialization, the provision of communication and navigation facilities for aircraft operating away from their home bases and a comprehensive range of air traffic control services. RAF Bampton Castle, a few miles south of Brize, provides long-range communications for all Strike Command aircraft and also services for the Meteorological Office at Bracknell.

RAF Bruggen

Resident units: No 9 Squadron (Tornado); No 14 Squadron (Tornado); No 17 Squadron (Tornado); No 31 Squadron (Tornado); No 37 Squadron Royal Air Force Regiment.

Named after the nearest railhead some four miles away, RAF Bruggen is actually situated just outside the North Rhine-Westphalia village of Elmpt. It is one of just two Royal Air Force stations supporting active squadrons in Germany, following recent defence expenditure cutbacks. Carved out of a large forest area and constructed on drained marshland in the remarkably short period of twelve months between July 1952 and July 1953, the station was built as part of an expansion of NATO forces in the early 1950s. RAF Bruggen's history can be divided into two distinct periods, the first being 1953–57 when the station was a fighter base and the second the period from 1957 to the present day, during which Bruggen has remained active as a strike/attack base.

During the early years of RAF Bruggen's existence No 23 Squadron Belgian Air Force and Nos 67, 71, 112 and 130 Squadrons RAF operated from the base. No 55 Wing RAF Regiment and No 5004 Airfield Construction Wing also operated from Bruggen, together with the General Equipment Park, better known as No 431 Maintenance Unit—which is the only RAF unit to have remained active at Bruggen continuously since 1953.

RAF Bruggen became predominantly a Canberra ground attack/bomber station when Nos 80 and 213 Squadrons arrived during the summer of 1957. No 87 Squadron also arrived at this time, maintaining the station's association with fighters until 1961. No 80 Squadron operated the Canberra PR.7 in the reconnaissance role from Bruggen until the unit's

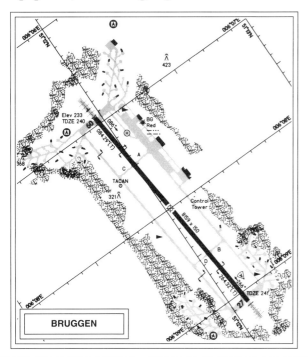

disbandment in 1969, while No 213 Squadron operated the Canberra B(I).6 interdictor in the ground attack and bomber role. The Canberras were eventually replaced by McDonnell Douglas Phantoms, beginning in 1969, and ground attack operations with Phantoms continued until 1975 when the first Jaguars arrived, enabling the Phantoms to be reassigned to air defence duties. Jaguars remained active at Bruggen until 1984, when the first Tornado GR.1 strike/attack bombers arrived, and the base is currently host to four Tornado squadrons, Nos 9, 14, 17 and 31.

The station has a uniformed strength of 2,900, assisted by 700 German, Dutch and British civilians, and is also responsible for 3,900 dependants of servicemen and women. Each of the four squadrons is equipped with twelve Tornado GR.1s, including a pair of GR.1(T) dual-control aircraft which are used for pilot proficiency and continuation training (but remain fully combat-capable). Also stationed at Bruggen is No 37 Squadron RAF Regiment, a Rapier short-range surface-to-air missile unit.

RAF Catterick

Resident units: *No 2 Squadron RAF Regiment; No 645 Volunteer Gliding School (Viking).*

RAF Chivenor

Resident units: *No 7 Flying Training School, comprising No 19(R) Squadron (Hawk) and No 92(R) Squadron (Hawk); 'A' Flight, No 22 Squadron (Wessex); No 624 Volunteer Gliding School (Vigilant).*

Aircraft operations from what eventually became RAF Chivenor first started in April 1934, when the North Devon Airport was created on the site as a large grass airfield, with a clubhouse and workshop building. The first RAF aircraft to use the airfield was a Hawker Hart, carrying out a survey of Exmoor in 1935. Potential RAF pilots were trained at the airfield prior to the Second World War as part of the Civil Air Guard scheme.

RAF Chivenor was completed in 1940 as a training station for Coastal Command, the first resident unit being No 3 Operational Training Unit, which arrived in October 1940. Equipped with Beauforts, Blenheims and Ansons, the unit was later joined by two Flights from No 1 OTU. RAF Chivenor became the principal source of trained air crews for squadrons equipped with Beaufort torpedo bombers.

In December 1940 No 252 Squadron became the first operational unit to be based at Chivenor, initially equipped with Blenheims but later converting to Beaufighters, flying long-range convoy protection missions. During the spring of 1941 the importance of the airfield was recognized by the *Luftwaffe* and it was attacked several times, sustaining substantial damage. In August 1941 Coastal Command's OTUs were reorganized and part of No 3 OTU moved to Cranwell, the remainder becoming the nucleus of No 5 OTU, training Beaufort, Blenheim and Anson crews.

A detachment of 502 Squadron Whitleys arrived in November 1941 and one of the unit's aircraft successfully sank *U206* on the 20th of the month—the first U-boat to be dispatched by an aircraft equipped with ASV (air-to-surface-vessel) radar. In January 1942 a special Flight was formed at Chivenor with Wellington aircraft, tasked with the evaluation of the Leigh light, a powerful airborne searchlight. The equipment was found to be very successful in

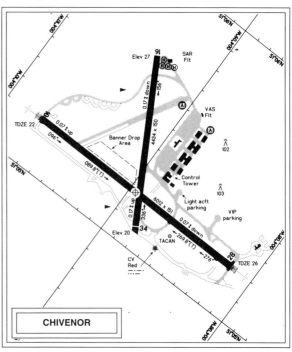

Above: Hawk trainers in front of Chivenor's modern control tower complex.

locating U-boats at night (when they surfaced to recharge their batteries), and the Flight was later expanded into a full squadron (No 272). During the spring of 1942 the station was transferred to No 19 Group, concentrating on anti-submarine operations over the Bay of Biscay, through which all enemy submarines had to pass in order to reach their bases in France. Nos 51 and 77 squadrons were 'loaned' to Chivenor by Bomber Command in May 1942, to join the anti-submarine effort.

From July 1942 Beaufighters began to fly interception missions against Ju 88s and FW 200s over Biscay. Nos 235 and 404 Squadrons were stationed for this purpose at Chivenor, which also acted as a forward base for Beaufighters from at North Coates and Talbenny. The Whitleys were later replaced by Wellingtons and Fortresses, and the introduction of a new version of ASV radar countered the Germans' newly acquired ability to detect aircraft with ASV. Chivenor was regularly used by aircraft in transit to and from the Middle East, including US aircraft such as the P-38s of the 27th Fighter Squadron, which were sent to Algeria in November 1942.

Towards the end of the Second World War the airfield was principally the home of Wellington squadrons, and as the Allied forces advanced into Western France the U-boats withdrew from the Biscay ports, moving submarine activity further north. Most of Chivenor's squadrons transferred to Scotland and Northern Ireland, their places being taken by units returning from the Middle East. Anti-submarine patrols continued for several weeks after the war.

During the first year of post-war activity, a strike wing was formed at Chivenor, which was quickly replaced by meteorological units, and by April 1946 the sole occupier was No 21 Holding Unit. The station was transferred to Fighter Command on 1 October 1946, and No 691 Squadron arrived at the base, flying Spitfires, Oxfords and Martinets on anti-aircraft co-operation duties.

In September 1947 No 203 Advanced Flying School arrived, and it remained until 1950 when

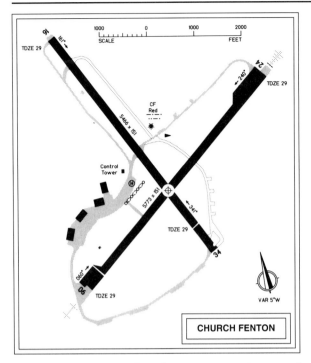

being re-numbered Nos 19(R) and 92(R) Squadrons, tasked with advanced flying and tactical weapons training. No 7 FTS disbanded late in 1994, leaving only the Sea King SAR unit in residence. The base is being considered as a site for Harrier operations.

RAF Church Fenton

Resident units: None.

Relief landing ground for Linton-on-Ouse.

RAF Colerne

Resident units: No 3 Air Experience Flight (Chipmunk); Bristol University Air Squadron (Bulldog).

RAF Coltishall

Resident units: No 6 Squadron (Jaguar); No 41 Squadron (Jaguar); No 54 Squadron (Jaguar); 'E' Flight, No 22 Squadron (Wessex).

The construction of Royal Air Force Coltishall began in February 1940. It was initially planned as a bomber station but was pressed into use as a fighter airfield in May 1940 while incomplete. The first squadron to operate from the station was No 66, flying Spitfires, and this unit was joined by No 242 Squadron, equipped with Hurricanes, in June 1940. The latter had returned from France to refit and was placed under the control of Squadron Leader Douglas Bader.

Coltishall was part of No 12 Group during the Battle of Britain, and a pilot from No 66 Squadron destroyed the first enemy aircraft in the battle, a Dornier 17, in the early hours of 10 July 1940. Although the station was used as a base for resting squadrons from No 11 Group in south-east England, its own squadrons played an aggressive part in the battle, belonging to the celebrated Duxford Wing, and destroyed a total of eighty enemy aircraft.

Following the end of the Second World War Coltishall became the home of Nos 23, 141 and 264

the station was transferred to Transport Command as a base for No 1 Overseas Ferry Unit. However, the airfield was too far west for peacetime operations of this nature, and Fighter Command resumed control, No 229 Operational Conversion Unit arriving from Leuchars in March 1950, equipped with Meteor T.7s and Vampire FB.5s and later with Sabres and Hunters. The Air Ministry was reluctant to consider Chivenor a long-term permanent RAF station, and despite the construction of concrete runways, hardstandings and taxiways, the accommodation facilities remained very basic for many years; only recently has a rebuilding programme been undertaken.

Joining the Hunters of No 229 OCU, a pair of Sycamore helicopters arrived in 1957 as 'E' Flight of No 275 Squadron. Following replacement by Whirlwinds (No 22 Squadron), the helicopter search and rescue detachment remains active at Chivenor, currently equipped with Wessex HAR.2s. In September 1974 the Hunters and Meteors of No 229 OCU left for Brawdy, and Chivenor closed as an active airfield. However, it reopened in August 1980 when the first Hawks arrived to form No 2 Tactical Weapons Unit, comprising Nos 63 and 151 Squadrons. Chivenor was transferred to Support Command in 1992, the TWU becoming No 7 Flying Training School and the component squadrons

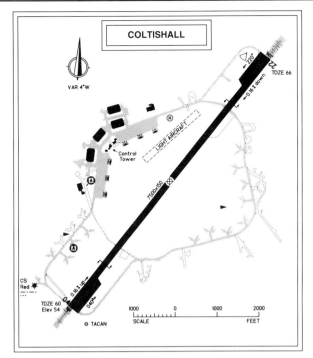

Squadrons flying Mosquitos, all of which moved temporarily to Church Fenton in 1949 while Coltishall's facilities (including the runway) were modified. No 23 Squadron re-equipped with Vampires in 1951 and No 141 Squadron received Meteors, followed by Venoms; No 264 Squadron transferred to Linton-on-Ouse. The two Coltishall squadrons then re-equipped with Javelins during 1957, becoming the first RAF Javelin Wing.

Following a period of reconstruction in 1958, the Air Fighting Development Squadron of the Central Fighter Establishment arrived at Coltishall, becoming the first unit to receive the English Electric Lightning. No 74 became the first RAF Lightning squadron during August 1960 (at Coltishall), and No 226 Operational Conversion Unit arrived in 1964 with a mix of single and twin-seat Lightnings, replacing No 74 Squadron which had earlier moved out. Until March 1976 Coltishall was the home of the RAF Battle of Britain Memorial Flight, with Spitfires and Hurricanes. No 202 Squadron's search and rescue Whirlwinds were replaced by a No 22 Squadron detachment ('E' Flight) equipped with Wessex helicopters, and the Lightning fighters have now gone.

Coltishall is now the Royal Air Force's main Jaguar base, and the home of Nos 6 and 54 Squadrons, which arrived in 1974. They were joined by a Jaguar reconnaissance squadron (No 41) in 1977, and all three units remain active at the station. After having been heavily committed to Operation 'Desert Storm', many of the Jaguars are now regularly deployed to support continuing operations in Bosnia.

RAF Coningsby

Resident units: *No 5 Squadron (Tornado); No 29 Squadron (Tornado); No 56(R) Squadron (Tornado).*

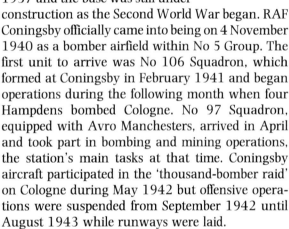

Construction work on the airfield site at Coningsby began during 1937 and the base was still under construction as the Second World War began. RAF Coningsby officially came into being on 4 November 1940 as a bomber airfield within No 5 Group. The first unit to arrive was No 106 Squadron, which formed at Coningsby in February 1941 and began operations during the following month when four Hampdens bombed Cologne. No 97 Squadron, equipped with Avro Manchesters, arrived in April and took part in bombing and mining operations, the station's main tasks at that time. Coningsby aircraft participated in the 'thousand-bomber raid' on Cologne during May 1942 but offensive operations were suspended from September 1942 until August 1943 while runways were laid.

No 617 Squadron, the famous 'Dambusters' under the command of Wing Commander Guy Gibson VC, flew Lancasters from Coningsby from August 1943 until January 1944, when the unit moved a few miles north to Woodhall Spa. The Squadron's Mess is now the popular Petwood Hotel. Early in 1944 a special Marker Force was formed within No 5 Group, operating from Coningsby and the satellite airfields at Woodhall Spa and Metheringham. The Marker Force achieved outstanding results, and the skill of its crews was largely responsible for the night bombing successes achieved during the last fifteen months of the war.

Lincolns arrived at Coningsby after the end of the Second World War, and Mosquitos in 1946. These aircraft departed during March 1950, leaving the airfield inactive for six months until Boeing Washingtons first arrived. The resident squadrons re-equipped with Canberra jet bombers in 1953. During the following year the station was closed to flying and a large construction programme began, which included the laying of a new concrete runway and associated hardstandings and taxiways. It re-opened for flying in 1956, Canberras taking up residence until 1961.

From 1962 until November 1964 three squadrons of Vulcan V-bombers (Nos 9, 12 and 35) were based at Coningsby and in May 1963 the station received the Freedom of the Borough of Boston. In 1964 it was selected as the prospective base for the BAC TSR-2 which was then in pre-production. Following the untimely cancellation of the latter project, RAF Coningsby was placed under care and maintenance until 1966, when it was selected as the first base for the TSR-2's chosen replacement, the McDonnell Douglas Phantom, and was transferred from Bomber Command to Fighter Command. The first Phantoms arrived in December 1967.

As the Phantom was initially intended to perform in the air support and ground attack role, the station was transferred to Air Support Command and during August 1968 the first Phantom air crew training

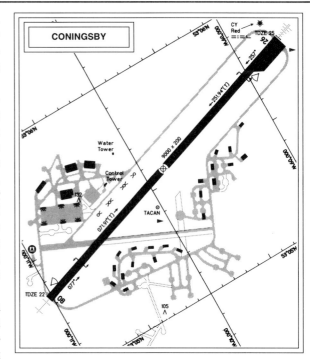

Below: Inside RAF Coningsby's control tower.

course was commenced within No 228 Operational Conversion Unit. In October 1974 the station was transferred again, to No 11 Group Strike Command, reflecting the Phantom's change to the air defence role. The RAF's famous Battle of Britain Memorial Flight moved to Coningsby from RAF Coltishall in March 1976 and continues to operate a fleet of Spitfires, together with a Hurricane, a Lancaster, a Devon and a Dakota.

In 1977 HRH Princess Margaret became Honorary Air Commodore of Royal Air Force Coningsby, and she visited the station in 1979, 1982 and 1985, and in 1987 she presented No 29(F) Squadron with a new Standard. In June 1981 an airfield 'hardening' programme began and the resident squadrons were dispersed into hardened aircraft shelter (HAS) sites around the airfield. The main runway was resurfaced in 1984, and during this period the squadrons operated from RAF Waddington.

The first Tornado F.2 fighter arrived at Coningsby in November 1984; No 229 OCU had re-formed on the 1st of the month and began the training of Tornado air crews shortly thereafter. No 29 Squadron re-equipped with Tornado F.3s during 1987. In April that year the Phantom OCU moved to Leuchars and during the following February No 5 Squadron arrived from Binbrook and re-equipped with Tornado F.3s. The Tornado Aircraft Interceptor Trainer was installed in 1985, followed by the Air Combat Simulator in 1987, reflecting Coningsby's role as the main Tornado interceptor base. An RB.199 engine deep-strip servicing facility was also developed at nearby Woodhall Spa.

RAF Cosford

Resident units: No 2 School of Technical Training; Joint Services School of Photography; RAF School of Physical Training; University of Birmingham Air Squadron (Bulldog); No 633 Volunteer Gliding School (Vigilant).

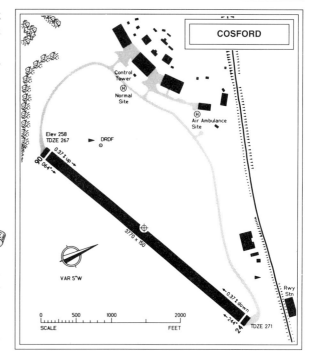

The Royal Air Force station at Cosford was opened in 1938 as part of the Government's pre-war expansion policy for the armed services. It was intended to become primarily a technical training school, but, although this has always been the station's main role, it has also been the home of an important RAF hospital, and it has hosted a number of maintenance and training units over the years.

From 1939 until 1942 Cosford was one of three Officer Training Schools for ground branch officers. Between 1942 and 1943 the three Schools were amalgamated at Cosford, as the Officer Cadet Training Unit. This unit then transferred to Spitalgate in 1948 and currently resides at Cranwell. The RAF School of Catering was based at Cosford from 1954 until 1958, when it moved to Hereford.

The second unit to be set up at Cosford was No 9 Maintenance Unit (MU) which first opened as an Aircraft Storage Unit in 1939. Its task was to store, assemble, repair and maintain all types of aircraft, ranging from Tiger Moths to Wellington bombers, and to ferry each aircraft handled to the appropriate squadron. The main aircraft types handled by No 9 MU were the Spitfire, Mosquito, Beaufighter and Wellington. In July 1942 the until went into full-time production of the Airspeed Horsa. The first Horsa glider was produced on 30 July 1942, and more than fifty had been completed by the following November. Cosford was one of only two bases where Horsa production was undertaken, the other being Brize Norton. Many of the gliders assembled at Cosford participated in the invasion of Europe, and in particular in Operation 'Market Garden', the Allied airborne assaults at Arnhem and Nijmegan.

Throughout the Second World War many enemy attacks were made on the Birmingham and Wolverhampton area, and, as a result, Vickers-Supermarine moved Spitfire production to Cosford and that aircraft became one of only a few types to have been manufactured and assembled at the base. Cosford suffered only one enemy air raid, which took place on 11 March 1941. The *Luftwaffe* launched a major attack on the Birmingham area, and more than 76 raids took place over a two-hour period. At one point, some 135 Heinkel He 111 and Junkers Ju 88 bombers were targeted on Birmingham, but the raid was hampered by cloud and only a few aircraft were able to make visual bombing runs. Birmingham's anti-aircraft guns fired nearly 7,000 rounds of ammunition against the formations, but with little success. However, some aircraft strayed off course and appeared over Cosford. Incendiary bombs landed on the grass airfield, but these were extinguished by unit personnel as the raid continued. Two high-explosive bombs narrowly missed a hangar but succeeded in causing heavy damage to its end wall. Further high-explosive bombs detonated in open countryside and caused some damage to roads leading to aircraft dispersal sites. After the raid it was discovered that only two Lysander aircraft had been damaged inside a hangar, and no injuries had been sustained by base personnel.

When No 9 MU disbanded in 1956 its place was taken by No 236 Maintenance Unit, specializing in mechanical transport. A Royal Air Force Hospital opened at Cosford in 1940, equipped with 503 beds, and this remained in use until a decision was made to close the hospital in 1975; at the request of the National Health Service, the unit remained open for use by the local civilian population until 1977. The main unit is now No 2 School of Technical Training, which has been at Cosford ever since the station first opened. Tasked with the training of armourers and aircraft fitters, engine and airframe mechanics, electrical technicians and telegraphists, the unit is also responsible for the training of many overseas students and now encompasses many diverse training tasks, such as avionics and specialist weapons instruction.

The RAF School of Photography moved to Cosford in September 1963, and the RAF School of Physical Training returned there in 1977. The University of Birmingham Air Squadron, equipped with Bulldog T.1s, moved to Cosford in 1978, with approximately 20 officers and 35 students.

RAF Cottesmore

Resident unit: Trinational Tornado Training Establishment (Tornado).

Situated on the eastern side of the ancient county of Rutland, the area between the villages of Cottesmore and Thistleton was first surveyed as a possible site for an airfield in 1935, and the station opened as a grassed aerodrome in 1938, when Battles of Nos 35 and 207 Squadrons arrived from Worthy Down in April of that year. Cottesmore remained active as a bomber flying training station until 1943, operating a variety of aircraft types.

During 1943 the station was transferred to the United States Army Air Force, becoming USAAF Station 489. Runways and taxiways were constructed prior to the arrival of Douglas C-47 Skytrains, C-53 Skytroopers and Waco gliders of the 316th Troop Carrier Group in March 1944. It was from Cottesmore that troops of the 82nd Airborne Division took part in Operation 'Overlord', the invasion of Europe, and later participated in Operation 'Market Garden', the biggest airborne operation of the Second World War, with paratroop drops into Holland near Nijmegan. The American forces returned the station to RAF control in May 1945, at the end of hostilities in Europe, and the base resumed bomber flying training with Lancasters and Beaufighters.

In 1946 Cottesmore became the home of No 16 OTU, later renamed No 204 Advanced Flying School, operating Mosquito and Oxford aircraft. For a period of six years beginning in 1948 Cottesmore was the home of No 7 Flying Training School, flying Tiger Moths, Harvards, Prentices and Balliols. The jet age came to the station in 1954 when the first Canberras of Nos 15, 44, 55, 57 and 149 Squadrons arrived. The Canberras remained for only a short period before the station was placed under care and maintenance while major reconstruction work began on both the airfield and the main station site.

RAF Cottesmore reopened as a V-bomber station with the arrival of No 10 Squadron's Victor B.1s in April 1958, with No 15 Squadron's Victor B.1s and B.1As arriving shortly afterwards. For eighteen months until March 1963 the two squadrons were joined by 'C' Flight of No 232 Operational Conversion Unit, flying Victor B.2s. After a brief one-week respite following the departure of the last Victor (from No 15 Squadron), the first Vulcans arrived in November 1964, and Nos 9, 12 and 35 Squadrons operated the Vulcan B.2 as part of the RAF Cottesmore

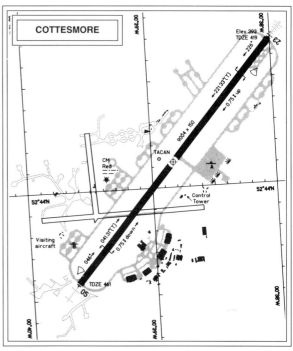

Above: **The unmistakable shape of a *Luftwaffe* Tornado IDS, seen through the security wires at Cottesmore. RAF students may fly British, German or Italian Tornados during their training at Cottesmore, the trinational fleet being 'pooled'.**

Vulcan Wing until February 1969, when the last aircraft, from No 12 Squadron, left the station.

For the next seven years the base was home to Nos 98 and 360 Squadrons, flying specialized versions of the Canberra. The Canberra Operational Conversion Unit (No 231 OCU) also operated from Cottesmore, together with No 115 Squadron, with Varsitys and Argosys. At the end of March 1976 the station was again placed under care and maintenance and another reconstruction programme began, in preparation for the next major phase in RAF Cottesmore's history.

In July 1980 the first RAF Tornado GR.1 arrived, beginning a two-year delivery period with new-build aircraft flying in at frequent intervals. The Trinational Tornado Training Establishment (TTTE) formed in January 1981 and RAF, German and Italian instructors began training students to fly the Tornado GR.1. The TTTE remains active at Cottesmore, and students destined to fly the Tornado GR.1 with the RAF, German Air Force and Navy, and Italian Air Force are all trained here.

RAF Cranwell

Resident units: *No 3 Flying Training School (Tucano); Royal Air Force College; Department of Air Warfare; Department of Specialist Ground Training; Department of Initial Officer Training; Headquarters University Air Squadrons; Officer and Aircrew Selection Centre.*

In 1915 the Admiralty requisitioned some 3,000 acres of farmland west of Cranwell village for use as a Royal Naval Air Service training station. The construction of a hutted camp and hangars began almost immediately, and on 1 April 1916 RNAS Cranwell opened. The establishment, known as HMS *Daedalus*, was tasked with the training of pilots on aircraft types such as the B.E.2c, Sopwith Pup and Maurice Farman S.7 and on airships and kite balloons. Training continued until 1 April 1918, when the RNAS and RFC amalgamated to form the Royal Air Force and base was renamed RAF Cranwell. Training then resumed, and a wireless school was also established.

During 1920 Air Marshal Sir Hugh Trenchard introduced a number of measured intended to consolidate the position of the Royal Air Force as an

Above: **The Royal Air Force College, Cranwell.**

independent service. An apprentice school was formed at Cranwell in 1920, remaining there until 1926 when RAF Halton assumed responsibility for this task. The wireless school became the Electrical and Wireless School and later the Radio School, moving to Locking in 1952. Another of Trenchard's steps was to establish a Cadet College to train flight cadets as officers and pilots, and Cranwell was selected as the permanent home.

In the late 1920s and 1930s Cranwell was associated with a series of historic long-distance flights: the first non-stop flight to India was made in 1929, and a similar mission to South-West Africa took place in 1933. However, the most historic flight to be made from Cranwell took place on 15 May 1941 when the first British jet-powered aircraft, the Gloster E.28/39, took off from the South Airfield.

Between 1920 and 1939 more than 1,100 flight cadets were trained at Cranwell. The Royal Air Force College closed at the outbreak of war in 1939 and the base became the home of a number of Flying Training Schools. The RAF College reopened in 1946 and the pattern of training gradually broadened to include supply and secretarial officers, navigators and RAF Regiment officers (these officers currently receive their specialist training at other stations).

In 1965 the RAF Technical College at Henlow merged with the RAF College to become the Department of Engineering. In 1971 RAF Cranwell assumed control of all of the University Air squadrons, and in 1974 the College of Air Warfare moved to Cranwell from Manby, to become the Department of Air Warfare (being incorporated as part of the RAF College along with the Department of Engineering). The Supply and Secretarial Officer Training squadrons at Upwood were also transferred to Cranwell and the Department of Engineering became the Department of Specialist Ground Training. The Secretarial Officer Training Squadron moved to Hereford in 1980. In April 1976 the Headquarters of the Central Flying School transferred to Cranwell from Little Rissington before moving to Leeming in 1977. In August 1979 RAF Cranwell officially established its own Flying Training School (No 3 FTS). The Officer Cadet Training Unit arrived from Henlow in 1980 and all RAF officers now complete their initial training at Cranwell. The Officer and

Aircrew Selection Centre also moved from Biggin Hill in 1992. Having operated a variety of aircraft types as part of the RAF's flying training requirement, Cranwell relinquished the last Jet Provosts in 1992 and No 3 FTS currently operates a fleet of Tucano T.1 turboprop trainers.

RAF Finningley

Resident units: *No 6 Flying Training School, Air Navigation School (Bulldog, Dominie, Tucano, Hawk); Air Electronics Engineer and Loadmaster School (Dominie, Nimrod); No 45(R) Squadron (Jetstream); No 100 Squadron (Hawk); Yorkshire Universities Air Squadron (Bulldog); No 9 Air Experience Flight (Chipmunk); Joint Forward Air Controller Training and Standards Unit (Hawk); No 9 Signals Unit.*

The airfield site at Finningley originally lay across the borders of Yorkshire and Nottinghamshire, hence the rose and sprig of oak featured in the Station badge, and the Station Club, the 'Rose and Acorn'. The airfield was constructed on agricultural land during 1936, the first aircraft arriving in September of that year in the shape of Handley Page Heyford bombers. For the first eighteen months of the Second World War the station played host to operational bomber units, before becoming the home of an Operational Training Unit in February 1941, training air crew to join the bombing onslaught on Hitler's Germany. Despite the station's training status, some thirty Wellingtons joined a thousand-bomber raid over Germany on 30 May 1942.

From 1946 until 1955 No 616 (South Yorkshire) Squadron of the Royal Auxiliary Air Force was based at Finningley, initially equipped with Mosquito fighters and then with Meteors. The station ceased flying operations in the mid-1950s while a major redevelopment programme was completed, which included the construction of a 1.7 mile long concrete runway, in anticipation of the arrival of V-bombers. The first Vulcans from No 101 Squadron arrived in October 1957, followed a few months later by Valiants of No 18 Squadron. The Bomber Command Development Unit moved to Finningley in 1960, and in June 1961 the Vulcan Operational Conversion Unit (No 230 OCU) moved to Finningley from Waddington.

After the departure of the operational squadrons, Finningley continued to act as the RAF's Vulcan training base, and even after February 1970, when the station was transferred to Training Command, various Vulcan training and support units remained

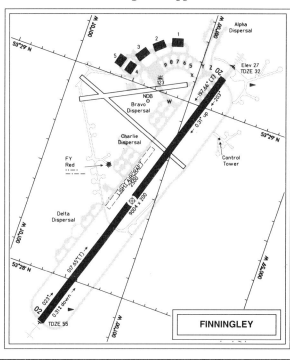

at the station, despite the fact that the OCU had moved on to Scampton. No 2 Air Navigation School arrived from Gaydon in May 1970 and was joined by No 1 Air Navigation School from Stradishall during September the same year. The units combined to form No 6 Flying Training School, equipped with Vickers Varsitys, Hawker Siddeley Dominies and Hunting Jet Provost T.4s , which were later replaced by Jet Provost T.5s. The Air Electronics and Air Engineers' School was transferred to Finningley from Topcliffe during October 1973, at which time No 6 FTS became one of the Royal Air Force's busiest training units (as indeed it is today). The Yorkshire Universities Air Squadron arrived in September 1975, and in September 1976 the Headquarters of the UK helicopter Search and Rescue Wing was established at Finningley as part of No 18 Group Strike Command, comprising Nos 22 and 202 Squadrons. No 6 FTS retired the last RAF Varsity in April 1976.

Following the merger of Training and Air Support Commands, Finningley became part of Support Command in 1977, and during April 1979 the Multi Engine Training Squadron (METS), equipped with Jetstream T.1s and a Dynamic Simulator, transferred from Leeming and was integrated into No 6 FTS. In March 1991 the first female RAF navigator graduated from No 6 FTS, followed in June 1991 by the first female pilot from the METS. Civilian contractors began to assume responsibility for certain duties in April 1991, and Short Brothers took over the station's engineering, supply and ground support facilities, drastically reducing the numbers of RAF personnel assigned to the base.

The first Shorts Tucano T.1 turboprop trainer arrived at Finningley on 2 April 1992, followed on 10 September by the first Hawk jet trainer, which led to the retirement of the last remaining RAF Jet Provosts during September 1993. The Multi Engine Training Squadron received the designation No 45(R) Squadron on 22 July 1992, although the unit remains as part of No 6 FTS. The SAR Headquarters closed down on 1 December 1992, No 22 Squadron moving to St Mawgan and No 202 Squadron being transferred to Boulmer. No 100 Squadron was relocated at Finningley from Wyton during August 1993, bringing with it a fleet of Hawk target facilities aircraft, effectively swelling the number of resident machines still further and making Finningley one of the Royal Air Force's most active airfields. The station has staged an annual Open Day for thirty-six years, and the event is currently the largest one-day air show to be held in the United Kingdom each year, attracting crowds of more than 150,000.

RAF Gibraltar

Resident units: *None.*

Gibraltar's strategic position at the 'gateway' to the Mediterranean has long made the location a vital military asset. The site was also ideal for development as a seaplane base, and the Royal Navy began operations from the area in 1915 when spotter aircraft flew in search of German U-boats. The seaplanes operated from the harbour area, while land-based aircraft flew from the racecourse under the north face of the Rock. The latter location was eventually developed into an airfield and was named RAF North Front from 1942 to 1966.

The first RAF squadron at Gibraltar was No 265, created from the amalgamation of three RNAS Flights in 1918, and various Navy units continued to operate from the airfield following the end of the First World War. RAF units also began to appear,

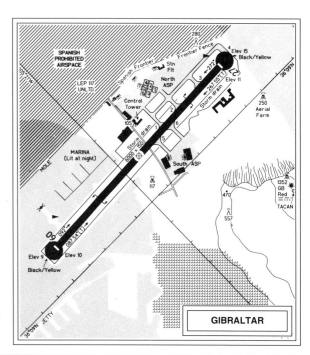

first No 210 Squadron with Rangoons and Singapores and then No 228 Squadron with Singapores. No 202 Squadron moved to the station when the Second World War broke out, and the unit's Saro Londons were later joined by Swordfish floatplanes. Sunderlands from No 228 Squadron arrived in July 1940, and No 202 Squadron converted to Catalinas in May 1941. Other RAF units operated from Gibraltar for varying periods of time, with many different aircraft—including No 200 (Hudson), 89 (Beaufighter), 540 (Mosquito), 43 (Hurricane), 81 and 242 (Spitfire) and 13 (Blenheim) Squadrons—as did several Royal Navy squadrons. During 1942 Royal Engineers constructed a 1,400yd runway, extending into the sea, together with parking areas capable of accommodating up to 600 aircraft, in preparation for the Allied invasion of North Africa, in which Gibraltar playing a vital part as a major staging base.

After the end of the Second World War the airfield remained active as a major maritime base, with regular detachments of Lancasters from both the United Kingdom and Malta. No 520 Squadron remained operational as a meteorological reconnaissance unit until its disbandment in 1946, when a detachment of Halifaxes from No 518 Squadron arrived. The latter was eventually renumbered No 202 Squadron and was joined by a Halifax detachment from No 224 Squadron, the whole unit eventually moving to Gibraltar.

Meteorological flights were gradually widened to encompass maritime reconnaissance sorties, and after a period in which the unit was a combined No 224/No 269 Squadron, No 269 was established as a separate entity before moving back to the UK in 1952. No 224 Squadron re-equipped with Shackletons in May 1953 and continued to operate from Gibraltar until it disbanded in 1966 as the last complete RAF squadron to be based at the station.

Since that time Gibraltar has been utilized as a base for a wide range of exercises and deployments, and many maritime squadrons have maintained a presence at the airfield, together with Royal Auxiliary Air Force fighter units which established summer camps there. During a period of tense relations with Spain in 1969, a Hunter detachment was maintained at Gibraltar until August 1978, when the last pair of aircraft (from No 2 TWU) returned to the UK. Detachments and exercises continue, and various combat aircraft transit through Gibraltar, not least No 6 FTS's Dominies on long-range navigational flights. RAF aircraft detached to the Armament Practice Camps at Decimomannu in Sardinia also regularly visit Gibraltar, and the Royal Navy operates from the airfield, especially during annual exercises when FRADU Hunters are deployed from Yeovilton. US Navy units are also regularly seen at Gibraltar, and the station also serves as a civil airport.

RAF Halton

Resident units: *No 612 Volunteer Gliding School (Vigilant); No 613 Volunteer Gliding School (Vigilant); No 1 School of Technical Training.*

RAF Henlow

Resident units: *No 616 Volunteer Gliding School (Vigilant); Signals Engineering Establishment.*

RAF Honington

Resident units: *No 20 Squadron RAF Regiment.*

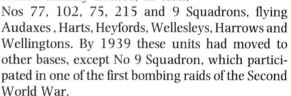

RAF Honington first opened on 3 May 1937 on land purchased from the Duke of Grafton. The station initially housed, in turn, Nos 77, 102, 75, 215 and 9 Squadrons, flying Audaxes, Harts, Heyfords, Wellesleys, Harrows and Wellingtons. By 1939 these units had moved to other bases, except No 9 Squadron, which participated in one of the first bombing raids of the Second World War.

During 1940 the station supported No 311 (Czech) Squadron, flying Wellingtons and Ansons, No 103 Squadron flying Battles and No 105 Squadron flying Battles and Blenheims. No 214 Squadron, equipped with Wellingtons, operated from Honington during 1942. A trio of Beam Approach Training Flights were also based here, instructing pilots in the use of blind landing equipment. The *Luftwaffe* made a total of sixteen recorded attacks on the station, mainly during the Battle of Britain. Hangar 'E' was hit twice by bombs, and a Junkers Ju 88 was shot down by ground fire close to hangar 'D' (the soldier respon-

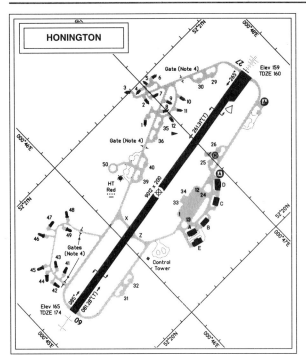
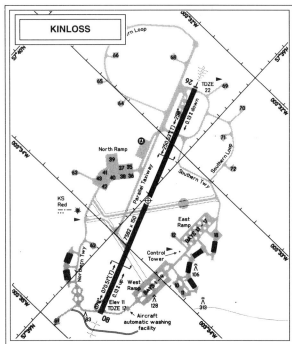

sible was reprimanded for firing without orders, but was later decorated!). The Station Commander and Senior Medical Officer were both awarded the George Medal for rescuing the crew of a crashed Wellington.

During 1942 the station was handed over to the United States Eighth Air Force as a depot for repairing and modifying the 3rd Bomber Division's Boeing B-17 Flying Fortresses. In 1943 the unit was renamed the 1st Strategic Air Depot. In 1944 the P-38 Lightnings and P-51 Mustangs of the 364th Fighter Group (comprising the 383rd, 384th and 385th Fighter Squadrons) arrived at Honington. During operations from the airfield they accounted for some 450 German aircraft destroyed, against 134 losses, earning a Distinguished Unit Citation for flying fighter escort on a bombing raid over Hamburg. Honington was the last wartime USAAF base to be returned to RAF control.

Between 1946 and 1950 Transport Command units were based at Honington, playing a vital part in the Berlin Airlift. From 1950 to 1956 the station housed No 94 Maintenance Unit, and from 1955 to 1957 it saw the arrival of Nos 10, 15, 44 and 57 Squadrons, each equipped with Canberra bombers. The first three of these squadrons were detached overseas for bombing operations during the 1956 Suez Crisis. For some ten years beginning in 1956 RAF Honington was one of the main V-Force bases, accommodating Nos 7, 90 and 199 Squadrons equipped with Vickers Valiants. Nos 7 and 199 Squadrons were later replaced by Nos 55 and 57 Squadrons, flying Victor B.1As. During 1966 the airfield was closed in anticipation of the arrival of the F-111K, which had been ordered for the RAF but was later cancelled.

In 1969 RAF Honington became the home of the first Buccaneers to enter RAF service, and Nos 12, 15, 208 and 216 Squadrons all operated from the base at various times during the 1970s and early 1980s. In addition, No 237 Operational Conversion Unit was based here before moving to Lossiemouth, and the station was the home base for the Royal Navy's 809 Naval Air Squadron. In 1971 the station began a year-long association with the Avro Shackleton when No 204 Squadron arrived. The last Buccaneers left for Lossiemouth in 1984. Meanwhile in 1981 the Tornado Weapons Conversion Unit was formed at Honington, followed by No 9 Squadron in 1982, which later moved to Germany. No 13 Squadron re-formed at the base on 1 January 1990, moving to Marham in 1994. The TWCU was retitled No 15(R) Squadron before moving to Lossiemouth early in 1994, at which stage Honington became a non-flying station, housing the RAF Regiment Depot, and Nos 2 and 66 Squadrons RAF Regiment, together with the Rapier Training Unit.

RAF Kinloss

Resident units: *No 42(R) Squadron (Nimrod); No 120 Squadron (Nimrod); No 201 Squadron (Nimrod); No 206 Squadron (Nimrod); No 663 Volunteer Gliding School (Vigilant).*

The origins of RAF Kinloss date back to 1938 when the airfield was first constructed. The base was intended to provide the home for a Flying Training School, far away from the likely 'operational' areas of the United Kingdom, especially East Anglia (attacks from the direction of Norway were considered unlikely at that time). No 14 FTS was established at Kinloss in 1939 with a fleet of Harvards and Oxfords and remained active at the station for approximately a year before moving south to Cranfield, making way for Bomber Command operations. Detachments from Nos 77 and 102 Squadrons followed earlier detachments of Whitleys and Hampdens from Nos 10, 49, 50, 51 and 102 Squadrons, which had all operated temporarily from the airfield as reinforcements for 18 Group's attacks on Stavanger, Trondheim and other Scandinavian ports. No 609 Squadron flew Spitfires from the airfield for two months beginning in December 1939, although the aircraft did not engage any enemy forces.

No 45 Maintenance Unit arrived at Kinloss during April 1940 and began to concentrate on the preparation of Halifaxes, Whitleys and Wellingtons for operational service; No 19 OTU formed at the station during the following month with Anson and Whitley bomber air crew trainers. A satellite airfield at Forres was established in 1941, and No 45 MU's activities expanded to include aircraft such as the Boston. As hangars continued to be constructed, fields surrounding the station were requisitioned for aircraft dispersal. RAF Kinloss was utilized as a forward base for Norwegian operations, and Halifax bombers were detached to the airfield for attacks on the German battleship *Tirpitz*, culminating in No 9 Squadron's final destruction of the vessel in 1944, flying from Kinloss.

The MU's activities expanded still further with the introduction of the Vickers Warwick, but by March 1944 attention was concentrated on the Halifax. During the same month a Swedish Airlines DC-3 flew familiarization sorties from the base, which became the company's diversion field for Dyce Airport. The OTU suffered a fairly high accident rate because of frequent bad weather, the surrounding high ground and the age if its aircraft, although training operations continued throughout the war.

Below: RAF Honington, formerly the home of the Tornado Weapons Conversion Unit. The huge airfield is today largely unused, although Rapier squadrons are now based at the station.

With the end of the war the MU was tasked with the handling of huge numbers of surplus aircraft; a total of 1,059 was reached by October 1946, although numbers then began to drop as scrap merchants disposed of the aircraft. The OTU closed in June 1945 and Kinloss was transferred to Coastal Command as the home of No 6 OTU, which flew Beaufighters. The OTU was designated No 236 Operational Conversion Unit in July and began to train crews for, in turn, the Lancaster, Neptune, Shackleton and Nimrod. No 120 Squadron's Lancasters arrived in December 1949, and the unit converted to Shackletons in 1951, moving to Aldergrove a year later. No 217 Squadron arrived with Neptunes in April 1952, and Nos 201 and 206 Squadrons flew Shackletons at Kinloss from 1965.

After a long association with the Shackleton and Neptune, the airfield was modified in preparation for the arrival of Nimrods, which re-equipped Nos 120, 201 and 206 Squadrons. No 8 Squadron re-formed at Kinloss in 1972 with Airborne Early Warning Shackletons before moving to nearby Lossiemouth during the following year. Nos 120, 201 and 206 Squadrons continue to operate a combined (and recently reduced) fleet of Nimrods from Kinloss, together with No 42(R) Squadron, the Nimrod Operational Conversion Unit, which arrived from St Mawgan during 1992.

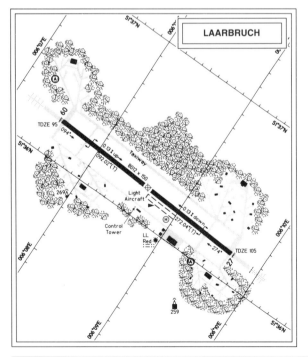

RAF Kirknewton

Resident unit: No 661 Volunteer Gliding School (Viking).

RAF Laarbruch

Resident units: No 3 Squadron (Harrier); No 4 Squadron (Harrier); No 18 Squadron (Chinook, Puma); No 220 Signal Squadron; No 1 Squadron RAF Regiment; No 26 Squadron RAF Regiment.

Situated close to the Dutch border, Laarbruch was the last airfield to be constructed by Germany as part of a reparation agreement after the end of the Second World War. Building work—which required the clearance of a huge area of forest—began in 1953 and flying started the following year.

Laarbruch was initially designated a reconnaissance base, and Nos 79, 541 and 69 Squadrons, equipped with Meteor FR.9s, Meteor PR.10s and Canberra PR.3s respectively, were transferred there. Three more Canberra units, Nos 31, 214 and 80 Squadrons, arrived during 1955, and in order to ease the consequent congestion the two Meteor units moved to Wunstorf in November 1955. No 214 Squadron was renumbered 80 Squadron and moved to Bruggen in 1957 and No 69 Squadron was transferred to Malta in April 1958. No 31 Squadron remained active with Canberra PR.7s until March 1971, when the unit disbanded (it later re-formed as a Phantom unit).

No 68 Squadron moved to Laarbruch from Wahn during July 1957, with Meteor fighters, and, after taking over No 5 Squadron's number, re-equipped with Javelins at Laarbruch early in 1960, moving to Geilenkirchen three years later. In March 1958 No 16 Squadron re-formed at Laarbruch with Canberra B(I).8 interdictors and was joined in January 1968 by No 3 Squadron, equipped with the same Canberra variant. Early in 1971 the first Buccaneers arrived, when No 15 Squadron was transferred from Honington. No 25 Squadron's 'C' Flight was also established at the base, equipped with Bloodhound surface-to-air missiles. No 16 Squadron disbanded in June 1972 but it re-formed six months later with Buccaneers. No 3 Squadron disbanded in

December 1971, reappearing as a Harrier unit at Wildenrath. No 31 Squadron also disbanded, in March 1971, but later re-formed on Phantoms at Bruggen.

No 2 Squadron arrived at Bruggen in May 1971 with Phantom reconnaissance fighters, which remained active until Jaguars were established in the reconnaissance role, and No 2 Squadron became an all-Jaguar unit at Laarbruch in October 1976. The Buccaneers of Nos 15 and 16 Squadrons were replaced by Tornado GR.1s during the 1980s, No 15 Squadron re-forming on the type in September 1983, followed by No 16 Squadron in March 1984 and by No 20 Squadron a year after that. After some thirteen years of RAF Jaguar operations in Germany, the last Jaguar sortie was flown by No 2 Squadron from Laarbruch in December 1988, after which No 2 Squadron became a Tornado GR.1A reconnaissance unit.

During 1992 two Laarbruch Tornado squadrons were disbanded; the TWCU at Honington became No 15(R) Squadron, and the Jaguar Operational Conversion Unit (No 226 OCU) became No 16(R) Squadron. No 2 Squadron retained its aircraft and was transferred to Marham. Following the Government decision to close RAF Gütersloh, the two RAF Germany Harrier units (Nos 3 and 4 Squadrons) arrived at Laarbruch, accompanied by No 18 Squadron, which was re-established with a mixed fleet of Chinook and Puma support helicopters.

RAF Leeming

Resident units: *No 11 Squadron (Tornado); No 25 Squadron (Tornado); No 15 Squadron RAF Regiment; No 11 Air Experience Flight (Chipmunk); Northumbrian Universities Air Squadron (Bulldog).*

Early in 1938 parts of Clapham Lodge Farm and Wilson's Farm were made into an airfield for Yorkshire Air Services, which was one of the first English flying clubs. Then came the expansion of the Royal Air Force to counter the threat posed by the *Luftwaffe*,

Below: A Tornado GR.1A climbs past Leeming's new control tower. For obvious reasons the locals refer to the complex as the 'Happy Eater'!

and the whole area of land was acquired by the Crown in the latter part of 1938. Work started immediately to level and drain the land, and the construction of a permanent airfield began.

RAF Leeming officially opened on 3 June 1940 and, although it had been built as a bomber base, its first aircraft were Blenheims from No 219 Squadron, detached from nearby Catterick. The first resident unit was No 10 Squadron, equipped with Whitleys, which arrived on 10 July and flew their first operational sorties on 20 July, attacking a factory at Wejendorf. Operations from Leeming were difficult, especially at night or in bad weather, as no concrete runways were laid at this time. No 7 Squadron formed at the station on 1 August 1940 with Stirlings but remained for only three months; No 35 Squadron arrived with Halifaxes, although this unit stayed for only two weeks. In April 1941 No 76 Squadron re-formed at Leeming, also flying Halifaxes, but their stay was also a very short three months.

During this period of the 'Phoney War' many squadrons were re-formed and re-equipped as the RAF expanded but quickly dispersed to newer airfields. No 10 Squadron was joined at Leeming by No 77 Squadron on 5 September, with more Whitley bombers, although No 10 re-equipped with Halifaxes in November, quickly followed by No 77. Both units continued their raids against continental targets, and No 10 joined other units in attacks on the German battlecruisers *Gneisenau* and *Scharnhorst* in Brest and on the battleship *Tirpitz* in Trondheim.

Concrete runways were laid in 1941, improving the station's all-weather capability and providing better conditions for the heavy Halifax bombers. No 77 Squadron relocated to the newly constructed RAF Elvington in June 1942. Two Canadian squadrons, Nos 419 and 420, arrived from Mildenhall in August 1942, equipped with Wellingtons, No 419 quickly moving to Topcliffe and No 10 then moving to Melbourne. In September No 420 Squadron converted to the Halifax and were joined by No 408 Squadron RCAF, formerly a Hampden unit. The Canadian units flew numerous operational missions against targets in France and the Low Countries and against German targets such as Aachen, Munich and Berlin. In March 1943 No 405 Squadron RCAF arrived at Leeming, leaving for Grandsden Lodge a few weeks later, their departure being followed by that if No 420 Squadron, which relocated to the

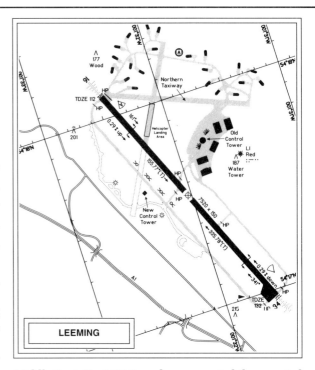

LEEMING

Middle East; No 427 Squadron occupied the vacated space at Leeming. No 408 Squadron moved to Linton-on-Ouse in August and was replaced by 429 Squadron RCAF. The two resident units remained at Leeming until May 1946. Towards the end of 1943 the main runway was improved and extended to the south-east.

On 4 March 1945 Leeming suffered its first (and only) air raid when *Luftwaffe* intruders attacked a returning bomber mission, shooting down three aircraft and strafing two hangars with cannon fire. Leeming's two squadrons converted to the Lancaster during 1945, but as the war in Europe drew to a close the units flew their last operational missions on 25 April against gun positions on Wanganye Island. After VE-Day the units were mainly occupied with the ferrying of Allied troops and prisoners back to the United Kingdom from Italy. The squadrons were subsequently disbanded and the station reverted to RAF control on 30 June 1946.

Whilst many RAF stations quickly closed after the end of the Second World War, Leeming remained active as the home of No 228 Operational Conversion Unit, equipped with Brigands and Mosquitos. Towards the end of 1951 the main runway was again improved and lengthened, in anticipation of the arrival of the first jet aircraft, Meteor NF.11s). In April 1956 the main runway received yet more attention and was extended to its present-day length of 7,500ft, ready for the introduction of the Javelin fighter. The OCU's Meteors were joined by Valetta radar trainers, and the first Javelin arrived at Leeming in June 1957. No 33 Squadron was transferred from Middleton St George for a one-year detachment beginning in October 1957, and in 1959 the OCU's Valettas were replaced by radar-equipped Canberra T.11s, the Meteor NF.11s being replaced at the same time by NF.14s. The OCU disbanded on 14 September 1961 as a result of the RAF's gradual reduction in fighter aircraft strength, in line with the Government's (mistaken) belief that air defence would eventually be conducted almost exclusively by surface-to-air missiles.

Leeming again survived closure and was transferred to Training Command as the home of No 3 Flying Training School. Pilot training on the Jet Provost T.3 began on 4 October 1961. The Royal Navy's Elementary FTS arrived at Leeming in 1973, equipped with Bulldogs, and the School of Refresher Flying's Jet Provost T.4s moved to Leeming in December the same year. More Bulldogs arrived in 1974 when the Northumbrian Universities Air Squadron was transferred from Ouston, and still more in 1976 when the Central Flying School's Bulldog Squadron moved from Cranwell, followed by the remainder of the CFS in November 1977. In May of 1977 the Multi Engine Training Squadron was activated at Leeming, equipped with Jetstreams, and the congested airfield traffic pattern relied on the use of relief landing grounds at nearby Topcliffe and Dishforth. In order to ease congestion still further, the Jetstreams moved to Finningley in 1979.

At this time the Ministry of Defence was busy completing a reappraisal of the United Kingdom's air defence needs, and in 1979 it was decided that there would be an overall increase in the number of RAF air defence squadrons, together with the introduction of a new long-range interceptor. In 1982 the MoD announced that Leeming would again become a fighter base, and in 1984 the CFS and 3 FTS vacated the airfield. Strike Command took control of the station on 1 October. The main runway was resurfaced, the taxiways were improved and the airfield facilities were 'hardened', while new shelter complexes were constructed in anticipation of the first Tornado F.3 arrivals. In May 1988 No 11 Squadron re-formed at Leeming, followed by No 23 Squadron in November and No 25 in July 1989. The three units were reduced to two with the disbandment of No 23 Squadron in March 1994 as part of defence spending reductions announced the previous year.

RAF Leuchars

Resident units: No 43 Squadron (Tornado); No 111 Squadron (Tornado); No 27 Squadron RAF Regiment; Aberdeen, Dundee and St Andrews University Air Squadron (Bulldog).

Leuchars has been associated with aviation for more than eighty years, the first such activities at this location having taken place in 1911 when the Army flew balloons from Tentsmuir Forest. The airfield was originally developed by the Royal Navy as a training base during the First World War.

Following the formation of the Royal Air Force in 1918, the station was officially named RAF Leuchars in March 1920. During the 1920s Leuchars hosted aircraft such as Nieuport Nighthawks, Parnall Panthers and Fairey IIIDs and Flycatchers, and the station's training activities including reconnaissance, artillery spotting and aerial combat. Much of the training was conducted by Royal Navy units, which continued to share the station's facilities with the RAF, and various Flights at Leuchars were detached to aircraft carriers. The nearby St Andrews golf course also became involved with aviation at Leuchars, and many golfing enthusiasts used the station for travelling to and from the course. In 1935 the base became the home of No 1 Flying Training School, and bombing ranges were established in Tentsmuir Forest.

As the Second World War approached, No 1 FTS moved to Netheravon and Leuchars was transferred to Coastal Command, with Nos 224 and 233 Squadrons arriving in August 1938. Initially equipped with Avro Ansons, both units converted to Lockheed Hudsons before hostilities began. On the second day of the war, a No 224 Squadron Hudson attacked a Dornier 18 over the North Sea, thus becoming the first British aircraft to engage the enemy during the Second World War.

As the war progressed, Leuchars became home to further maritime units engaged in patrol duties over

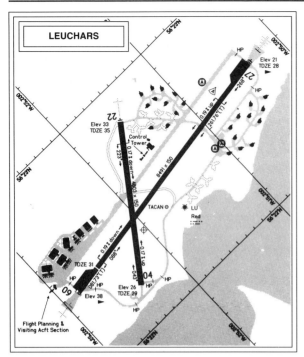
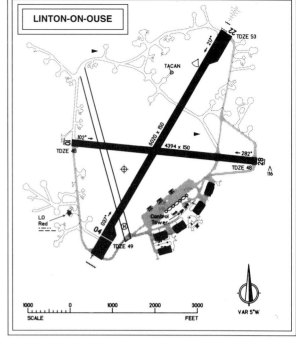

the North Sea and Atlantic Ocean. In February 1940 another No 224 Squadron Hudson successfully located the German prison ship *Altmark*, enabling the destroyer HMS *Cossack* to intercept her and liberate over 200 British prisoners being held on board. Units from the Netherlands, Norway, Australia, Canada and New Zealand were eventually transferred to Leuchars, and with more advanced aircraft such as the Beaufort, Blenheim, Hampden and Beaufighter the Leuchars-based units were able to extend offensive patrols to the Norwegian coast. Reconnaissance missions were flown as far as Berlin and Stettin, although sorties were concentrated on the Norwegian fjords, the German battleship *Tirpitz* occupying Leuchars' aircraft for some time. Mosquitos were assigned to these reconnaissance missions but were also used to attack and destroy a number of German aircraft.

A detachment of BOAC personnel and aircraft was also based at Leuchars, flying a civilian service to Stockholm and bringing back valuable engineering materials such as ball bearings, and an American unit operated Liberators from the airfield, dropping supplies and agents into occupied Norway and flying civil-marked aircraft into Sweden to recover refugees.

After the end of the Second World War, RAF Leuchars became the home of the St Andrews University Air Squadron, equipped with Tiger Moths, and, after the station had been transferred to Fighter Command, Meteors of No 222 Squadron arrived in May 1950. The Meteors were later joined by Vampires and progressively superseded by Hunters, Javelins and, in 1964, English Electric Lightnings. The fixed-wing aircraft were joined by Sycamore helicopters for search and rescue duties in 1954, and these were subsequently replaced by Whirlwinds, which were in turn supplanted by Wessexes. As the 'Cold War' developed, Soviet long-range bomber and reconnaissance aircraft made increasingly numerous flights into the United Kingdom's airspace, and Leuchars-based Lightnings were regularly scrambled to intercept such intrusions.

The first McDonnell Phantom FG.1 arrived in 1968, No 43 Squadron's fleet being joined by No 111 Squadron and eventually re-equipping with Phantoms which had formerly been operated by the Royal Navy on board HMS *Ark Royal*. As part of their regular air defence duties, the Phantom squadrons were employed on Soviet interception flights. The Phantom Operational Conversion Unit moved to Leuchars from Coningsby for a brief period, before the wind-down of the Phantom force began. No 43 Squadron flew its last Phantom mission in June 1989, and No 111 Squadron's last flight took place in January 1990. Tornado F.3s re-equipped both units. These aircraft continue to operate from Leuchars, and are also still assigned to the UK's QRA (Quick Reaction Alert) role, although the number of flights by Russian intruders into UK airspace has dwindled almost to zero. Leuchars hosts an annual Open Day, normally on the same day as RAF Finningley's event and sharing with that station many of the participating aircraft.

RAF Linton-on-Ouse

Resident units: No 1 Flying Training School (Tucano); No 642 Volunteer Gliding School (Vigilant).

RAF Linton-on-Ouse was built as a bomber airfield and officially opened on 13 May 1937, becoming the Headquarters of No 4 Group until 1940. The Air Officer Commanding at the time was Air Commodore A. T. Harris, who later became Marshal of the Royal Air Force Sir Arthur T. Harris.

At the outbreak of the Second World War Whitley bombers of Nos 58 and 51 Squadrons took off from Linton-on-Ouse to drop propaganda leaflets over Germany, and by 1940 bombing raids were being mounted over targets in Holland, Germany and Italy. A particularly memorable event in the history of the station occurred during the night of 12/13 November 1940 when Group Captain Leonard Cheshire, then a Flying Officer, brought a Whitley back from an attack over the Cologne area with a 12ft by 4ft hole in the aircraft's fuselage. For this exploit Cheshire was awarded the first of his three DSOs. Cheshire later returned to Linton-on-Ouse as Commanding Officer of No 76 Squadron, while No 78 Squadron was commanded by another famous RAF officer, Wing Commander Willie Tate. Linton-on-Ouse was attacked by enemy aircraft during the night of 10/11 May 1941, and the Station Commander, Group Captain F. M. F. Conway, was killed during the raid.

By 1942 Linton-on-Ouse was a major bomber station. It participated in the first thousand-bomber raids on Cologne and Bremen. In 1942 and again in 1944 the station was honoured by visits from HM King George VI and HM Queen Elizabeth. From 1943 until after the end of the war the station was part of No 6 Group Royal Canadian Air Force, equipped mainly with Lancaster aircraft, and it continued to play a major role in the bombing offensive against Germany. The Canadians finally departed in October 1945. After a few months as a Transport Command station, tasked with repatriating passengers and freight from overseas in York and Stirling aircraft, Linton-on-Ouse settled into a peacetime routine within Fighter Command, operating Mosquitos, Hornets and Meteors, followed by Sabres, Hunters and Meteor night fighters. It also became the home of Yorkshire Sector Headquarters and in 1956 was chosen to represent the Royal Air Force at the parading of the Queen's Colour on the occasion of Her Majesty's birthday—the first time that this ceremony had been carried out by the Royal Air Force.

Linton-on-Ouse was placed under care and maintenance during February 1957 but reopened on 9 September 1957 as the home of No 1 Flying Training School, as part of Flying Training Command, equipped with Provost T.1 and Vampire T.11 aircraft. From 1957 until 1969 No 1 FTS trained both Royal Air Force and Royal Navy pilots. Naval fixed-wing training was then suspended, and the school returned to the task of training RAF students and officers from Commonwealth and foreign forces. No 23 Group moved to Linton-on-Ouse from Dishforth during July 1966 and remained there until 1975, when the Group disbanded. The station was honoured with the Freedom of the City of York in April 1968.

In addition to operations from Linton-on-Ouse, No 1 FTS also operates from RAF Church Fenton some ten miles to the south, easing congestion in the Linton air traffic area. Until 1993 No 1 FTS also supported the Royal Navy Elementary Flying Training Squadron, detached to RAF Topcliffe some eighteen miles north of Linton. However, the RNEFTS combined with the RAF EFTS in 1993 to form a new independent and civilian-contracted unit at Topcliffe. No 1 FTS was the first RAF unit to be transferred to private contractors during 1985, when all engineering and supply services were handed over to civilian control. Jet Provost T.3 and T.5 aircraft were operated from Linton-on-Ouse until 1993, when deliveries of Shorts Tucano T.1 turboprop trainers enabled the last of No 1 FTS's Jet Provosts to be retired. Linton is now the home of one of only two fixed-wing basic flying training schools, the other being at Cranwell (q.v.).

RAF Little Rissington

Resident unit: No 637 Volunteer Gliding School (Vigilant).

RAF Lossiemouth

Resident units: No 12 Squadron (Tornado); No 617 Squadron (Tornado); No 15(R) Squadron (Tornado); No 16(R) Squadron (Jaguar); 'D' Flight No 202 Squadron (Sea King); No 48 Squadron RAF Regiment.

Royal Air Force Lossiemouth was built in 1938–39, and No 15 Flying Training School was formed at the new station in April 1939. The first aircraft to use the airfield were Oxfords and Harvards, but because of the airfield's location and good climate a wide variety of aircraft were frequently diverted there, even during these early days when the station was part of Training Command.

As the Second World War approached, the station was transferred to Bomber Command and No 20 Operational Training unit was formed during April 1940. The station's first recorded success during the war occurred on 11 October 1940 when an aircraft on an operational training flight shot down a Junkers Ju 88 after having been attacked. The only raid on the airfield took place on 26 October 1940, although little damage was sustained and one of the attacking Heinkel He 111s was destroyed. Fourteen Wellingtons from Lossiemouth participated in the first thousand-bomber raid on Cologne, and perhaps the most famous raid to be launched from the station took place on 12 November 1944 when No 617 Squadron successfully attacked the German battleship *Tirpitz*.

Following the end of the Second World War the station became a satellite of nearby Milltown, as part of RAF Coastal Command, and on 5 July 1946 both airfields were handed over to the Fleet Air Arm. At this point the station became HMS *Fulmar*, RNAS Lossiemouth. Various basic training units were located there, deck-landing training taking place at Milltown. The aircraft carrier HMS *Theseus*, positioned in the Moray Firth, was used for shipboard training. The Naval Air Fighter School was moved to Lossiemouth from Culdrose during the early 1950s, requiring Lossiemouth's runways to be extended and strengthened. Various fighter and trainer types operated from the station, and two Royal Navy aerobatic demonstration teams were formed, flying Sea Hawks and Hunters.

The Fleet Air Arm returned the station to the Royal Air Force at a Sunset Ceremony on 28 September 1972. As major reconstruction work took place on the airfield, flying operations were kept to a minimum, although the Whirlwind helicopters of 'D' Flight No 202 Squadron arrived during 1972 (the Flight is currently equipped with Sea Kings), joined by the Gannets of 849 Naval Air Squadron, which thereby maintained a link between the station and the Fleet Air Arm.

During May 1973 the first Jaguar arrived, to begin the formation of the Jaguar Operational Conversion Unit (No 226 OCU), and three months later the venerable Shackletons of No 8 Squadron were transferred to Lossiemouth from nearby Kinloss. No 2 Tactical Weapons Unit formed at the station in September 1978, flying single- and twin-seat Hunters on weapons and tactical training missions as part of the RAF's pilot training system. The Gannets of 849 Naval Air Squadron were retired in December 1978 and the unit disbanded, leaving No 8 Squadron's Shackletons as the United Kingdom's only Airborne Early Warning (AEW) asset.

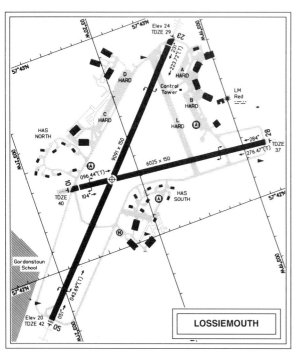

same time the Buccaneers of No 208 Squadron arrived from Honington. The Buccaneer Operational Conversion Unit (No 237 OCU) was also transferred from Honington in 1984, bringing a fleet of Buccaneer-instrumented Hunters used as part of the OCU training course. No 216 Squadron moved from Honington during 1980 but enjoyed only a brief period of activity at Lossiemouth before disbanding.

The OCU disbanded on 1 October 1991, and on 1 July 1992 No 8 Squadron finally retired its Shackletons, prior to re-forming at Waddington with E-3 Sentrys. Buccaneer operations continued to wind down in 1993, and No 12 Squadron converted to Tornado GR.1Bs in October that year. No 208 Squadron disbanded in April 1994, and No 617 Squadron was transferred to Lossiemouth from Marham, also equipped with maritime strike-configured Tornado GR.1Bs. The Jaguar OCU, now given a 'shadow' designation as No 16(R) Squadron, continues to operate from the base and was joined by No 15(R), the Tornado Weapons Conversion Unit, early in 1994.

Above: The Shackleton may be gone, but No 12 Squadron's HAS complex at Lossiemouth lives on. The Squadron's Buccaneers were replaced by Tornado GR.1Bs in 1993.

No 48 Squadron RAF Regiment arrived in December 1978, tasked with the short-range air defence of the station and equipped with Rapier missiles. No 2622 (Highland) Squadron RAuxAF arrived at Lossiemouth in July 1979 as a ground defence unit. The Tactical Weapons Unit moved to Chivenor during May 1981.

Although Fleet Air Arm Buccaneers had, from time to time, operated from Lossiemouth, the station's association with the Buccaneer officially began in July 1980 when No 12 Squadron was transferred from Honington. The station became part of No 1 Group Strike Command in July 1981, assigned the primary task of providing tactical air support to maritime operations. The station was transferred to No 18 Group in July 1983, and at the

RAF Lyneham

Resident units: No 24 Squadron (Hercules); No 30 Squadron (Hercules); No 47 Squadron (Hercules); No 70 Squadron (Hercules); No 57(R) Squadron (Hercules).

RAF Lyneham came into being during May 1940 with the establishment of No 33 Maintenance Unit, responsible for the storage of aircraft which were not in regular service use. Flying activities began in August 1941 when No 14 Flying Training School arrived, equipped with Airspeed Oxford twin-engine trainers. However, the FTS moved on just six months later and Lyneham became the centre of training for air crew engaged on ferry duties to overseas destinations, and for the preparation and dispatch of aircraft being recovered from storage for service overseas.

Since these early days of Ferry Command, Lyneham has always been a terminal for international flights, including a period between 1943 and 1945 when BOAC operated civil scheduled services from the airfield.

Following the formation of Transport Command in 1943, York and, later, Hastings transports operated from Lyneham, serving with particular distinction during the Berlin Airlift. No 216 Squadron re-equipped with a VIP variant of the 2 airliner during 1955 and later converted to the more advanced Comet 4. An example of the earlier Comet variant is now positioned within the grounds of the station as a tribute to the world's first jet airliner. In December 1959, with the Hastings force now concentrated at nearby Colerne, Lyneham became the home of two Britannia squadrons, Nos 99 and 511, and throughout the 1960s the station was the hub of the RAF's long-range freighting, trooping and VIP operations.

The first Lockheed Hercules destined for squadron service was delivered to Lyneham on 1 August 1967, to begin the re-equipment of No 36 Squadron. Crews from No 48 Squadron also took delivery of Hercules aircraft at Lyneham before departing in October 1967 for Changi in Singapore.

Following a major rationalization in service air transport policy in 1970, the Britannia fleet moved to Brize Norton to join the VC10 strategic transports already based there. In 1971 the two Hercules squadrons which had formed at Fairford in 1968, Nos 30 and 47, transferred to Lyneham, to be joined by No 48 Squadron later in the year following that unit's withdrawal from the Far East. Lyneham

Above: The Lockheed Hercules fleet at Lyneham is 'pooled', with aircraft assigned to each squadron as required on a daily basis.

became the home of five of the RAF's six Hercules squadrons which existed at that time, the sixth being No 70 Squadron based at Akrotiri in Cyprus.

Further rationalization took place in 1975 following a major defence review in 1974. No 242 Operational Conversion Unit moved to Lyneham from Thorney Island, and the Hercules deep servicing organization was transferred from Colerne. No 70 Squadron returned to Lyneham from Akrotiri, and Nos 36 and 48 Squadrons disbanded, together with the Comet-equipped No 216 Squadron. RAF Lyneham is now the home of the RAF Hercules force, with the exception of just one aircraft which is assigned to the Meteorological Research Flight at Farnborough. The OCU is now designated No 57(R) Squadron, and all first- and second-line servicing of the Hercules is carried out at Lyneham, together

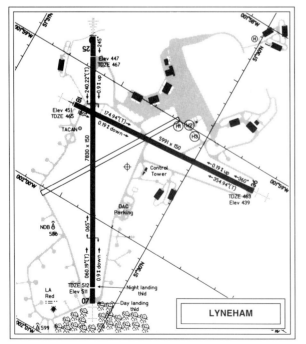

with the training of all associated ground personnel, equipment support personnel and other technical, engineering, supply and administrative personnel required for the Hercules fleet.

The Lyneham Transport Wing's Hercules fleet reached one million flying hours on 27 March 1990. The aircraft were heavily committed to both Operation 'Granby' ('Desert Storm') and Operation 'Haven' during 1990–91 and the Hercules crews became proficient in the skills of low-level desert flying and rough-strip operations. Over 40,000 hours were flown in a seven-month period, with approximately 50,000 tonnes of freight carried. In 1992 RAF Lyneham celebrated the 25th anniversary of the Hercules' service entry into the Royal Air Force.

RAF Machrihanish

Resident units: None.

NATO standby airfield.

RAF Manston

Resident units: No 1 Air Experience Flight (Chipmunk); Fire Services Central Training Establishment.

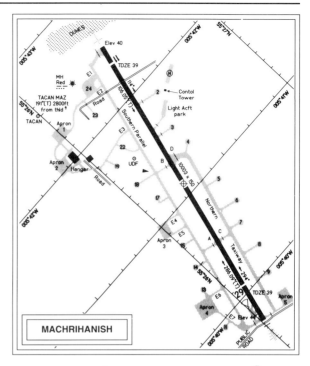

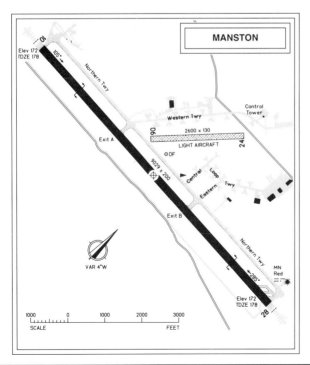

RAF Marham

Resident units: No 2 Squadron (Tornado); No 13 Squadron (Tornado); No 39 (1 PRU) Squadron (Canberra).

During the summer of 1916 a Royal Air Force station site of some eighty acres was established three miles south-west of Narborough, at Marham. This became the headquarters of No 51 Home Defence Squadron and its subordinate 'C' Flight, flying F.E.2bs. From November 1917 No 191(N) Training Squadron was also located at Marham, commanded by Major A. T. Harris, who became Commander-in-Chief of Bomber Command during the Second World War. This squadron moved out in July 1918, although No 51 Home Defence Squadron remained until the station was closed in 1919.

Marham remained closed until 1935, when a rebuilding programme began. It reopened on 1 April 1937 as a heavy bomber station within No 3 Group. No 38 Squadron arrived on 5 May, equipped with Fairey Hendons. One month later No 115 Squadron re-formed at the station with Handley Page Harrows, re-equipping with Wellingtons in May 1939.

During the early months of the Second World War the Marham squadrons were employed on

AIRFIELD DIRECTORY

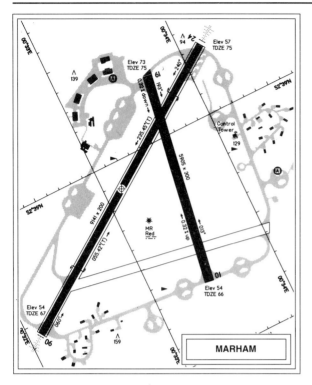

Below: A Panavia Tornado GR.1 from No 9 Squadron takes off from Marham for its home base at Bruggen in Germany.

coastal sweeps and leaflet raids but during March 1941 they were involved in attacks on the battlecruisers *Scharnhorst* and *Gneisenau*. In May 1941 aircraft from Marham participated in the first thousand-bomber raid on Cologne and in August No 115 Squadron carried out the first trials with 'Gee', a new navigational and bombing radar aid. In September 1942 Nos 218 and 115 Squadrons left Marham and were replaced by Nos 105 and 139 Squadrons, equipped with Mosquitos. No 139 was then replaced by No 109 Squadron and Marham became part of No 8 (Pathfinder) Force in July 1943. The Mosquito force was equipped with 'Oboe', a blind-bombing device which enabled the Marham crews to drop target indicator flares in all weathers, and in July 1943 nine Pathfinder Mosquitos led more than 600 bombers to Krupp's armament works in Essen.

Marham closed in April 1944 while runways were laid, and it reopened in 1946 as the home of the Central Bomber Establishment, which, however, moved to Finningley two years later. In July 1948 the first US Air Force squadrons moved into Marham with Boeing B-29 bombers, remaining at the base until 1950, when the airfield returned to RAF control. B-29s remained active at Marham, since

four RAF Washington squadrons and an OCU were formed at the station. The Washingtons were replaced by Canberras early in 1954, but in 1956 Marham became a V-bomber station when Valiants arrived.

Valiant operations continued until the latter part of the 1960s, when Nos 55, 57 and 214 Squadrons re-formed at Marham with Victor aerial refuelling tankers. Air-to-air refuelling was, at that time, a relatively new skill, but the Marham squadrons demonstrated their capabilities in 1969 when Victor tankers supported RAF Harriers and Royal Navy Phantoms in the Transatlantic Air Race. The Strike Command Air-to-Surface Missile Support Unit formed at Marham in December 1970, initially tasked with the servicing of the Martel missile and later becoming responsible for the Sea Eagle, used by the Buccaneer force and, more recently, the Tornado GR.1B. No 100 Squadron moved to Marham in January 1976 as a target facilities unit, and the Canberra OCU (No 231) also moved in; these two units transferred to Wyton in January 1982 and July 1982 respectively. RAF Marham was awarded the Freedom of King's Lynn and West Norfolk in November 1981.

On 1 March 1983 No 2620 Squadron RAuxAF Regiment formed at Marham. The first Tornado unit to take up residence was No 617 Squadron, which re-formed in March 1983. No 27 Squadron arrived three months later, and both squadrons were heavily committed to Operation 'Desert Storm' during 1991 and 1992, supported by the resident Victor tanker force. Following the reduction in the RAF forces assigned to Germany, No 2 Squadron, equipped with reconnaissance-configured Tornado GR.1As, moved to Marham from Laarbruch in December 1991. The RAF's second Tornado reconnaissance squadron, No 13, also moved to Marham during 1994.

RAF Marham's long association with the Victor ended in 1993 when No 55 Squadron disbanded in October and the remaining seven Victor tankers were retired, effectively bringing to a close an important chapter in RAF history as these last V-bombers were withdrawn. No 27 Squadron was renumbered 12 during the same month and moved to Lossiemouth, the 27 Squadron number plate being transferred to the Chinook/Puma OCU at Odiham. No 617 Squadron moved to Lossiemouth during April 1994.

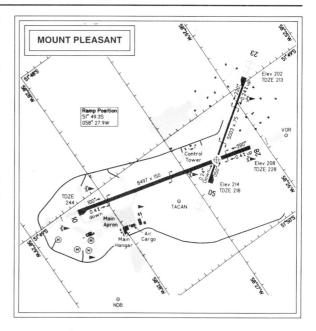

RAF Mount Pleasant

Resident units: No 1435 Flight (Tornado F.3); No 1312 Flight (Hercules C.1K); No 78 Squadron (Chinook, Sea King).

RAF Newton

Resident units: East Midlands University Air Squadron (Bulldog); No 7 Air Experience Flight (Chipmunk); RAF Police School; School of Education; School of Management Training; Guided Weapons School.

RAF Northolt

Resident units: No 32 Squadron (BAe 125, Andover, Gazelle); Northolt Station Flight (Islander).

Northolt was one of the first military airfields to be constructed in the United Kingdom. Surveys had begun as early as 1910, and the official opening took place on 1 March 1915 when No 4 Reserve Aeroplane Squadron arrived from Farnborough, becoming No 18 Squadron, Royal Flying Corps, two

AIRFIELD DIRECTORY

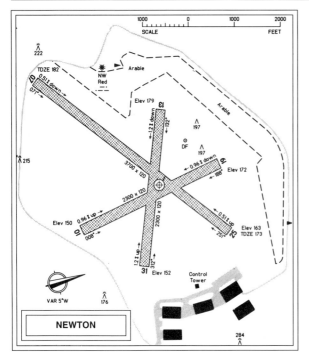

months later. The first flights took place in June 1915 when B.E.2cs mounted an anti-Zeppelin sortie from the airfield. No 11 RAS was formed in October, followed by No 39 Squadron, No 40 RS, No 43 Squadron RFC and other units. The Fairey Aviation Company established a base at Northolt in 1917, conducting flight tests with such aircraft as the Kennedy Giant. Northolt continued to operate primarily as a training base, and during 1918 the resident squadrons were amalgamated into No 30 Training Depot Station.

After the end of the First World War all fighter training operations ended and the South-Eastern Communications Flight arrived. During the following year Northolt became a joint RAF/civil airfield with the arrival of the Central Aircraft Company. Military activity increased when the Coastal Area Flight arrived, followed by No 12 Squadron's D.H.9As in 1923. New arrivals over the following years included Nos 41 and 24 Squadrons, together with Nos 600 and 601 Squadrons RAuxAF. In 1938 No 111 Squadron, which at that time was a resident unit, became the first in the RAF to be equipped with Hurricanes.

Northolt was heavily involved in fighter operations throughout the Second World War, and huge numbers of Spitfires and Hurricanes operated from the airfield at various times, resident squadrons including Nos 1, 16, 17, 25, 65, 92 and 111. A satellite airfield was constructed at nearby Heston during 1939 and a decoy airfield was built on Barnet golf course. The station hangars were also camouflaged, but instead of being finished in the usual disruptive green, black and brown they were painted to represent rows of houses, in an effort to blend them in with the surrounding suburbia. Whether the camouflage was effective remains unclear, but the airfield received relatively little attention from the *Luftwaffe*.

Major reconstruction work took place in 1945, including the laying of a new runway and the building of a new parking apron and associated freight and passenger buildings. In February 1945 No 271 Squadron began flying a scheduled passenger service to Brussels and the resident ADGB Communications Squadron absorbed the VIP Flight of the Metropolitan Communications Squadron, receiving Douglas Skymasters before moving to Lyneham. While work proceeded on the development of the former RAF airfield at Heathrow into an international air terminal, Northolt became London's main airport, BOAC's European Division (which later became BEA) operating flights to various European destinations. In March 1946 the main runway was reopened and airline operations gradually expanded to include companies such as Alitalia, Aer

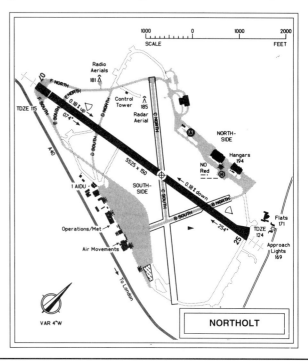

Lingus and Swissair, flying principally DC-3s, DC-4s and Vikings while the RAF continued to operate mainly Yorks and Dakotas from the airfield. During the mid-1950s the airfield was modernized, and the Metropolitan Communications Squadron arrived from Hendon in 1957.

Following the gradual development of Heathrow as London's main airport, civil operations from Northolt slowly decreased and the airfield is now used exclusively by the RAF. It is the home of No 32 Squadron, which flies BAe 125s, Andovers and Gazelles on communications duties.

RAF Odiham

Resident units: *No 7 Squadron (Chinook, Gazelle); No 33 Squadron (Puma); No 27(R) Squadron (Chinook, Puma); Joint Helicopter Support Unit.*

The airfield at Odiham was completed in 1925 as a summer camp for army co-operation aircraft, utilizing a grass runway. The site was used for flying from April to September each year and reverted to grazing land during the winter. Under the Government's Air Expansion Scheme in the early 1930s Odiham was turned into a permanent airfield, and on 18 October 1937 the new station was opened by *General* Erhard Milch, Chief of Staff of the *Luftwaffe* (!). Milch was impressed with what he saw, and later commented to Hitler, 'When we conquer England, Odiham will be my Air Headquarters.' Reputedly, as a result, he ordered that Odiham should not be bombed, and certainly the airfield was not attacked during the war.

When hostilities began the resident Army Co-operation Wing (No 614 Squadron) moved to France and No 225 Squadron, flying Westland Lysanders, took its place. There followed Free French, Belgian and Canadian training units. In June 1943 Fighter Command took control of Odiham, flying Mustangs and Typhoons, and on D-Day the station assumed a transit role for 'follow-up' elements and later became a prisoner-of-war camp; an old chalk quarry close to the airfield still contains some tin huts in which German POWs were held. During the summer of 1945 a Canadian Transport Wing was formed in the United Kingdom, and for just over a year Odiham became a part of the Royal Canadian Air Force.

Following the end of the Second World War, Fighter Command resumed operations from Odiham and a variety of aircraft types were flown from the airfield, including Spitfires, Hunters and Javelins. In July 1948 six Vampires from No 54 Squadron departed from Odiham to make the first jet crossing of the Atlantic, flying via Iceland, Greenland and Labrador. After impressing American audiences with an aerobatic display, they returned in time to perform at the 1948 SBAC show at Farnborough. One of the most famous days in RAF Odiham's history was 15 July 1953, when, as part of the nationwide Coronation celebrations and ceremonies, HM the Queen and HRH the Duke of Edinburgh reviewed the Royal Air Force at Odiham. The static display contained 318 aircraft and a further 641 took part in the fly-past.

Early in 1955 Odiham became the RAF's third Hunter station, and No 54 Squadron formed the RAF's first Hunter aerobatic team, known unofficially as the *Black Knights*. In February 1956 No 46 became the first Javelin squadron, and this unit continued to operate from Odiham until 1959, when the station was placed under 'care and maintenance'. It reopened in February 1960 as part of Transport Command and thus began a long associa-

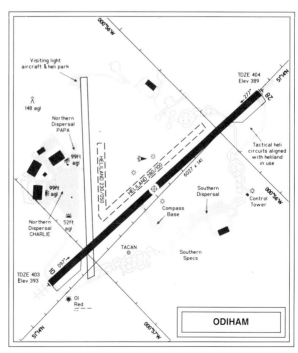

tion with helicopters, starting with the Sycamore, followed by the Whirlwind, Belvedere and Wessex. In 1971 the Pumas of Nos 33 and 230 Squadrons arrived and in 1972 the Wessex and Puma Operational Conversion Unit (240 OCU) was formed. During 1981 No 72 Squadron's Wessex helicopters were transferred to Benson, their place being taken by Boeing Chinooks assigned to Nos 7 and 18 Squadrons. The Pumas of No 230 Squadron moved to RAF Gütersloh in Germany during November 1980 and were followed by No 18 Squadron's Chinooks.

No 7 Squadron continues to operate from Odiham with Chinooks (and one Gazelle) and No 33 Squadron continues to operate the Puma. No 240 OCU, flying Pumas and Chinooks, was renumbered No 27(R) Squadron during October 1993. The station has standing commitments to support deployments to the Falkland Islands and Belize, and No 33 Squadron's Pumas deploy to Norway each year for a winter exercise and to Turkey in the summer in support of the ACE Mobile Force.

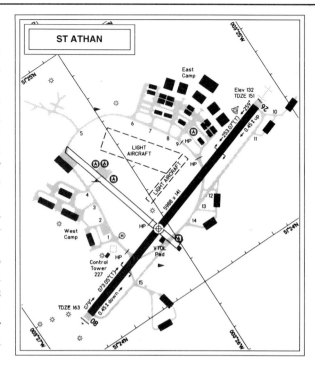

RAF St Athan

Resident units: *No 4 School of Technical Training; University of Wales Air squadron (Bulldog); No 634 Volunteer Gliding School (Viking); Support Command Ground Defence School.*

The area surrounding RAF St Athan is steeped in legend and folklore. Just one mile from the station lies the village of Boverton, which possesses a ruined castle dating from before the year 1199. A mile away is Llantwit Major, a locality where education and Christianity were reputedly introduced into the United Kingdom. The station is built on what was known, from the time of King Henry I, as the East and West Orchards. The site was purchased by the Air Ministry in 1936, and the base existed as a hutted training station until 1939, when the construction of permanent buildings began.

RAF St Athan officially opened on 1 September 1938, the first unit to take-up residence being No 4 School of Technical Training. In 1939 the scope of the station's activities expanded with the arrival of a fighter Group Pool, a Maintenance Unit and a School of Air Navigation. The station was already equipped to handle a large variety and complexity of tasks, which it continues to do at present.

During the Second World War the St Athan expanded to a peak number of over 14,000 personnel as units were transferred to and from the station. The training units turned out thousands of flight engineers, ground mechanics, wireless and radar operators, physical training instructors, navigators and others, despite being subjected to enemy air raids throughout 1940. Nos 19 and 32 Maintenance Units serviced a variety of aircraft types at St Athan, ranging from Whitleys to V-bombers, before disbanding in 1968.

Since the end of the war, RAF St Athan has evolved to meet present-day requirements, although the station's role is essentially unchanged. It boasts a vast engineering complex, responsible for the deep servicing of all types of RAF aircraft, and possesses a large manufacturing support facility, required by the maintenance role. The repair of engine and mechanical components of various RAF aircraft is also performed at the base. Training functions are exercised through No 4 School of Technical Training and the RAF Support Command Ground Defence School. The University of Wales Air Squadron was formed at St Athan in 1963, initially equipped with Chipmunks, and continues to operate with a fleet of

Scottish Aviation Bulldogs. The Regional Headquarters of the Air Training Corps is located at the base, which is also responsible for the maintenance of one of the RAF's eight Mountain Rescue Teams.

RAF St Mawgan

Resident units: No 22 Squadron (Wessex); Sea King Training Unit (Sea King); School of Combat Survival and Rescue; No 3 Maritime Headquarters Unit; No 2625 (County of Cornwall) Squadron RAuxAF.

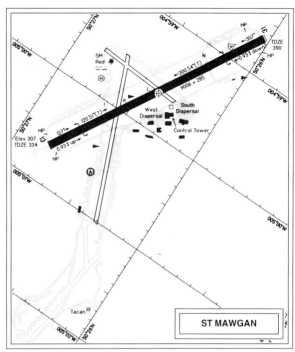

The present-day Royal Air Force St Mawgan lies to the north of a forty-acre site which in 1936 was known as Trebelzue Big Field. No record was made of when the first aircraft arrived at Trebelzue, but Western Airways, in conjunction with the Great Western Railway, started a passenger service which called at the airfield.

As the Second World War approached, a relatively large aerodrome was built a few miles north, at St Eval, and Trebelzue became a satellite landing ground for this station, all civil passenger flying having ceased. Trebelzue was used to support squadrons engaged in anti-shipping and U-boat patrols. At the end of 1941 the airfield was transferred from No 19 Group Coastal Command to No 44 Group Ferry Command and a wide variety of aircraft types called in en route to or from overseas theatres. Two Royal Canadian Air Force squadrons carried out patrols over the Bay of Biscay from the end of 1942 until February 1943, flying Mustangs and Mosquitos from the airfield. The station was renamed St Mawgan on 24 February 1943, and by the end of that year three concrete runways had been built to the northeast, enabling heavy, long-range bombers to transit also.

The airfield closed shortly after the end of the war but reopened as part of No 19 Group Coastal Command in April 1951, housing an advance party from the School of Maritime Reconnaissance. Flying operations resumed in June 1951, and the station became a Master Diversion Airfield in November 1955. The School of Maritime Reconnaissance moved to Kinloss during October 1956, its place being taken by Nos 220 and 228 Long Range Maritime Reconnaissance Squadrons, equipped with, respectively, Avro Shackleton MR.1s and MR.2s; these units were later renumbered Nos 201 and 206 Squadrons and were joined by No 42 Squadron. St Mawgan also became the Headquarters of No 22 Squadron, a search and rescue helicopter unit, which remained at the station until April 1974 when it was transferred to Thorney Island.

In 1965 Nos 201 and 206 Squadrons moved to Kinloss and at the same time the Maritime Operational Training Unit (MOTU) moved south to St Mawgan from Kinloss. Shackleton operations continued from St Mawgan until September 1971, when No 42 Squadron exchanged its Shackleton MR.3s for Nimrod MR.1s. The MOTU also re-equipped with Nimrods and was redesignated No 236 Operational Conversion Unit.

During July 1970 No 7 Squadron was re-formed at St Mawgan. Equipped with Canberra TT.18s, T.19s and T.4s, it flew target-facilities missions in support of RAF, Royal Navy and Army units before being disbanded on 18 January 1982. The Squadron's old standard was laid up in Truro Cathedral. No 42 Squadron converted to the Nimrod MR.2 during 1983 and the OCU temporarily moved to Kinloss the same year to undergo a similar transition, before returning to St Mawgan. However, No 42 Squadron disbanded during 1992, and the Nimrod OCU moved back to Kinloss, where it was redesignated No 42(R) Squadron.

The School of Combat Survival and Rescue moved to St Mawgan from Mountbatten during 1992, and No 3 Maritime Headquarters (RAuxAF) also moved from the latter base, which then closed down. No 22 Squadron returned to St Mawgan from Finningley during the same year, and the Sea King Training Unit was transferred from nearby RNAS Culdrose. No 2625 (County of Cornwall) Squadron RAuxAF was formed at St Mawgan during November 1982 and currently remains active at the base as a ground defence unit. Following the construction of hardened aircraft shelters, the station continues to act as host to various unit detachments and exercises, and it also serves as a forward base for No 12 Squadron.

RAF Scampton

Resident units: *Central Flying School (Tucano, Bulldog); The* Red Arrows *(Hawk); No 643 Volunteer Gliding School (Vigilant).*

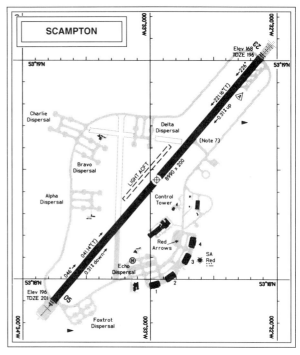

RAF Scampton's origins can be traced back to November 1916 when an airfield on the present site was first opened. Referred to as Brattleby Airfield, it was, apart from the hangars, essentially a temporary establishment for training operations. A variety of aircraft used the site, including F.E.2s, Avro 504s, R.E.8s and Martinsyde Elephants. Following the end of the First World War the RAF's training requirement was drastically reduced and the resident aircraft at Brattleby were transferred to South Carlton during April 1919. By the following year the airfield had been completely demolished and the land returned to agricultural use. However, when the RAF began to expand in the 1930s the Brattleby site was re-surveyed and in 1935 it was repurchased. A grass airfield was quickly constructed, and it opened as RAF Scampton on 27 August 1936. The first unit to arrive was No 9 Squadron, followed in turn by Nos 214, 148, 49 and 83 Squadrons, flying aircraft such as the Heyford, Virginia, Harrow, Audax, Wellesley and Hampden.

At the beginning of the Second World War the Scampton squadrons quickly became involved in both bombing and minelaying activities. During November 1941 No 1518 BAT Flight arrived with Oxfords, and No 83 Squadron began to re-equip with Manchesters during the following month, followed by No 49 Squadron. However, a series of technical problems with the Manchester saw the aircraft quickly replaced by the Lancaster. No 57 Squadron moved to Scampton in September 1942, replacing No 49 Squadron, which moved to Wyton. No 467 Squadron RAAF arrived during November, and No 49 Squadron moved to Fiskerton in 1943. On 21 March 1943 No 617 Squadron formed at Scampton, and after a six-week training period, the 'Dambusters' launched their historic raid on 16 May.

Bomber operations continued from Scampton until August 1943, when the resident squadrons moved out, enabling a reconstruction programme to begin, including the laying of concrete runways. The first unit to arrive at the rebuilt airfield was No 1690 Bomber Defence Training Flight. This unit departed in October 1944, in which month No 153 Squadron arrived with Lancasters, to be joined by No 1687 BDTF two months later with Spitfires, Hurricanes and Martinets. No 625 Squadron arrived in April 1945, disbanding five months later, as did No 153 Squadron.

After the end of the Second World War the station remained active. No 57 Squadron returned in November 1945, followed by No 100 Squadron, both units moving to Lindholme in May 1946. The Bomber Command Instructors' School arrived in 1947 with Lancasters, Lincolns, Mosquitos and Wellingtons, and in July 1948 the USAF's 28th Bomb Group took up residence with B-29 Superfortresses, later replaced by the 301st Bomb Group. The Americans left after only a few months, and in February 1949 No 230 OCU arrived with Lancasters and Lincolns. In 1952 Nos 120 and 240 Squadrons operated Shackletons from Scampton for a few weeks, and in June 1952 the 3930th Air Base Squadron was established there, with two B-17s and a pair of US Navy Constellations. No 230 OCU disbanded in 1953 and the BCIS moved to Binbrook, while the American unit also disbanded. In January that year No 10 Squadron's Canberras moved to the station, followed by Nos 27, 18 and 21 Squadrons, which remained at Scampton with Canberras until 1955, when the airfield was closed for another major reconstruction programme in anticipation of the arrival of Vulcan V-bombers.

RAF Scampton reopened in 1958, and No 617 Squadron returned, this time with Vulcans, followed by Nos 83 and 27 Squadrons. No 83 Squadron continued to operate the Vulcan until July 1969 when the unit disbanded, and five months later No 230 OCU (now the Vulcan OCU) arrived from Finningley and was joined by Hastings rear crew trainers from what had been the Strike Command Bombing School and was now unofficially known as '1066 Flight'. No 27 Squadron disbanded in 1972, reforming the following year as a Vulcan maritime radar reconnaissance unit. No 35 Squadron arrived from Cyprus in 1975.

Vulcan operations continued until March 1982, when No 27 Squadron transferred the last Vulcans from Scampton to nearby Waddington, where they joined No 44 Squadron. Following another period of reconstruction, Scampton reopened as the new home of the Central Flying School, with an assortment of Bulldogs, Chipmunks, Hawks and Jet Provosts. The Central Flying School's most famous squadron, the *Red Arrows*, also transferred to Scampton, establishing a new home in one of the former Lancaster hangars. The Jet Provosts were replaced by Tucanos in 1992.

Below: RAF Scampton, illustrating the station's layout as the *Red Arrows* streak over the airfield.

AIRFIELD DIRECTORY

RAF Sealand

Resident units: No 631 Volunteer Gliding School (Viking); No 30 Maintenance Unit.

RAF Shawbury

Resident units: No 2 Flying Training School (Wessex, Gazelle); Central Flying School Detachment (Gazelle); Central Air Traffic Control School; No 8 Air Experience Flight (Chipmunk).

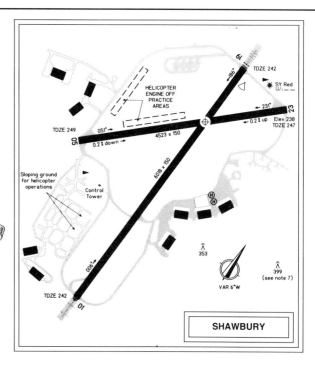

During the First World War the Royal Flying Corps began a search for suitable sites in western England where pilots could be trained prior to being posted to the Front. Shawbury was one of several selected, and the McAlpine Construction Company transformed 260 acres of farmland into an active airfield. Two grass landing strips were established, each being approximately 1,000 yards long. Seven wooden hangars were constructed, six for aircraft storage and the seventh for an aeroplane repair section.

The first aircraft arrived during the summer of 1917, and No 29 (Training) Wing took up residence on 1 September with three squadrons, Nos 10, 29 and 67. The remainder of the Wing formed during November at nearby Ternhill. The number of different aircraft types operated by the Wing was considerable and included Avro 504s, D.H.5As, Bristol Scouts, Nieuports and Sopwith Camels, although the Avro 504 quickly established itself as the most suitable aircraft for flying training duties. During October 1917 No 90 (Fighter) Squadron arrived, eventually receiving their own fleet of Aero Monos, Scouts and Sopwith Dolphins, and after a gradual increase in the number of overseas pilots posted to Shawbury the latter became known as No 9 Training Depot Station.

As the First World War began to move towards a conclusion, the RFC's (and later the RAF's) training needs diminished and in June 1919 the TDS and Training Wing disbanded. RAF Shawbury closed just one year later. The site was returned to agricultural use, but history repeated itself and during 1937 the farmland was again transformed into an airfield, ready to begin training pilots in anticipation of the Second World War. The overall size of the airfield was increased, and twelve hangars were eventually constructed. The first unit (No 27 MU) arrived on 1 February 1938, together with its associated aircraft, which included Audaxes, Harts, Blenheims, Battles and Gladiators.

The huge numbers of aircraft being held by the MU led to the widespread dispersal of airframes to various satellite landing grounds, but by 1940 more than 500 aircraft were being stored at Shawbury. This led to the construction of even more hangars, scattered around the perimeter of the airfield and suitably camouflaged to blend in with the local housing. The first training unit to arrive was No 11 FTS on 14 May 1938 with a fleet of Harts, Audaxes, Gauntlets, Furys and Tutors; another two years passed before the RAF standardized on the twin-engine Airspeed Oxford trainer. The large number of aircraft using Shawbury's grass field led to the construction of two concrete runways, one 4,500ft long and the other just under 4,000ft long, by the summer of 1942. The associated taxiways were also concrete, though many of the smaller tracks leading to the hangars remained as hardcore until after the war.

Shawbury first saw enemy action on 27 June 1940 when bombs were dropped on the airfield as night flying training was in progress. Two more raids took place during September and another during November. As the end of the Second World War approached, the RAF's training requirement decreased (a great deal of training activity having already been relocated overseas). The Central Navigation School arrived early in 1944 with Wellingtons and Stirlings, breaking Shawbury's association with pilot training and beginning what was to become the Station's best-known contribution to RAF history. During the war the Air Staff had become increasingly concerned with the relative inaccuracy of bomber aircraft navigation, especially at night, and the Central Navigation School was formed at Cranage, tasked with the training of navigation specialists and given the overall objective of improving navigational techniques. By the time the unit moved to Shawbury the accuracy of the bomber crews' navigation had improved dramatically, and the School's remit was expanded to include the conduct of research into worldwide navigation.

One of the School's first record-breaking flights, and certainly the most famous, was that made by Lancaster B.1 PD328 *Aries* during 1944—the first round-the-world flight by a British aircraft. During 1945 *Aries* began a series of pioneering flights to the North Pole, examining the peculiarities of Arctic air navigation. The aircraft continued in service until 1947, when it was replaced by a Lincoln.

By 1954 Shawbury's role had changed considerably, with the training of air traffic control students now a major undertaking, and by 1955 over 200 ATC students were in residence. Vampire T.11 trainers were delivered to Shawbury during 1957, giving the station a relatively high-performance aircraft with which to teach the increasingly complex techniques of air traffic control. The runways were also modernized, and the main runway was increased to 6,018ft in length. The Navigation Wing moved to Manby during 1963, and the Central Air Traffic Control School formed on 11 February that year, with Marshalls flying Provosts, Vampires and finally Jet Provosts on behalf of the School. The CATCS became an 'all-synthetic' unit during 1989 when the Jet Provosts were retired, thanks to the increasing capabilities of the RAF's simulator equipment.

No 27 MU had meanwhile disbanded on 30 June 1972, having performed sterling work for very many years. Sadly, the MU's final tasks had included the scrapping of large numbers of surplus airframes, including Ansons, Beverleys, Hastings, Mosquitos, Vampires, Argosys, Jet Provosts, Shackletons and Javelins, all of which had made their final flights to the station.

Flying training returned to Shawbury on 1 October 1976 when No 2 (Advanced) Flying Training School arrived from Ternhill, together with the Central Flying School (Helicopter) Squadron, flying Whirlwinds and Gazelles respectively. In 1977 the

Below: A Westland Gazelle HT.3 inside one of Shawbury's servicing hangars. (John Hale)

AIRFIELD DIRECTORY

Wessex replaced the Whirlwind as the RAF's advanced helicopter trainer, the Gazelle taking over as the basic trainer type. Recent changes in RAF helicopter crew training have led to the introduction of a renamed No 1 Rotary Wing AFT course, which began in May 1992, training pilots, navigators and crewmen and restoring Shawbury's historical links with navigator training.

RAF Swanton Morley

Resident units: Central Servicing Development Establishment; No 611 Volunteer Gliding School (Viking).

RAF Syerston

Resident units: Air Cadet Central Gliding School (Vigilant, Viking, Valiant, Kestrel); No 644 Volunteer Gliding School (Vigilant).

RAF Ternhill

Resident unit: No 632 Volunteer Gliding School (Vigilant).

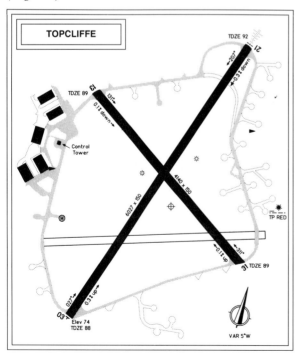

RAF Topcliffe

Resident unit: Joint Elementary Flying Training Squadron (Slingsby Firefly).

RAF Turnhouse

Resident units: No 12 Air Experience Flight (Chipmunk); East Lowlands University Air Squadron (Bulldog).

RAF Valley

Resident units: No 4 Flying Training School, comprising No 74(R) Squadron (Hawk) and No 234(R) Squadron (Hawk); Central Flying School Detachment (Hawk); 'C' Flight No 22 Squadron (Wessex); Search and Rescue Training Unit (Wessex).

RAF Valley, first referred to as RAF Rhosneigr, opened on 13 February 1941 as part of No 9 Group Fighter Command. The station's location made it an ideal base for a Sector Operations Centre, controlling fighter defences in the approaches to Merseyside and Belfast, and for the protection of shipping in the Irish Sea. No 312 (Czech) Squadron's Hurricanes arrived on 3 March 1941 and began flying convoy patrols over the Irish Sea, and before the unit relocated to the Isle of Man two months later a Ju 88 was destroyed during one sortie from Valley. No 615 Squadron then arrived, followed by 'A' Flight of No 219 Squadron, with Beaufighters, and sections of Nos 302 (Polish) and 68 Squadrons. On 30 June 1941 No 456 Squadron RAAF was formed at the station, equipped with Defiants, and this unit was followed by No 275 Squadron in October with air/sea rescue Walruses and Lysanders.

The airfield was by now beginning to take shape, and the three tarmac runways were extended, whilst improvements were made to the very basic domestic site. Another squadron arrived at Valley in November 1941, this time No 350, a Belgian-manned Spitfire unit. More squadrons used Valley as an operating base over the following months, including Nos 125, 131, 157, 315, 406 and 452, flying Spitfires, Beaufighters and Mosquitos. By

1943 enemy air activity over the Irish Sea had diminished considerably and Valley was identified as a suitable terminal for transatlantic ferry flights made by American aircraft destined for RAF or USAAF squadrons. In October 1943 the Sector Operations Centre closed, leaving just No 125 Squadron's Beaufighters for air defence and No 275 Squadron's air/sea rescue aircraft, which departed to Warmwell in 1944.

For the remainder of the Second World War Valley was almost entirely devoted to the receipt of incoming transatlantic aircraft from the USA and Canada, prior to assignment to front-line bases in Britain. The USAAF Movements Section handled most of these ferry flights, although the RAF took care of British aircraft. After the end of the war in Europe, Valley handled large numbers of USAAF aircraft which were transferred from Europe to the Far Eastern theatre for the war against Japan.

The USAAF Transit Unit vacated the airfield in September 1945, leaving only No 1528 Beam Approach Training Flight, with Oxfords, until that unit also left, for Blakehill Farm in December. The station was transferred to Flying Training Command on 29 July 1946, by which time Valley was virtually inactive, under care and maintenance and with only occasional diversions and detachments for night flying, refresher flying and gunnery training.

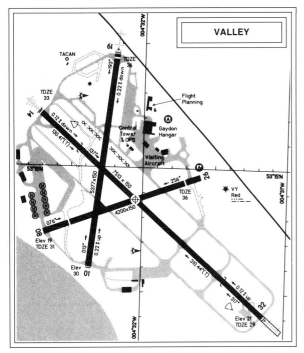

The airfield changed commands yet again in April 1948, when No 12 Group Fighter Command assumed control, and No 20 squadron arrived with Vampires in July 1949. No 202 Advanced Flying School's Vampires began jet training duties at Valley in February 1951; the unit was redesignated No 7 Flying Training School on 1 June 1954. In 1955 No 7 FTS was joined by No 6 Joint Services Trials Unit, a 'lodger' organization established to undertake trials with the Fairey Fireflash air-to-air missile; redesignated No 1 Guided Weapons Development Squadron in 1957, the unit operated a fleet of ten Swifts modified to carry this weapon. On 1 January 1959 the unit was redesignated yet again. this time No 1 Guided Weapons Training Squadron, and was equipped with six Javelins, devoted largely to the testing of the Firestreak infra-red missile.

In 1958, meanwhile, the station had taken over from RAF Worksop the role of advanced flying training for student pilots, and on 15 August 1960 No 4 Flying Training School re-formed at Valley, with Vampire T.11s. The Vampires were replaced by Gnat T.1s during 1962, and in 1964 the unit formed an aerobatic team with five yellow-painted aircraft; named the *Yellowjacks*, they were the predecessors of the world-famous *Red Arrows*. From 1967 the Gnats were supplemented by Hunter F.6 single-seat and T.7 twin-seat trainers, and all three aircraft types remained in service with No 4 FTS until 1976, when Hawk trainers were delivered and the Gnats and Hunters retired. The Hawk also equipped the Central Flying School's detachment at Valley, tasked with the training of instructors for the RAF, Fleet Air Arm and other air services.

No 1 Guided Weapons Training Squadron was disbanded in May 1962, to be replaced by the Fighter Command (later Strike Command) Missile Practice Camp. Still in residence at Valley, the unit is now known as the Strike Command Air-to-Air Missile Establishment (STCAAME). Another 'lodger' unit at Valley was the Central Flying School Helicopter Detachment, which arrived from Ternhill in 1962. Later replaced by No 2 (SAR) Squadron of No 2 FTS, the unit became the Search and Rescue Training Unit in 1979, before moving to RAF St Mawgan. No 4 FTS remains in residence at Valley, divided into two component squadrons, these being No 74(R) and No 234(R) Squadrons. Valley is one of the RAF's busiest stations, and nearby RAF Mona is maintained as a relief landing ground (RLG).

RAF Waddington

Resident units: No 8 Squadron (Sentry); No 51 Squadron (Nimrod).

Situated south of the historic city of Lincoln, RAF Waddington first opened in November 1916 as a flying training station. No 97 Squadron RFC formed at the station in December 1917 but moved to Stonehenge a few weeks later. During the First World War a variety of aircraft types operated from the airfield on training duties, including D.H.4s, D.H.9s, Avro 504s and Maurice Farman Shorthorns.

The station closed in 1919 but reopened seven years later as the home of No 503 (Bombing) Squadron, equipped with Fairey Fawns. This unit was later renumbered No 503 (County of Lincoln) Squadron, of the Royal Auxiliary Air Force, re-equipping with Hyderabads in 1929 and then with Westland Wallaces in 1935.

A major rebuilding programme took place during the 1930s, and in May 1937 No 110(B) Squadron re-formed at Waddington with Hawker Hinds, followed by Nos 50(B) and No 88(B) Squadrons. In June 1937 No 44 Squadron arrived at the station, re-equipping with Blenheims in December the same year.

At the outbreak of the Second World War Nos 44 and 50 Squadrons were based at Waddington with Hampdens, and these units quickly became actively involved in reconnaissance and bombing missions. No 142 Squadron came to Waddington in June 1940 with Fairey Battles but soon moved out, as did No 50 Squadron. In November 1940 No 207 Squadron re-formed at the station as the first Avro Manchester unit, and No 97 Squadron re-equipped with Manchesters three months later, before moving to Coningsby. The first Lancaster unit was No 44 Squadron, following re-equipment at Waddington early in 1942. Towards the end of 1941 No 420 Squadron RCAF formed, and in August 1942 No 9 Squadron arrived from Waddington and re-equipped with Lancasters.

The construction of three concrete runways began in May 1943, and by the end of the year the airfield was again active as the base for Nos 467 and 463 Squadrons RAAF. In addition to almost continuous participation in the RAF's heavy bombing campaign, Waddington also accommodated the RAF Film Unit, which was attached to No 463 Squadron. The *Luftwaffe* flew bombing missions against the station too. Indeed, during the night of 3/4 March 1945 Waddington's Lancasters returned from a raid to find the airfield under attack by German aircraft; however, all the Lancasters managed to land safely.

After the end of the Second World War the station continued to support bomber operations. No 617 Squadron arrived from Woodhall Spa in June 1945, only to be replaced by No 61 Squadron seven months later. The latter unit re-equipped with Avro Lincolns in May 1946 and was joined by No 57 Squadron in October the same year. More Lincolns arrived in March 1950 when No 100 Squadron arrived, but the jet age was fast approaching and in August 1953 the three resident Lincoln squadrons (Nos 49, 61 and 100) moved to Wittering. Waddington was then placed under care and maintenance while the station was reconstructed in preparation for the arrival of V-bombers. One of the three runways was rebuilt and extended in length to 9,000ft. Aircraft dispersals were also constructed around the perimeter, and in June 1955 the station reopened to receive Nos 21 and 27 Squadrons from Scampton flying Canberra B.2s.

Above: RAF Waddington's control tower, with the familiar shape of a Vulcan bomber in the background.

The first Vulcans arrived in 1955, and by the end of 1957 the Canberras had left, leaving Waddington as the home of the Vulcan Operational Conversion Unit (No 230 OCU). No 83 Squadron formed at Waddington before moving to Scampton, and Nos 44 and 101 Squadrons re-formed at Waddington, the latter unit taking the place of the OCU, which moved to Finningley. No 50 Squadron re-formed in 1961 and No 9 Squadron arrived from Cyprus in 1975, bringing the Waddington Vulcan Wing up to full strength.

Waddington's long association with the Vulcan continued into the 1980s, and the station became heavily involved in the 1982 Falklands conflict when Vulcans were assigned to bombing and anti-radar attacks in the South Atlantic. Following the final withdrawal of the Vulcan bombers, No 50 Squadron remained at Waddington with Vulcan K.2 refuelling tankers until March 1984, after which the station was devoid of any resident flying units: just one Vulcan, XL426, remained, retained by the RAF for display flying. This aircraft was replaced by XH558, which made its final flight from Waddington in March 1993. No 8 Squadron re-formed at Waddington during 1991 with Boeing Sentry AEW.1s, and was to be joined by No 51 Squadron's Nimrods in 1995.

RAF Wattisham

Resident unit: No 22 Squadron (Sea King HAR.3).

RAF West Raynham

Resident unit: No 66 Squadron RAF Regiment.

RAF Wethersfield

Resident unit: No 614 Volunteer Gliding School (Viking).

RAF Wittering

Resident units: No 1 Squadron (Harrier); No 20(R) Squadron (Harrier); RAF Armament Support Unit.

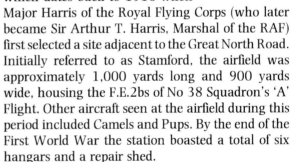

RAF Wittering has enjoyed a particularly long and varied history which dates back to 1916 when Major Harris of the Royal Flying Corps (who later became Sir Arthur T. Harris, Marshal of the RAF) first selected a site adjacent to the Great North Road. Initially referred to as Stamford, the airfield was approximately 1,000 yards long and 900 yards wide, housing the F.E.2bs of No 38 Squadron's 'A' Flight. Other aircraft seen at the airfield during this period included Camels and Pups. By the end of the First World War the station boasted a total of six hangars and a repair shed.

American forces were also stationed at Wittering from October 1917 when, as part of an international agreement, the RFC trained American pilots on D.H.6 and Curtiss JN aircraft. The Aeroplane Repair Section at Wittering was also American, this being the 831st Aero Repair Squadron. The station was officially named RAF Wittering on 10 April 1918, following the official formation of the Royal Air Force on the 1st of that month.

After the end of the First World War the airfield was closed down and it remained inactive until

1924, when it was re-built in order to accommodate the Central Flying School, which moved in in October 1926. When the CFS was transferred to Upavon nine years later, No 11 Flying Training School arrived at Wittering; it remained until May 1938, by which time the station had become an operational fighter airfield. Nos 23 and 213 Squadrons arrived in May, followed by No 610 Squadron, equipped with Spitfires, in October 1939. Wittering's fighters were largely involved in convoy patrol duties until the situation in France deteriorated, when aircraft were sent to cover the retreat of the British Expeditionary Forces from that country.

As the build-up to the Battle of Britain began, No 213 Squadron left Wittering, to be replaced by No 229 Squadron, equipped with Hurricanes. No 1 Squadron's Hurricanes arrived in September 1940 to replace No 229 Squadron, and the station suffered two light incendiary raids on 24 September and 28 October, although no damage was sustained during either. Towards the end of 1940 the resident squadrons left, to be replaced by Nos 25 (Blenheims and Beaufighters) and 151 (Defiants and Hurricanes). Tasked primarily with night-fighter duties, these units were successful in intercepting bomber formations heading to the Midlands. RAF Wittering suffered its heaviest attack on 14 March 1941 when six 500lb bombs and some 100 incendiaries hit the station. Seventeen people were killed.

In July 1941 No 1453 Flight was formed, its Havocs fitted with powerful searchlights. These aircraft operated in conjunction with No 151 Squadron's Hurricanes, attempting to illuminate targets for interception by the fighters.

In 1942 RAF Wittering was joined to the nearby satellite field at Collyweston by removing trees, ditches and hedges. The result was a large airfield with a landing area almost three miles long, which became useful for the recovery of damaged bombers returning from raids over Germany. A Bomber Command Servicing Unit was established, and numerous Lancasters, Stirlings and Halifaxes were successfully recovered. In March 1943 No 1426 (EAC) Flight was formed at Wittering, tasked with the evaluation of captured *Luftwaffe* aircraft. The Flight formed a 'touring circus' which visited various RAF stations around the country to aid enemy aircraft recognition, and during the unit's stay at Wittering such aircraft as the Heinkel He 111, Junkers Ju 88 and Messerschmitt Bf 109 were flown. The Fighter Interception Unit and the Night Fighter Interception Unit arrived in April 1944 and stayed for five months, flying Mosquitos and Typhoons. During this period RAF Wittering was home to an astonishing variety of aircraft types, including Tempests, Meteors, Dauntlesses and the Junkers Ju 88 which currently resides in the RAF Museum.

The Gunnery Research Unit moved in from Exeter during April 1944, bringing with it one of the few remaining Fairey Battles, and following the departure of the Fighter Interception Unit the Central Fighter Establishment was formed at the station later that year. No 68 Squadron operated from Wittering for a short period in February 1945, flying interception sorties against low-level nuisance raids by He 111s, and following the departure of this unit the base's wartime activity effectively ended. The USAF's 55th Fighter Squadron had arrived late in 1943, and the unit's P-38 Lightnings were employed on long-range escort missions. After re-equipping with P-51 Mustangs, the 55th FS left England in October 1945.

After the end of the war Wittering was returned to Flying Training Command, although no active flying units were based there until 1946, when the station returned to Fighter Command and Nos 19,

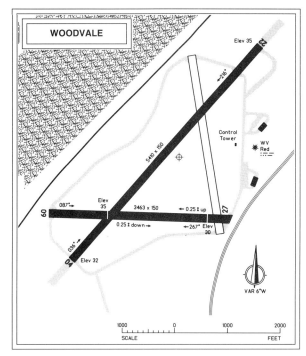

OCU, the Harrier Operational Conversion Unit, was formed. Wittering's Harrier GR.1s and GR.3s have now been replaced by the more capable Harrier GR.5/7s, although 'early-generation' Harrier T.4 conversion trainers are still in use, pending delivery of new Harrier T.10s. No 233 OCU was redesignated No 20(R) Squadron during 1992, and although RAF Laarbruch continues to support two Harrier squadrons, Wittering is very much the 'Home of the Harrier'.

RAF Woodvale

Resident units: *No 10 Air Experience Flight (Chipmunk); Manchester University Air Squadron (Bulldog).*

RAF Wyton

Resident units: *No 360 Squadron (Canberra); No 51 Squadron (Nimrod); Electronic Warfare Operational Support Establishment; Royal Naval Electronic Warfare Operational Support Unit; Army Electronic Warfare Operational Support Unit; Electronic Warfare and Avionic Division RAFSEE; Joint School of Photographic Interpretation; 7010 Flight RAF Volunteer Reserve.*

23, 41, 141 and 219 Squadrons arrived, flying Spitfires, Mosquitos and Hornets. These units all departed in April 1947 but were replaced by No 264 Squadron, flying Mosquito night fighters. During the previous year Wittering had acted as a test airfield for the Handley page Hastings transport, taking advantage of the three miles of available runway.

A new concrete runway was laid in 1952 and Bomber Command's Nos 49, 61 and 100 Squadrons arrived in 1953, equipped with Lincolns. Canberras quickly replaced the Avro bombers, and in July 1955 the first Valiant V-bombers arrived. The Bomber Command Development Unit joined No 138 Squadron at the base and was responsible for the testing of Britain's first nuclear weapons. A No 49 Squadron Valiant made the first air-drop in 1956, and during the following year another 49 Squadron aircraft, XD818, dropped Britain's first H-bomb.

Following the retirement of the Valiant force, Nos 100 and 139 Squadrons re-formed at Wittering with Victor B.2s, equipped with Blue Steel stand-off bombs. Victors remained active at Wittering until 1968, and in February 1969 the station was transferred to Air Support Command, receiving No 230 Squadron's Whirlwinds in March and the first Harriers in August of that year. No 1 Squadron re-formed in August, and in October 1970 No 233

The original airfield at Wyton was built in 1914 as a training base for Army and Royal Flying Corps pilots, but after the end of the First World War the site was sold and restored to agricultural status. As the Royal Air Force expanded to meet the growing German threat in the 1930s, the land was re-purchased and developed into a Royal Air Force station. Nos 114 and 139 Squadrons formed there in 1936, flying Hawker Hinds, and two years before the outbreak of the Second World War these aircraft were replaced by Blenheims.

A Blenheim from Wyton was credited with the first oper-ational sortie of the Second World War, photographing Kiel harbour, as the Prime Minister made his sombre announcement to the world on 3 September 1939. Shortly afterwards the HM King George VI and HM Queen Elizabeth visited RAF Wyton and the first investiture of the war was held in one of the hangars; five Wyton air crewmen were decorated.

Wellingtons and Stirlings replaced the Blenheims, and in 1942 Wyton became the home of the Pathfinder Force, transforming the RAF's bombing techniques through new navigation and target-marking procedures. In 1943 the King and Queen paid a second visit, inspecting the new headquarters of No 8 (Pathfinder) Group. The units based at Wyton at this time were Nos 83, 139 and 163 Squadrons and No 1409 Flight, all equipped with the Mosquito. The year 1944 saw the addition of a Meteorological Flight, to provide vital weather information for the Allied air offensive.

After the end of the war the station became the home of a Photographic Reconnaissance squadron, which proved its value by providing extensive coverage of the East Coast flood disaster in March 1953, and three months later three Wyton Canberras flew film of the HM Queen Elizabeth II's Coronation to Canada, where it was shown just eight hours after having been taken in London. In 1955 No 543 Squadron arrived with Vickers Valiant strategic reconnaissance aircraft, joining No 58 Squadron with Canberras and the Radar Reconnaissance Flight with Victors. The last disbanded in September 1961, but eighteen months later No 51 Squadron arrived. In 1965 No 543 Squadron disposed of its Valiants and became a Victor SR.2 unit, and in February 1969 No 26 Squadron re-formed as a light transport unit, with Bassets and Devons. No 58 Squadron disbanded in 1970 and was replaced by No 39 Squadron with Canberra PR.9 reconnaissance aircraft.

In addition to their normal training activities, the Wyton squadrons were engaged in various tasks around the world. In 1967–68 No 543 Squadron made a photographic survey of Denmark and in 1969–70 Nos 58 and 543 Squadrons made a similar survey of Norway. No 543 Squadron finally disbanded in May 1974, passing the radar reconnaissance task to No 27 Squadron at Scampton. In 1977 No 39 Squadron carried out another aerial survey of Denmark. In 1978 a third reconnaissance unit arrived at Wyton, when No 13 Squadron transferred from Malta. No 100 Squadron's Canberras arrived from Marham in January 1982, and at the same time No 13 Squadron disbanded, followed by No 39 in June of the same year. As that squadron disbanded, No 1 Photographic Reconnais-

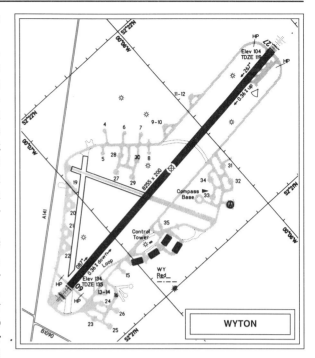

sance Unit was formed to continue this work. In July 1982 No 231 OCU's Canberras arrived from Marham. No 25 Squadron arrived from Germany in January 1983 and was absorbed into No 85 Squadron, equipped with Bloodhound SAMs.

Wyton also became home to some lodger units. The JARIC Model section arrived in 1951, the Joint School of Photographic Interpretation in 1969, the Electronic Warfare and Avionic Unit (now renamed the Electronic Warfare and Avionic Division) in 1971, No 1 Air Survey Section Royal Engineers in 1977, the Strike Command Canberra Maintenance School in 1981 and the RAF Electronic Warfare Operational Support Establishment in 1983. No 85 Squadron disbanded in August 1990.

After re-equipping with Hawks, No 100 Squadron moved to Finningley in September 1993, and following the disbandment of 231 OCU only two operational RAF Canberra squadrons remained active, both based at Wyton. No 360 Squadron (which arrived in 1975) remains at Wyton with Canberra electronic warfare trainers but is disbanding at the end of 1994. No 39(R) Squadron (formerly No 1 PRU) moved to Marham in 1993, and No 51 Squadron will move its Nimrods to Waddington in January 1995. Although Wyton thus becomes a non-flying station, the base remains active as the home of RAF Logistics Command.

AIRCRAFT DIRECTORY

AIRCRAFT DIRECTORY

BAe 125/Dominie

125 CC.3 (CC.1 and CC.2 similar): *Span 47ft; length 50ft 8½in; height 17ft 7in. Weight 12,845lb (empty), 25,500lb (max). Maximum speed 436kts. Maximum range 2,500nm. Two Garrett TFE731-3-1 turbofans rated at 3,700lb thrust.*

Dominie T.1: *Span 47ft; length 47ft 5in; height 16ft 6in. Weight 10,000lb (empty), 21,200lb (max). Maximum speed 365kts. Maximum range 1,300nm. Two Rolls-Royce Viper Mk 301 turbojets rated at 3,120lb thrust.*

The Dominie was developed from the hugely successful De Havilland 125 executive jet, which first flew on 13 August 1962. It was selected to replace the Varsity and Meteor in the advanced navigation training role, and some twenty aircraft were ordered, all of which were eventually assigned to No 6 Flying Training School at Finningley. The Dominie T.1 accommodates a pilot and co-pilot, up to three navigator students, and two instructors. Doppler radar is fitted, and the emphasis is placed on low-level (500ft) radar navigation training, although high-altitude navigation is also taught as part of the current No 6 FTS syllabus. Part of the Dominie T.1 fleet is scheduled to undergo a major modification programme, introducing new equipment more appropriate to navigator training in the 1990s.

The BAe 125 CC.1 was introduced in 1971 as a high-speed communications and staff transport aircraft, based on the civil Series 400 model. It was initially powered by Viper turbojet engines, although turbofans have been retrospectively fitted. The CC.2 is based on the Series 600 aircraft, incor-

Above right: A Dominie receives pre-flight attention at Finningley.
Below: A BAe 125 CC.3 from No 32 Squadron.

BAe 125/DOMINIE

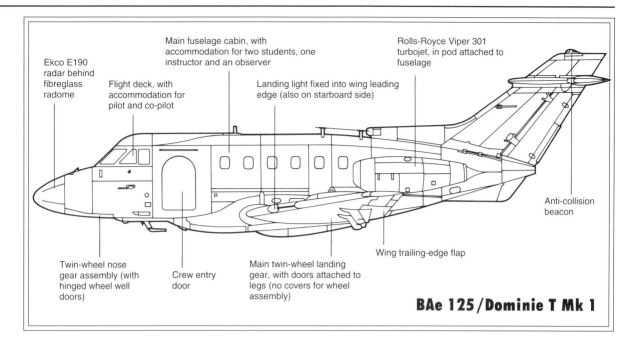

BAe 125/Dominie T Mk 1

porating a stretched fuselage and uprated Viper turbojets, which, again, have now been replaced with turbofans. The CC.3 is the latest variant to enter RAF service, based on the Series 700, with Garrett turbofan engines fitted as standard. The BAe 125 is a cost-effective passenger aircraft, used to transfer personnel between RAF establishments around Britain and Europe. Despite its value to the RAF, it is possible that expenditure cutbacks will see most, if not all, of the fleet withdrawn from use.

UNITS
125: *No 32 Squadron (Northolt).*
Dominie: *No 6 Flying Training School (Finningley).*

Below: A Dominie T.1 taxies out to begin a navigator training mission.

AIRCRAFT DIRECTORY

BAe 146

146-100: *Span 86ft 5in; length 85ft 10in; height 28ft 3in. Weight 47,000lb (empty), 76,000lb (max). Maximum speed 426kts. Maximum range 1,500nm. Two Avco Lycoming ALF502R-3 turbofans rated at 6,700lb thrust.*

Following its maiden flight on 3 September 1981, one British Aerospace 146-100 was leased by the Ministry of Defence for evaluation as a potential VIP transport in The Queen's Flight. After a trial period with No 242 OCU at Brize Norton, this aircraft was re-sold on the civilian market. The BAe 146-100 was selected for The Queen's Flight, and three aircraft were purchased for medium-range transport of members of the Royal Family and other VIPs. The aircraft have an increased fuel capacity and a specially designed 'Royal Suite' interior.

UNIT
The Queen's Flight (Benson).

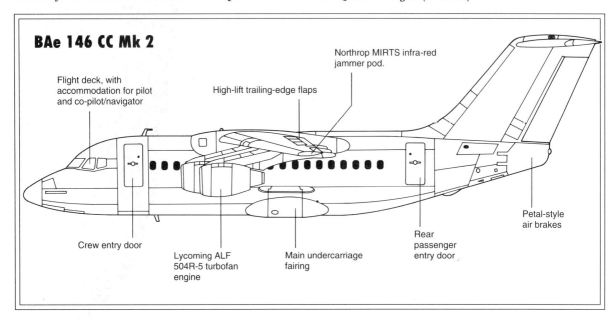

BAe Andover

Andover E.3A: *Span 98ft; length 77ft 11in; height 29ft 5in. Weight 28,295lb (empty), 50,000lb (max). Maximum speed 278kts. Maximum range 2,500nm. Two Rolls-Royce Dart RDa.12 turboprops rated at 3,245ehp.*
Andover CC.2: *Span 102ft 5½in; length 67ft; height 24ft 10in. Weight 28,432lb (empty), 46,500lb (max). Maximum speed 233kts. Maximum range 1,100nm. Two Rolls-Royce Dart RDa.7 turboprops rated at 2,280ehp.*

Above: An Andover E.3.

Flying for the first time on 24 June 1960, the Avro 748 was developed into a successful medium-range passenger and cargo transport aircraft. Shortly after the type's certification trials began, the Royal Air Force opted to purchase a redesigned version of the aircraft for tactical transport operations. The Avro 780 was designated Andover C.1 and entered service in July 1966. Following a reduction in the RAF's overseas commitments, the majority of the Andovers were withdrawn from service, but seven aircraft were converted to radar calibration configuration. Andovers were later purchased for passenger transport duties, and were operated by The Queen's Flight until BAe 146s were acquired.

The Andover E.3A was developed from the Andover C.1 and was operated by No 115 Squadron until October 1993 on radar calibration duties. The latter role has been temporarily transferred to a civilian contractor for a trial period, while some of the Andover E.3As have been transferred to No 32 Squadron for passenger and transport duties. The E.3A variant retains the rear-loading door and 'kneeling' undercarriage of the C.1. The Andover CC.2 is the RAF equivalent of the civil Avro 748, used for VIP and communications flying.

UNITS
E.3A: *No 32 Squadron (Northolt).*
CC.2: *No 32 Squadron (Northolt).*

Below: An Andover E.3A as operated by No 115 Squadron until late 1993.

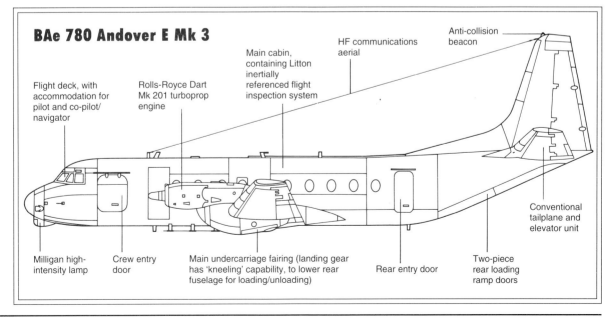

BAe Bulldog

Bulldog T.1: *Span 33ft; length 23ft 3in; height 7ft 5¾in. Weight 1,430lb (empty), 2,350lb (max). Maximum speed 130kts. Maximum range 600nm. One Avco Lycoming IO-360-A1B6 air-cooled piston engine rated at 200hp.*

A military trainer version of the Beagle Pup, the Bulldog was produced by Scottish Aviation until 1982, by which time the company had become part of British Aerospace. The Bulldog is the standard RAF basic trainer, having replaced the venerable Chipmunk. An order for 132 aircraft was placed in 1972, and deliveries began the following year. The Bulldog T.1 is the basic (and only) RAF variant, strengthened for service use and fitted with a wide range of avionics and instrumentation. The aircraft is operated primarily by the RAF's University Air Squadrons scattered around the United Kingdom.

UNITS
Central Flying School (Scampton); No 6 FTS; University Air Squadrons.

Above: A BAe (Scottish Aviation) Bulldog T.1
Below: A Bulldog of the Central Flying School.

BAe Canberra

Canberra PR.9: *Span 67ft 10in; length 66ft 8in; height 15ft 7in. Weight 30,000lb (empty), 57,500lb (max). Maximum speed 475kts. Maximum range over 5,000nm. Two Rolls-Royce RA24 Avon Mk 206 turbojets rated at 11,250lb thrust.*

Famous as Britain's first jet bomber, the Canberra has now virtually disappeared from RAF service: just one unit remains active at Marham, operating a small fleet for photographic reconnaissance and photographic survey work. The Canberra, in its original bomber form, first flew on 13 May 1949 and was quickly recognized as being an outstanding design in terms of capability and manoeuvrability, prompting the USAF to adopt the aircraft for light bombing and interdiction duties under the designation B-57. No 360 Squadron's Canberra T.17 electronic countermeasures (ECM) trainer aircraft are due to be withdrawn from service in late 1994,

Above: Canberra PR.9 nose section, illustrating the navigator's instrument panel and table.

Below: A Canberra PR.9 wearing the markings of No 29 (1 PRU) Squadron.

when the task is to be handed over to Flight Refuelling Ltd.

The Canberra PR.9 is the main Canberra variant in service with the RAF. Manufactured by Short Brothers, it features a significantly enlarged wing and uprated engines optimized for high-altitude photographic reconnaissance. The cockpit area is also revised, with a single-seat fighter-style canopy, the navigator sitting ahead of the pilot, enclosed in the forward nose section. Up to nine cameras can be carried internally, including the F.96 vertical camera with lenses ranging from 4in to 48in in focal

Above left: Canberra PR.9 camera bay in port forward fuselage.
Above: Nose section, illustrating the navigator's ejection seat and instrument consoles.
Below: The PR.9's canopy is offset to port. Grey/green camouflage has now given way to Hemp.

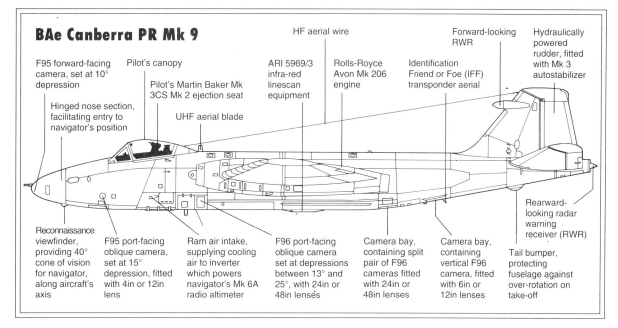

length. Infra-red linescan equipment can also be carried, giving the Canberra an all-weather and night capability, and flares can be used for night operations. Other, less publicized equipment can also be carried, including a long focal-length camera system housed in an underfuselage pod. Regular sorties are currently flown over Bosnia.

No 39 Squadron also operates three Canberra T.4 dual-control trainers for pilot conversion and continuation training, together with a pair of PR.7s on radar calibration duties.

UNIT
No 39 (1 PRU) Squadron (Marham).

BAe Harrier

Harrier GR.7: *Span 30ft 4in; length 47ft 1½in; height 11ft 7¾in. Weight 15,542lb (empty), 31,000lb (max). Maximum speed 575kts. Maximum range 2,263nm. One Rolls-Royce F402-RR-408 Pegasus Mk 105 turbofan rated at 21,500lb thrust.*

First entering service with the Royal Air Force in 1969, the Harrier was the world's first fixed-wing vertical/short take-off and landing aircraft. The initial GR.1 variant was upgraded to GR.3 standard, incorporating a new nose section to house a Ferranti LRMTS (Laser Ranging and Marked Target Seeker), and remained in RAF service until 1993 with No 1417 Flight in Belize and No 20(R) Squadron at Wittering. The GR.3 was used operationally during the 1992 Falklands conflict.

McDonnell Douglas purchased the rights to Harrier development and produced the AV-8B, a radical re-design of the basic Harrier airframe using an uprated version of the original powerplant and with a 50 per cent increase in fuel capacity, a 70 per cent increase in ordnance capability and a 60 per cent improvement in maintenance man-hours. BAe produced the AV-8B for the RAF under the designation Harrier GR.5, the first development aircraft making its maiden flight on 30 April 1985 and the first production machine being delivered to the RAF on 1 July 1987.

The Harrier GR.7 is a night-attack development of the GR.5 (and the interim GR.5A version), featuring a FLIR (forward-looking infra-red) system which connects with the pilot's NVGs (night vision goggles) and gives the aircraft the ability to operate by day or by night, in all conditions except thick fog. The GR.5/5As have progressively been upgraded to GR.7 standard. Weapons options include 1,000lb free-fall and retarded bombs, BL.755 cluster bombs, 400lb Type 155 rocket pods (each containing eighteen 68mm rockets) and Paveway laser-guided

Above: The Harrier GR.3 (bottom) was replaced by the 'new-generation' Harrier GR.5 (top), which, in turn, has now been developed into the GR.7 night attack variant. (BAe)

Below: Harrier GR.7 nose, illustrating the Angle Rate Bombing System window and forward-looking infra-red equipment.

1,000lb bombs. The Harrier GR.7 fleet will also eventually receive the twin ADEN 25mm cannon (each with 100 rounds) which is currently under development.

The GR.7 has a reconnaissance capability, with a Vinten VICON 18 Series 403 pod attached to the centreline hardpoint. The pod contains a Vinten 4000 infra-red linescan camera and a Type 753 panoramic camera. For long-range oblique photography a VICON 57 pod can be carried, containing a Type 690 camera (with 18in and 36in telephoto lenses) plus a fan of three cross-track cameras, together with a BAe Type 401 IR linescan and a Type 751 panoramic camera. Self-protection measures include AIM-9L Sidewinders and BOL-34 chaff and flare dispensers incorporated into the rear of the Sidewinder launch rails, together with tail-mounted radar warning receivers.

The Harrier T.4 is the twin-seat trainer derivative of the Harrier GR.3 single-seater. Retaining the

BAe HARRIER

single-seater's combat capability, at least one T.4 is attached to each Harrier squadron for pilot continuation training. The majority of the twin-seat Harriers are assigned to the Harrier Conversion Unit, No 20(R) Squadron at Wittering. The Harrier T.10, a combat-capable twin-seat trainer derivative of the GR.7, was ordered by the RAF in March 1990 and will enter service in 1995, replacing the aged T.4s.

Above: A No 1 Squadron Harrier GR.7.
Below: Starboard rear fuselage, illustrating the semi-extended air brake.

UNITS
Nos 1 and 20(R) Squadrons (Wittering); Nos 3 and 4 Squadrons (Laarbruch).

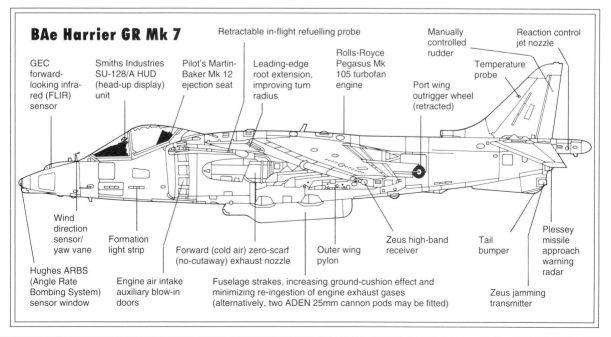

BAe Harrier GR Mk 7

- GEC forward-looking infra-red (FLIR) sensor
- Smiths Industries SU-128/A HUD (head-up display) unit
- Pilot's Martin-Baker Mk 12 ejection seat
- Retractable in-flight refuelling probe
- Leading-edge root extension, improving turn radius
- Rolls-Royce Pegasus Mk 105 turbofan engine
- Manually controlled rudder
- Port wing outrigger wheel (retracted)
- Reaction control jet nozzle
- Temperature probe
- Wind direction sensor/yaw vane
- Formation light strip
- Forward (cold air) zero-scarf (no-cutaway) exhaust nozzle
- Outer wing pylon
- Zeus high-band receiver
- Tail bumper
- Plessey missile approach warning radar
- Hughes ARBS (Angle Rate Bombing System) sensor window
- Engine air intake auxiliary blow-in doors
- Fuselage strakes, increasing ground-cushion effect and minimizing re-ingestion of engine exhaust gases (alternatively, two ADEN 25mm cannon pods may be fitted)
- Zeus jamming transmitter

BAe Hawk

Hawk T.1A: Span 30ft 9¾in; length 38ft 11in; height 13ft 1¼in. Weight 8,845lb (empty), 12,566lb (max). Maximum speed 575kts. Maximum range 1,313nm. One Rolls-Royce/Turboméca Adour 151-01 turbofan rated at 5,200lb thrust.

One hundred and seventy-six British Aerospace Hawks were ordered for the RAF as replacements for the Gnat advanced trainer and the Hunter advanced and tactical weapons trainer, and the aircraft first flew on 21 August 1976, deliveries beginning in November that year. The Hawk remains in widespread use with a variety of RAF units. No 4 Flying Training School at Valley and No 7 Flying Training School at Chivenor both operate a large fleet for advanced training and tactical weapons training, No 100 Squadron operates the aircraft as an airborne 'silent' target and banner target-tug, and No 6 Flying Training School uses it for advanced low-level navigation training. Perhaps the most famous operator of the Hawk, however, is the Royal Air Force Aerobatic Team, the *Red Arrows*.

The Hawk T.1 is the basic trainer variant used by the RAF. The advanced trainer does not normally carry any external stores, although the *Red Arrows* Hawks carry an externally mounted diesel fuel pod,

Top: Hawk T.1As belonging to the Royal Air Force Aerobatic Team, the *Red Arrows*.
Above: Sidewinder attached to the Hawk's starboard weapons pylon.
Below: A Hawk T.1 with No 6 Flying Training School's badge applied to the fuselage.
Below right: A Hawk T.1A of the Central Flying School.

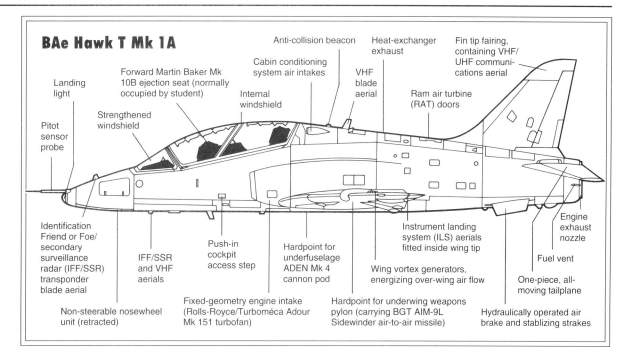

on the fuselage centreline, to generate coloured smoke during aerobatic demonstrations. The Hawk T.1A is a modified version of the basic airframe, equipped to carry two AIM-9L Sidewinders. It can also be fitted with a centreline-mounted 30mm ADEN cannon and wing-mounted Mk 100 CBLS (Carrier, Bomb, Light Store) practice-bomb carriers. The T.1A is also able to carry the Matra 155 rocket pod, although this weapon has not figured in the Hawk training syllabus for some time.

Although the Hawk is employed as an advanced trainer, the T.1A would be used operationally as a

point defence fighter in conjunction with radar-equipped Tornado F.3s, as part of the RAF's MFF (Mixed Fighter Force) concept.

UNITS
T.1/1A: *No 4 FTS, comprising Nos 74(R) and 208(R) Squadrons (Valley); No 7 FTS, comprising Nos 19(R) and 92(R) Squadrons (Chivenor); No 6 Flying Training School (Finningley); No 100 Squadron (Finningley); Central Flying School (Valley); The Red Arrows (Scampton).*

Right: Hawk port wing trailing-edge flap assembly.

BAe Jetstream

Jetstream T.1: *Span 52ft; length 47ft 1½in; height 17ft 5½in. Weight 9,600lb (empty), 14,550lb (max). Maximum speed 263kts. Maximum range over 1,000nm. Two Turboméca Astazou XVI turboprops rated at 940shp.*

Designed as a turboprop-powered executive transport aircraft, the Handley Page HP.137 Jetstream first flew on 18 August 1967. Full production was under way when Handley Page was declared bank-

Right: A Jetstream T.1 from No 45(R) Squadron, pictured during a training sortie.
Below: A Jetstream T.1, its undercarriage and flaps extended.

BAe JETSTREAM

Above: A Jetstream on the taxiway at Finningley.

rupt during 1970 and the assembly line was transferred to Scottish Aviation at Prestwick, now part of British Aerospace. The Jetstream T.1 was ordered for the RAF as a twin-engine pilot trainer to replace the Varsity. After entering service in June 1973 the aircraft were placed in storage following a change in RAF pilot training policy. From the initial batch of 26 aircraft, fourteen were eventually transferred to the Royal Navy as observer trainers (redesignated Jetstream T.2), while eight aircraft returned to RAF service. These latter are now operated by No 45(R) Squadron, the Multi Engine Training School (part of No 6 Flying Training School) at Finningley. The aircraft are used for twin-engine pilot training and for limited transport and communications duties.

UNIT

No 45(R) Squadron (Finningley).

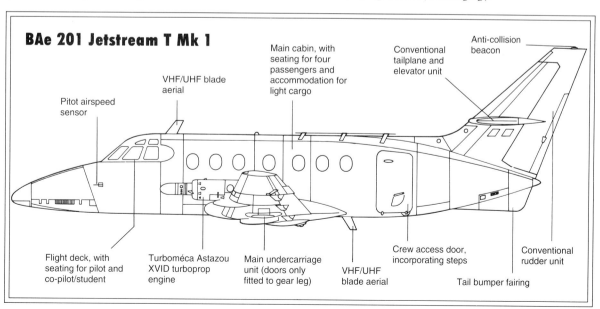

AIRCRAFT DIRECTORY

BAe Nimrod

Nimrod MR.2P: Span 114ft 10in; length 129ft 1in; height 29ft 8½in. Weight 86,000lb (empty), 192,000lb (max). Maximum speed 500kts. Maximum range 5,750nm. Four Rolls-Royce RB.168-20 Spey Mk 250 turbofans rated at 12,140lb thrust.

Purchased as a replacement for the venerable Avro Shackleton, the Nimrod started life in 1964 when Hawker Siddeley Aviation first began work on a long-range maritime patrol aircraft based on the proven De Havilland Comet airframe. The Nimrod's maiden flight took place on 23 May 1967 from Hawker Siddeley's Woodford aerodrome (where the Avro Shackleton had also been manufactured). The first production Nimrod MR.1 took to the air on 28 June 1968 and the first aircraft entered service with No 236 Operational Conversion Unit at St Mawgan on 2 October 1969. Nimrods were assigned to Nos 120, 201 and 206 Squadrons at Kinloss and to No 42 Squadron (together with No 236 OCU) at St

Below: A No 51 Squadron Nimrod R.1P. (John Hale)

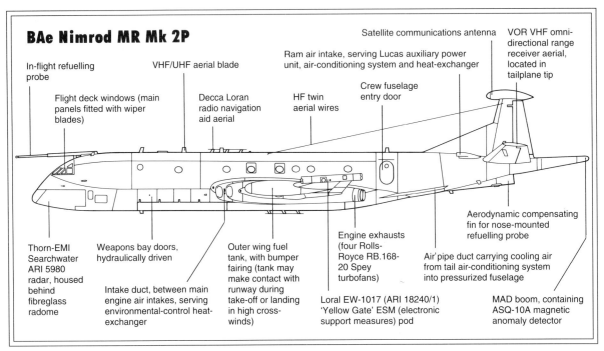

Mawgan. They were also based on Malta, with No 203 Squadron at Luqa. Three Nimrods were produced for electronic intelligence-gathering duties, becoming operational in 1974, and the aircraft was also intended to serve in the airborne early warning role as a replacement for the Shackleton AEW.2, but persistent problems with the radar system led to the cancellation of the programme and the purchase of Boeing E-3D Sentrys. The Nimrod's weapons options include Mk 44, Mk 46 and Stingray torpedoes, 1,000lb free-fall and retarded bombs, BL.755 cluster bombs and Martel and AGM-84A Harpoon anti-ship missiles. Self-protection equipment includes AIM-9L Sidewinders and BOZ-107 chaff/flare dispensers.

The Nimrod MR.2P is the variant currently allocated to the maritime reconnaissance, anti-submarine warfare and air/sea rescue roles. The fleet of MR.1s was modified to MR.2 standard during the early 1980s, the upgrade incorporating a new avionics suite, EMI ARI 5980 Searchwater radar and twin Marconi AQS-901 sonobuoy listening equipment. Following the 1982 Falklands conflict the Nimrod fleet was fitted with in-flight refuelling probes taken from retired Vulcan bombers, aircraft thus modified being designated Nimrod MR.2P. Loral 1017A ESM pods have also been fitted to the aircraft's wing tips.

Above: Nimrod nose detail, with radome removed.
Below: The RAF's Nimrod fleet is 'pooled' among four units and the aircraft rarely wear squadron markings, apart from representative badges applied for special events.

AIRCRAFT DIRECTORY

The Nimrod R.1P is a specialized elint (electronic intelligence) aircraft, three of which are currently in Royal Air Force service with No 51 Squadron at Wyton (moving to Waddington). The Nimrod AEW.3 was flown in pre-production form but never entered RAF service. One aircraft has been retained for ground instructional duties at Finningley.

UNITS
MR.2P: Nos 42(R), 120, 201 and 206 Squadrons (Kinloss).
R.1P: No 51 Squadron (Waddington).

Right: A Nimrod MR.2P turns at low level over home base at Kinloss in Scotland.

BAe VC10

VC10 K.2 (C.1K similar): *Span 146ft 2in; length 166ft 1in; height 39ft 6in. Weight 134,200lb (empty), 299,000lb (max). Maximum speed 505kts. Maximum range over 3,000nm. Four Rolls-Royce Conway Mk 550B turbofans rated at 21,800lb thrust.*
VC10 K.3: *Span 146ft 2in; length: 179ft 1in; height 39ft 6in. Weight 155,000lb (empty), 322,000lb (max). Maximum speed 505kts. Maximum range over 3,000nm. Four Rolls-Royce Conway Mk 550B turbofans rated at 21,800lb thrust.*

Originally a long-range airliner, the Vickers VC10 was developed into two variants, a Standard VC10 optimized for 'hot and high' performance and a Super VC10 featuring a lengthened fuselage and an additional fuel tank inside the tail, for transatlantic flights. Having flown for the first time on 29 June 1962, the VC10 was purchased by airlines such as BOAC, BUA and East African Airways. Early Royal Air Force interest in the aircraft was translated into

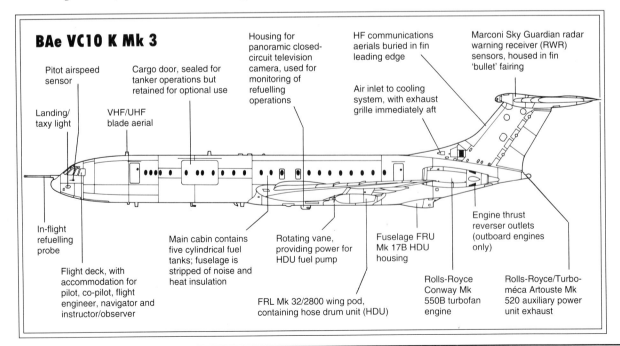

BAe VC10

Above: A VC10 C.1K taking off from Marham's runway.

an order for fourteen VC10 C.1s, the first of which made its maiden flight on 26 November 1965. The VC10 has proved to be an excellent strategic transport aircraft, and it was heavily involved in the 1982 Falklands conflict and also in the more recent Gulf War.

During 1978 the Ministry of Defence opted to purchase surplus VC10 airliners for conversion into air-to-air refuelling tankers, and a second batch of aircraft has recently begun conversion to this role. The C.1 is the original strategic transport variant, constructed for the RAF. During 1993 these aircraft began to be refitted with underwing refuelling HDUs, enabling them to operate both as transports and as refuelling tankers, with the new designation C.1K. The aircraft are now regularly fitted with bolt-on refuelling probes, giving them an even greater range.

The VC10 K.2 designation applies to five former Gulf Air Type 1101s which were converted to the refuelling tanker role by British Aerospace at Filton, the first conversion flying on 22 June 1982. Fitted with two underwing Mk 32 HDUs and a centreline-mounted Mk 17B HDU under the rear fuselage, this variant is also equipped with a closed-circuit TV system, enabling the crew to monitor the refuelling operations from the flight deck.

The VC10 K.3 is the tanker designation applied to four Type 1154 Super VC10s formerly operated by East African Airways. Like the K.2s, they were converted by BAe during the period 1982–84, and by September 1985 all five VC10 K.2/3s were in service with the RAF. The K.3 features a longer fuselage and retains the cargo door fitted to the Type 1154, and the inboard engine thrust reversers have been removed in order to standardize the VC10 engines across the fleet. The K.3's internal layout differs considerably from that of the K.2, most notably in the cockpit, where a navigator's station has been added (the position was designed as 'standard' in the K.2).

The K.4 designation applies to the latest batch of VC10s currently undergoing conversion to the tanker role. These former British Airways Super VC10s were purchased by the RAF and stored for many years at Abingdon before the latest conversion programme was initiated.

UNITS
C.1K: *No 10 Squadron (Brize Norton).*
K.2: *No 101 Squadron (Brize Norton).*
K.3: *No 101 Squadron (Brize Norton).*

AIRCRAFT DIRECTORY

Boeing Chinook

Chinook HC.2: *Rotor diameter 60ft; fuselage length (inc. rotors) 98ft 10¾in; height 18ft 11in. Weight 23,402lb (empty), 50,000lb (max). Maximum speed 161kts. Maximum range 1,093nm. Two Textron Lycoming T55-L-712 turboshafts rated at 3,000shp.*

Design work for the Boeing-Vertol CH-47, an all-weather medium transport helicopter for the United States Army, began in 1956 and the first YCH-47A prototype made its maiden flight on 21 September 1961. A total of 33 Chinook HC.1s were ordered for the RAF in 1978, the first example flying on 23 March 1980. The Chinook was heavily committed to operations in the South Atlantic during the 1982

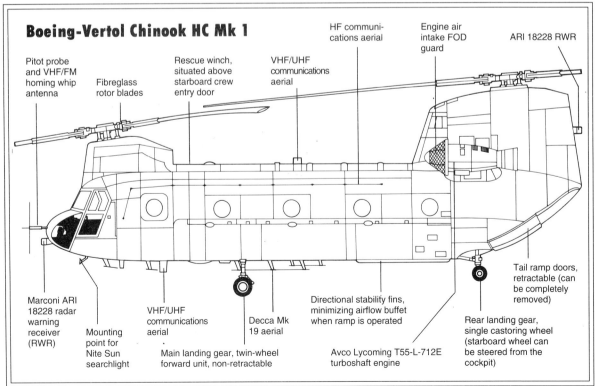

Falklands conflict, and three aircraft were destroyed when their transport ship was sunk; eight more Chinooks were ordered as a result.

HC.1B is the latest standard to which the fleet has been upgraded, but a further modification programme is currently under way to bring it to HC.2 standard, equivalent to the US Army's CH-47D. Modifications include a new automated flight control system, updated modular hydraulics, a stronger transmission, an improved T62-T-2B auxiliary power unit, airframe reinforcements, a new, low-infra-red-signature paint scheme and the addition of an infra-red jammer, chaff/flare dispensers, missile approach warning receivers and machine gun mountings. The programme will be completed during 1995.

UNITS
Nos 7 and 27(R) Squadrons (Odiham); No 18 Squadron (Laarbruch); No 78 Squadron (Mount Pleasant).

Left: Boeing Chinook HC.1,
Below: Chinook port engine detail.
Below right: Starboard fuselage winch pod detail.

Boeing Sentry

Sentry AEW.1: *Span 147ft 7in; length 152ft 11in; height 41ft 9in. Weight 332,500lb (max). Maximum speed 460kts. Maximum range over 5,000nm. Four CFM56-2A-3 turbofans rated at 24,000lb thrust.*

The Boeing E-3 was developed during the 1970s, the first aircraft entering service with the United States Air Force on 24 March 1977. Some 34 examples were produced for the USAF, and the 1,010th (and final) Boeing 707 airframe has been retained by Boeing for further E-3 development work. Following the cancellation of the Airborne

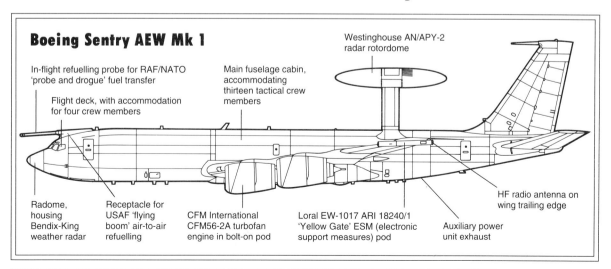

Early Warning Nimrod programme, the British Ministry of Defence announced an order for six E-3Ds on 18 December 1986, exercising an option for a seventh aircraft in October 1987. The first RAF E-3D made its maiden flight on 11 September 1989 and arrived in the United Kingdom during November 1990. The first handover to the RAF took place on 24 March 1991 at Waddington, where No 8 Squadron re-formed on the type before disposing of its fleet of aged Shackletons at Lossiemouth.

The E-3D, referred to as the Sentry AEW Mk 1 in RAF service, carries a flight crew of four and a specialist AEW crew of thirteen, although this latter figure can vary according to the type of mission being flown. The rotating pod attached to the upper fuselage contains a Westinghouse AN/APY-2 surveillance radar and IFF/TADIL-C antennae. In addition, Loral 1017 'Yellow Gate' (ARI.18240) ESM pods are attached to the wing tips.

USAF E-3s were used operationally during the Gulf War, and RAF E-3Ds fly regular AEW missions over the Bosnia region, normally direct from Waddington.

UNIT

No 8 Squadron (Waddington).

De Havilland Chipmunk

Chipmunk T.10: *Span 34ft 4in; length 25ft 5in; height 7ft. Weight 1,425lb (empty), 2,014lb (max). Maximum speed 120kts. Maximum range 250nm. One De Havilland Gipsy Major 8 air-cooled piston engine rated at 145hp.*

Designed immediately after the Second World War, the venerable Chipmunk still plays an important part in the modern Royal Air Force. Thirteen Air Experience Flights are equipped with the type, allocated to the Air Training Corps and flying large numbers of air cadets in order to foster an interest in aviation and the RAF. Many ATC cadets eventually join the Service, and the Chipmunk often provides them with their first taste of flying.

The T.10 was developed from the Chipmunk prototype, which first flew on 22 May 1946. Some 735 aircraft were purchased for the RAF, used for primary flying training for many years, notably with the University Air Squadrons, until Bulldogs were purchased as replacements. Two are assigned to the Berlin Station Flight at Gatow: for many years they were used to police the East/West German border, and to exercise Britain's right to fly in the area. but since the removal of the Berlin Wall they have been used primarily for communications and liaison.

UNITS

Berlin Station Flight (Gatow); Battle of Britain Memorial Flight (Coningsby); Air Experience Flights.

Below: A De Havilland Chipmunk T.10 from the now-defunct Elementary Flying Training School.

Lockheed Hercules

Hercules C.1: *Span 132ft 7in; length 97ft 9in (C.3 112ft 9in); height 38ft 3in. Weight 76,469lb (empty), 175,000lb (max). Maximum speed 325kts. Maximum range 4,250nm. Four Allison T56-A-15 turboprops rated at 4,508shp.*

The Royal Air Force was one of the first overseas customers for the Lockheed Hercules, a total of 66 C-130K variants being ordered, the first of which was delivered in September 1966. The C-130K is essentially a C-130H (as used by the USAF) but with British avionics. Designed as a versatile tactical transport, the Hercules is capable of flying from semi-prepared airstrips, and can operate over long distances if necessary through the use of air-to-air

Above: Hercules starboard fuselage detail.

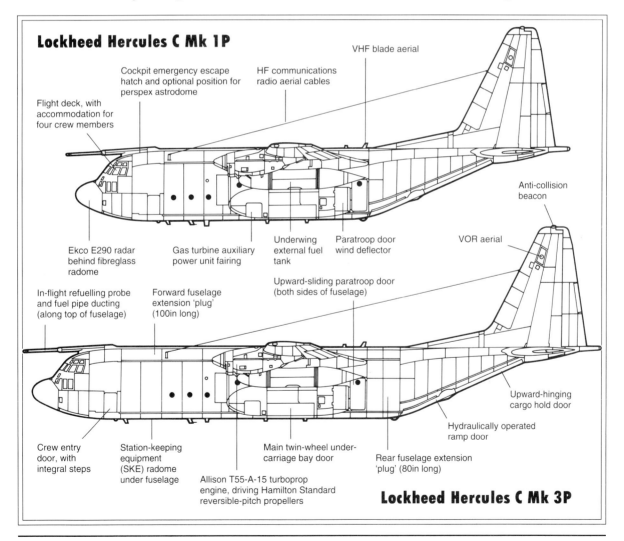

refuelling. The Hercules was heavily committed to transport operations during the 1982 Falklands conflict, and the aircraft was similarly employed in the Gulf during Operation 'Desert Storm'. Current duties include regular transport flights to and from Bosnia.

The C.1P is the basic RAF Hercules variant, fitted with a refuelling probe and associated piping running along the upper fuselage. Some aircraft are equipped with AN/ALQ-157 infra-red jammers, while most are now also fitted with AN/APN-169B station-keeping equipment. The C.1K is a modified tanker version of the C.1P, fitted with cylindrical fuel tanks (in the cargo hold) and a refuelling hose drum unit (HDU) on the rear cargo door. Racal 'Orange Blossom' ECM equipment is contained in wing-tip pods. Six aircraft were modified to this standard, although some are gradually being reconverted to C.1Ps.

The C.3P is a 'stretched' derivative of the C.1P, incorporating two 'plugs' which lengthen the fuselage by 15ft, thus increasing the aircraft's cargo-carrying capacity. Like the C.1s, these aircraft are fitted with refuelling probes. The Hercules W.2 is a specialized Hercules dedicated to meteorological research. One aircraft was converted to this configu-

ration by Marshalls of Cambridge and delivered to the RAF Meteorological Research Flight at Farnborough.

UNIT
Nos 24, 30, 47, 70 Squadrons (Lyneham); Meteorological Research Flight (Farnborough).

Above: Hercules C.1P flight deck: main instrument panel.
Below: A Lockheed Hercules C.1P from the Lyneham Transport Wing.

Lockheed TriStar

TriStar K.1: *Span 155ft 4in; length 164ft 2½in; height 55ft 4in. Weight 240,963lb (empty), 496,000lb (max). Maximum speed 525kts. Maximum range 6,000nm. Three Rolls-Royce RB.211-524B turbofans rated at 50,000lb thrust.*

Production of the Lockheed L-1011 began during 1968, leading to the first flight of the prototype on 16 November 1970. The TriStar design competed directly with aircraft such as the DC-10 and Boeing 747, which naturally restricted the potential sales success of the aircraft, and production was terminated after a relatively modest run of 250 aircraft, the last being completed in August 1983. The 1982 Falklands conflict highlighted the need for a greater RAF transport and tanker capability and resulted in the purchase of six TriStars from British Airways. The first aircraft to enter RAF service arrived at Brize Norton on 24 March 1986.

Below: A No 216 Squadron TriStar with No 74 Squadron F-4Js in trail. The Phantoms have long since been retired, although the TriStar is expected to remain in RAF service into the next century.

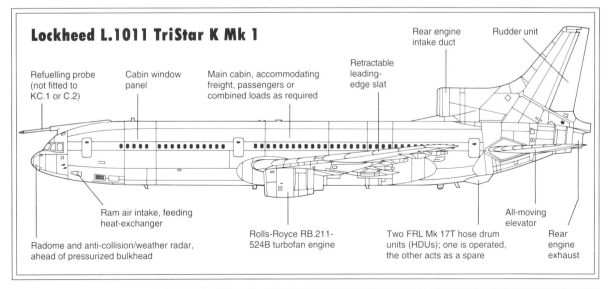

The TriStars are allocated air-to-air refuelling and strategic transport duties and are equipped with refuelling probes to enable them to maintain a global capability. Two K.1 aircraft are currently in service, configured for passenger operations and aerial refuelling, with a centreline-mounted twin HDU. Four KC.1s (including two additional TriStars purchased from Pan Am) are configured for combined passenger and cargo-carrying operations, with a 140 × 102in cargo door fitted to the fuselage and a roller conveyer system capable of accepting up to twenty cargo pallets or seating for up to 196 passengers. The aircraft also have a refuelling-tanker capability, with a twin HDU fitted to the rear fuselage. Two C.2 transports are also in service, capable of carrying up to 265 passengers and 35,000lb of freight. These aircraft will be fitted with underwing refuelling pods.

UNIT
No 216 Squadron (Brize Norton).

Panavia Tornado

Tornado GR.1: *Span 45ft 7½in (spread); length 54ft 10¼in; height 19ft 6¼in. Weight 30,620lb (empty), 61,620lb (max). Maximum speed over 800kts. Maximum range 2,420nm. Two Turbo-Union RB.199-34R Mk 103 turbofans rated at 16,075lb thrust with afterburning.*

Tornado F.3: *Span 45ft 7½in (spread); length 61ft 3½in; height 19ft 6¼in. Weight 31,970lb (empty), 61,700lb (max). Maximum speed over 800kts. Maximum range 2,420nm. Two Turbo-Union RB.199-34R Mk 104 turbofans rated at 16,520lb thrust with afterburning.*

The Tornado programme began in 1968 when a multi-national feasibility study was initiated, resulting in the Multi-Role Combat Aircraft (MRCA) which flew for the first time on 14 August 1974. The first production interdictor/strike (IDS) Tornado, designated Tornado GR.1 by the Royal Air Force, made its first flight on 10 July 1979 and the first aircraft to enter service was delivered to RAF Cottesmore, the home of the Trinational Tornado Training Establishment, on 1 July 1980.

The Tornado GR.1 is a low-level strike and ground attack aircraft which replaced the Vulcan and partially replaced the Buccaneer and Jaguar in RAF service. The aircraft are assigned to NATO, with four squadrons currently active in Germany and one reserve unit based in Great Britain. A variety of weapons can be carried, including 1,000lb free-fall and retarded bombs, laser-guided bombs, BL.755 cluster bomb units, JP.233 airfield denial weapons, BAeD ALARMs (Air-Launched Anti-

Below: A Tornado GR.1 carrying ALARMs. (BAe)
Right: A No 15(R) Squadron GR.1 carrying a BOZ-107 chaff/flare dispenser (starboard wing) and a Sky Shadow ECM pod (port wing).

PANAVIA TORNADO

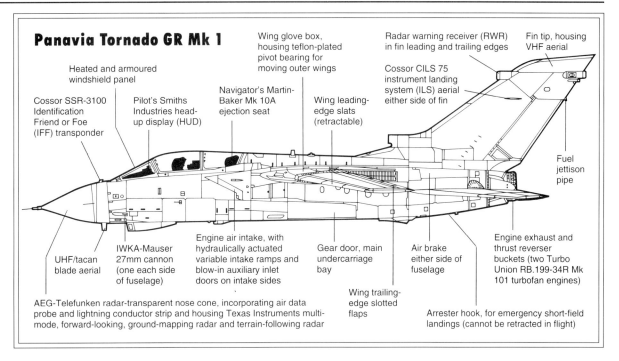

AIRCRAFT DIRECTORY

Above: Tornado GR.1 nose gear assembly.
Right, top: Starboard undercarriage bay.
Right: Port main undercarriage
Below: GR.1 engine exhaust pipes.

Radar Missiles) and the WE177B nuclear bomb. The GR.1 is also equipped with two Mauser 27mm cannon, each with 180 rounds of ammunition. For self-protection, an AIM-9L Sidewinder missile can be carried on each inboard pylon.

The aircraft was used extensively by the RAF during Operation 'Desert Storm', in the course of which the TIALD (Thermal Imaging and Laser Designating) pod was introduced, giving the Tornado a highly accurate laser designation capability which had previously been provided by Pave Spike-equipped Buccaneers. In addition to a pair of internally mounted GEC-Marconi passive radar warning receivers (giving fore and aft protection), the Tornado normally carries an ARI.23246/1 Sky Shadow electronic countermeasures pod and a BOZ-107 chaff and flare dispenser.

The Tornado GR.1A is a day/night all-weather tactical reconnaissance aircraft. The first development Mk 1A flew on 11 July 1985, the first service delivery following on 3 April 1987. The GR.1A carries no optical camera equipment, relying on synthetic electro-optical sensors which provide a better all-weather performance and easier interpretation. The primary sensors are a BAe sideways-looking infra-red system (SLIR) and a Vinten Linescan 4000 infra-red surveillance system. The recorded video film can be replayed in flight and transmitted

to a ground unit in 'real time' if necessary. This variant is fully combat capable, although the twin Mauser cannon have been removed in order to accommodate the reconnaissance sensors. It was first used operationally on 19 January 1991 during the Gulf War.

The Tornado GR.1B has replaced the Buccaneer in the maritime strike role: No 12 Squadron re-equipped in October 1993 and No 617 was assigned

Above: Hunting JP.233 munitions dispenser pods under a Tornado GR.1.
Below: A Tornado GR.1 armed with four Sea Eagle missiles. (BAe)

AIRCRAFT DIRECTORY

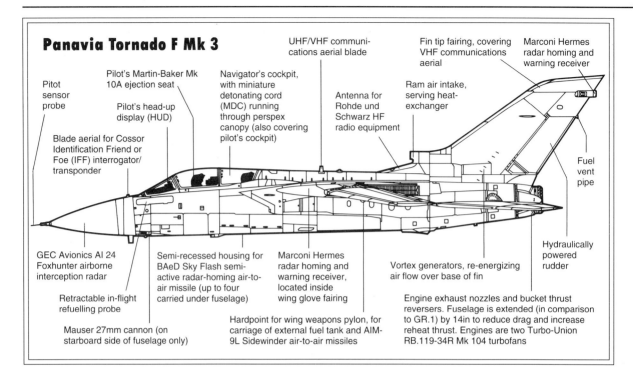

the task the following April. Some 24 aircraft were modified to this standard, equipped to carry four (eventually five) BAeD Sea Eagle anti-ship missiles. The GR.1B retains its original combat capability and will also assume the Buccaneer's 'buddy–buddy' refuelling capability.

Tornado GR.4 will be the designation applied to Tornado GR.1s which undergo a MLU (mid-life update). Modifications will include a new Marconi Defence Systems electronic warfare suite, an updated weapons control system, an advanced video recording system (with a ground replay facility) and

PANAVIA TORNADO

Below left: A Tornado F.3 of No 1435 Flight in front of a hangarette at RAF Mount Pleasant. (RAF Strike Command)
Above: A Tornado F.3 turning hard at low level.

a new computer loading system. The GR.4 will also be equipped with a new Ferranti head-up display (HUD) with computer-generated symbology and with a Smiths Industries colour CRT head-down display (HDD).

The Tornado F.3 is the air defence variant (ADV) of the airframe and currently equips six squadrons together with a reserve unit assigned to air crew training. The first ADV prototype's maiden flight took place on 27 October 1979 and the F.3 first flew on 20 November 1985. Deliveries to the RAF began on 5 November 1984 when the Tornado F.2 arrived at Coningsby. This first batch of aircraft was delivered without radar, and the much-publicized problems with the radar continued until the early 1990s, when full-capability equipment was finally fitted to the entire ADV fleet except for the F.2s, which by this time had been withdrawn to storage. The Tornado F.3 carries four BAeD Sky Flash air-to-air missiles, which will eventually be replaced by the Hughes AIM-120 AMRAAM. The aircraft also carries four AIM-9L Sidewinders and is equipped with a single internal IWKA-Mauser 27mm cannon.

UNITS
GR.1: *Nos 9, 14, 17 and 31 Squadrons (Bruggen); No 15(R) Squadron (Lossiemouth); Trinational Tornado Training Establishment.*
GR.1A: *Nos 2 and 13 Squadrons (Marham).*
GR.1B: *Nos 12 and 617 Squadrons (Lossiemouth).*
F.3: *Nos 11 and 25 Squadrons (Leeming); Nos 43 and 111 Squadrons (Leuchars); Nos 5, 29 and 56(R) Squadrons (Coningsby); No 1435 Flight (Mount Pleasant).*

Below: Retractable refuelling probe, Tornado F.3.

AIRCRAFT DIRECTORY

Pilatus Britten-Norman Islander

Islander CC.2: *Span 49ft; length 35ft 6½in; height 12ft 9¼in. Weight 4,114 (empty), 6,600lb (max). Maximum speed 150kts. Maximum range: 600nm. Two Allison 250-B17C turboprops rated at 320hp.*

The Britten-Norman Islander first flew on 13 June 1965, powered by a pair of Avco Lycoming piston engines. The quieter and more economical turbine-powered Islander is a direct development of the basic model, flying for the first time during August 1980. Although the Turbine Islander has not enjoyed huge sales success, the aircraft is still in production. The CC.2 designation applies to two aircraft purchased by the Ministry of Defence for the RAF Northolt Station Flight. Both are used for communications, liaison and light transport duties.

UNIT
Northolt Station Flight.

Below: One of a pair of Pilatus Britten-Norman Islanders used by RAF Northolt's Station Flight. (John Hale)

SEPECAT Jaguar

Jaguar GR.1A: *Span 28ft 6in; length 55ft 2½in; height 16ft 0½in. Weight 16,292lb (empty), 34,172lb (max). Maximum speed 625kts. Maximum range over 1,750nm. Two Rolls-Royce/ Turboméca Adour Mk 104 turbofans rated at 7,900lb thrust with afterburning.*

The Defence Ministries of Great Britain and France initiated the Jaguar project on 17 May 1965, a company named SEPECAT (Société Européenne de Production de l'Avion ECAT) being formed to manage the project. Although the Jaguar began life as an advanced trainer, the design was, largely because of RAF requirements, developed into a capable ground attack aircraft. The first example, a twin-seat trainer, made its maiden flight on 8 September 1968. Deliveries to the Royal Air Force began in 1973 and ended in 1978. Although the Jaguar was expected to be withdrawn during the early 1990s, the MoD decided to retain the aircraft on the RAF's inventory beyond the year 2000 (although a 1994 study suggests that withdrawal may in fact occur at an earlier date).

The Jaguar GR.1A is a single-seat, low-level, ground attack aircraft which replaced the Phantom in the interdiction and counter-air role. Delivered with Adour Mk 102 turbofans rated at 7,305lb thrust, the RAF Jaguars were fitted with uprated Adour Mk 104s (8,040lb) between 1978 and 1984. The GR.1 was modified to GR.1A standard when the original inertial navigation system was replaced by a Ferranti FIN 1064. Weapons include 1,000lb free-

fall and retarded bombs, Paveway laser-guided bombs, CBU-87 cluster bombs, BL.755 cluster bombs and 19-round LAU-500B/A pods of CRV.7 rockets. AIM-9L Sidewinders can also be carried, on overwing missile rails. Self-protection equipment also includes the Phimat chaff and flare dispenser and the ALQ-101 ECM pod. Radar warning receivers are fitted in a pod attached to the GR.1A's vertical tail.

The Jaguar GR.1A is also flown in the reconnaissance role by No 41 Squadron. A centreline-mounted 1,102lb BAe reconnaissance pod is carried for this task, containing five Vinten F.95 cameras together with one vertical infra-red linescan camera, although for Gulf War operations the linescan kit was replaced by an F.126 survey camera. One Jaguar carried a Vinten VICON LOROP (Long-Range Optical Pod). The reconnaissance-configured Jaguar remains fully combat-capable and retains the GR.1A's internally mounted pair of 30mm ADEN cannon, each with 180 rounds of ammunition. GR.1As have

Above: A Jaguar GR.1A wearing No 6 Squadron titles on the tail.
Below: A line-up of Jaguars at RAF Lossiemouth.

AIRCRAFT DIRECTORY

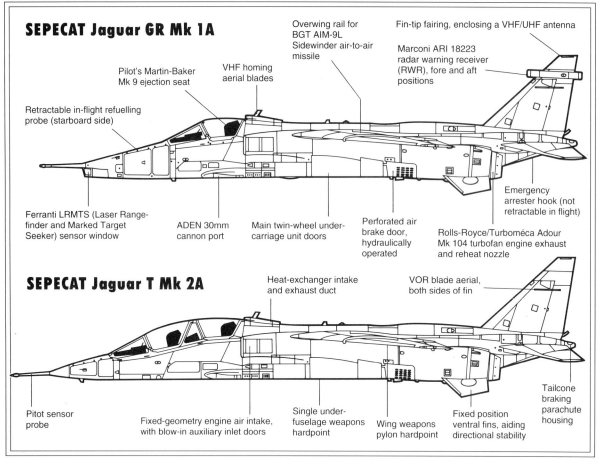

SEPECAT Jaguar GR Mk 1A
- Pilot's Martin-Baker Mk 9 ejection seat
- VHF homing aerial blades
- Overwing rail for BGT AIM-9L Sidewinder air-to-air missile
- Fin-tip fairing, enclosing a VHF/UHF antenna
- Marconi ARI 18223 radar warning receiver (RWR), fore and aft positions
- Retractable in-flight refuelling probe (starboard side)
- Ferranti LRMTS (Laser Range-finder and Marked Target Seeker) sensor window
- ADEN 30mm cannon port
- Main twin-wheel under-carriage unit doors
- Perforated air brake door, hydraulically operated
- Emergency arrester hook (not retractable in flight)
- Rolls-Royce/Turboméca Adour Mk 104 turbofan engine exhaust and reheat nozzle

SEPECAT Jaguar T Mk 2A
- Heat-exchanger intake and exhaust duct
- VOR blade aerial, both sides of fin
- Pitot sensor probe
- Fixed-geometry engine air intake, with blow-in auxiliary inlet doors
- Single under-fuselage weapons hardpoint
- Wing weapons pylon hardpoint
- Fixed position ventral fins, aiding directional stability
- Tailcone braking parachute housing

Below: Jaguar Laser Ranger and Marked Target Seeker window.

Below: Phimat chaff/flare dispenser under starboard wing.

also been progressively fitted with ALE-40 ECM equipment, attached to the lower rear fuselage.

The Jaguar T.2A is a twin-seat conversion trainer derivative of the single-seat GR.1A, retaining a similar combat capability. Although two T.2As are attached to each Jaguar squadron for continuation training, the majority of the twin-seat aircraft are assigned to the Jaguar Operational Conversion Unit, No 16(R) Squadron, at Lossiemouth. Like the GR.1, the T.2 was upgraded to T.2A standard with the introduction of FIN 1064 INS equipment; unlike its French Air Force twin-seat equivalent, and unlike the GR.1A, the T.2A does not have a retractable in-flight refuelling probe.

Above left: Starboard air brake, looking forward.
Above: Jaguar nose landing gear assembly.

UNITS
GR.1A/T.2A: *Nos 6, 41 and 54 Squadrons (Coltishall); No 16(R) Squadron (Lossiemouth).*

Shorts Tucano

Tucano T.1: *Span 37ft; length 32ft 4¼in; height 11ft 2in. Weight 4,872lb (empty), 7,937lb (max). Maximum speed 330kts. Maximum range over 1,000nm. One Garrett TPE331-12B-701A turboprop rated at 1,100shp.*

Purchased as a replacement for the Jet Provost basic jet trainer, the Tucano T.1 was developed jointly by Shorts and Embraer of Brazil from the EMB-312 airframe. The aircraft was selected from a short list of contenders primarily on grounds of cost (although the prospect of job creation in Northern Ireland also influenced the decision), and the first

Right: Front cockpit instrument panel and consoles, Tucano T.1

AIRCRAFT DIRECTORY

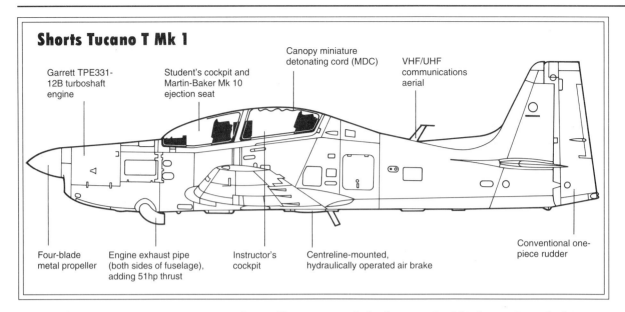

Shorts Tucano T Mk 1

- Garrett TPE331-12B turboshaft engine
- Student's cockpit and Martin-Baker Mk 10 ejection seat
- Canopy miniature detonating cord (MDC)
- VHF/UHF communications aerial
- Four-blade metal propeller
- Engine exhaust pipe (both sides of fuselage), adding 51hp thrust
- Instructor's cockpit
- Centreline-mounted, hydraulically operated air brake
- Conventional one-piece rudder

Below: Shorts Tucano ZF406 in a special overall blue scheme for 1993 air display appearances. **Opposite top:** A Tucano with its landing gear extended, photographed high over Lincolnshire. **Opposite lower left:** Tucano nosewheel detail. **Opposite lower right:** Vertical tail and rudder.

production T.1 made its maiden flight on 30 December 1986. The first example was delivered to the RAF during September 1988.

Used by the RAF as a basic trainer, the Tucano features a tandem seating arrangement, unlike the Jet Provost, which has a side-by-side layout. The Tucano's instrument layout is designed to resemble that of the Hawk in order to ease the student's transition from basic to advanced trainer. The final Tucano delivery to the RAF was made during January 1993. Students fly approximately 150 hours on the aircraft, after completing up to 60 hours of *ab initio* training on the Bulldog or Firefly.

UNITS
No 1 Flying Training School (Linton-on-Ouse); No 3 Flying Training School (Cranwell); No 6 Flying Training School (Finningley).

Westland Gazelle

Gazelle HT.3: *Main rotor diameter 34ft 5½in; length (inc. rotor) 39ft 3¼in; height 10ft 5.2in. Weight 2,022lb (empty), 3,968lb (max). Maximum speed 142kts. Maximum range 400nm. One Turboméca Astazou IIIA turboshaft rated at 590shp.*

Designed as a light observation helicopter for the French Army, the Aérospatiale SA.340 first flew on 7 April 1967. The Gazelle was produced under a joint agreement between Britain and France, and the RAF, Royal Navy, Army and Royal Marines purchased the type. The first production aircraft made its maiden flight on 6 August 1971.

The Gazelle HT.3 is operated by the RAF as a basic helicopter trainer, allocated to No 2 Flying Training School at Shawbury. After basic training, students progress to the larger Wessex. The HT3 is also operated by the Central Flying School detachment at Shawbury. The Gazelle HCC.4 is operated by No 32 Squadron from Northolt on a variety of communications duties.

UNITS
HT.3: *No 7 Squadron (Odiham); No 2 Flying Training School (Shawbury); Central Flying School (Shawbury).*
HCC.4: *No 32 Squadron (Northolt).*

Below: A Gazelle HT.3 used for communications duties and liaison flights, based at Northolt with No 32 Squadron.

Westland Puma

Puma HC.1: *Main rotor diameter 49ft 2½in; length (inc. rotors) 59ft 6½in; height 16ft 10½in. Weight 7,560lb (empty), 14,111lb (max). Maximum speed 143kts. Maximum range over 300nm. Two Turboméca Turmo IIIC4 turboshafts rated at 1,575shp.*

Manufactured by Britain and France as a joint design, the Puma was ordered for the RAF in part as a replacement for the Wessex, in the tactical support role. The first prototype SA.330 made its maiden flight on 15 April 1965, the first Westland-built Puma taking to the air on 25 November 1970. The Puma HC.1 was first delivered to the RAF in 1971.

Capable of performing a variety of roles, the Puma can carry up to sixteen fully equipped troops or six stretchers with four attendants. Equipment up to 5,500lb in weight can also be carried as an underslung load. Recent improvements to the Puma fleet have included compatibility with night vision goggles, the fitting of upgraded navigation aids and radar warning receivers and the installation of ECM.

UNITS
No 18 Squadron (Laarbruch); Nos 27(R) and 33 Squadrons (Odiham); No 230 Squadron (Aldergrove); No 1563 Flight (Belize).

Right: A Westland Puma HC.1, wearing a recently introduced two-tone green camouflage scheme.

WESTLAND PUMA

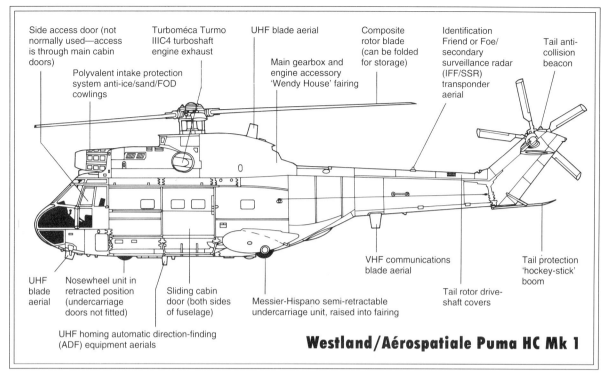

Westland/Aérospatiale Puma HC Mk 1

Westland Sea King

Sea King HAR.3: Main rotor diameter 62ft; fuselage length 55ft 9¾in; height 15ft 11in. Weight 13,762lb (empty), 21,000lb (max). Maximum speed 112kts. Maximum range over 700nm. Two Rolls-Royce Gnome H.1400-1T turboshafts rated at 1,660shp.

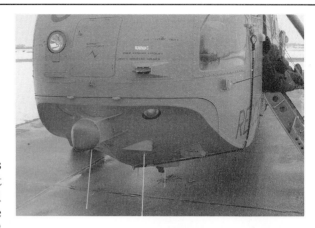

Developed from the Sikorsky SH-3, the Sea King was ordered by the Ministry of Defence as a replacement for the ageing Whirlwind helicopter in the SAR (search and rescue) role. The first deliveries were made during 1977, equipping Nos 22 and 202 Squadron. No 78 Squadron, based at Mount Pleasant on the Falkland Islands, also operates the Sea King on SAR and transport duties. Further deliveries of Sea Kings (Mk 3As) will enable No 22 Squadron to replace its remaining SAR Wessex helicopters, producing an all-Sea King SAR fleet with detachments at Chivenor, Valley, Lossiemouth, Boulmer, Leconfield and Wattisham.

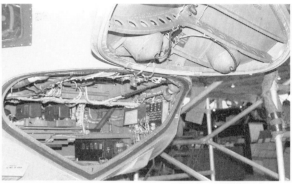

The Sea King HAR.3 features a MEL ARI 5955 radar, a Decca TANS (Tactical Air Navigation System) and a variety of rescue equipment. Although

WESTLAND SEA KING

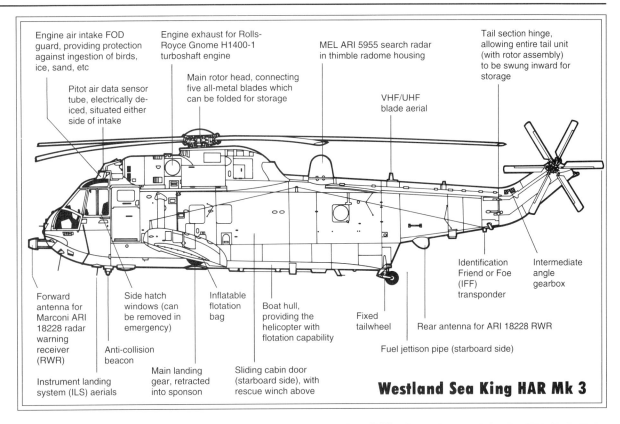

- Engine air intake FOD guard, providing protection against ingestion of birds, ice, sand, etc
- Pitot air data sensor tube, electrically de-iced, situated either side of intake
- Engine exhaust for Rolls-Royce Gnome H1400-1 turboshaft engine
- Main rotor head, connecting five all-metal blades which can be folded for storage
- MEL ARI 5955 search radar in thimble radome housing
- VHF/UHF blade aerial
- Tail section hinge, allowing entire tail unit (with rotor assembly) to be swung inward for storage
- Forward antenna for Marconi ARI 18228 radar warning receiver (RWR)
- Anti-collision beacon
- Instrument landing system (ILS) aerials
- Side hatch windows (can be removed in emergency)
- Main landing gear, retracted into sponson
- Inflatable flotation bag
- Boat hull, providing the helicopter with flotation capability
- Sliding cabin door (starboard side), with rescue winch above
- Identification Friend or Foe (IFF) transponder
- Fixed tailwheel
- Fuel jettison pipe (starboard side)
- Intermediate angle gearbox
- Rear antenna for ARI 18228 RWR

Westland Sea King HAR Mk 3

Left, top: A small number of Sea Kings have been retrofitted with tail- and nose-mounted radar warning receivers (RWR).
Left, centre: Nose section, with access panel open
Left: Sea King HAR.3s of No 202 Squadron.
Below: Starboard landing gear.
Right: Tailwheel, with access door open.

AIRCRAFT DIRECTORY

primarily assigned to the rescue of military personnel, the SAR Sea Kings are more regularly deployed on civilian rescues and casualty evacuation missions. No 78 Squadron's Sea Kings are fitted with radar warning receivers (RWR) and chaff/flare dispensers.

Above: A Sea King HAR.3 from No 202 Squadron.

UNITS
No 22 Squadron (HQ St Mawgan); No 202 Squadron (HQ Boulmer); No 78 Squadron (Mount Pleasant); Sea King Training Unit (St Mawgan).

Westland Wessex

Wessex HU.5C: *Main rotor diameter 56ft; length (inc. rotor) 65ft 9in; height 16ft 2in. Weight 8,657lb (empty), 13,500lb (max). Maximum speed 115kts. Maximum range 400nm. Two Bristol Siddeley Gnome turboshafts rated at 1,350shp.*

Following the success of Westland's turboshaft-powered version of the Whirlwind helicopter, negotiations were initiated to produce a similarly modified variant of the later Sikorsky S-58 design. After initial difficulties with the programme, the first converted airframe took to the air on 17 May 1957, leading to the production of a wholly Westland-built airframe powered by a pair of Napier Gazelle engines. The Wessex was purchased by the Royal Navy for anti-submarine warfare duties and by the Royal Air Force as a tactical airlift and SAR helicopter.

The Wessex HC.2 is powered by two Gnome turboshafts and first flew in 1962. For support and transport duties it can carry up to twelve troops or up to seven stretchers. Cargo can also be airlifted up to a weight of 3,600lb, either internally or as an underslung load. For search and rescue duties the helicopter is fitted with additional rescue equipment, and a third crewman (a winch operator/navigator) is also carried. It is also used for advanced helicopter training, following basic training on the Gazelle.

WESTLAND WESSEX

The Wessex HCC.4 is a specialized VIP variant of the HC.2; The Queen's Flight currently operates a pair of these, transporting members of the Royal Family and other important people. The HU.5C designation applies to five former Royal Navy airframes currently operated by No 84 Squadron at RAF Akrotiri on support and search and rescue duties.

Above: A Wessex from No 84 Squadron. (John Hale)

UNITS

HC.2: *No 22 Squadron (HQ St Mawgan); SARTU (Valley); No 28 Squadron (Sek Kong); No 60 Squadron (Benson); No 72 Squadron (Aldergrove).*
HCC.4: *The Queen's Flight (Benson).*
HU.5C: *No 84 Squadron (Akrotiri).*

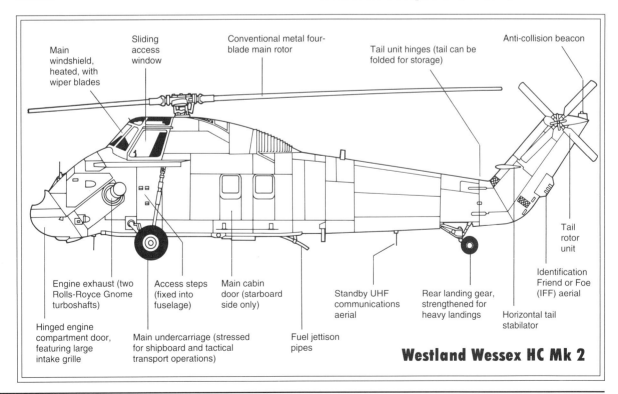

Westland Wessex HC Mk 2

AIRCRAFT DIRECTORY

Above: A Westland Wessex HC.2 from No 22 Squadron.

Below: A Westland Wessex HCC.4 of The Queen's Flight.

OPERATIONS PROFILES

BAe

OPERATIONS PROFILES

Tornado F.3

During the 1970s, as the Soviets introduced a new generation of long-range attack aircraft such as the Su-24 and Tu-26, it quickly became clear that the Royal Air Force required a new air defence fighter which was capable of countering this threat. Various fighter designs were studied and evaluated, including the hugely successful F-16 and F-15 interceptors. However, the former was found to be lacking in terms of weapons, avionics and range. The new fighter would have to be relatively sophisticated, with a sizeable weapons load, long range and a significant loiter capability, and able to handle multiple targets simultaneously. The F-15 was judged to be the more appropriate, but it was a single-seat design and a two-man cockpit was considered more suited to the RAF's needs. The F-14 Tomcat was virtually perfect for the role, but it was estimated that the cost would be significantly higher than that of a development of the Panavia MRCA (Multi-Role Combat Aircraft); moreover, the Tomcat's Phoenix missiles would be vastly more expensive than the Sky Flash which was being developed by British Aerospace. Consequently, the British Government opted for the MRCA's ADV (Air Defence Variant) design, and two prototypes were ordered during 1977.

After flying for the first time in 1979, the Tornado F.2 interceptor entered RAF service during 1984 with No 229 Operational Conversion Unit at Coningsby. The Tornado F.2's development proceeded very smoothly, with only a slight delay in delivery schedules, but the initial success was dogged by persistent problems with the GEC AI-24 Foxhunter radar, which fell far short of its predicted performance. As the Tornado F.2s were delivered to Coningsby, the radar was still being developed, and national media reports of aircraft flying with concrete ballast instead of radar units did little to improve the aircraft's reputation. Fortunately, these 'teething troubles' were eventually solved, and in 1987 the first Tornado F.3s were delivered to the RAF's first operational Tornado fighter unit, No 29 Squadron.

The F.3 was fitted with production-standard radar from the start (although further radar improvements continued for some time) and was powered by uprated Turbo-Union RB.199 engines. The early batch of eighteen Tornado F.2s was withdrawn and placed in long-term storage, and deliveries of F.3s continued as the Phantom and Lightning fleet was gradually replaced. Certainly, the Tornado F.3 has had to battle against an unfavourable reputation, thanks to the initial difficulties with the Foxhunter radar, but is fair to say that the aircraft has matured into an outstanding interceptor. As a Tornado pilot explains,

> You want an aeroplane that can detect targets at long range, looking up and down, coping with lots of targets simultaneously. You also need to carry lots of weapons over a long range. The Tornado F.3 meets these criteria in every respect apart, perhaps, in radar performance, which isn't quite as good as the manufacturer originally said it would be. But, having said that, it still performs very well indeed, so its range is more than adequate. For example, if I can't successfully intercept a target after picking it up at maybe fifty miles, then there's something wrong with me. Okay—a supersonic target might need to be detected at about seventy miles, but in that kind of situation the target would probably be fairly high, so our ground radar would pick him up and vector me on to it. So the F.3 is in no way deficient. It was never designed to be an air superiority fighter, so I wouldn't want to 'mix it' with a MiG-29 or a Su-27, but, having said that, I'd be much happier fighting against that kind of aircraft in a Tornado F.3 than in a Phantom.

The Tornado F.3 performs well, and more than matches the specifications for which it was designed. Unfortunately, the global political situation has moved on, and it is the role for which the aircraft was designed that is now almost obsolete. However, it would be unfair to suggest that the aircraft is incapable of meeting the air threats of the 1990s, as, in the right hands, it would be a formidable opponent. An F.3 instructor explains:

> The Tornado is much better suited to my job than an F-16 for example. I wouldn't want to be 150 miles out over the North Sea on my own in an F-16. Its radar is very limited in range. I've flown the F/A-18 and, okay, it's very nice, but to go the same distance and do the same things that we do in the Tornado, flying clean without external tanks, the Hornet would have to carry a belly tank, which would significantly reduce its performance. It's the fastest aeroplane around: there's absolutely nothing that could run away from us.

The days of regular Quick Reaction Alert (QRA) scrambles have long since gone, and Russian intrud-

TORNADO F.3

Above: Tornado pilot and navigator in front of their interceptor.

scenario for the mission, establishing the expected threat, the position of friendly forces, refuelling support, AWACS assistance and so on. The full flight plan, with turning point positions, refuelling tanker positions and rendezvous points, CAP (combat air patrol) patterns and missile engagement zones, will be fed into the Tornado's onboard computer system, either through a pre-programmed magnetic cassette tape or directly through the onboard multi-function keyboards. This information will then be available to the navigator on his CRT display screen and can be repeated on the pilot's electronic head-down display (HDD), although steering commands are normally routed to the head-up display (HUD).

Each Tornado is housed in an individual hardened aircraft shelter (HAS), and after a walk-round check has been completed the crew board the aircraft, complete the pre-start checks and start the two RB.199 Mk 104 turbofans before taxying out of the shelter. Once cleared on to the runway, the two aircraft take up their positions in line abreast and each pilot runs up the engines to full 'dry' power before selecting 50 per cent afterburner. Holding on the Tornado F.3's strong wheel brakes, the formation leader signals to his wingman and both aircraft release their brakes, simultaneously selecting 80 per cent reheat. With a combined thrust of 32,000lb, the powerplants produce an impressive take-off performance, and at 135kts the nosewheel leaves the runway before the aircraft lifts gently into the air at 150kts. After climbing away from the airfield, the two aircraft will settle into a transit 'battle' formation, flying line abreast and separated by about one mile. For larger formations of four or more (two-versus-two intercepts and so on), the second pair will fly in trail, keeping the lead aircraft in radar contact. Even without in-flight refuelling, the F.3's range is very impressive, more than twice that available to the Phantom. In January 1982 a Tornado F.2 prototype flew a demonstration CAP mission from Warton, covering 375 miles at altitude before flying a CAP pattern at low level for 2hrs 20mins. After flying back to Warton, the aircraft loitered for a further fifteen minutes before the it landed, 4hrs 13mins after take-off, with 5 per cent of its fuel remaining.

Inside the Tornado's cockpit the navigator's instrument panel is dominated by two multi-function CRT display screens (the pilot has a single screen which can repeat information available to the navi-

ers are now seen only very rarely. When a scramble is ordered, only a single aircraft is launched, largely as a token demonstration of capability, and the ensuing East–West encounter is invariably a friendly one. For more regular training exercises, Tornado F.3s are operated in pairs, providing the aircraft with mutual support through the use of pre-planned and well-rehearsed defensive and offensive tactics.

The pre-flight briefing for a typical training mission with an operational squadron takes place inside the unit's NBC-resistant (Nuclear, Biological and Chemical-resistant) Personnel Briefing Facility (PBF), where the details for the planned sortie are discussed. In addition to the usual 'domestics' (radio frequencies, weather, weapons and fuel loads, callsigns and so on), the briefing will describe the gator). With the radar in 'search' mode, the navigator will begin looking for targets once the aircraft is established in the appropriate CAP pattern. Most interception sorties revolve around a basic CAP pattern, which will be positioned around a specific point as pre-briefed or as directed by ground or airborne controllers. The CAP pattern is essentially a 'racetrack' circuit, in which one pilot flies towards the direction of the anticipated threat ('up-threat') while his wingman flies the opposite 'down-threat' leg of the pattern. There are variations on this basic arrangement, however, such as a visual search CAP, which is another 'racetrack' but flown 'broadside' to the anticipated direction of the threat. Used primarily by single aircraft, this pattern ensures that the aircraft is positioned 'tail-on' to the anticipated threat for as little time as possible. Ship protection CAP patterns are essentially the same as a basic CAP, but with a moving datum point, to keep pace with the ship or convoy that is being protected. Finally, a 'figure-of-eight' CAP pattern can be flown if necessary, to maintain a higher cruising speed (and thus retain more energy for manoeuvring) and to allow a single aircraft to keep important turns 'up-threat'. The position, speed and height of the CAP will vary, depending upon the nature of the threat, the weather, the available friendly forces and so on. The navigator will keep a careful watch on each radar return, the individual plots being displayed as short vertical lines, with a horizontal crossbar to indicate IFF (Identification Friend or Foe) response. By moving a four-quadrant marker (by joystick) over any of these plots, the target can be automatically tracked, the display format being switched to 'track-while-scan'. The speed, heading and height of the target can be displayed, and one CRT will normally be switched to the Tactical Evaluation Display, a north-orientated view of the entire surrounding area, featuring all available information from data-linked sources such as an AEW aircraft and other fighters, plus ground stations. This overall picture enables the crew to plan their activities and tactics effectively, and select the most appropriate targets.

With the radar in attack display mode, the navigator will select the most suitable weapon, probably a Sky Flash medium-range missile, while the radar constantly illuminates the selected target. An aiming dot appears over the target, providing a collision-course steering vector, with an allowable steering

Above: Hawk T.1As escorting a Tornado F.3. (BAe)

error (ASE) circle surrounding the dot. The circle diameter will vary, depending upon the missile's parameters and the distance to the target. Maximum and minimum launch ranges are also displayed, and provided the ASE circle is positioned over the aiming dot a successful missile 'hit' is likely. The Sky Flash is a very effective weapon, and it has demonstrated good reliability and 'kill probability' during trial launches. It can be used against both subsonic and supersonic targets from any aspect. It can also discriminate between targets flying in close formation, and it will continue to operate in hostile ECM (electronic countermeasures) environments. Perhaps the only disadvantage is that the Tornado must continue to illuminate the target after the missile is launched, sometimes causing the aircraft to close to within range of the target aircraft's own armament. However, with a new 'fire-and-forget' missile perhaps on the way, this weakness should also eventually be overcome.

Should a close-in 'dogfight' become necessary, the Tornado F.3 would still perform well. Despite the fact that the aircraft was not designed to 'turn and burn', the RAF's fighter crews are well trained to use the Tornado in this kind of situation. By depressing an air-to-air override button on the throttles, the pilot can obtain full HOTAS (hands on throttle and stick) control. The first depression of this button arms all missiles and the internal cannon and selects radar 'air combat' mode. Sky Flash missiles are selected, but a second depression of the button will select Sidewinders, and a third will select the cannon. With AIM-9 Sidewinders selected, steering cues will be displayed in the head-up display. With a diamond symbol in the HUD, signifying that the missile is locked on to the target, the missile is ready to launch.

The Tornado features a spin prevention and incidence limiting system (SPILS), which will automatically ensure that the aircraft cannot be flown beyond its limits. This enables the pilot to 'mix it' with hostile fighters in a relatively carefree fashion, safe in the knowledge that the aircraft will not allow him to do anything which would cause it to depart from normal flight. The AMDS (automatic manoeuvre device system) enables the Tornado to operate flaps, slats and wing sweep as necessary, leaving the pilot to concentrate on combat manoeuvring. Should the fight turn to the opponent's advantage, the Tornado pilot can simply 'unload' the high-g manoeuvres, sweep the wings back, slam the throttles into 100 per cent afterburner and fly away. With a top speed in excess of 800kts, the Tornado can easily exceed the structural limiting speed of most other combat aircraft, and the crew will have an opportunity to escape and re-engage as necessary.

Training missions often incorporate a variety of intercept profiles, sometimes including a rendezvous with a refuelling tanker. The Tornado F.3 can perform well without tanker support, but a 'hook-up' with a VC10 or TriStar is often made in order to maintain pilot proficiency. After refuelling, the Tornado formation may be vectored to a new CAP pattern, or back to base, depending upon the requirements of the sortie. Once back to base, the aircraft will close in to a relatively tight line-abreast formation before arriving over the airfield and breaking down-wind to land. The F.3's landing performance is particularly impressive, thanks to the combination of flaps, slats, air brakes, wheel brakes and thrust reversers, which will bring the aircraft to a standstill within 1,600ft from an approach speed of approximately 135kts. This capability enables the aircraft to be deployed to semi-prepared airfields in time of war, even stretches of public highway, should the home base be unavailable. Prior to landing, the throttles can be pre-armed to deploy the thrust reverser buckets as soon as the mainwheels make contact with the ground. However, on many peacetime training missions a more gentle arrival is practised, often with the nose held high along the runway, using aerodynamic drag to slow the aircraft in order to avoid unnecessary wear on the brakes.

Once the aircraft is safely back in its protective shelter, the crew will de-brief while it is refuelled for another mission. The single pressure refuelling point will allow a fuel flow of 2,400lb/min, which enables the ground crew to achieve fast turn-around times. Minimal servicing between flights is required, thanks to built-in fault location and ratification equipment and easily accessible LRUs (line-replaceable units). Largely as a result of the Gulf War (in which the RAF's Tornado F.3s participated), the F.3 fleet has been progressively modified, not least with the introduction of the latest Foxhunter radar, which has an improved close-combat capability and a better ECM resistance. The pilot's control column has been changed to an F/A-18-style stick, with all the main combat controls now comfortably within the pilot's grip. The radar warning receiver (RWR) equipment has been improved, and a combat boost switch has been added to the throttles, giving the engines an additional 5 per cent of thrust. Tracor ALE-40 chaff/flare dispensers have been introduced (with Vinten VICON 78 series dispensers in prospect), and Philips-Matra Phimat chaff dispenser pods can be carried as necessary. Radar-absorbent material has been added to the leading edges of the wings and tail and to other radar-sensitive areas. The Sidewinder launch rails also now incorporate Celsius Tech BOL chaff dispensers. Additionally, the Tornado F.3 is now being fitted with the US Joint Tactical Information Distribution System (JTIDS), which will give the aircraft a secure data link with other RAF and USAF fighters as well as airborne and ground-based command and control centres.

As a result of a series of seemingly endless Government expenditure reductions, the Tornado F.3 force is gradually being reduced in size. No 23 Squadron disbanded early in 1994, leaving Nos 11 and 25 Squadrons at Leeming, Nos 43 and 111 Squadrons at Leuchars and Nos 5 and 29 Squadrons, together with the Operational Conversion Unit, No 56(R) Squadron, at Coningsby and No 1435 Flight at Mount Pleasant.

Despite a less than auspicious entry into RAF service, the Tornado F.3 has slowly emerged as a very capable interceptor, which will provide the RAF with a very credible defensive capability until the Eurofighter 2000 eventually enters service.

Helicopter Operations

The Royal Air Force has maintained an active involvement in helicopter operations for almost as long as the helicopter has been in existence. The versatile 'chopper' has proved its value both as a flexible support aircraft and as a search and rescue platform. More recently, following drastic changes in defence needs, the helicopter has attained an even greater importance within the RAF, providing an ideal medium and heavy-lift transport capability in many inhospitable and remote areas: as conflicts of varying intensity continue around the globe, the need for helicopter support becomes even more vital. The Royal Air Force's medium-lift helicopter transport capability is currently provided by the Aérospatiale/Westland Puma assigned to No 33 Squadron at Odiham, No 18 Squadron at Laarbruch and No 230 Squadron at Aldergrove. In addition, the Puma/Chinook Operational Conversion Unit, No 27(R) Squadron, operates a small number of Pumas for training duties—this unit has a reserve wartime role as a support squadron—and a detachment of Pumas is also operated by No 1563 Flight in Belize.

The Puma's primary task is to support the British Army, transporting personnel and equipment as necessary, and the helicopter frequently participates in Regular and Territorial Army exercises. It also has a national contingency role, supporting flood relief efforts and transporting food supplies to isolated areas cut off by snow. Aeromedical flights are also sometimes made to transport patients or equipment. Although in wartime the Puma would probably be flown by a two-man flight crew, in peacetime the Puma has just one pilot, together with a crewman. The spacious cabin interior can accommodate up to sixteen troops, and the seats can be quickly removed, transforming the aircraft into a flexible cargo-carrier. Particularly large items of equipment can be carried, thanks to the installation of a heavy-duty cargo hook. Underslung load-carrying does have disadvantages, however, not least the need to fly at a relatively high altitude, which would naturally expose the aircraft to ground fire and radar detection. The cargo hook also requires the removal of an underfloor fuel tank, thus reducing the Puma's range. However, there are many advantages, including a rapid turn-round at the landing zone and an ability instantly to jettison a potentially hazardous load if necessary. Artillery units regularly take advantage of the Puma's capabilities, moving both ammunition and the 4,200lb Light Gun. In the aeromedical role, the helicopter can accommodate up to six stretchers together with attendants, and under wartime conditions a larger number of casualties could be carried, albeit in rather less comfort. A winch can also be used to extract personnel from otherwise inaccessible areas.

The Puma force would operate from dispersed locations in wartime, with perhaps four aircraft assigned to each dispersed site. Consequently the RAF Puma crews regularly deploy on field exercises, maintaining proficiency in off-site operations. Overseas exercises are also undertaken, not least in Norway, where the British Army regularly trains in recognition of the need to protect NATO's northern flank. The Puma can be transported in the cargo hold of a Hercules with relatively little disassembly, enabling the helicopter to be deployed around the world efficiently.

For heavy-lift helicopter transport, the Royal Air Force operates a fleet of Boeing Chinooks, equipping No 7 Squadron at Odiham, No 18 Squadron at Laarbruch and No 27(R) Squadron (see above). In addition, No 78 Squadron operates the Chinook from Mount Pleasant in the Falkland Islands. Although essentially the same as the US Army's CH-

HELICOPTER OPERATIONS

Left, upper: A Wessex of No 2 FTS. (John Hale)
Left, lower: A Puma HC.1 equipped with nose- and tail-mounted RWR.
Above: A Boeing Chinook HC.1 makes a low pass along St Mawgan's main runway.

47D, the RAF's Chinook HC.1 and HC.2 helicopters are fitted with updated transmission systems, a triple hook system and single-point pressure refuelling. Like the Puma, the Chinook is assigned primarily to the support of the British Army, and its introduction into RAF service led to fairly drastic changes in the Army's concept of air-mobile operations, thanks to the huge increase in capability which the helicopter provided.

The Chinook is manned by two pilots and two crewmen, but a small number of navigators are also assigned to the fleet, taking the second seat on the flight deck when necessary. The helicopter can carry loads both internally and externally, being capable of lifting up to 20,000lb on the front and rear hooks or 28,000lb on the centre hook. Internally, a pair of Land Rovers or a pair of 105mm guns can be accommodated, and seats for up to 44 troops can be installed. However, the Chinook's personnel-carrying capability is limited by capacity rather than weight. During the 1982 Falklands conflict a Chinook carried 81 paratroopers on one sortie, and during the Vietnam War a US Army CH-47 lifted 140 passengers. For casualty evacuation, up to 24 stretchers can be carried. Equipment and personnel can be loaded relatively easily thanks to the clamshell rear doors, and a winch can be fitted to lift personnel from inaccessible areas. RAF Chinook crews are trained for search and rescue (SAR) operations, giving this versatile helicopter a useful additional capability, although the huge rotor blades create a strong downwash, requiring a high hovering altitude. The Chinook can land on water if necessary, as the fuselage is seaworthy, although RAF Chinooks are not waterproofed and the dangers of corrosion preclude such operations except in an emergency.

Like the Puma force, the RAF Chinooks would be deployed to field sites in wartime, and regular off-site exercises are conducted, almost always in conjunction with the Army. Overseas exercises are also made to various destinations, largely within Europe. Improvements to the Chinook airframe and avionics continue, the most recent including a night vision capability.

As an indication of the increasing importance of helicopter support, the Royal Air Force formed an additional unit in 1992 when No 60 Squadron re-formed with Wessex helicopters at Benson, joining No 72 Squadron in Northern Ireland, No 28 Squadron in Hong Kong and No 84 Squadron in Cyprus. Although the Westland Wessex is a somewhat aged design, the need for more and more support helicopters has ensured that it is likely to remain in service for some considerable time, although replacements in the form of EH.101s are likely to be acquired in due course.

The Wessex is less capable than the Puma in terms of its lifting capability, and the emphasis is placed on the airlifting of personnel rather than the transport of equipment. However, up to eight fully equipped troops can be accommodated, providing the Army with a useful capability additional to the heavily committed Puma and Chinook force. The trend towards Army night operations has led to the introduction of night vision goggles (NVGs) for the Wessex crews, and, like the Puma and Chinook, the helicopter can be fitted with a Nightsun searchlight (producing some 30 million candlepower) and an infra-red filter for night operations.

Perhaps the best known aspect of RAF helicopter activity is the search and rescue (SAR) role performed by a fleet of Wessex and Sea King helicopters. The Wessex is gradually being withdrawn from the SAR role as new Sea Kings are delivered, equipping Nos 22 and 202 Squadrons, together with No 78 Squadron (a combined Chinook/Sea King support/SAR unit) on the Falkland Islands. The RAF search and rescue service provides all-year round emergency cover for both sea and land incidents. Although intended primarily for military service, the SAR fleet flies most of its sorties in support of civilian emergencies. The Wessex has a 90nm range and a capacity to carry up to fourteen survivors, together with the three-man crew of pilot, navigator and winchman. The Sea King is much more capable, with a 280nm range and a capacity for eighteen survivors. The Sea King's automatic flight control system enables the helicopter to move from forward flight into an automatic doppler-controlled hover which can be used in conjunction with other homing aids and radar, giving the aircraft a true all-weather and night capability which has been used to advantage during a variety of emergency rescues. The Sea King's crew comprises a pilot and navigator, a radar/winch operator and a winchman.

In May 1990 the RAF completed one of the world's longest rescue missions when a Sea King from RAF Brawdy recovered an injured crewman from a yacht participating in a 'round-the-world' race. The rescue took place some 610 miles off Land's End and required a thirteen-hour flight, involving refuelling stops in Ireland and on board the Royal Fleet Auxiliary *Argus*.

Hercules

The Lockheed C-130 Hercules has enjoyed a long and distinguished association with the Royal Air Force since first entering service during 1967, when the first aircraft arrived at RAF Thorney Island on 3 May. Without doubt, the famous 'Herky Bird' has earned a place in aviation history as the most successful transport aircraft ever to have been built, and its success continues, with more rolling off the production line in Georgia for military and civilian operators around the world. Although the RAF has sometimes been forced to operate aircraft types which were less than ideal for their tasks (usually because of inept Governmental decision-making), the Hercules is a rare example of a 'perfect' aeroplane, so much so that, a quarter of a century after its entry into RAF service, there is still no clear candidate to replace it... except perhaps another Hercules!

RAF Lyneham near Chippenham in Wiltshire is the home of the RAF's Hercules fleet (known collectively as the Lyneham Transport Wing), which reached a staggering one million flying hours on 27 March 1990. All previous records would be broken, however, when the Hercules began its participation in Operations 'Granby' and 'Haven' during 1990-91. Throughout these operations the RAF crews became expert in the skills of low-level desert flying and rough-strip landings. Over 40,000 hours were flown in a seven-month period, and approximately 50,000 tonnes of freight were carried.

During 1992 RAF Lyneham celebrated the Silver Jubilee of the Hercules' entry into RAF service. RAF Lyneham has a conventional four-Wing organization covering Operations, Engineering, Administration and Supply. However, the span of control for the Station Commander is somewhat larger than at most RAF establishments. UK Mobile Air Movements Squadron (UKMAMS) is technically a lodger unit at Lyneham, although its function is obviously an integral part of air transport operations. Equally important is the part played by other lodger units— No 47 (Air Dispatch) Squadron and the Royal Logistics Corps—in the preparation, loading and dispatch of air-dropped stores.

With all engineering at Lyneham fully centralized, the four squadrons (Nos 24, 30, 47 and 70) are made up of aircrew only. Currently there are 22 or 23 five-man crews assigned to each squadron. All four squadrons are employed in the basic air transport (AT) role, carrying freight and passengers around the world. The squadrons each have other roles, however, Nos 24 and 30 Squadrons specializing in airborne refuelling operations whilst Nos 47 and 70 are tasked with tactical support (the airdropping of paratroops and supplies). No 57(R) Squadron is the Hercules Operational Conversion Unit, where new C-130 crews are trained. With a staff of more than 130, it is the RAF's largest OCU, comprising six component units. The Groundschool and Hercules Conversion Squadron deal with the initial training of some 28 crews each year. The Hercules Training Squadron provides annual refresher training for approximately 90 crews a year, together with short co-pilot-to-captain courses. The Simulator Squadron operates three Hercules flight simulators, providing conversion and refresher training for the RAF and also operating 'on hire' to overseas air forces. The Support Training Squadron trains tactical crews for Nos 47 and 70 Squadrons, and the Tanker Training Flight trains crews in air-to-air refuelling techniques. RAF Lyneham's Operations Wing operates 24 hours a day, 365 days a year, simply because the Station's air transport movements cannot be constrained by normal working hours.

UKMAMS comprises two fairly distinct elements, the Base Movements Flight, which is responsible for the processing of all passengers and freight through Lyneham, and the Mobile Teams, which may be deployed at short notice anywhere in the world to load or unload any of the RAF's transport aircraft. Thanks to a somewhat anomalous (but thoroughly workable) arrangement, an Army unit is responsible for the preparation, loading and dispatch of all stores which are air-dropped from RAF aircraft. Personnel from No 47 (Air Dispatch) Squadron RLC fly as crew members when assigned to air-drop operations. Lyneham's Engineering Wing boasts some 1,300 personnel and is the Station's largest section by far. All Hercules servicing is centralized, and the Engineering Wing carries out all first- and second-line servicing on all the RAF's Hercules, including the second-line servicing of the single Hercules W.2 devoted to meteorological research at Farnborough. The periodicity for aircraft servicing is based on flying hours, which reduces the servicing cycle and provides some relief of pressure on the limited amount of hangarage at Lyneham.

Lyneham is one of only a few RAF stations to retain its own Supply Wing, which also includes responsibility for MT operations (known collectively as the Supply and MT Wing), providing logistics and spares support for the Station and its aircraft, wherever the latter may be deployed around the world. The Administrative Wing provides service support for a uniformed civilian staff of more than 3,300, and their dependants (numbering up to 10,000) and an estate covering some 2,500 acres containing some 690 working buildings and 900 married quarters. In addition, the base also has a Royal Auxiliary Air Force Defence Flight with an establishment of 103 personnel, tasked with the defence of the station's facilities.

RAF Lyneham, like any front-line station, is constantly prepared to assume a Transition to War (TTW) posture should an armed conflict develop. In a TTW situation, Lyneham's principal task would be the support of NATO. The Hercules fleet would also be heavily involved in the recovery of any British forces in overseas locations, for example the Falkland Islands, and would then become totally committed to the deployment of British forces to whatever locations might be specified, within the NATO area. Reinforcement and re-supply tasks would probably continue beyond the outbreak of hostilities, with routes and tactics amended where possible to reduce the threat to the unarmed and poorly protected transport aircraft. Outside the NATO area the Hercules force could be engaged in operations to deploy and support British forces almost anywhere in the world. Indeed, the two tactical squadrons (Nos 47 and 70) are tasked in peacetime to provide air mobility for the United Kingdom's out-of-area intervention force, No 5 Airborne Brigade, should that force be deployed to conduct an evacuation of British nationals. However, not all non-NATO emergency situations require the seizure of an airhead and the intervention of an armed force—in many cases a standard airlift will suffice. Nevertheless, the Hercules brings an impressive list of capabilities to any out-of-area operation.

Primarily, the Hercules is a tactical support aircraft, normally flying medium-altitude transits using built-in station-keeping equipment (SKE) to maintain formations as necessary. Low-level approaches to drop zones or airheads can be performed when required. Special Forces operations are also a major activity for the LTW Hercules crews, and low-level air-drop missions can be flown with night-vision equipment. Airfield assault insertion flights play a part within this role. As a secondary duty, the Hercules can fly maritime reconnaissance missions, and the aircraft can also operate as a search and rescue (SAR) platform, able to drop air/sea rescue equipment and fly patrols of up to ten hours. The Hercules fleet is also capable of refuelling in flight, giving the aircraft a very flexible endurance. A small

Below: Hercules C.3P XV177 was the first C-130K to enter regular service with the RAF. In its original guise it was an 'unprobed', 'unstretched' C.1.

number of the aircraft are equipped to operate as airborne refuelling tankers, although this capability is scheduled to be withdrawn in order that these aircraft may be reconfigured for the transport role.

Since first entering service in 1967, the RAF Hercules fleet has been involved in a range of operational tasks worldwide, in addition to the normal trooping and freighter activities. Some of the notable activities have included 'Khana Cascade' (the annual Nepal famine relief exercise), the Cyprus evacuation (following the Turkish invasion), Managua (earthquake relief), Cambodia (famine relief), Rhodesia (support of the ceasefire-monitoring force), 'Corporate' (the capture of the Falkland Islands), 'Bushel' (Ethiopian famine relief), 'Granby' (the Gulf War), 'Haven' (Northern Iraq: Kurdish relief), 'Cheshire' (Sarajevo: humanitarian relief) and 'Vigour' (Somalia: famine relief).

The Royal Air Force's C-130Ks are essentially standard C-130H aircraft fitted with British avionics, and with major airframe sections constructed in the United Kingdom. Sixty-one aircraft from a batch of 66 remain in use, developed into four versions. The C.1P is the 'standard' aircraft, essentially unchanged since entry into RAF service, the 'P' suffix referring to an aerial refuelling capability, the Hercules fleet having been progressively fitted with the necessary probes and associated piping. Capable of carrying 92 ground troops, 66 paratroops, 74 stretcher cases or vehicles and freight up to 20 tons in weight over distances of up to 4,600 miles and at speeds of about 340kts, the Hercules is equipped with reversible-pitch propellers, enabling the aircraft to 'backtrack' and perform three-point turns—a useful capability when it is operating from small, semi-prepared airstrips.

The C.3P was introduced from 1980 as a 'stretched' version of the basic C.1. The weight-carrying capability of the Hercules C.1 often exceeds the size restriction placed upon freight by the dimensions of the C-130's cargo hold. Consequently Lockheed introduced a 'stretch' option which lengthened the fuselage, enabling more cargo to be carried up to the aircraft's weight limits. Thirty of the RAF's Hercules fleet were converted to C.3 standard by adding an extra fifteen feet of fuselage structure through the insertion of two 'plugs', one forward of the wing section and one behind. The lengthened fuselage increases the volume of the cargo compartment by 37 per cent, which, in simple terms, means

Above: The Lockheed Hercules W.2—the sole aircraft operated by the Meteorological Research Flight at Farnborough.

capacity for an extra Land Rover or 24 more paratroops. In all other respects the C.3P remains essentially the same as a C.1P. The standard crew for the Hercules consists of a pilot (Captain), co-pilot, navigator, flight engineer and air loadmaster.

The Hercules C1.KP is a C.1P aircraft converted to the air-to-air refuelling tanker role. Four large long-range fuel tanks are fitted inside the aircraft's cargo hold, and a Mk 17 HDU (hose drum unit) is installed on the rear ramp door. Four aircraft were converted to this standard in just 87 days by Marshall Engineering, in response to an urgent requirement in 1982 as a result of the Falklands conflict. More recently the increasing need for transport aircraft has prompted a decision to reconfigure these tankers as standard freight/troop carriers. The most unusual Hercules variant is the W.2, operated by the Royal Air Force Meteorological Research Flight at Farnborough. A modified C.1, it is a flying weather research laboratory, affectionately known as 'Snoopy' because of the huge instrumentation boom attached to its nose.

The Hercules fleet has been established in RAF service for more than 25 years and the aircraft have been the subject of various upgrades and modifications, some of which are as follows:

About 1969: Replacement of some integral wing fuel tanks which suffered corrosion owing to the use of contaminated fuel.

1978 onwards: The stretching of 30 airframes to C.3 standard. The 15ft extension increased the volume of the cargo hold by 37 per cent, effectively adding nine new airframes to the fleet without the necessity for any additional equipment or personnel.

About 1979: A specimen wing centre-section failed under fatigue test and the entire RAF Hercules fleet was fitted with a redesigned assembly.

1979–85: Fatigue life extension programme, involving modifications to the outer wing sections, wing joints and engine mounts.

April 1982: Marshalls completed the first installation of an air-to-air refuelling probe on a Hercules, just ten days after the requirement was issued.

June 1982: Marshalls completed the first of six tanker conversions.

Post-1982: Omega navigation equipment was installed, and refuelling probes were fitted to the entire Hercules fleet.

Post-1983: Station-keeping equipment (SKE) was fitted to a portion of the C.3P fleet.

Post-1991: Updated tacan was fitted to the entire fleet.

The operational highlights of the past 25 years reflect the innate flexibility of the Hercules and the diversity of the air transport task:

1967: Withdrawal from Aden—52 evacuation sorties to Bahrain, all but one achieving a turn-around time at Aden of less than 30 minutes. Recovery of the RAF El Adem Desert Rescue Team from the Kufra Oasis.

1968: Resupply of the British Transarctic Expedition. Recovery of a Hawker Hind from Kabul, Afghanistan.

1969: Deployment of Marines and police to quell the Anguillan rebellion.

1970: Red Cross relief support in Jordan. Airlift of relief supplies to Turkey and Peru following earthquakes, and to East Pakistan following a cyclone disaster.

1971: Airlift of medical supplies to Calcutta to help stem a cholera epidemic. Indo–Pakistani War—extraction of British nationals from Karachi and Chakala to the safety of Masirah.

1972: Initial withdrawal of British troops from Malta. Rapid deployment of troops to Belize to counter threat of invasion by neighbouring Guatemala. Assistance with typhoon relief in the Philippines. Emergency airlift of relief supplies to Nicaragua (on Christmas Day) following an earthquake.

1973: Mercy missions to famine areas in Southern Sudan and in Mali, Senegal and other areas of West Africa. Operation 'Khana Cascade'—a four-aircraft detachment to Nepal to drop food to starving people in the remote western regions of the country (1,964 tons of food air-dropped in 29 days). Airlift of 900 non-British troops into Cairo to establish the UN peace-keeping force in the wake of the Yom Kippur War.

1974: Relief supplies dropped to St Helena. Assistance given in the Darwin area following its devastation by Cyclone 'Tracy'. Further famine relief in North Africa. Following a *coup* in Cyprus and a Turkish invasion, an intensive airlift to extract Service families and international tourists from Kingsfield airstrip in Dhekalia, to the safety of RAF Akrotiri and thence to the United Kingdom (some 5,148 people of 46 nationalities evacuated).

1975: Evacuation (under mortar fire in one instance) of the British Embassy staff in Saigon, following the fall of the city. Reinforcement of Belize following a heightening of tension in the area.

1976: Relief supplies flown to the Van area of Turkey following an earthquake.

1977: Rapid airlift of Harriers, Rapier missiles and troops to Belize to counter a seemingly imminent invasion by Guatemala.

1979: Evacuation of British and other Western nationals from Teheran and a minor airfield in Southern Iran following the overthrow of the Shah. Relief supplies airlifted to civil war-torn Nicaragua. Disaster relief flights to Yugoslavia following an earthquake. Support of Red Cross activities in Cambodia (Kampuchea), ferrying food and medical supplies to refugees in Phnom Penh, from Bangkok. Advance elements of the Commonwealth ceasefire monitoring force airlifted to Rhodesia.

1980: Operation 'Agila'—support for the Commonwealth forces protecting the Patriotic Front guerrillas at widely dispersed assembly points in Rhodesia. Operation 'Khana Cascade 80', a re-run of the 1973 operation. Eight aircraft deployed to Vanuato, New Hebrides, following an attempted *coup*.

1982: Less than 24 hours after the invasion of the Falklands, the first Hercules was en route to Ascension Island. As the Task Force deployed, the dispatch rate increased to one Hercules every four hours.

OPERATIONS PROFILES

Some 163 sorties arrived on Ascension in the first three weeks of the emergency, carrying 3.75 million pounds of supplies. In order to extend the range of the Hercules as far as the Falklands, aircraft were modified to carry ex-Andover long-range fuel tanks in the freight bay, giving 1,000nm of extra range though at the expense of vital freight space. Equipped with four tanks, the aircraft were used to drop high-priority items over the Falklands. Aircraft were fitted with an air-to-air refuelling capability, and the first long-range AAR sortie to drop parachutists and stores to the Task Force within the Total Exclusion Zone was completed on 16 May with a flight time of 24hrs 5mins. On 18 June a sortie to drop supplies to Mount Kent established a world endurance record for the Hercules, at 28hrs 4mins. Four aircraft were modified to the tanker role. The first RAF Hercules landed at Port Stanley on 24 June, another arriving the next day with the Falkland Islands' Governor. While Port Stanley's runway was closed for lengthening, mail supplies were dropped by Hercules and outward mail was collected by a 'grappling hook' snatch technique. A Hercules tanker detachment was established on the Falklands to support air defence operations.

1983: Deployment and subsequent withdrawal of British elements of UN peace-keeping force in the Lebanon.

1984: Famine relief flights to Upper Volta. Beginning of Operation 'Bushel'—detachment established at Addis Ababa to fly sorties to remote strips in drought-stricken areas.

1985: Operation 'Bushel' continues, developing into an air-drop operation. Some 32,000 tonnes of relief supplies delivered, of which 14,000 were air-dropped.

1986: Disaster relief flights to Mexico City and Columbia. Operation 'Balzac' in support of the rescue of refugees from Aden.

1990: Support for the Electricity Board following severe gales. Relief flights to Montserrat following Hurricane 'Hugo'. Assistance to Western Samoa following a typhoon. Operation 'Granby' begins on 6 August following the invasion of Kuwait by Iraq. The first RAF Hercules departed less than 24 hours after the operation began and was the first Allied aircraft into the Gulf region. Lyneham assumed an intensive 24-hour shift system with more than twice the normal tasking rate. Over 40,000 hours were flown in seven months—typically fourteen months' worth. Some 24 million gallons of fuel were consumed during the operation, and the Hercules fleet flew some 12 million miles carrying 100 million pounds of freight.

1991: Operation 'Provide Comfort', following 'Granby'—three aircraft operating from Incirlik in Turkey drop over 1 million pounds of relief supplies to Kurdish refugees in the mountains of the Turkey/Iraq border region. Operation 'Haven' involved the movement of support equipment and vehicles required by 3 Royal Marine Commando Brigade as part of its duty to protect Kurds in the 'safe haven' camps.

1992: Operation 'Cheshire' begins in July, providing humanitarian relief to the besieged city of Sarajevo in the former Yugoslavia. A Hercules aircraft from No 47 Squadron was the first UN-sponsored aircraft to fly into the city's airport. By mid-January 1993 this aircraft had air-landed 10 million pounds of supplies into Sarajevo. Because of an increasing danger to aircrews operating from Zagreb, the RAF detachment moved to Ancona in Italy in February 1993. Operation 'Vigour' involved a two-aircraft deployment to Mombasa in Kenya, flying relief missions into Somalia, often arriving at dirt-strip airfields before US Marines had secured the area. British participation in the operation ended on 28 February 1993, 6 million pounds of relief supplies having been flown into the area.

The foregoing list of activities covers just part of the LTW's continuing schedule of activities both within the United Kingdom and around the world. Aircraft also regularly participate in exercises, airlift competitions and exchange programmes, provide support for diplomatic staff worldwide and fly impromptu search and rescue missions in addition to regular training and categorization sorties. There is little doubt that the RAF Hercules fleet is in heavy demand, and the illustrious 'Herky Bird' is a valued aircraft which performs excellently.

Nimrod

Designed around the De Havilland Comet airframe, the British Aerospace (formerly Hawker Siddeley) Nimrod could easily be regarded as being little more than a 'militarized' airliner, dedicated to rather sedate and uninteresting patrol duties over hundreds of miles of featureless seascape. In reality, the

Nimrod is something very different—it is a 'high-tech' weapons system capable of locating and destroying hostile sub-surface targets. A powerful and sophisticated aircraft, the Nimrod remains at the forefront of anti-submarine warfare technology. Despite the reduction in East–West tensions, Russia still possesses a large submarine and surface fleet which, if not a direct threat to NATO, is still very much in business and therefore presents a potential threat to either NATO or, more particularly, Britain's maritime safety. However, following the end of the 'Cold War', the Royal Air Force has scaled down Nimrod operations and the fleet of more than thirty aircraft has been reduced by almost a quarter. Operations from St Mawgan have been terminated, and all the aircraft are now concentrated at Kinloss in Scotland.

After entering RAF service during 1969, the Nimrod MR.1 enjoyed a long and successful career which encouraged the introduction of a fleet improvement programme during the late 1970s. This resulted in the Nimrod MR.2, whose completely revised sensor fit effectively gave the RAF a new aircraft. The 1982 Falklands conflict prompted more modifications, and refuelling probes, wingtip-mounted ESM (electronic support measures) pods and self-protection Sidewinder missiles were introduced, increasing the Nimrod's capabilities still further.

The mission performed by the RAF Nimrod crews is essentially twofold—maritime reconnaissance and anti-submarine warfare. Patrol missions require flexibility, and briefings for each sortie are usually relatively short, covering the basics such as transit to the search area, fuel details, target information and so on. Patrols often last for up to five hours, and if a long-range transit is required the total mission length could extend beyond twelve hours, especially if in-flight refuelling is utilized. Intelligence is a vital aspect of the briefing, relying upon satellite information, reconnaissance photography and other data. The Nimrod's Tactical Navigator will brief the crew on the current intelligence picture while the Air Electronics Officer explains surveillance tactics, detailing the way in which the mission will be conducted—perhaps an 'active' search with radar or a 'silent' watch relying on ESM equipment. Once the other basics of the flight have been covered (communications, weather, etc), the crew board a bus and drive out to the flight line, where one

Above: The view from the flight deck of a Nimrod MR.2P during a low-level visual identification.

aircraft will have been drawn from the collective Nimrod 'pool' and prepared for the sortie, the complex avionics suite having been thoroughly checked and appropriate equipment installed into the huge weapons bay. For a reconnaissance mission, the most likely stores would be air/sea rescue equipment or sonobuoys, and Sidewinder self-protection missiles may be fitted to the underwing hardpoints. The twelve-man crew board the Nimrod and make their way through the masses of equipment which has been progressively 'squeezed' into the fuselage, taking up their positions in the aircraft. Because of the complexity of the Nimrod's systems, the pre-start checks are extensive and the crew is normally on board for at least an hour before the scheduled departure time. Once the checks are complete, the four Rolls-Royce Spey turbofan engines are started up and the aircraft is taxied to the active runway. Once the pre-take-off checks have been successfully completed, the aircraft departs, climbing to a transit altitude around 20,000ft.

Like many other combat aircraft, 'stealth' is an important part of operational activity, and the Nimrod crew endeavour to maintain anonymity whenever possible. Radio communications are kept to a minimum, and operational transmissions are made via a secure data link. After arriving at the designated search area, a descent to around 10,000ft will be made, at which height the Tactical Navigator will activate the Searchwater radar, making wide sweeps over a range of approximately 200 miles. Naturally, an active radar will be easily detected by shipping in the area, but any potential target ship can make little response other than turn off its own radar. The Searchwater radar is capable of estimating the size of each radar target, which enables the TacNav to identify most if not all of the likely targets within the search area. The tracks of each target will be plotted and projected on to the TacNav's display screen, and eventually a pattern of activity will emerge, the most important targets being selected for further investigation. In an operational environment a target group would be selected and the Nimrod Captain would run in towards the area with the Searchwater radar switched off, the ESM operator maintaining a watch for radar emissions from the ships. When a radar is identified, the ESM operator will obtain a strength and bearing, while the pilot quickly descends to around 5,000ft. The radar signal is then relocated, and the pilot brings the aircraft down still further, maintaining ESM contact at the very edge of the ship's radar picture. This will enable the Nimrod to arrive within visual range of the target without being identified on the target ship's radar.

Down at low level—often well below the overland minimum height of 250ft—the Nimrod runs in towards the target, the crew keeping a careful watch on the aircraft's radar warning systems as it enters the ship's missile engagement zone. If the mission were being flown 'for real', the crew would be ready to deploy chaff and flare decoys as necessary before launching a torpedo at the target; in peacetime, the crew is more likely to overfly and photograph the target, making an 'operational' departure at high speed and low level. The Nimrod is more than capable of performing such torpedo bomber attacks, although the aircraft is more likely to be used as a control centre from which Tornados or Sea Harriers armed with Sea Eagles could be directed on to the selected targets. However, the Nimrod fleet is now capable of carrying Harpoon anti-ship missiles, which can be launched 'blind' (against a predetermined position) from a range of more than 50 miles. Once

Below: A Nimrod MR.2P, illustrating the 'double-bubble' fuselage construction.

launched, the Harpoon descends to wave-top height and acquires the target with its own radar, making final course adjustments en route.

The Nimrod is also a highly sophisticated anti-submarine warfare aircraft. While submerged, submarines are more likely to be hunted by friendly submarines, but a surfaced (or near-surface) submarine is a potential target for the Nimrod. Operating in isolation, or under the direction of friendly naval forces, the Nimrod will sow a number of sonobuoys through which submarines will have to pass, thereby giving away their position. The sonobuoys are of two basic types, a passive version which will listen for targets, giving a bearing but not range, and an active type, which transmits a signal, recording any echoes and thus producing a range. A detailed data bank enables the Nimrod's crew to determine the type of submarine through an analysis of the target's sound signature. The aircraft's Searchwater radar is capable of locating and tracking a surfacing submarine's schnorkel and periscope, the synthetic radar display enabling the operator to maintain contact easily. However, the active radar emissions will naturally be picked up by the target submarine's ESM equipment, and the Searchwater therefore cannot be relied upon. The most effective passive search system is the human eyeball, and the Nimrod can fly extensive patrols at low level for many hours, often powered by just two engines. The two pilots maintain a careful watch of the search area, assisted by two crewmen positioned at the fuselage bubble windows. When a target periscope is located, a smoke marker is quickly launched to establish its position and the aircraft is thrown into a tight turn to overfly it, at low level (perhaps just 50ft in wartime). The now-submerged target is enclosed within a search circle, while the magnetic anomaly detector (MAD) operator looks for a tell-tale change in the magnetic field. The circle is maintained until the submarine's position is established, the Nimrod often being flown to its limit, sometimes through its own slipstream. More sonobuoys are now launched to establish the target's speed, depth and track, active systems being required to produce an echo as the submarine captain will no doubt have shut down engines so as to maintain silence.

This engagement would probably mark the end of a peacetime mission, but in wartime a torpedo attack would be initiated. The Nimrod's relatively aged Mk 44 and Mk 46 torpedoes are now being supplemented by the new Stingray, an 'intelligent' weapon which is pre-programmed with all appropriate target data and, once launched, will make its own search patterns, discounting decoys in favour of the required noise signature. For fast-moving and thick-skinned submarine targets, even the Stingray might not be a suitable match, and B57 nuclear depth charges could also be deployed if necessary. After maintaining a long patrol, or after successfully engaging surface or sub-surface targets, the weary Nimrod crew return to base for a well-earned rest.

In the post-Cold War era, the opportunity to pursue Russian submarines is relatively rare, but training operations continue, relying upon NATO naval forces to provide suitable simulations of the 'real thing'. The Nimrod crews are consequently able to maintain their skills, and their highly capable aircraft remain active, ready to fly into action whenever or wherever it might be needed.

Sentry

The Royal Air Force's airborne early earning (AEW) capability was drastically transformed during 1992 when the Boeing E-3D Sentry entered service with No 8 squadron at Waddington. The venerable Shackleton radar platforms which had been operated continuously since the 1970s relied on radar technology dating back to the 1950s, and a replacement for these aircraft was long overdue. The Nimrod was initially selected as a suitable airframe to carry a new radar system, but after lengthy and expensive developmental difficulties the AEW Nimrod programme was cancelled and the Boeing E-3 was ordered. (Unfortunately, funds were not made available to convert the AEW Nimrods back to their original maritime reconnaissance configuration.) The Shackletons are now retired, and the Sentry has settled into operational service with the RAF.

The airborne early warning aircraft was developed largely in response to the Soviet offensive capability evident during the Cold War, but following the thaw in East–West relations the need for an 'eye in the sky' increased still further when many areas of Europe became politically unstable. The Sentry forms part of NATO's 'crisis management' capability, providing a real-time monitoring/control centre which can be deployed around the world as

Above: A pair of Tornado F.3s from No 5 Squadron escort a Sentry AEW.1. (BAe)

necessary. No 8 Squadron's aircraft enable the RAF to gather and evaluate large amounts of information which can be processed and transferred via data links to commanders on the ground, at sea or in the air, and fighter assets can be directly controlled from inside the airborne aircraft. Seven Sentrys (probably reducing to six) are currently in service with the RAF, operating in conjunction with NATO's eighteen E-3As based at Geilenkirchen in Germany.

Controlled collectively by the NATO AEW Force Command at SHAPE, the combined fleet is tasked on a daily basis to fly AEW missions as required throughout NATO's areas of interest. One of the more significant undertakings is a continual presence over Bosnia, and just two weeks after No 8 Squadron declared an Initial Operational Capability the unit's Sentrys were tasked to support UN sanctions against Serbia. The E-3D is widely considered to be the most capable AWACS (Airborne Warning and Control System) variant, equipped with fuel-efficient CFM56 turbofan engines, a Westinghouse APY-2 radar and Loral 1017 'Yellow Gate' ESM equipment.

The Sentry's crew comprises two pilots, one navigator, one Tactical Director, one Data Link Manager, two Weapons Controllers, one Communications Technician, one Flight Engineer, one Communications Officer, one Surveillance Controller, one ESM Operator, one Fighter Allocator, one Display Technician and one Radar Technician. Although the aircraft is crewed by 'traditional' flight deck personnel, the 'heart' of the Sentry lies within the fuselage, where the specialists perform their mission. Starting with the communications specialists, the Sentry's radio fit includes three ARC-165 HF, two ARC-166 and six ARC-17 UHF/SATCOM transceivers, together with two ARC-187 UHF transceivers which feature 'Have Quick' ECCM (electronic counter-countermeasures) modules. Secure data links are available, to link the controllers with American fighter aircraft, air and ground stations and ship-based stations. In addition, the Joint Tactical Information Distribution System (JTIDS) is gradually being introduced, enabling RAF fighters and bombers to be controlled directly from the Sentry via a secure data link. The Computer Display Technician works with a pair of IBM 4 Pi CC-2 computers, each with a 665,360-word capacity, and two digital multiplexers, three tape drives and a line printer.

The main cabin is dominated by nine high-resolution situation display consoles (SDCs) divided into three banks of three. The Westinghouse S-band radar's range is classified, but for a typical cruising height of 30,000ft the limiting radar horizon is almost 300 miles. The radar system operates in several modes—PRF (pulse repetition frequency), PDNES (pulse-doppler non-elevation scan, in which target elevation is not available), PDES (pulse-doppler elevation scan, in which target elevation is available) and BTH (beyond the horizon, in which pulse radar without doppler is employed). The radar can also operate in Maritime mode (high resolution, with low 'clutter') or in Passive mode, in which the Sentry remains 'silent' while the onboard receivers and processors continue to function. The individual modes can be combined if necessary, and the radar's 360-degree scan can be segmented into 32 sectors, each of which can be monitored in a different mode. Target information is processed by the onboard computers (and 'cleaned-up' by the Surveillance Controller) before being presented to the other operators. After being combined with data from the ESM and IFF systems, the information is evaluated by each of the appropriate operators, under the supervision of the Tactical Director (who monitors the overall radar picture) before being passed down the data links to commanders on the ground. Fighter aircraft can be vectored by the Weapons Controller to identify or engage targets.

The Sentry is well equipped to fly long-endurance sorties, being capable of flying up to twelve hours without any need for aerial refuelling. However, the aircraft is fitted with a refuelling probe and (uniquely for an RAF aircraft) a USAF-style receptacle, giving the E-3D an even greater range and endurance. The Sentry is the cornerstone of NATO's Rapid Reaction Force, and, as the number of worldwide 'trouble spots' continues to grow, the E-3D's importance and value will increase still further.

VC10, TriStar

The Royal Air Force's strategic transport and aerial refuelling operations have traditionally been carried out by a variety of aircraft types, ranging from the Comet, Britannia and Belfast transports to the Victor, Valiant and Vulcan tankers. In response to reductions in overseas commitments, defence budget cut-backs and the easing of East–West tension, the variety of operational tanker and transport types has gradually decreased, leaving the RAF with just two aircraft types, the VC10 and TriStar. These aircraft are capable of performing both the tanker and transport role, giving the RAF a great increase in flexibility, although the recent increase in overseas commitments has ensured that the tanker/transport fleet is never less than extremely busy.

The majestic VC10 was originally designed in response to a BOAC requirement for a long-range jet airliner capable of operating from 'hot and high' airfields which were then part of BOAC's 'Empire' routes. Unfortunately, the need for a good short-field performance made the VC10 less than ideal for other airline operators, who preferred the less-expensive (and lighter) Boeing 707. The outstanding success of the latter overshadowed any significant interest in the VC10, and only 54 were built. However, the RAF also required a new jet-powered strategic transport during the 1960s, and the new VC10 appeared to be the ideal aircraft for the role. Initially, it was proposed that a batch of multi-role VC10s be purchased, capable of performing transport, tanker, maritime reconnaissance and bomber roles. (It is perhaps ironic, that thirty years later, the VC10 has now adopted a dual-role capability, indicating that this early proposal was not such a wild idea.) Eventually, fourteen VC10 Type 1106s were acquired for the RAF, designated VC10 C Mk 1 and allocated to the strategic transport role, and the first aircraft (XR806) completed its maiden flight on 26 November 1965. The fleet was delivered to No 10 Squadron at Brize Norton, the last aircraft arriving in August 1968.

The VC10 proved to be the perfect aircraft for the RAF's diverse needs. Capable of high speeds and possessing a long range, the aircraft was, thanks to the original BOAC specification, ideal for regular flights to places such as Gan, Kai Tak, Washington, Luqa, Goose Bay, Akrotiri, Belize and Muharraq. One aircraft (XR809) was sold to Rolls-Royce for engine development work (primarily the RB.211 turbofan), while the remaining thirteen continue to operate with No 10 Squadron on passenger and cargo transport operations and casualty evacuation duties. The VC10s were heavily involved in both the Falklands conflict and the Gulf War, and they continue to fly sorties in support of the RAF's overseas commitments. Members of the Royal Family and Government ministers also make use of the VC10s for long-range overseas flights. Thanks to the large cargo door, the VC10's internal layout can be quickly rearranged to suit a variety of passenger and cargo-carrying configurations, providing the RAF with an excellent multi-role transport for which, thirty years after the C.1's first flight, there is still no obvious replacement in sight.

In 1978 the Ministry of Defence turned its attention back to the VC10 in response to an increasing need for more aerial refuelling tanker aircraft. The Victor tankers were quickly reaching the end of their usefulness, and the RAF had a much greater need for refuelling support; this was to increase still further, not least because of post-Falklands War operations, which required regular transport flights to be refuelled en route to and from the islands—a commitment which also accelerated the usage of the Victor's remaining fatigue life. Consequently, a contract for nine VC10 tankers was placed in 1979, covering the conversion of airliners which were now available for purchase. Five standard Type 1101 VC10s formerly operated by Gulf Air and four Type 1154 Super VC10s (with a longer fuselage, uprated engines and a fin fuel tank, for transatlantic operations) last used by East African Airways were purchased for the RAF and delivered to Filton, where the conversion work was undertaken by British Aerospace under the direction of the company's Weybridge office, where the VC10 had originally been designed and developed.

Great efforts were made to develop 'commonality' between these aircraft and the VC10 C.1s which were already in RAF service. The engine fit was standardized for the entire fleet, with thrust reversers removed from the Super VC10s' inboard engines, and an auxiliary power unit was installed. However, it is fair to say that the two tanker variants and the transport derivative remain distinctly different in terms of both airframe size and configurations. The VC10 C.1 is in effect a 'hybrid' design, incorporating the standard VC10's short fuselage and the uprated engines and fin fuel tank of the Super VC10. The five converted standard aircraft were designated VC10 K.2 and the four 'Supers' K.3, the first of these aircraft flying in converted form in June 1982. Deliveries to the RAF began in July 1983, the first K.3 entering service in February 1985.

The tanker conversion involved the installation of two underwing refuelling points and a third under the centre fuselage. Soundproofing and insulation were removed from the fuselage, apart from the forward section of the cabin, where a new bulkhead was installed, and the emptied fuselage interior was fitted with five cylindrical fuel tanks, plumbed into the aircraft's fuel system. The four Super VC10s incorporated large cargo doors which enabled BAe to install the fuel tanks relatively easily, and, once fitted, the doors were sealed shut. However, the standard VC10s required a hole to be cut into the cabin roof, through which the tanks could be installed. Much of the rear fuselage is completely empty, in order to restore the aircraft's centre of gravity. The wing-mounted Flight Refuelling Mk 32 hose drum unit (HDU) pods were fitted relatively easily, but the installation of the Mk 17B HDU in the rear lower fuselage posed much greater problems, requiring the pressurized fuselage to be opened up and new bulkheads to be constructed. A closed-circuit television system was also fitted, enabling the Flight Engineer to monitor refuelling operations from his position on the flight deck, and lighting units were installed to help receiver pilots to locate and line up on the aircraft during night operations. Internally, the flight deck layout of the K.3 was redesigned to accommodate a navigator's station, the standard VC10s (K.2s) having been designed with this additional seat from the start. Consequently, the K.3's flight deck is somewhat cramped. Behind the flight deck, the K.2 is fitted with six rows of three seats, while the K.3 has five rows of three seats, with a further two seats in a forward area (without windows). Thus the tankers' aircrews can carry ground crew with them whenever necessary, and other personnel can occupy these seats as required.

With a total of 22 VC10s in regular RAF service, the Ministry of Defence purchased more former VC10 airliners, placing them in open storage at Abingdon. From a collection of fifteen aircraft, ten airframes were scrapped, but five Super VC10s were retained for modification to tanker configuration,

Above: A Lockheed TriStar in formation with a VC10 K.3, a VC10 C.1, two Buccaneers and two Royal Navy Sea Harriers.

and conversion to K.4 standard is now under way. Four aircraft are expected to enter RAF service in 1994; the fifth may be retained as a source of spares. The conversion of these VC10s was more complicated than originally envisaged, the years of open storage having had a significant effect upon the condition of the airframes. Unlike the earlier VC10 conversions, the K.4 will not carry additional fuel tanks in the fuselage and will thus retain a transport capability.

The Royal Air Force's air-to-air refuelling capability was originally developed as a means of extending the range of the Valiant, Vulcan and Victor strategic bomber force, but, as the flexibility of the RAF's air power was widened, the role of the tanker aircraft has grown dramatically, and virtually every front-line RAF aircraft is now capable of refuelling in flight. Consequently, the Service's main refuelling unit, No 101 Squadron at Brize Norton, is committed to support a wide variety of operations, usually tasked on a weekly basis, although day-to-day changes to mission requirements are made as necessary. Once the 'customers' have been established, the Squadron's planning staff prepare a 'Details of Tasking' sheet which is posted daily to the Squadron's crews, providing details of aircraft, call-signs, navigation, times, fuel required and so on. These details are then transferred to individual crews for pre-flight briefing, at which stage further information concerning the tanker's status (fuel load, etc) is established, together with details of weather, routings and so on. Some 90 minutes before the scheduled take-off time, the Flight Engineer drives out to the aircraft with the Crew Chief, to begin pre-flight preparations. There is a careful walk-round check, and the VC10's internal power is switched on to allow the inertial navigation system to be set up. About fifteen minutes later the pilot, co-pilot and navigator arrive and begin their own pre-flight preparations.

The aircraft is started up and taxied to the active runway, and a 'low-noise' take-off is usually performed, involving a maximum-rate climb to altitude before a more fuel-efficient climbing attitude is assumed. Interestingly, although the VC10's throttles are positioned in the traditional location between pilot and co-pilot, it is usually the Flight Engineer who makes throttle changes, his own controls being located beside his station. The majority of refuelling missions take the aircraft north from Brize Norton, then east, out over the North Sea where one of the RAF's designated refuelling areas is located. Most flights are made in support of fighter and bomber training missions and involve refuelling over the North Sea from inside a designated area (known as a 'towline'). Ground radar units will vector fighters and bombers towards the tanker, which will be established inside the towline, flying a racetrack pattern, with refuelling drogues extended. As the receivers close in towards the tanker, the final rendezvous is made by radar, followed by a visual join-up as directed by the tanker's crew. Smaller aircraft such as the Tornado, Jaguar and Harrier will use a wing-mounted drogue unit to refuel, moving into formation off the VC10's port wing tip. Often refuelling in pairs, the aircraft are directed to a pre-contact position behind each trailing drogue, and after final clearance from the VC10 crew they close in towards the refuelling basket, to make contact, waiting for an amber light on the HDU. Once safely 'plugged in', the receiver will push the basket slightly, to register full contact, after which the amber light changes to green and the flow of fuel begins. Once refuelling is complete, the green light changes back to amber and the receiver reduces speed slightly, pulling the refuelling probe out of the basket before edging away to take up formation on the VC10's starboard wing tip. Once the receivers have been replenished, they will depart to continue their own missions, leaving the VC10 to continue flying the towline pattern.

The VC10's refuelling altitude varies according to the requirements of the receivers, but 25,000ft is an average figure. The 'probe and drogue' refuelling system enables successful and safe transfers to be made at much lower altitudes, however, and tactical aircraft often take on fuel at these levels in order to avoid an unnecessary climb from their normal low-level environment. The VC10's Flight Engineer is responsible for the transfer of fuel to each receiver, and he also maintains a careful watch over the VC10's fuel supply, ensuring that the offload of fuel does not take the tanker's centre of gravity beyond safe limits. The Flight Engineer monitors all three refuelling positions through a swivelling TV camera mounted under the fuselage, and, should a dangerous situation develop, he can quickly cut the supply, switching the HDU lights to red and prompting each receiver to pull away. Although radio communication between receiver and tanker is maintained, some rendezvous are performed in total radio silence, as a wartime refuelling would naturally require an absolute minimum of radio chatter and an exclusive reliance on the HDU 'traffic lights'. Likewise, night refuellings are performed, and the VC10 can, if required, light up like the proverbial Christmas tree, making the receiver's task much easier.

Larger aircraft such as the Nimrod and TriStar—and, indeed, the VC10 itself—refuel from the centreline Mk 17B HDU, which delivers a greater flow of 500 Imp gal/min as opposed to the wing-mounted Mk 32 HDU's 300 Imp gal/min. The approach is made from astern the tanker, displaced to port. For the final rendezvous the receiver moves right to line up behind the HDU basket, before edging in to plug into the drogue. The Hercules (often encountered in the towline over Cornwall) presents the VC10 crew with a specific challenge, in that its speed is naturally much slower than theirs. An 'overtake' rendezvous is performed, in which both the Hercules and VC10 enter a gentle descent, the tanker slowly overtaking the receiver, after which the Hercules tucks in behind the tanker to take on fuel. In this way both aircraft can maintain a safe speed during the rendezvous.

After the tanker crew have fulfilled the mission's allotted tasks, the VC10 heads back to Brize Norton to land. The crew then de-brief, the tanker's performance being relayed directly to the ground crews who will prepare the aircraft for its next mission, which may take place just a few hours later. Despite the age of the VC10's airframe, serviceability is remarkably good, and with a variety of redundant back-up systems (left over from airliner days) the aircraft is perfectly suited to tanker operations. The VC10 C.1 strategic transports belonging to No 10 Squadron are currently being modified to carry underwing Mk 32 HDU pods, giving the aircraft a very useful refuelling tanker capability. Thus No 10 Squadron's VC10 C.1Ks will become multi-role tanker/transports.

Brize Norton is already the established home of a fleet of tanker/transport aircraft in the shape of six Lockheed L.1011 TriStars, which entered service with No 216 Squadron from 1986. Following the successful conversion of VC10s to the tanker role, a need for a further increase in both tanker and transport capacity was identified by the MoD, and the purchase of six surplus British Airways TriStars, together with three formerly operated by Pan American Airways, was authorized. These aircraft were converted by Marshalls at their Cambridge factory and emerged as four TriStar KC.1s, two K.1s, two C.2s and one C.2A. These designations apply to the variations in aircraft configurations, the K.1 being a combined tanker and passenger transport (with a refuelling probe fitted), the KC.1 a tanker/passenger/cargo transport (no longer fitted with a refuelling probe), the C.2 a freight/passenger transport and the sole C.2A an enhanced version of the C.2. The K.1s and KC.1s are fitted with a twin Mk 17T HDU assembly in the rear lower fuselage and have additional tanks installed in the underfloor cargo holds, providing an extra 100,000lb of fuel. Unlike the VC10 tankers, the TriStar tankers remain fully capable as large-capacity passenger and freight carriers, with 140 × 102in cargo doors and seats (when fitted) for up to 204 people in the K.1 and 196 in the KC.1. The transport-dedicated C.2/2A can carry 265 passengers plus 35,000lb of freight. Linked pallets can be installed to carry vehicles, and the forward end of the cabin includes space for up to twelve additional crew members. With a payload of 50,000lb and a cruising speed of around 525kts, the TriStar has an unrefuelled range of more than 6,000 miles. However, the K.1s also retain an in-flight capability, giving the aircraft an almost limitless range.

Following the retirement of the RAF's Victor tankers in October 1993, the Royal Air Force's aerial refuelling capability is now tasked to this mixed force of multi-role VC10 and TriStar tanker/transports. Although the fleet of VC10s is far from new, and the TriStars are also effectively embarking upon a second lease of life, the RAF's tanker/transports are well placed to enjoy long and valued service until a new purpose-built multi-role 'large aircraft' is made available, probably after the turn of the century.

Jaguar

No 54 Squadron, Royal Air Force, is one of three Jaguar units stationed at Coltishall in Norfolk. It is allocated to NATO's ACE Mobile Force, and its primary role has been to support, from bases in Denmark, NATO's Northern Flank in the event of a war with the now-defunct Warsaw Pact. However, following the break-up of the Soviet Union, the RAF's Jaguars have been employed in different roles—not least during 'Desert Storm', when they were operated very successfully, without incurring a single loss. Jaguars remain in the Middle East, a presence being maintained in Turkey. Low running costs, ease of deployment and high reliability were all factors which favoured the Jaguar, and, contrary to earlier plans for its early replacement by the European Fighter Aircraft, it will remain in RAF service for some time, following a decision first to re-equip the RAF's Tornado F.3 squadrons with EFAs (although this is probably an indication of the RAF's regard for the Tornado F.3 rather than an eagerness to retain the Jaguar indefinitely).

Coltishall is home to two other Jaguar squadrons, Nos 6 and 41, while No 16(R) Squadron at Lossiemouth acts as the Jaguar Operational Conversion Unit. Each squadron is equipped largely with single-seat Jaguar GR.1As, although small numbers of two-seat T.2As are also operated (the majority with the OCU), for check-rides, dual control instruction etc. The GR.1A is primarily a ground attack aircraft, although some export models of the Jaguar are employed as air defence fighters.

At present, approximately twelve aircraft are assigned to No 54 Squadron, together with sixteen pilots. The number and type of missions flown each week depend largely upon aircraft serviceability and whether the Squadron is working up to any major exercises. For example, a pilot could fly perhaps three sorties in one day and none the next day. However, on average, a pilot can expect to fly thirty hours a month. A typical mission will last for roughly ninety minutes, unless the sortie includes air-to-air combat, in which case the duration drops significantly to around forty minutes because of the thirsty characteristics of the Jaguar's Rolls-Royce Adour engines when reheat is selected.

The tasking for each mission is normally received two hours before the scheduled take-off time, the standard NATO time scale. The briefing begins with a time check, followed by the aims of the sortie, callsigns, a listing of the pilots, the aircraft serials, the weapons fit each aircraft is carrying and the aerodynamic limits to which each can be flown. Spare aircraft are detailed, together with the weather for the local and target areas, the amount of fuel needed to return to base, who will be responsible for making the various fuel calls and radio frequencies—which are pre-briefed to avoid the need to broadcast such details when in the air. The Jaguar is equipped with 'Have Quick' frequency-agile radios, which are virtually resistant to jamming. The briefing continues with details of the take-off, recovery, routes to be flown, heights, 'notams' (Notices to Airmen), Royal flights, safety altitudes, emergencies, air-to-air refuelling (if it is to be employed) and so on. The evasion brief will detail the types of aircraft which the Jaguar pilots will be avoiding, the limits to which evasion will be flown, and the tactics which are to be employed. The whole briefing will last up to forty minutes, depending on the experience of the pilots. If the formation includes a 'new boy', the brief will have to include precise details of what is going on so that he is left in absolutely no doubt as to what he will be expected to do.

The planning for each mission is time-consuming, but it is vital to the success of each sortie. The Jaguar pilots adhere to a much-used acronym, 'KISS'—'keep it simple and safe'. The target is first examined, and weapons are then assigned as appropriate, after which the ground crews will be advised of the weapons fit required for each aircraft. The route to the target is studied, threats are taken into account (with a great deal of input from an Army ground liaison officer assigned to the Squadron) and the delivery techniques—level bombing, dive bombing, etc—are chosen. The Jaguar is equipped with a FIN 1064 inertial navigation platform, a very accurate system which runs a projected map display and generates steering information in the head-up display. If times for waypoints are programmed into the computer, it will also give demanded ground speed and actual ground speed, enabling the pilot to arrive at his designated target precisely on time, provided he adheres strictly to the HUD information. TOT (time on target) is vitally important, so as to avoid conflict with other strikes, reconnaissance overflights or friendly manoeuvres on the ground.

The INS requires specific target details, such as its latitude and longitude; its height, so that the HUD can generate a bar over the predicted target position before it becomes visible to the pilot; and the initial point (IP) position, so that any 'wandering' by the INS can be updated between thirty and ninety seconds before the aircraft arrives at the target. Some pre-IP updates can also be fed into the INS, the most accurate means of revising the INS's data being to use the Jaguar's laser target seeker head, although this is strictly a wartime option as the Jaguar's laser is not 'eye-safe'. Indeed, the laser can be used in peacetime only over weapons ranges, and only within a few hundred yards of the target position. The IP and target co-ordinates become two of a series of waypoints which form the complete route that is fed into the INS.

The RAF Jaguar fleet utilizes a Total Avionics Briefing System (TABS), which enables the pilot to feed all the relevant data into the aircraft swiftly and easily. He lays his map on a digitizing map table and programmes each waypoint into a data store by means of a small hand-held cursor. A TV monitor displays the information as it is programmed, enabling errors to be corrected as required. Once the route is properly programmed, the 32k-memory portable data store (PODS) is ready to be 'plugged' into the aircraft. A record of the flight is given to an operations officer, who will book the aircraft into the low-flying system and also into whatever weapons ranges are required. Departure out of the airfield is also booked with air traffic control so that the Jaguars can be handed over to a radar control authority if required, although for many missions the aircraft will depart visually at low level. Part of this planning must include careful timing of the attack phase, so that a first-run attack on a weapons range is timed to coincide with the operating periods at the range (which closes at various times to allow, for example, targets to be changed). Therefore TOT and time on range must match. A formal flight plan is filed only if the aircraft are expected to enter the airways network or if they are flying overseas.

When planning has been completed it is time to gather the appropriate flying kit together, which includes the bulky immersion suit if sea temperatures are below 10°C. An anti-*g* suit is worn, together with the usual gloves, life preserver and flying helmet. Once the pilot has been fully kitted out, it is time to 'walk', the next stop being the Operations desk, where a final 'out-brief' is given by the authorizing officer. The crews then walk to the line hut to sign out each aeroplane (on RAF Form 700), checking that each is fuelled correctly, is carrying the required weapons fit and is fully serviceable. Unacceptable defects are always noted in red ('I always look for missing wings or wheels,' commented one pilot), and acceptable defects are also noted, these being regarded as relatively unimportant provided the pilot is aware of them. Individual aircraft also develop specific problems which tend to recur, and each pilot is therefore careful to note any previous defects in case they arise again during the flight.

Arriving at his aircraft, the pilot makes a preliminary inspection, ensuring that it is parked correctly, that chocks are fitted under the wheels, that safety pins are fitted to each weapon, that external equipment is available and that a fire extinguisher is present. He then climbs into the aircraft, checking

Above: A Jaguar GR.1A carrying a pair of overwing-mounted AIM-9L Sidewinder missiles. (BAe)

that the cockpit's circuit-breakers are all set and that the battery, ignition and parking brake are all 'on'. The ejection seat pins are confirmed as being fitted, and then the rudder pedals and the seat are adjusted as required.

Looking to the left side of the cockpit, the pilot checks that the undercarriage handle is down, that the canopy jettison handle is flush and that the arrester hook handle is fully forward. Behind each throttle is an igniter re-light button, and a clicking sound will confirm that this is functioning correctly. The master armament safety bus bar key is then fitted into its slot, and the pilot climbs out of the aircraft again to complete a full external check. The first task is to look into the nosewheel bay, where he selects a number of switches to indicate the weapons fit and the ballistic mode in which the weapons will be dropped. The AN/ALE-40 chaff and flare dispenser selections are also made in the nosewheel bay. The checks then continue with a look at the various vents, to ensure that they are all unblocked. The hydraulic accumulators are checked for the correct pressure, and the safety pins are confirmed as being removed. On a more general note, the pilot will look for any leaks and, if necessary, check with an engineer that they are within limits. He will also look for any loose panels and unusual cracks, check inside the engine intakes for foreign objects, check the exhausts, confirm that the afterburner rings are in good condition and also ensure that the fuel shield inside the engine bay is not likely to fall off. The removal of the arrester hook pins and brake parachute pins is also checked.

The Jaguar is fitted with an internal starter unit, which incorporates a microswitch which needs to be placed in the correct position, and the starter's oil level is checked at the same time. It is also customary to see pilots shaking the various external stores on their pylons, ensuring that they are all properly secured. Once satisfied that the aircraft is in good condition, the pilot can climb back into his cockpit to complete the pre-start checks. Strapping in is the first task, working from left to right, attaching the personal equipment connector (oxygen, anti-g air pressure), personal survival pack (dinghy, etc), leg restraints, lap and shoulder straps, RT and helmet and removing the seat safety pins, at which stage the 'liney' (the member of the ground crew who assists with strapping-in) will remove the access ladder.

Working from left to right again, almost every item of equipment in the cockpit is checked, starting with the wanderlamps and autostabilization systems (pitch, yaw and roll) and also checking that the laser is off. The flaps are moved 'up', although without hydraulic pressure nothing happens at this stage. The inertial navigation system is normally switched on prior to the pilot's climbing in, giving the equipment time to heat up and align itself with its position. The pilot plugs in his data pod and selects 'DTS' (data transfer), checking that the route is programmed into the computer properly. Throttles are checked for full and free movement, and the main flight instruments are all scrutinized to ensure that they are functioning properly. The HUD is turned to the correct mode, usually 'radalt' (radio altimeter) for take-off. On the right-hand side of the cockpit are various fuel gauges and warning panels: the fuel cross-feeds are checked, as is the EHP (electro-hydraulic pump, which supplies hydraulic pressure if both pumps fail in flight). The engine instruments are examined, and then the alternators and transformer/rectification units are switched on. The air-conditioning is switched to 'ground', and the tacan is switched on. It is now time to start the engines.

The pilot makes a hand signal to the ground crew and the micro-turbo starter is switched on, taking four or five seconds to run up to 85 per cent. Once the unit is at this idle setting, the pilot holds one finger in the air, vertically, to signify engine No 1 start. He opens the low-pressure cock and presses the start. When the engine has wound up to around 52 per cent, the pilot checks that the relevant captions are out and that the flaps are being raised to their selected positions. No 2 engine is then started, and the external power is switched off. Each engine incorporates a dump valve which releases excess air from the compressor during start-up, and advancing the throttles to 61 per cent will close the bleed valves, confirmed by a slight reduction in the TGT (turbine gas temperature). The engines idle at between 54 and 57rpm on the ground. The flying controls are checked, and the autostabilization system is checked. Flaps can be moved to one of eight settings, half-flap being 20 degrees and full flap 40 degrees. The flaps and leading-edge slats run along the entire leading and trailing edges of the wing, turning being achieved by the use of spoiler devices. For take-off, flaps are set at 20 degrees.

Radio check-in with the rest of the formation begins at a pre-briefed time, the pilots using twenty pre-set frequencies, 'Stud One' being for 'ground' (start-up and taxy). The INS is switched from its alignment mode, and with nosewheel steering selected (by means of a switch on the control column, which also operates cameras in the Jaguar reconnaissance model) the aircraft is ready to taxy. With roughly 70 per cent power on each engine, the parking brake is released and the aircraft rolls forward, at which stage the pilot tests the foot brakes and returns the throttles to idle before turning left or right so as to avoid damaging other aircraft (or personnel!) with engine blast. While the pilot is taxying to the active runway there is time to consider emergency procedures for take-off. If an engine fails on the run below 100kts, the take-off can be aborted by bringing the throttles back to idle and streaming the brake parachute; the aircraft will be very heavy, putting a great deal of strain on the undercarriage. Above 100kts the 'one-shot' arrester hook can be extended (it has to be raised by an engineer). Alternatively, a single-engine take-off can be made by raising the undercarriage and dumping all external stores (by means of a single emergency switch). However, the pilot must be careful not to dump weapons on top of the travelling undercarriage. 'Speed is life' as far as Jaguar pilots are concerned: the faster the aircraft flies, the lower the angle of attack (AOA), and the primary aim on a single-engine take-off is therefore to achieve speed, not altitude.

At the end of the runway, the INS clock is started and the radio frequency is changed to 'Tower', enabling the pilot to obtain departure instructions. The aircraft then lines up on the runway, perhaps with others. Four aircraft is the largest number which can be accommodated line-abreast on the runway, and, once in position, each pilot checks the runway caravan for any safety signals, checks that all warning captions are out and checks that the INS clock is running. The throttles are then pushed to full dry power while the aircraft is held on the foot brakes and the EGT is within its limit of 700°C. With a 'thumbs-up' from the wingman, the leader will make a chopping motion with his hand, to signal brake release, and the aircraft begin their take-off roll. Aircraft depart solo, in pairs or in 'pairs of pairs', separated by thirty seconds (equivalent to about three miles).

After another nod from the leader as his aircraft passes about 40kts, the pilots release catches on the throttles to select afterburners, checking that flow of fuel increases (although the Adour engine is very reliable, and faults rarely occur). At the pre-briefed rotation speed (dependent upon weight and temperature, although it is normally around 180kts heavyweight and 140 lightweight) the aircraft is rotated to 14 degrees AOA and the Jaguar is swiftly airborne, normally at around 5,000ft from brakes release. Once airborne the aircraft quickly move into formation, achieved by lining up wing and tail aerial positions visually. The undercarriage gear and flaps are retracted, and the AOA audio warning and the air-conditioning are switched on (air-conditioning drains 4 or 5 per cent of thrust from the engines, so it is not switched on until the aircraft is safely airborne).

The Jaguar is a very sprightly performer when flown 'clean', requiring only 2,000ft to take off, but most missions are flown with a pair of 924kg (2,035lb) external fuel tanks under each wing. Moreover, in hot weather the Adours do not perform very well, and in extreme conditions of perhaps 30°C, with a full fuel and weapons load the Jaguar would require a runway of 7,000ft or more. However, the engines can be modified to give additional thrust, as was the case during 'Desert Storm'.

Once airborne, the pilot will ensure that the Jaguar's defensive systems are functioning, these being the ECM (electronic countermeasures), RWR (radar warning receivers) and chaff/flare dispensers. The formation will then adopt tactics which are appropriate to either a ground or an air threat as necessary. The Jaguar is fitted with a radar altimeter, which is considered to be very accurate (pilots confirm that it reads 'five feet' whilst taxying), and this enables the aircraft to be flown at ultra-low altitudes—a mere fifteen feet above the sea is quite practical, the only real limits being the risk of 'scraping' external stores and the nerve of the pilot! However, such low flying is an exception rather than the rule, and in the United Kingdom the normal 250ft minimum applies and only occasionally is special permission granted for 100ft AGL flights, in strictly designated areas.

Jaguars normally fly in battle formation, in line abreast with 2–3,000yds' separation, ensuring that a hostile aircraft cannot close in on the tails of the aircraft. The entire formation can fly in line abreast or in 'card' formation, in trailing pairs. Low flying is still considered to be a key to survival in a hostile environment, even though RAF Jaguars operated at medium altitudes over Iraq and Kuwait. The Allied air forces were able to maintain a 'sterile' air environment in the Gulf War, allowing attack aircraft to operate at altitudes which would normally invite surface-to-air missiles and anti-aircraft artillery. Obviously the same kind of relatively benign operating conditions may not be available in any future conflict in which the Jaguar might participate. The high wing-loading characteristics of the Jaguar make the aircraft a good performer at low level, offering a safe, smooth and quiet ride, with no smoke trail and only a small radar return. Indeed, during severe contour flying, the Jaguar can 'hug' the landscape, the pilot rolling the aircraft through 180 degrees to make a positive-g pull downhill rather than the usual negative-g 'bunt'. However, such manoeuvring tends to be reserved for lightly loaded aircraft, as a full weapons load will significantly reduce the aircraft's roll rate.

As the aircraft reaches each turning point, the HUD changes to a loose navigation mode and a marker appears over the predicted position of the waypoint. As the aircraft flies over the waypoint, the pilot will update the INS position if necessary and select the 'change destination' button, switching the HUD back to navigation mode. When the aircraft approaches the initial point, the INS will display a cue in the HUD, 60 seconds from the IP. The pilot will check his bomb selection, and check that the pylons are 'on' and the weapons fused, check the 'stick spacing' (the interval between each bomb drop) and select auto attack by computer or manual attack and guns 'on' or 'off'. Then the late arm safety switch is selected, making the whole system live. Finally, a small catch on top of the control column is activated, enabling the computer to drop the bombs at the required time. Targets are usually acquired visually, although the laser can be used, giving an appropriate cue on the HUD.

For a typical automatic attack, the pilot places a target bar over the target position, using a small controller located behind the throttles. This ground-stabilized image is automatically connected to the laser ranger, which fires at the target and measures the range by calculating the time taken for reflected laser light to return to the aircraft. Keeping the fire committal button pressed confirms the attack, and when the CCIP (continuously computed impact point) and target become coincident, the weapons are released automatically. The attack sequence takes place in a matter of seconds, as the Jaguar pilots will try to 'unmask' (reveal themselves to the target and its associated defences) at the last possible moment, thus leaving themselves very little time to acquire the target. Terrain-masking is still recognized as being tactically valuable, and the Jaguar pilot will try to dash in and out of the target area as rapidly as possible before disappearing in the surrounding 'clutter' again.

On departure from the target area, reheat can be used to pick up extra speed if necessary, although, as one pilot commented, 'If you select afterburners, every heat-seeker in the vicinity will be going "Yum-yum, there's a heat source", so you have to be careful.' The Adour engines are not immensely powerful, so they are not particularly hot either, and they give the Jaguar a fairly small heat signature, especially when compared to aircraft such as the Tornado. Once back over friendly territory, the formation can raise its altitude and assume a 'non-warlike' flight attitude so as to avoid being shot down by friendly forces. IFF is a vital piece of equipment for sorting the 'good guys' from the 'bad guys'. The flight back to base is normally made at around 360kts—this is a good speed for low fuel consumption in most weapon configurations.

On a peacetime return to Coltishall, the formation will make radio contact with Squadron Operations, giving prior notice of its return to the waiting ground engineers. Selecting 'Stud Three' puts the formation back into contact with air traffic control, and a visual recovery is normally made. The final arrival over the airfield is made on the 'Tower' radio frequency, the aircraft flying in a loose arrow formation. Thirty seconds before arrival overhead, the call 'Initials' is made and the aircraft break left at 1,200ft, in a 4–5g turn, air brakes deploying and throttles moving back to idle. The aircraft lose speed rapidly, and by the time they are established on the downwind leg of the circuit it has been reduced to 260kts. Flaps are now extended 40 degrees, air brakes are in and speed is down to 230kts. 'Gear down' selection can now take place, and a radio call is made to state intentions, either to land or overshoot. The harness is checked tight and locked. Fuel is checked to be sufficient, with hydraulics working, three greens (undercarriage down and locked) and rudder sensitivity changed from small to large, and full flap is extended before a 12-degree AOA turn is made on to final approach.

Engines are set at roughly 93 per cent, and the turn will be tightened or widened to take the direction and speed of the wind into account. The 12-degree AOA is maintained, and a careful check is made that the engines are functioning correctly—if one fails at this stage, the pilot is obliged to eject. Once the aircraft is established on finals at about a mile from touch-down, the gear is confirmed as down again and the aircraft is positioned on the correct glidepath to the runway, usually relying on PAPIs (precision approach path indicators), which should read as two reds and two white lights, changing to three reds and one white just prior to touch-down. The aircraft is aimed to land 'on the numbers' just beyond the 'piano key' threshold markings at a touch-down speed of around 140kts. Once it is down, the throttles are closed and the aircraft is flared by rotating to 14 or 15 degrees alpha (AOA)—anything greater would probably cause the underfuselage strakes to make contact with the runway. The nose will fall at around 120kts, and nosewheel steering is engaged, with braking commencing at below 100kts. A heavy or fast landing can be retarded by releasing the brake parachute, the deployment handle for which is located on the left-hand side of the cockpit.

Once the aircraft is clear of the runway, one engine is shut down. A lightweight Jaguar tends to 'run away' with its occupant: with both engines running at idle this not a particular problem, but it can cause the brakes to overheat. Armament switches are 'safed', ejection pins are replaced, the canopy is partially opened and, once the ground marshal is spotted, the taxy lights are switched off, prompting the marshal to guide the pilot back into the parking position. A final INS fix is taken, to establish the system's accuracy, and the engine is shut down. After signing for the aircraft, giving details of the INS performance, sortie, fatigue counts, etc, the pilots return to the Squadron building to de-brief. This establishes whether the mission achieved its aims and what may be learned from it. The formation leader will conduct the de-brief, the supervising officer raising appropriate points as necessary.

The Jaguar does possess one or two vices, not least the T.2's inability to recover from a spin. The GR.1 can assume a dangerous flat spin from which a pilot is unable to eject, and it is therefore important to recover or get out of the aircraft quickly. The overall speed is good, and with afterburners the Jaguar can achieve Mach 1 at low level. Maintenance demands are very light: the Jaguar force can be deployed and return home without any major unserviceabilities, an achievement that can be matched by few other aircraft. The weapons capability is good, the RAF force carrying 1,000lb bombs with retarded or slick tails and air burst, impact or delay fuses, laser-guided bombs, CRV-7 air-to-ground rockets (Mach 4 speed, 10lb warhead), two ADEN 30mm guns, CBU-87 or BL.755 cluster bombs, ALQ-101 ECM pods and chaff/flare dispensers. Performance is good, especially when flown clean ('basically a Hawk with afterburners'), although the aircraft normally carries a hefty weapons and fuel load. It can also carry overwing AIM-9L Sidewinders, a capability developed for operations in the Gulf, and although they rely on boresight positioning they do enable the aircraft to defend itself.

The Jaguar is almost 25 years old, and a degree of 'imperfection' might therefore be expected: as one pilot has commented, 'A perfect Jaguar would have a new HUD, twin fins, a bubble canopy and a grey paint scheme!' On the other hand, the aircraft is well respected by its crews, and the RAF's reluctance to dispose of its Jaguar fleet is indicative of the aircraft's effectiveness.

Tornado GR.1

In terms of both offensive capability and numerical strength, the Panavia Tornado is without doubt the most important aircraft on NATO's inventory. The air forces of the United Kingdom, Germany and Italy all operate considerable numbers of Tornado GR.1 strike/interdiction aircraft, and the RAF also operates a fleet of Tornado F.3 interceptors.

The Royal Air Force's F.3 fighters have received more than a little criticism from media observers, who were quick to highlight the seemingly endless development and production problems experienced with the aircraft's Foxhunter radar system. Likewise, the Tornado's fighting capability—when compared to that of aircraft such as the F-15 and Su-27—is still questioned. Perhaps the concept of a Multi Role Combat Aircraft *was* a little over-ambitious, but while the Tornado ADV (Air Defence Variant) might have enjoyed a controversial career, the IDS (Interdictor/Strike) variant has become recognized as a truly outstanding combat aircraft.

The basic task of the RAF Tornado GR.1 squadron is to maintain a Combat Ready status, to support NATO operations as and when required. This involves a period of training for those who are new to front-line Tornado flying, having come from the TWCU (Tornado Weapons Conversion Unit) and originally the TTTE (Trinational Tornado Training Establishment) at RAF Cottesmore. Once a pilot has achieved Combat Ready status, continual training is required to maintain the level of skills which he has learned. Each squadron will also take part in various exercises and deployments each year, aimed at improving tactics, flying skills, inter-squadron co-operation and command procedures. The lead-in time for these tasks will vary from several months for a full detachment (that may last for two or three weeks) to a few hours for an exercise simulating wartime conditions.

The tasking for each individual sortie comes from a variety of sources, many flights being self-generated within the Squadron. In a combat situation, for example, RAF Germany's Tornado squadrons would receive details of each mission from 2 ATAF's ATOC (Air Task Operations Centre), from where an ATM (air task message) would be issued. This is then allocated to the appropriate aircrew, with an input from the Squadron's Intelligence Officer and GLO (Ground Liaison Officer—an Army officer attached to the Squadron) to assist with intelligence-gathering and to co-ordinate the air activity with ground operations. Once the crews for the mission have been selected, planning will begin. The first consideration is the aim of the mission, which in peacetime might be an exercise for a Combat Ready work-up, or against a specific target, as part of a NATO operational exercise. The second consideration is the weather, and which parts of the United Kingdom and Germany are fit for flying. Once the most suitable areas have been selected, the details which change daily are considered, for example navigation

Below: Aircrew hard at work drawing up mission routes prior to a sortie. (RAFG)

warnings (landing aids and beacons which are unserviceable), 'notams' or Notices to Airmen (indicating areas of danger, or those areas to be avoided), Royal flights (to be avoided) and 'birdtams' (warnings of large flocks of birds).

Once all the information has been collated, the detailed planning can begin, with a look at the target and a decision as to which weapon (or simulated weapon) would be the most suitable in order to maximize the amount of damage. The attack profile is to some extent dictated by the type of weapon which is being carried, and once these details have been established the route into and out of the target area is chosen, taking into account all the appropriate tactical considerations (surrounding terrain, enemy defences, etc) and peacetime restrictions. The pilot will now draw up the target, highlighting the main visual and radar features, on an Ordnance Survey map. While the pilot is busy with the target maps, the navigator plans the route to and from the target area, including a flight plan if required (necessary if flying through an airway), a low-level airspace booking, a range slot booking, fuel usage and all the warnings described earlier.

The navigator plans the target split and checks the route for each Tornado, ensuring that all the aircraft are separated throughout the mission. This will enable the route to be flown in cloud or at night and at low level (a minimum of 250ft in the United Kingdom), subject to flying regulations. The navigator plans the routes at the CPGS (Cassette Preparation Ground Station), where he places a 1:500,000 ('half mil') map on an electronic map table. The CPGS computer is aligned with the map by positioning the cursor over two grid intersections and inputting the corresponding latitude and longitude. The route is then fed into the computer by moving the cursor to each turning point, the target and so on. Once complete, the data are loaded on to an audio cassette, ready to 'plug in' once the crew are inside the cockpit. Hard copies are also produced of the data, in case the system should fail. Likewise, the traditional maps are carried too, each crew member being given a copy of the maps, thanks to the advent of the colour photocopier ('the most useful member of the Squadron', according to the popular view!).

The lead pilot and navigator now prepare the flight briefing, the mnemonics, abbreviations and other jargon in vogue becoming familiar to the crews, for example:

'Altex'	Alternative exercise.
'Bingo'	A pre-briefed fuel state radio call.
'Call-sign'	The word used for air traffic identification.
'Chicken'	The fuel state at which recovery to an airfield must be initiated.
'Combat Fuel'	Spare fuel, i.e. the difference between the planned amount and the minimum required.
'Datum'	A time nominated for reference purposes.
'Divs'	Diversion airfields, which dictate the minimum amount of fuel required for landing.
'Emcon'	Emission control to prevent detection.
'Ifrep'	In flight report.
'Sutto'	Start-up, taxy, take-off.
'TOT'	Time on target.
'TRP'	Timing reference point.

With the briefing complete, the crews collect their flying equipment and prepare to move to their aircraft. The standard RAF flying kit can be supplemented by a full NBC (Nuclear, Biological and Chemical) protective outfit, which is worn during some exercises and would of course be worn in a real war if there were a serious threat of NBC conditions. (Aircrew carried NBC equipment with them at all times during the 1991 Gulf War.) Leaving the PBF (Personnel Briefing Facility), the crews either walk or take a minibus (armoured personnel carriers would probably being used in time of war) to their respective aircraft in the hardened aircraft shelters (HAS). The aircraft documentation, covering its servicing history and maintenance schedule, is checked and the aircraft 'signed for'.

The pilot walks round the aircraft, looking for signs of damage and checking the security of panels, doors and external stores. The tyres are checked for excessive wear or cuts, the brake leads for damage or leaks. The covers and blanking plates are all confirmed as being removed, as are the various safety and restraining pins. Before climbing into the cockpit, both pilot and navigator check their own ejection seats for serviceability and make sure that the seats' safety pins are inserted. They then climb into their seats and begin the 'power-off checks', ensuring that no equipment will operate unexpectedly when power is switched on. After external electrical power is introduced, the radios are checked and the navigator begins aligning the INS. Power-on checks are completed, the pilot starts the engines and external power is disconnected. Meanwhile the navigator is loading the route data into the computer and bringing the navigation and weapon aiming system on line. The team of three ground crew conduct a series of tests to make sure that the flying controls, engines and weapons systems are functioning correctly, and when these checks are complete the aircraft is ready to taxi.

Clearance to taxi from the HAS to the holding point at the end of the active runway is obtained from the Ground Controller, and after each aircraft has 'checked in' with the rest of the formation the Tornado GR.1s rumble out from their protective shelters and weave their way through the HAS complex before joining the main taxiway. During the short journey to the runway each pilot and navigator runs through the series of pre-take-off checks, ensuring that the aircraft is in the correct configuration for departure. At the holding point the crews change from 'Ground' to 'Tower' frequency and details are given to cover the initial outbound heading and height, the local wind direction and speed and the radio frequency for departure.

Once the aircraft is lined up on the runway, full power is applied and reheat selected, the Tornado being capable of holding on the brakes at full thrust. As soon as the 'burners are functioning, the brakes are released and the first aircraft blasts down the runway, trailing a plume of flame over twenty feet long in its wake. Acceleration is very brisk, and once the machine is airborne the undercarriage and flaps are immediately raised and the wings are swept back to 45 degrees. The nature of each departure varies greatly according to the destination, the weather, the number of aircraft present and so on. Many sorties from Bruggen are flown to the United Kingdom, to take advantage of the lower (250ft) minimum height limit available in non-restricted British airspace. These flights are normally 'hi–lo–hi' profiles, involving a high-level transit to and from a low-level route, requiring a SID (standard instrument departure) from Bruggen, flown under instructions from various air traffic authorities along the route as detailed in the flight plan filed during the mission planning stage. Once cleared through German and Dutch airspace, the aircraft enter the United Kingdom ADIZ (Air Defence Identification Zone) and descend to low level.

The aim of most peacetime missions is to locate and destroy a simulated target, and the hours of planning will be wasted if the target attack is not carried out. If the weather permits, a low-level visual formation will be flown en route to the target, maximizing mutual cross-over cover to thwart an enemy attack from the six o'clock position (many sorties include a simulated attacker, in the form of a 'bounce' aircraft, which launches separately from Bruggen). Thanks to its accurate terrain-following radar (TFR) system, the Tornado can fly automatically at 250ft. Inside the GR.1's radome, the TFR dish projects a monopulse beam ahead of the aircraft, nodding above and below the Tornado's flight path. The TFR projects an imaginary curved line (often referred to as a 'ski toe' shape) ahead of the aircraft, and if any obstruction intrudes into the 'ski toe' the TFR commands the Tornado autopilot to climb until the obstruction is avoided. The 'ride comfort' can be adjusted to fly a fairly smooth course over the terrain; for a more warlike ride, the TFR will haul the aircraft up and down each hillside fairly aggressively.

On the approach to the target area, the navigator will update his navigation equipment with radar fixes and regularly monitor the fuel state, engine instruments, oxygen and electrical and hydraulic systems. Likewise, great attention is paid to the weapons systems as the target gets closer. At the

Below: Tornado GR.1 aircrew strap in prior to a mission over Germany. (RAFG)

OPERATIONS PROFILES

pre-briefed split point, each aircraft will separate on to different headings, sweep the wings back to 67 degrees and accelerate towards the target; each will arrive over the target from different directions, separated from the next aircraft by a few seconds. One of several types of delivery profile may be flown, each being relevant to the type of weapon being carried. Laydown attacks require a direct overflight of the target and its defences—a risky tactic, but a necessary one for the delivery of some munitions, including the JP.233 airfield-denial weapon used so successfully during the Gulf War. Conventional 1,000lb bombs can also be delivered in this manner, but the resulting shallow angles of impact will generally reduce quite significantly the amount of damage caused. Loft attacks, involving a pull-up 'toss' release several miles from the target, allow a generous stand-off distance from the target, avoid a potentially dangerous overflight and also give a larger angle of impact for the bombs, which thus may cause much greater damage. The RAF Tornado force would use this profile to deliver nuclear free-fall bombs if required.

A shallow dive attack will give the aircraft some protection from being detected. The Tornado approaches the target at low level before 'popping up' at the last moment to acquire the target visually, the bombs thereby descending steeply while the aircraft is exposed to the enemy for the minimum amount of time. Where the enemy defences have been suppressed, as happened in the Gulf War, a medium-level dive attack can be used, again giving a good angle of penetration for the bombs. Laser-guided bombs (LGBs) were also dropped from medium level during the Gulf War, the targets being designated by other Tornados or by Buccaneers. The JP.233, however, did require the Tornado to fly at low level, directly over the airfield which the weapon was intended to destroy, and consequently a sizeable number of aircraft were damaged or destroyed during the early days of 'Desert Storm', because of the dangerous environment through which the crews were flying. The Allies quickly neutralized Iraq's air force, however, making further airfield attacks unnecessary. All these different types of attack are regularly practised during training sorties, with the crew flying either 'visual' with the target or 'blind' because of weather or distance.

As the Tornado approaches to within two minutes' flying time of the target, the navigator will

Top: Front cockpit, Tornado GR.1A.
Above: Rear cockpit, Tornado GR.1A.

search for his pre-briefed radar fix points, which the pilot will also look for visually. The target can be marked by laser or radar, or visually through the HUD, and, likewise, the bombs can be dropped automatically or manually. The Tornado's computer system is particularly accurate. For example, a typical lay-down attack normally achieves a delivery within ten feet of the designated impact point. The JP.233, unique to the Tornado GR.1, dispenses 215 area-denial mines and 30 cratering munitions, rendering the runway unusable and very difficult to repair.

'Bombs gone—recover' is the instruction from the navigator, signifying that the weapons have been delivered and enabling the pilot to re-join the rest of the Tornado formation as planned, ready to resume the correct positions for defensive cross-cover. On peacetime training missions it is normal for the aircraft to attack two or three different simulated targets, some purely visually, or to use small practice bombs against weapons-range targets. This ensures that all aspects of weapon-aiming, radar-handling and weapons-selection are practised again and again. Bombs dropped on the weapons ranges are scored relative to the precise target position, and the element of competition between crews provides an extra incentive to achieve the best results.

The range of possible in-flight emergencies is quite large, although every system in the Tornado has a back-up or reversionary mode. Even the complete failure of one engine will not prevent the aircraft from flying safely. In peacetime, however, any major systems failure will normally require a sortie to be terminated. The aircraft will be flown to the nearest suitable and available airfield, and engineering advice will be sought. In wartime the mission would naturally have a higher priority, and the Tornado would be flown with a greater level of 'acceptable' systems failures. In some cases, battle damage may require an aircraft to be coaxed home with severe and multiple problems, and the Tornado aircrews regularly practise such 'worst case' situations in ground simulators. Coping with emergencies is a vital skill when one considers the number of things which could go wrong, ranging from major malfunctions such as hydraulic or electric failure, bird-strikes, a loss of aerodynamic control (stalling, spinning, etc), burst tyres on take-off or landing and brake failures (leading to an arrester cable landing), to less catastrophic malfunctions such as instrument or radio failure. For every problem there exists a set procedure to assist the crew in achieving a safe solution. The flight crew check-list (FCC), backed up with personal knowledge of the systems, will help the crew to solve the problem.

When no other safe solution is available, however, the final option is the ejection seat. The Martin Baker seat is a 'zero/zero' escape system, able to operate at zero forward speed and zero altitude if necessary, thanks to an internal rocket pack which will fire the seat and occupant clear of the aircraft at a staggering initial acceleration of $25g$! The seat includes stabilization equipment, an oxygen supply and an automatic separation system, putting the occupant quickly under a fully deployed parachute. Attached to the pilot's harness is a personal survival pack, with a dinghy and emergency rations, enabling the downed crew member to survive in a hostile sea (or land) environment until rescue arrives.

Recovering back to base, the formation will call air traffic control three or four minutes before arrival to obtain the latest airfield status information. Instrument approaches are often necessary in typical German weather, but otherwise, when conditions permit, a visual recovery is made, running in over the airfield, breaking individually down-wind, reducing speed and extending the wings to their fully forward position, with flaps, slats and undercarriage all deployed. The final approach is flown at about 135kts, and once the aircraft is safely down on the runway the nose can be held high to achieve some aerodynamic braking. The thrust reverser buckets can also be deployed when required, and for a full-performance, ultra-short landing the reversers can be pre-armed to deploy as soon as the main wheels make contact with the ground.

When the aircraft is clear of the runway, one engine will be shut down and the weapon aiming equipment, some navigation equipment and the flight systems will also be switched off. The Ground Controller directs the crews back to their individual shelters, where the aircraft is winched backwards into the HAS and the engineers get to work on any problems reported by the aircrew. Back in the PBF the crews complete the usual supply of forms, detailing the route flown, the weapons dropped, the fuel used etc, before attending the de-brief. The first topic will be any flight safety points which may have arisen during the sortie, and any lessons to be learned will be stressed. The Flight Leader will then ascertain whether the object of the mission was achieved—whether each of the crews hit their targets and what the range scores were. Then each stage of the sortie will be discussed in detail, from brief through start-up, take-off and attack profiles to recovery and landing. After this, the radar and HUD film recordings will be assessed to verify the crews' claims regarding their results. This done, the mission is complete. From the beginning of the planning stage the whole exercise may have taken up to six hours, only two of which may have been spent in the air.

The Tornado GR.1 is a true 'fly-by-wire' design, allowing the aircraft to be flown 'freely' without any risk of accident. However, the Tornado systems do have limits, and the aircraft has to be kept within its design envelope. Even so, it handles well, and it is often referred to as a 'big Hawk' by its pilots. For its size and weight it possesses a good range and can carry a big payload, and compared with other bombers it has a proven record for the accuracy of its weapons delivery. Serviceability is excellent, thanks to the many LRUs (line replaceable units). The Tornado is scheduled to receive an avionics upgrade which should equip it for service well into the next century.

TARGET IRAQ
The following is a Tornado navigator's account of 'Desert Storm':

We'd always make sure that we were as full of fuel as possible before crossing the Iraqi border, at which stage the tanker would leave us and we'd press on in radio silence, although the AWACS E-3 would be listening to us all the time. On night sorties there was always a fairly large number of aircraft crossing the border, and it always amazed me that nobody hit each other. Most of the aircraft by this time had switched their lights off, but if you put on your night vision goggles it was like Piccadilly Circus— literally hundreds of aircraft going in, and quite often you'd hear them checking in with AWACS before crossing the border. It was complete pandemonium.

The run-in would start to get rather tense then, and we'd be busy double-checking all of our equipment. If any of your electronic warfare package wasn't working, that was the point at which you'd turn back, because you'd need to know whether you're going to get shot down by something and you'd also need to know that your EW system is going to block any radar emissions which might be looking at you. So if that's not working you have to go home, which is something I had to do on one occasion. If you haven't been talking to your pilot before, this is the point at which you begin talking to him non-stop, as he will want to know everything you're doing in the back seat, and vice versa, so things get a little busy. Your eyes are on stalks, looking for anything you might see or hear, or see on the radar warning receiver. You're constantly talking to each other about how the timing is going, how the speed is, how you're feeling, and the conversation increases the closer you get to the target.

Below: A Tornado GR.1 taxying into a protective sun shelter at Muharraq during 1991. The self-protection Sidewinder missile rails can be seen, attached to the inner wing weapons pylons.

Most of the targets that we went for in the Tornado were quite heavily defended, the airfields being the worst, but later in the war, even if we were going against the bridges, these too had triple-A [anti-aircraft artillery] sites close to them, as the Iraqis gradually realized which targets we were going for. Most of the airfields and POL [petrol, oil and lubricants] sites we had intelligence on, so we knew roughly what kind of defensive systems were around them, although sometimes we were surprised, finding completely different systems there. It was very comforting to be going in with American support beside you, so if any of the radar emitters on the ground did light up, then the Americans would have a go at them with their radar-seeking missiles. The Americans were very interesting to us. Their fighter boys weren't getting the number of kills they wanted, so quite often they'd be flying along beside us with all their lights on, flickering their afterburners on and off so that any Iraqi fighter pilots would see them and hopefully have a go at them. But that didn't work—it just made us more nervous!

One of the most amazing things I've ever seen is triple-A coming up at me. Obviously I'd never seen it before, and to be suddenly looking straight at it was quite frightening. It just snaked up at you, and always seemed to reach the height we were flying at, so we'd be talking about it the whole way through. It just lights up the whole sky around you. Some of it cones straight up at you or around you [and] some snakes up towards you, and it was quite obvious that the guys on the ground were lying on their backs and were just waving the guns backwards and forwards in the hope of catching something. There was lots of flak around too, and you often felt it exploding around you as you went in towards the target. I didn't see many surface-to-air missiles, and many of them were unguided because as soon as their radar systems came on they'd be knocked out by the Americans. They tended to launch them blind most of the time, with no radar image, hoping that they'd hit something, and I saw a few of those come quite close to me. You don't see any sign of them on your RWR, but you'd suddenly see a missile come whistling over your canopy, fully armed and ready to go bang if it hit you.

As for evasion, well, you'd try to go round a triple-A battery the best way you could if you saw it, and, likewise, if you saw a missile you'd pull hard to avoid it if at all possible. You talk to the pilot all the time and he talks to you, because if he's going to pull the aircraft violently to one side you obviously want to know what he's doing. Contrary to popular belief, the Iraqi fighters were airborne in the early stages of the war. There weren't all that many, but they were definitely there and I was locked-on by something on the third or fourth night . . . You do what you can to avoid it and you drop chaff out the back or you fly some fairly violent manoeuvres—whatever you can to break that fighter's lock on you—otherwise he's going to launch a missile at you. As we closed in on the target the pilot would basically want to know how far away we were and how the timing was going. The level of conversation goes up one hundred per cent. You're talking non-stop. The radar was switched on at quite a late stage, so as not to warn the Iraqis that we were coming in, and you only used it for short bursts at any one time, to identify the radar offsets and eventually to identify the target. You'd be looking at fixed points all the way along the route from Bahrain, but only for very short periods, so that the radar is never on for very long. However, you have to make sure that your navigation equipment is very good, so that by the time you get to the target you don't have any problem finding it on radar.

The radar is very good, and you get an excellent picture in the back cockpit of the target area. As long as you've done your route study correctly, you'll have no problem finding your target and the exact point that you want to hit. The pilot is more concerned with looking outside the aircraft, watching for other aircraft, missiles or triple-A, while the navigator is more concerned with making sure that the bombs go off on target and that the timing and navigation are working okay. You make sure that the bombs are live. It's a two-man aircraft, so both people have some means of controlling bomb release, and you have to make sure that you're both happy before they're dropped. You go through all your switches, making sure everything is live and ready to drop on command. It's all computer-controlled, and all the navigator can do is to tell the computer where to drop the bombs. It will then work out the trajectory, where the bombs will go, and it will drop the bombs automatically when you reach the release point. The bombs will fall off, and you'll hear them drop in sequence—*pop . . . pop . . . pop*—as they come off, and you count them to make sure they do all drop . . . maybe you'll make a quick jinking manoeuvre to actually see them going down to the target. You then turn and head for home as fast as you possibly can.

The pilot is obviously concerned that you're marking the right place, and he'll be continually talking about this. He'll want to know that all the bombs are off and that the switches are all looking good. The aircraft is much lighter now, much more manoeuvrable, as you've just got rid of quite a few thousand-pounders. If you do feel under threat at all, you can plug in the afterburners to give you a bit of extra speed in the turn to get you back home again. It's basically a race to get back over the border and rendezvous with the tanker, although quite often you didn't need [one]. But he'd always be there, and wait until the last man was over the border. If one of the boys didn't come back, the tanker captain would wait . . . until there was absolutely no hope at all of the guy coming back. The tankers guys were excellent . . . It's the navigator's job to guide the pilot into the refuelling basket, and if the pilot was feeling a little shaky after flying around Iraq it could take quite a while to get back into the basket. You always took just the minimum amount of fuel you needed as you didn't want to waste time—you wanted to get back on the ground to have a good rest—so you'd unplug from the tanker and get out of the way, ready for another receiver who might be shorter on fuel than you were. Once when we arrived back at Bahrain we were just listening to the controller giving us clearance to land when we heard the air raid siren go off in the background—a Scud inbound to Bahrain. We were completely exhausted but we had to hold overhead the airfield and plug into a tanker, staying up there for nearly half an hour.

How did the trip to the Gulf go? Well, I guess it went well because I came home, and that's the main thing. The big concern is not getting shot down, [but] it's a worry . . . making sure that you do your job right and . . . don't let down your mates. You're nervous when you go out to the aircraft and when you get back, but as soon as you get into that aircraft you've got a job to do and you have to put the nerves behind you. You have to make sure you do the job properly. The transit to the target, probably from the point you take off, to the rendezvous with the tanker [on the outbound leg] is the time when you can think about what you're doing and you can start to get nervous. When you're actually tanking you have a job to do so you're okay. You get very nervous indeed when you leave the tanker, before crossing the Iraqi border, but after that you have so much to concentrate on, you just haven't got time to be nervous. On the target run you're just too busy, and you just have to make sure you get those bombs on the target and destroy it. Coming home, you just want to get back as quickly as you can, and as soon as you step out on the ground you feel nervous again, thinking, 'My God, what the hell have I just been through?' Very mixed emotions, really.

Obviously one or two missions were particularly scary, and when we lost people it was particularly disappointing, but it's one of those things that you have to get over . . . you've got to go and fly the next day, probably to attack the same target, so if you do feel . . . sad because you've lost a colleague you have to put it behind you and get on with it. Sounds very cold, but you can't let things like that affect you, otherwise you might be the next one to go down. Sortie lengths varied from maybe three and a half hours to five and a half hours, the longest I flew being well to the north of Baghdad . . . I was feeling pretty shabby after that one.

Back home I'm now an instructor, and it's my job to train new navigators to go and fly in the Tornado. Because of what I did in the Gulf I can train them with an emphasis on actually fighting a war . . . when I was a student the last thing on my mind was fighting a war. However, when it did happen I was ready and prepared for it, and I like to think that I'm training my students with war in mind. I tell them Gulf stories, and if they do make mistakes I liken it to a war situation, which makes [for] a good learning environment. In a strange way the Gulf War was very satisfying as it was a chance to put into practice what I'd only done in theory before. You can always train for war, but you can never know how you'll really perform unless you've actually done it. Now that I have, and flown eighteen missions, I figure I must have done a good job to survive it, as did my colleagues. To have flown inside enemy territory is a very frightening experience, but to have come back from it . . . having achieved my job of putting bombs on the target makes me feel very good—makes me feel proud of myself and [of] the rest of my formation too. I'm far more confident now, and it's also made me appreciate the fact that life can stop at any moment—which makes you want to live life to the full. Certainly, that's something I've done since I came back, but maybe not something I'd done before the war. While I was actually out there in the war I realized that at any second I might no longer exist. So now I want to make sure that I live my life to the full.

Another interesting point, and a nice one for us, was the amount of media interest. The Press were very reasonable to us, and we had all kinds of people writing to us, ranging from mothers and grandmothers to . . . schoolchildren. We still correspond with some people now . . . We got letters and good-luck cards from lots of people—even chocolate bars and teddy bears, which we took flying with us. Valentine's Day was fantastic!

Much of the combat flying was essentially similar to peacetime flying. The planning stage was much the same, as we always simulated an EW environment, we often flew with package support and we dropped bombs on a range. The only real difference was that whereas much of the peacetime flying is good fun, the Gulf flying was taken much more seriously. But we'd never underestimate the value of training. Much of the specific planning was the same as during peacetime, the pilots choosing the actual places at the target to attack and choosing the offset points and so on. The navigators still did the routeing in and out of the target [area]. Perhaps the real peacetime difference is that you're not in danger from a Scud missile coming through the roof while you're planning or briefing, so you wouldn't be carrying your Nuclear, Biological and Chemical warfare suit around with you. However, no matter what training you do, you can never be . . . completely prepared for the real thing. We always thought that if we did go to war it would be an East–West conflict, and we didn't think we'd be flying in the Middle East. So to go and fight in the desert, and have camels to avoid, was very different! Above all, we proved that the Tornado GR.1 is more than capable for fighting in a modern combat environment. More than can be said for certain other aircraft!

Harrier

Harriers are different! There is no doubt that, in the world of ground attack operations, the British Aerospace/McDonnell Douglas AV-8 Harrier is a truly unique aircraft. Unlike any other combat aircraft, it does not require a runway to get airborne. The capacity to operate almost anywhere gives it total flexibility, and a truly outstanding survival capability in a modern battlefield scenario, where a fixed airfield is a highly vulnerable target. Naturally, the ability to operate 'in the field' is practised regularly, particularly in Germany, where RAF Strike Command maintains two squadrons (Nos 3 and 4) of Harrier GR.7s at Laarbruch. During a field deployment, each squadron is divided into three flights, each occupying a separate dispersed site. Likewise, No 1 Squadron, based at Wittering in the United Kingdom, also regularly deploys to its representative wartime area in Norway, where the unit would support NATO's Northern Flank.

Out in the field, each Harrier pilot, sitting in his cockpit, is connected to an operations cabin attached to each dispersal site. The ops cabin is staffed by a senior RAF officer who works in company with a Ground Liaison Officer (GLO) from the Army. He will receive a tasking signal which will arrive, via a Forward Wing Operations Centre (FWOC), from the central tasking agency conducting whatever operations are taking place at that time. The GLO will assemble an ATM (air task message) which is a formatted A4 sheet containing all the relevant details required by the Harrier pilot to conduct his mission. Details include the call-sign, the position of the target, the time of attack, how many aircraft will be required, what co-ordination there will be with other units if required, and so on. The ATM is handed to the pilot in his cockpit, and a 'runner' will be sent out with Ordnance Survey maps of the target area. The 'Auth' in the ops cabin will decide which pilot will lead the mission, and who will fly with him, based on his information about which aircraft are refuelled, which are combat capable and so forth.

The pilot can talk directly to the ops cabin, and to the GLO and other pilots as required, by land-line (plugged into the aircraft fuselage). Once the briefing is complete, the aircraft start up, taxy from their camouflaged 'hides' and begin their sorties. On completion of the missions, the pilots will quickly resume communication, by land-line, for an 'in-brief', which will include a 'MisRep' (mission report) from each pilot, outlining the effectiveness of the sortie, engine operations, times etc. This information is then quickly conveyed to the central tasking agency so that additional attacks, reconnaissance flights or a new tasking for new targets can be planned if necessary.

RAF field operations invariably take place deep in the German countryside in an effort to minimize the disturbance to the general public. However, in

Below: Harrier GR.5, illustrating the port wing weapons pylons and a Sidewinder missile training round.
Bottom: Harrier T.4 twin-seat conversion trainer.

wartime the Harrier force would be more likely to utilize urban locations such as petrol station forecourts and supermarket car parks—the local Safeway store could be a potential Harrier base! For peacetime training purposes, stretches of highway are often 'borrowed' as temporary runways, connected to the Harrier 'hides' by stretches of PSP (pierced steel planking), and it is not uncommon for road traffic to be stopped by the local police force while a Harrier rumbles out from nearby woodland to take off. A bizarre event like this is part of day-to-day life in Germany, although such sights are becoming less frequent as the shadow of the Cold War disappears.

How does the Harrier pilot plan his mission? First, having received an ATM, he checks its date and checks also that it includes sufficient time for the mission to be planned. The leader of the mission will then allocate specific tasks to each of his wingmen. For example, one pilot will be responsible for working out VSTOL (vertical take-off and landing) figures, while another will check the weather in the target area. The pilot will then locate the target on an OS map, be it a bridge, a troop concentration or a POL (petrol, oil and lubricants) installation, establishing what weapons should be used to attack it. Sometimes the decision will have been made for him by the tasking agency, who will have attempted to match weapons with appropriate targets. However, the pilots may have to change the plan. For example, there would be little point in attacking a bridge with a cluster bomb unit, this weapon having been designed to destroy light armour and troops not concrete walls, and in such an instance a conventional 1,000lb bomb would be much more effective.

The next task is to work out an attack track on to the target. For something like a bridge, it would be wrong to attack from an angle of 90 degrees, as it would be easy to straddle it with bombs rather than hit it. Attacking longitudinally would also be ineffective if the left/right positioning is in error. Therefore the optimum attack is a 30 to 45-degree oblique attack, and this must be planned into the route. Another important consideration is the 'unmask', the point at which the aircraft emerges from the hillside clutter and the pilot first sees his target. Unmasking too late will leave insufficient time to line up on the target. However, the target would normally be defended, and if the pilot can see his target the defenders can certainly see the aircraft. Unmasking ten miles before the target would thus be foolish, and the Harrier pilot would probably try to reveal his position approximately seven seconds before bomb release. Ensuring that the aircraft will be positioned in the right place, just seconds before the attack, means that the route must be very carefully planned, making use of lead-in visual features that will place the aircraft on the correct heading.

Other aircraft will be flying with the leader, in battle formation so that each six o'clock position can be watched. The leader's wingman may well need to approach the target from a different direction, perhaps cutting in on the leader's approach route a few seconds before bomb release. However, 1,000lb bombs create huge clouds of smoke and debris which he obviously would not want to fly through. Target separation thus becomes important, and a 'slash' attack may be flown, the wingman making a 45-degree attack some 20–30 seconds after the leader. For defensive purposes, too, it would be dangerous to fly two aircraft on exactly the same attack route. The separate attack tracks and times must therefore be individually planned.

Lead-in features are selected from the Ordnance Survey map, the most prominent and easily recognizable being chosen. In the United Kingdom it is fairly easy to find a lake, a wood, a motorway junction or some other similarly conspicuous landmark, and basic navigation techniques will then lead the pilot to the target. In the Harrier GR.3 the pilot simply overflew a suitable feature, set the stopwatch counting and flew the aircraft at a constant 480kts on the required heading. After a specific number of seconds, the Harrier would be over the target. With the arrival of the Harrier GR.7, the pilot can work out the latitude and longitude of the target and feed the co-ordinates into a computer, and a precise bearing and range in metres to the target will be produced. This information is then fed into the Harrier's onboard computer. When the pilot overflies the IP (initial point), he hits the WOF (waypoint overfly) switch. The Harrier then switches the pilot's head-up display (HUD) into an air-to-ground read-out mode and the aircraft's computer checks the radio altimeter in order to calculate the height and position of the pre-programmed target. Once the WOF has been selected the pilot will then check that the armament master switches are on, and having already selected the appropriate weapons release sequence he is ready to look through a green diamond symbol which is generated on the HUD. This is the computer's predicted target position, and the Harrier pilot can expect the target to appear inside the diamond. However, the traditional GR.3 style stopwatch-and-map navigation techniques are still used, to ensure that the computer is doing its job properly. Assuming that the computer's HUD prediction for the target position proves to be correct, the pilot can select a TV camera in the nose which provides 6–7× magnification, showing in greater detail where the computer is targeted. With another switch selection the Harrier's camera will track the target, and this will enable the computer to 'fine-tune' the accuracy of its weapon delivery. On this CCIP (continually computed impact point) attack, a cross will appear on the HUD, predicting where the bombs will impact, provided the pilot presses the 'pickle' button to drop the weapons. However, the bombs can be dropped automatically by selecting 'Auto'; in this mode the pilot still presses his 'pickle' button on the control column, ahead of the target, but the weapons are retained on their hardpoints until the computer's pre-calculated release point is reached.

Although the Harrier's computerized system makes his task sound simple, it must be remembered that the pilot expects to be flying towards a heavily defended target at 100ft AGL or less, at 480kts. In the circumstances, it would be incredibly difficult to devote much time to a TV screen or a computer display. For example, if the HUD diamond had appeared to the left or right of the actual target position, the pilot could slew the diamond on to the target visually, before locking-on, by physically flying the aircraft into the precise position, but the heavy workload for the pilot tends to preclude the exclusive use of TV attacks as a primary means of delivering weapons. The TV system is much more practical for medium-level attack—but the RAF has for a long time considered that anything other than a low-level attack would be suicidal. Following experience in the 1991 Gulf War, the situation has changed somewhat, and a greater emphasis is now placed on medium-level operations, for which the Harrier's computerized system is particularly suited. Nevertheless, it is important to recognize that the conditions which prevailed in the skies over Iraq may well be very different from those experienced in other situations, and the RAF still trains its Harrier pilots to attack at low level.

A typical day in the field in Germany, begins at 0530Z ('Zulu', or GMT), which normally equates to 0730 in Germany. After getting out of bed, washing, shaving, etc, the pilots collect their sleeping kit together, ready to move to a new dispersal site. They wear standard RAF flying suits, plus anti-*g* trousers. After collecting his flying helmet, each pilot will walk to his aircraft, pausing to sign for it at the hide, where a special 'aircraft turnaround' certificate is attached to the usual Form 700 book to enable him to endorse what would otherwise be a lengthy list of separate 'boxes'. Following a quick check of his aircraft's exterior, each pilot climbs into his cockpit and effectively stays there for the rest of the day—apart from brief trips to answer the calls of nature! He takes the Form 700 book with him and sits in his aircraft as it is refuelled and serviced, ensuring that the aircraft, pilot and servicing documents are all instantly capable of rapid re-deployment.

A small gas turbine starter is incorporated into the Harrier, which produces AC power, enabling the pilot to align the aircraft's computer before strapping in. The task of attaching oneself to the GR.7's seat is much easier than in the GR.3, simply because the cockpit is substantially larger. After the two leg restraints and PSP (personal survival pack) have been attached, the PEC (personal equipment connector) is fitted, to supply oxygen and a communications link and air pressure for the anti-*g* suit. The harness straps are routed through a lap restraint and into a QRB (quick release box), and once each strap is tightened the pilot is ready to start the aircraft. The first tasks are to turn the communications equipment on, then switch the fuel pumps on and activate the electronic fuel control (a manual fuel system is also fitted, and is checked). Still on the left side of the cockpit, other checks include the autostabilizers, the undercarriage ('down') and the flaps ('up'), then the pilot looks up to his left-hand TV screen to check the BIT (built-in test) list. Also located on the left side of the cockpit are the controls for the chaff/flare dispenser and the Harrier's unique nozzle vector lever.

The basic instruments are now checked, as is the UFC (up-front controller), which includes selection switches such as the WOF, the CCIP/Auto (in the GR.5—relocated on the throttle in the GR.7) and the tacan (tactical air navigation equipment). The appropriate altitude base height, below which the aircraft will automatically provide visual and audi-

OPERATIONS PROFILES

Above: A trio of Harrier GR.5s. The GR.5 has now been largely replaced by the night-attack GR.7.

ble warnings to the pilot, is also selected. The IFF (Identification Friend or Foe) frequency is selected, and 'WPS', the weapons selection, is checked, enabling the pilot to programme his weapons release on the options display unit, located to the left of the UFC (the weapons panel will have been checked before the pilot enters the aircraft). Just below the UFC is the HUD control panel, where the brightness can be adjusted and a back-up weapon aiming sight can be selected should the main system fail. Below this panel are the main aircraft instruments—the attitude indicator, heading reference, vertical speed indicator, altimeter, airspeed indicator, angle of attack indicator and turn and slip indicator.

Between the pilot's knees, low on the instrument panel, is the sensor control panel for the TV/laser tracker in the nose, the alignment knob for the inertial platform and the video recording switch, together with a few circuit breakers. Up on the right-hand side is the engine data panel, showing rpm, JPT (jet pipe temperature), duct pressure to the reaction controls, fuel flow and tailplane position. Further to the right is the engine nozzle position indicator. Below this is a moving map display, with an option for differing scales according to whether a sortie is to be flown at high, medium or low level. To the right of this is an ECM (electronic countermeasures) panel featuring Zeus, an onboard EW (electronic warfare) suite recognized as being an excellent system. Below this is a fuel panel. On the right-hand console is an array of caution lights—brake pressure, hydraulic pressure, cabin pressure etc. Further to the right are switches for the APU, standby radio and ACNIP (auxiliary communications and navigation identification) panel—a kind of back-up system for the UFC. Also on this side of the cockpit are controls for the internal lighting, which in the GR.7 is all-green—even including the warning lights.

Having completed the left-to-right switch selection, the pilot starts up the aircraft, and after taking out the safety pins for the seat and MDC (miniature detonating cord) he signals for the intake blanking plates to be removed. Once start clearance is obtained, the low-pressure fuel cock is turned 'on', the electronic fuel control master switch is 'on', the high-pressure fuel cock is 'off', the manual fuel system is 'off' and the booster fuel pumps are 'on'. The start switch, located on the electrical panel near the APU switch, is selected and the APU runs down initially, reverting to DC power if required, in order to maintain the onboard systems before the engine is engaged, after which the APU winds up again. As the engine starts up, the fuel HP cock is opened, initiating the rest of the start procedure, while the pilot checks the JPT. If the temperature rises too rapidly, a 'hot start' has occurred (the engine receiving too much fuel), so the throttle is closed slightly—the pilot checking that the ground marshal is not making a fire signal—before the start-up procedure is continued. The nozzles are set aft, to prevent hot air from being ingested and the problems of a 'hot start' thereby exacerbated.

Once post-start checks have been completed, the aircraft is taxied to the runway area. A check is made that the nozzles are working, before a 10-degree setting to avoid heat damage to the tail is made; the jet efflux flowing over the tailplane can be felt by the pilot through the control column while he is taxying. A take-off in the Harrier is always impressive: it is a 'punchy little jet', as any Harrier pilot will confirm. The initial rate of acceleration is greater than that attainable by almost any other combat aircraft, and even though it has no reheat the thrust-to-weight ratio is still dramatic. At light weights the Harrier will be airborne in just 200ft. The drag factor does begin eventually to overcome thrust as speed increases, but for low (including zero) speed handling the Harrier possesses some unique qualities. From a dispersal strip the take-off speed will be predetermined according to weight and ambient temperature. Likewise, the speed at which the nozzles are dropped to 50 degrees to 'punch' the aircraft into the air is also calculated in advance. The nozzles enable the aircraft to utilize both air and jet lift before they are vectored rearwards, allowing the aircraft to begin normal wing-borne flight.

The Harrier's fuel control system is complicated, as great emphasis is placed on engine reliability. An aircraft which hovers requires an almost instant response from its engine, which in turn requires a sophisticated means of supplying it with fuel. In order to check the system before take-off, the throttle is deliberately 'slammed' from idle to 55 per cent and then held while the time taken to achieve the greater thrust is established. It should be under five seconds.

Increasing the thrust to full power would cause the aircraft's tyres to slip on their mountings, although the brakes would hold. The nozzles are quickly checked for rotation to 50 degrees, and the engine duct pressure is checked. Finally, the IGVs (inlet guide vanes) are checked. These vanes move in flight to maintain inlet air pressures across the low-pressure intake stage of the engine.

After a final look to make sure the seat safety pins are out, and a glance at the right fuel and flap settings and the master arm safety switch, take-off clearance is obtained. Little verbal communication is necessary, and for two-ship and four-ship departures hand signals are sufficient—a deliberate nod to commence the take-off roll, another nod to 'STO' (short take-off) and another to raise the gear. The take-off attitude is 12 degrees AOA, creating a steep climbing attitude to clear trees or other potential obstructions around the field. On particularly hot days in Germany some take-offs are performed with less than full fuel loads, to enable the aircraft to make short take-off rolls within safety limits. The normal take-off speed is around 120kts, using slightly less than full power, in order to reduce engine fatigue. When full power is required, water injection is used, cooling the rear portion of the engine and enabling an extra 6–7 per cent rpm to be achieved, giving the Harrier an additional 1,000–1,500lb of thrust. However, the 50 gallons of water will last for only eighty seconds, and if ten gallons are used for take-off there may be less than a minute's reserve of water remaining. Consequently the pilot must be careful when identifying and coming in to his dispersed landing site, as his 'hover time' may be severely limited at certain weights.

Back with the take-off procedure, a check that the water is flowing is followed by a look at the engine rpm. This is a vital check, as some take-off clearings are small and if the engine's water injection fails to flow the engine will not develop full power. The pilot then has to make an instant decision whether to abort, and in such a small space, with rapid acceleration, there is virtually no time to think. If the trees are fast approaching, ejection may be the only option. Flap settings vary according to the take-off requirements, and 'Cruise' (up), 'Auto' (between 5 and 25 degrees) or 'STOL' (full deflection for short take-offs or landings) may be selected. During a normal 'pairs' take-off the flaps are usually set at 'Auto': full deflection causes the Harrier to bounce into the air, making close-formation manoeuvres tricky. On a dispersed strip, however, STOL flap is always used. The undercarriage gear is retracted once the aircraft is airborne.

RT communication varies of course, but a typical exchange might be as follows:

'Bottle formation is airborne, Stud Eight.' (Harrier)

'Roger, Bottle formation, cleared to Stud Eight.' (Tower)

'Stud Eight, go.' (Harrier, switching to radio channel)

'Bottle', 'Two', 'Three', 'Four'. (Each Harrier pilot)

'Bottle, four aircraft departing, VFR, one thousand feet.'

'Roger, no known traffic in the area, QNH is nine-eight-five. You're cleared on route, good day, Stud Fifteen.' (Tower)

'Bottle', 'Two', 'Three', 'Four.' (Harriers change frequency)

The aircraft leave the local area at 1,000–1,500ft in order to minimize the disturbance to the local population. Once the aircraft are clear of built-up areas the transit height is eased downwards—in the United Kingdom the low-level limit is 250ft, normally available in sparsely populated areas of Wales, Scotland, North Yorkshire, etc. Routes are always planned to avoid built-up areas: RAF pilots, like everybody else, are well aware of the nuisance which can be caused by jet noise.

The Harriers normally fly in battle formation, in line abreast, roughly 2–3,000yds apart, checking each other's six o'clock positions. With a four-ship formation, a second pair will fly in trail, about thirty seconds behind, sometimes displaced laterally. The planned routes are largely dictated by the areas of population which must be avoided. Although the entire United Kingdom land mass is treated as one huge low-flying area, the RAF pilot's low-level chart is crammed with avoidance areas, the result of which is a remarkably limited number of routes which can be flown. Turning points must be related to unique features which can be instantly recognized from the air, and many points tend to be chosen again and again simply because of the ease with which they can be recognized and because of the convenience of their position.

Forward air controllers regularly work with the Harrier force. The GR.5 and GR.7 have an excellent laser search system which will pick up even the smallest amount of reflected laser light and display its range and position extremely accurately in the cockpit, enabling the pilot to switch instantly to an auto attack if required. For attacks with CBUs (cluster bomb units), an over-the-target height of 100ft is used, or 150ft for a conventional 1,000lb bomb. The normal attack speed is 480kts or faster. The RAF Harrier force will eventually re-employ the Matra SNEB rocket launcher pod. Two Sidewinder self-defence missiles will probably be carried too, and the cockpit TV display will give the pilot a detailed layout diagram, showing where each weapon is carried

Returning to base, the Harriers approach at a fairly high level, to avoid causing too much noise disturbance, before descending to run in over the airfield to break into the traffic pattern at 1,500ft. Circuits are flown on AOA settings rather than speed. Conventional forward landings can be made at 140–150kts, but a lightweight Harrier can almost always be landed vertically and both field operations and conventional airfield approaches often culminate in this way. The aircraft is decelerated into the hover, the pilot having first noted the wind direction and speed. Pilots must be very wary of cross-winds, as they will have an increasing effect upon the aircraft as it slows towards the hover. During the transition from 90 to 30kts the Harrier can produce yaw-induced intake drag, which can kill. The wing is producing some lift, but if one wing produces more than the other the effect of a cross-wind in the huge intakes will produce a yawing movement which, when combined with the asymmetric wing lift, will cause the aircraft to flip over. The angle of attack is consequently kept low, and the aircraft is always flown into wind as it slows, the pilot picking up the landing site references as he comes into the hover.

Stabilizing at 50ft above the landing position, the aircraft is controlled by jet puffer ducts, located in the nose, tail and wings, which provide jet thrust bled from the engine. The system is connected directly to the control column and functions in exactly the same way as the normal flying controls. Once the pilot is satisfied that a safe landing can be achieved, the aircraft makes the final descent to the landing pad before taxying back to the dispersed hide or flight line. After engine shut-down there are various post-flight checks to be made before the pilot either returns to the flight line hut or simply hands the aircraft's Form 700 to the Crew Chief, giving details such as how long the aircraft has been airborne and how much fuel has been used. Airframe and engine fatigue data are noted, as are the type of landing and take-off and the weapons that have been carried—all vital information for the accurate recording of fatigue usage.

RAF Harrier pilots also regularly fly aerial combat sorties, maintaining a good proficiency in self-defence. The Harrier has a good turning capability —not quite as impressive as an F-16's perhaps, but excellent at slower speeds. The Harrier also possesses the unique VIFF (vectoring in forward flight) capability, whereby the engine nozzles can be swivelled forward to create an instantaneous and dramatic deceleration. The manoeuvre can be used, for example, at the top of a loop: the aircraft can be pitched back into the vertical very rapidly if the pilot pushes the nozzles into the 40-degree position. Pushing the nozzles into the braking stop while descending vertically will keep the aircraft stabilized at around 150kts. A conventional aircraft cannot hope to compete and would race past the Harrier into an embarrassing missile-kill position. Equally, such a manoeuvre can be employed in the horizontal plane, and if the Harrier pilot cannot push his aircraft into the correct missile firing position the application of nozzle vectoring will punch the nose quickly into the right place. VIFF is a useful facility— though by no means the answer to every problem.

Potential hazards for Harrier pilots include birdstrikes, although the aircraft is particularly robust in terms of the strength of its airframe and engine. RAF pilots would certainly like more thrust if such could be made available; indeed, Rolls-Royce are actively promoting a more powerful Pegasus engine for the Harrier, which the USMC and RAF may well eventually adopt, enabling the pilot to take on aircraft such as the F-16 with confidence. The engine relights easily, and flame-outs are not considered to be a major problem. The Harrier is very much an 'electric jet', however, having a multiplicity of systems which rely on electrical power, and generator failure can cause difficulties.

Any RAF Harrier pilot will proudly say that he is part of a unique breed of single-seat RAF combat pilots, making all the decisions himself in the world's only fully VTOL-capable jet aircraft. The navigation and weapons systems are very accurate and effective. That the aircraft is not fast is perhaps its only real disadvantage. A two-man cockpit might be an advantage: the pilot's workload is exceptionally high, and even he will admit that a second pair of eyes and hands would be very useful. However, the Harrier's ability to disperse away from conventional airfields is a recognized as being a vital asset, and the aircraft provides a flexible means of air cover for ground forces.

Hawk

RAF Valley, on the south-western coast of Anglesey, is the home of No 4 FTS, one of two Royal Air Force Flying Training Schools where would-be bomber and fighter pilots learn to use an advanced trainer—the Hawk—as a tactical fighter and attack aircraft. Until recently, the RAF trained its fast-jet pilots in a two-stage process, advanced flying instruction being completed at Valley before tactical weapons training was undertaken at Brawdy or Chivenor. These courses have now been combined, and both Valley and Chivenor operate identical courses, teaching Tucano pilots to become very competent fighter-bomber Hawk pilots. A Royal Air Force instructor explains:

We have now started a new combined syllabus, and although there have been some changes to the course the students are effectively doing the same training that they would have done under a separate FTS and TWU arrangement. There is a clear-cut division between the flying training and tactical training elements of the 4 FTS course, but the distinction is rapidly disappearing. However, it is, naturally, important to keep the students on a learning curve, and the advanced flying skills will obviously have to be learned before we introduce the tactical training, so what we have essentially done is join the two courses together rather than mix them.

There are still some general handling sorties within the tactical phase of the course anyway, so the new system is mixed, but only inasmuch as the whole course is done with just the one squadron on one airfield and the training is much more of a continual learning curve. The student comes here without having flown the Hawk, and he leaves having dropped bombs and having flown air combat. The flying hours are somewhat reduced when compared to the old arrangement, but we haven't removed anything of any significance from the course. Because the students aren't changing stations after the advanced flying phase, we don't need to fly any familiarization sorties after changing base, so we've saved on duplication. Some sorties have been lost though, but maybe only one or two fewer within the actual training elements, so nothing significant in that sense. We're anticipating a drop in the number of students passing through here, but so far we haven't seen any real reduction. We aren't working any less than we ever have done before, but we are talking about smaller courses in the future, reflecting the reduced commitments of the front-line squadrons.

The students all fly the same course, and there is no distinction between the potential fighter pilot or bomber pilots. We don't divide them into the two categories like we did a few years ago, and they all do the same combined course. At the end, we will decide where to post them. There is an advantage in this system, in that aircraft like the Tornado GR.1 and Harrier do sometimes fly combat, and we can give the student an overall impression of everyone's role, and that will be of some benefit to the students when they fly an operational type. When the student leaves Valley or Chivenor, it's fair to say that he will have learned more than just the basics. He will have learned how to lead an advanced air defence sortie, using a ground intercept controller, using Sidewinders and so on, and he'll have led a simulated attack profile, with a bounce aircraft trying to put him off track. That's a fairly demanding sortie, so the student is pretty capable by the time he completes the course. Moving to the Operational Conversion Unit is perhaps something of a quantum leap, however, in terms of the aircraft that he'll be flying. It's often said that the Tornado is just a big Hawk, but, believe me, it is a big Hawk in the same way you could say that a bus is just a big van. The operating constraints are different. You'll fly in bigger formations, maybe six-ships or eight-ships, and he'll fly further, maybe refuelling from a tanker, so the sorties will become more complicated.

Certainly, the 'Top Gun' movie image of the modern military fast-jet pilot is quickly shattered at Valley, where there is no time for anything other than plain hard work. The syllabus for No 4 Flying Training School is tough, and not every student will survive the course. Those who are successful will be posted to an Operational Conversion Unit (OCU), where they will continue their training on the aircraft type which they will fly when they finally join an operational squadron. However, there is no doubt that by the time each student leaves Valley (or Chivenor) he is already very capable. Towards the end of the course, the student will lead a SAP sortie, a simulated attack profile, which is a particularly arduous mission designed to resemble closely a 'real'

Above: Hawk T.1s from No 4 Flying Training School, RAF Valley.

operational attack sortie. The ultimate aim of a sortie flown by a strike/attack squadron is to deliver weapons accurately on to a designated target. The request for an attack sortie usually comes in the form of an air task message (ATM) and this, together with a target photograph (if available), the intelligence officer's briefing, the ground liaison officer's (GLO's) briefing and the meteorological forecast, provides all the information necessary for planning the attack. The ATM will include, amongst other things, the details of the task, the time on target (TOT), the position of friendly forces, the number and type of aircraft to be used and the weapons load to be carried. The intelligence briefing will include details of the positions of any SAM (surface-to-air missile) and AAA (anti-aircraft artillery) areas, the details of enemy fighter defences and CAP (combat air patrol) positions, target information from previous attacks or reconnaissance sorties, enemy radar coverage and escape/evasion and SAR (search and rescue) cover.

For a close air support mission, a briefing will normally be given by an Army GLO. He will provide details of radio frequencies, control agencies and call-signs, the position and description of contact points (CPs) and initial points (IPs), the position of friendly and enemy forces, the type of target marking (if any) and the position of entry and exit 'gates' in the area. Finally, the meteorological briefing will cover the weather conditions at base and at the diversion airfield or airfields, route weather, winds and contrail heights if any high-level flying is to be conducted. Because of the large amount of planning involved in an attack sortie, the leader of the mission (in the case of a SAP, this will be a student) must work back from the TOT and decide how long can be spent on planning and briefing. He must study the target maps and photographs, formulate an attack plan and decide on tactics. He may then allocate some tasks to other members of the squadron, such as domestic information, the met forecast, route planning and map preparation, fuel calculations, copying the attack plan and target maps and weapons briefing.

It is important to arrange the planning sequence correctly, otherwise the time taken to plan the sortie can become unnecessarily protracted. For a typical SAP mission, an instructor will provide the student with a target, from a range of some sixty potential sites situated around the United Kingdom (mostly in the West). The instructor will provide all the relevant details which would be included in a 'real' ATM, and the student is then expected to assemble a SAP plan based on the information. He will firstly plan the intelligence and meteorological briefings, and he will then draw up suitable maps, a low-level route chart (1:500,000 scale) and an IP-to-target chart (1:50,000 scale), with details of the route and all relevant intelligence included as necessary. Naturally, the route taken will depend upon the attack plan, and there are many considerations to bear in mind when preparing it. First, the available weapons must be considered, as each weapon type will require a different delivery technique. The target defences will vary in quality and quantity, and the chosen route must be designed to keep the attacking aircraft 'masked' from the target for as long as possible, but still with sufficient time for the pilot to acquire it visually and line up on it. The number of aircraft is another consideration, as the student must take into account the size of his formation. It would, naturally, be impossible to fly through narrow valleys with a four-ship SAP formation. Other considerations include the terrain surrounding the target, and the possibilities for re-attacking it. The best aiming point on the target must be chosen, so as to obtain the best effects with the available weapons. Likewise, the position of the sun can be

Above: Hawk front cockpit main instrument panel.

important, in providing good illumination of the target and obscuring the enemy's view of the attackers. The effect of the wind on weapons-aiming and smoke travel is also important.

The IP is a vital stage in the attack mission, from which the final target run is commenced. It must be a unique ground feature, easily visible from a reasonable distance. It should also be between five and ten nautical miles from the target. It must be undefended, and it should also provide a suitable map changeover point, thirty seconds before the IP, to give an accurate track check. The student will plan to overfly the IP on the target heading, as turns on to the IP are normally avoided—the aim is to be on track and on time at the IP.

Most SAP routes are planned 'lo–lo–lo' (i.e. at low level throughout), and the student should take this into account when examining the target's range from base, the positions of the enemy defences, the terrain, weather, combat fuel allowance and recovery fuel. The route should avoid built-up areas and defended areas (avoidance areas such as farms and hospitals are often classed as 'enemy SAM sites' etc for the purposes of a SAP exercise). Terrain is used to hide the SAP formation as much as possible, within the constraints of the 250ft minimum height restriction which is imposed for peacetime training. Terrain features are also used for navigation, and the most obvious features are chosen in order to make the visual navigation as easy as possible.

Most importantly, the student is advised to plan for the unexpected, for example a delayed take-off, bad weather en route to (or at) the target area, excessive fuel consumption, loss of contact with the other aircraft in cloud or aircraft unserviceability.

The SAP will include a 'bounce' aircraft in the form of an additional Hawk flown by an instructor. He will assume the role of an enemy aggressor, aiming to throw the student off course and generally distract him from his planned route. Navigational errors are also possible; indeed, the instructors emphasize that if the student is flying on track at all times his look-out for enemy fighters is obviously not good enough.

The planning stage is vitally important, as the mission will succeed or fail depending upon the quality of the pre-flight planning and briefing. The following is an extract from a SAP briefing:

> We will go as a pair, pushing out to battle formation for transit, then we'll close up for our descent into Shawbury, and that will be a full radar-to-visual approach to overshoot and depart at low level. If I see any opportunities to cut corners, we'll take them, otherwise we'll fly down Shawbury's centreline ... Flight level one-seven-zero to Shawbury, and we expect to be on runway two-three there.
>
> Formation is battle, and flying wing as required ... For recovery we will split for individual visual recoveries back here ... Bird-strike, we'll go as a pair, and I prefer to be pushed, so I'd be up front there ... Low level, we're heading one-two-zero, climbing through the airways, into Shawbury for a fast speed radar-to-visual. A three hundred knot transit, and as soon as we're Victor Mike with the ground we'll overshoot and depart on one-six-zero until we're clear of LFA nine, descending to low level. What have we got by way of visuals? Well, we have an enormous two-thirty-nine double mast here just by the railway line, and this tip of land with a two-ten mast on, and then sliding down the ridge we have a pair of six hundred and seventy foot masts. We don't want to hit them, and we want to be about a mile to the right of them. Then we're starting to pick up the woods, and we're time hacking on the lake in the woods just on the edge of LFA nine. Down past Bridgnorth and we obviously can't stray left–and keep an eye open for any civvies bumbling into Halfpenny Green—and we're looking to pick up the dam and the woods which feed into the bigger woods to turn on to the IP.
>
> We'll come off the target on one-six-six, down to the woods and low ground, around Bromyard, to pick up the distinctive ridge and the Wellington sheds complex, to turn onto our IP. Off target, we miss Ross-on-Wye and pick up the motorway, turning to come across the top of Abergavenny—fifteen-ninety-five spot height is a good lead there—and if we need to go south of Abergavenny, watch those red spots to avoid. Turning up the valley towards Brecon, we turn short of Brecon, into fighting wing if necessary, but maintaining battle if we can, as it's an air threat throughout, so I want you looking at my six o'clock all the time. Round we go, and we've got Sennybridge mast, Llandrindod Wells, and we're starting to think about pulling up to save some gas, and then it's three-four-zero from Newtown, back to Valley.
>
> So, the first target is on two-one-five, at thirty-six seconds from the IP. There's a reservoir to lead us in, the woods abeam, looking ahead in the two o'clock position for the next set of woods. Down past Highley, and my IP is Maxfields Coppice, and you'll be making a four-g turn through ninety degrees to get yourself behind me. Now, looking ahead I have the wood to the left, and the town on the right side, but I want to be looking for the valley line which will hopefully be quite distinctive. Then I'm looking for the wiggle in the river and then the railway line, leading us to the bridge and the complex at the target. If you look where the railway line is, I think I should be able to see where the railway crosses the river. So we're looking for the big bridge beyond the house for our target.

The briefing continues, covering further target details and a complete description of the second target which is included in the SAP mission. After almost an hour, the briefing will be complete and the aircrew are ready to walk to their aircraft after collecting their flying gear and 'signing' for their mounts. Out on the flight line, the conditions are not always as glamorous as one might expect. This is not a movie, and it's no time to make a Tom Cruise-style walk down the line. The weather is terrible, with driving rain and fierce winds, and the only sensible thing to do is to get inside the aircraft as quickly as possible. However, the external walk-round checks have to be completed first, while the ground crew are busy shovelling away the pool of water which has rapidly collected inside the Hawk's open canopy. With the checks complete, the crew can climb into the rain-soaked cockpits, strapping in before the canopies are quickly closed. After wiping rainwater from the instrument faces, the start-up sequence gets under way, and in just a few minutes the Hawk's Rolls-Royce/Turboméca Adour turbofan is quietly turning at idle speed.

After taxying to the active runway, the two-ship formation ('Bobcat One' and 'Bobcat Two') rolls on to the threshold and takes up position in line abreast, running engines up to full power. Although the Adour creates a considerable amount of noise, the conditions inside the Hawk are fairly comfortable, and all that can be heard through the 'bonedome' is a distant rumble, accompanied by a gentle airframe shudder. With a nod from the lead pilot (to cue the brake release for the wingman), the Hawk lurches forward and quickly begins to accelerate along Valley's runway. At 90kts the control column is moved slightly rearwards, raising the Hawk's nose into the airstream. At 120kts the stick is rotated further and the Hawk is airborne, accompanied by the wingman, both aircraft bobbing and weaving in the turbulent conditions. At 150ft the landing gear is retracted and the flaps are then raised, the pilot ensuring that they are fully up before he reaches 200kts.

After climbing through the cloud, the Hawks are positioned in battle formation, separated by about a mile. The high-level transit enables them to reach a suitable 'entry gate' into a low-level route without wasting fuel unnecessarily. With the assistance of a radar controller, 'Bobcat' formation is guided through the clouds towards RAF Shawbury, where the formation leader descends into the low-level phase of the mission after making visual contact with the ground. Back under the cloud cover, the two Hawks level off at 250ft, driving through the heavy rain, banging and rocking as they hit continual pockets of turbulence. The conditions are terrible, and occasional patches of thick, low-level cloud create further hazards, forcing the formation to make detours and adding to the student's navigational problems. After passing to the right of Telford on a heading of 160 degrees, the formation approaches the first IP, and at a speed of 420kts the student does not have much time to locate its position. With a 4g turn to starboard, the aircraft are positioned on a heading of 215 degrees, passing directly over the IP towards the target. Just 36 seconds later the target bridge flashes by, partially obscured by thick trees. Fortunately the formation leader had successfully identified the target and positioned the Hawk on a perfect simulated 1,000lb high-explosive (retarded) bombing approach, quickly followed by 'Bobcat Two'. Attacks such as this one demonstrate that target acquisition is incredibly difficult, although level attacks do make sighting somewhat easier—with a fixed approach altitude the pilot can simply wait until the target 'fills' the appropriate amount of his bomb sight.

Once clear of the target, both aircraft turn hard on to 166 degrees for a further two minutes, before

Above: Running in towards the bridge target, looking through the Hawk's gun sight.

turning right on to 255 degrees. Due south of Leominster another turn is made, this time on to the next target heading of 155 degrees, passing over the IP at 420kts and still at 250ft. One minute and eight seconds from the IP, the lead pilot pulls up to begin a dive attack, turning right 60 degrees at the top of the climb before establishing himself on a 10-degree dive at the second target, in this case another bridge. The weapons to be used in any attack will normally be predetermined by a higher authority, and three basic types are available: the 1,000lb high-explosive retarded bomb, which is used to best effect against bridges, dams and hardened buildings; the cluster bomb unit (CBU), used against armour, radar installations, aircraft on the ground and troop concentrations; and the cannon, used against soft vehicles, aircraft and rail facilities and for flak suppression. Each weapon type is simulated during the student's training course, although the cannon is only used as an option for attacks on weapons ranges, where both practice bombs and live ammunition can be used. The type of weapon to be used will directly influence the attack tactics. Some weapons, such as cannon, rockets and unretarded bombs, must be delivered in a dive, whereas the CBU and retarded bombs offer the choice of either a dive or a level attack. The type of weapon will also determine the tip-in altitude, and its accuracy and damage pattern on the ground will affect the attack direction.

The basic aim of each aircraft is to maximize the time available for target acquisition and weapons accuracy, but at the same time minimize the aircraft's exposure to enemy defences—contradictory considerations requiring compromise. On the Hawk, the recommended profile is to pull up from low level to achieve the required 10-degree dive angle and turn through 40–80 degrees (ideally 60 degrees) on to the attack heading. The SOP (standard operating procedure) distances give a reasonable compromise of minimum exposure time and acceptable tracking and acquisition time. As with the level attack, an untrained observer will find a dive attack both confusing and disorientating, although it is naturally much easier to acquire the target visually once the aircraft is positioned on the final attack dive.

Pulling up from the target, 'Bobcat Two' streaks in behind 'Bobcat One' to complete the simulated attack, turning hard right on to 260 degrees. The ride is still rough, the weather still poor, but provided the low-level visibility is adequate the SAP continues as planned—the RAF instructors recognize that operational missions are unlikely to be afforded the luxury of clear skies. It is therefore important to train as realistically as possible. After climbing out of the low-level route, 'Bobcat One' and 'Bobcat Two' make their way back to Valley at high level, descending over Bettws-y-Coed to run in over the airfield at 2,000ft and 350kts for a battle break into the circuit. The break is made at 4g, the downwind speed reducing to 150kts (the finals turn speed), and the touch-down is made at just over 110kts.

After taxying back to the flight line the crews gather for a de-briefing, during which the instructor examines every aspect of the sortie in detail, concentrating on what the student can improve upon. The instructor for the sortie flown by 'Bobcat One' and 'Bobcat Two' is suitably impressed:

He's a very good student. He was working really hard all around the cloudy areas, and the first target was a very difficult one. We had a little confusion at one stage, but he did very well—he's fine. I would say that the mission was better than average. It's not unusual to miss the targets sometimes, and that's okay as it's all a learning process. If the targets were easy ones and the student repeatedly missed them, we would naturally be concerned, so much would depend on why the student missed them, but by using hard targets we are able to prove that the navigation and acquisition techniques are working.

Towards the end of the course, the students are learning to do everything as a pair of aircraft. They could do that SAP sortie easily on their own, but when they're a pair, and the student's co-ordinating two aircraft, it gets tricky. Sometimes things just tend to start happening too quickly, and the student has to think ahead. The fact that he has to organize two aeroplanes flying in battle formation is like trying to handle an unstoppable train, and it takes a great deal of effort to keep everyone going in the right direction. Navigation is becoming almost second nature by now, but when he's working hard to stay in formation everything tends to degrade, so he has to work even harder. When we talk about capacity, we mean the ability to 'prioritize'—for example, he has to realize when he has to look at the map to avoid getting lost, or decide when he should be telling his wingman what to do, and so on. Capacity is vitally important, and if he can't cope with everything that's going on at the same time, then he's in trouble. Sometimes the student simply can't navigate well at low level, but we can teach anyone if they have the capacity to learn. We tend to lose maybe just one or so students on each course, but by this stage we tend to have weeded out most of the students who can't handle the job. We lost a student recently, and he was unable to think in three dimensions—just hadn't got the capacity to cope—so we dropped him, but he'll be offered a flying post on helicopters or transports in all probability.

Although the Air Force is contracting, we haven't been encouraged to be more selective, and we teach in the same way as we always have. Additionally, the new combined syllabus doesn't affect the students in any way. Much of the training is done within the OCU, however, so there's no point covering everything in the advanced and tactical training course. For example, the Hawk's bomb sight obviously isn't used on the Tornado, Jaguar or Harrier, so some of the training will naturally have to be done within the OCUs. The course here at Valley is different now, but it hasn't lost much, other than maybe a couple of sorties, so as far as the students are concerned things haven't really changed since the Tactical Weapons Units disappeared. The courses at Valley and Chivenor are identical, although Valley is eighty miles from the weapons range at Pembrey whereas Chivenor is only sixty miles away, so we take the students to Chivenor for three weeks on detachment, for the weapons phase of the course.

The students now fly tactical grey-camouflaged aircraft right from the beginning of their advanced training, and they will see people in their crew room who are actually doing the tactical weapons flying, so they feel that little bit closer to the action. We've moved away from the red-and-white-trainer attitude, and that must give the students the right kind of impression, right from the start!

WEAPONS DIRECTORY

BAe

WEAPONS DIRECTORY

500lb GP HE Bomb

Type: *Conventional general-purpose HE bomb.*
Length: *(Body) 3ft 5in (1.04m)*
Diameter: *1ft 1in (330mm)*
Launch weight: *534lb (242kg).*
Warhead: *(Mk 1) HE/RWA; (Mk 2) HE/Torpex.*

1,000lb GP HE Bomb

Type: *Conventional general-purpose HE bomb (data for Mk 13).*
Length: *(Body) 4ft 1½in (1.26m).*
Diameter: *1ft 4½in (420mm).*
Launch weight: *908lb (412kg).*
Warhead: *Torpex HE or RWA HE.*

Developed from the Second World War-type bombs, the 500lb and 1,000lb GP HE bombs feature improvements to combat kinetic energy effects caused by low-level and high-speed flight. Single and twin NATO-standard suspension systems and modern fuzing systems are also fitted. The 500lb Mk 1 and 1,000lb Mk 13 weapons have an RWA filling

Above: A free-fall 1,000lb bomb, as carried by the Harrier, Jaguar and Tornado.
Below: A Harrier GR.7 carrying BL.755 cluster bombs painted for test purposes with photo calibration markings. (BAe)
Right, top: A 1,000lb bomb with a retarding tail fitted, its parachute open for display purposes.
Right, centre: A 30mm ADEN cannon fitted to the centreline of a Hawk T.1.
Right, bottom: Part of the Harrier's armoury: six anti-armour rockets (carried in the Matra pod), cannon shells and an ADEN cannon.

suitable for high-temperature flight conditions. The 500lb Mk 2 and 1,000lb Mks 10, 18 and 20 feature a Torpex filling. Standard or retarded tails can be fitted.

ADEN 25mm Cannon

Type: Single-barrel revolver gun.
Length: 7ft 6in (2.29m).
Weight: 203lb (92kg).
Rate of fire: 1,650rds/min

ADEN 30mm Cannon

Type: Single-barrel revolver gun.
Length: 5ft 2½in (1.59m).
Weight: 192lb (87kg).
Rate of fire: 1,200rds/min.

The ADEN 30mm cannon was developed by the Royal Armament Research and Development Establishment following the end of the Second World War. The single-barrel, five-chamber gun uses belt ammunition and is housed in a light alloy cradle unit attached to the underside of the Harrier T.4 (when required). The 30mm cannon—largely used by the Harrier GR.1/3 fleet—is being withdrawn in favour of the ADEN 25mm, which will be carried by the Harrier GR.7/T.10.

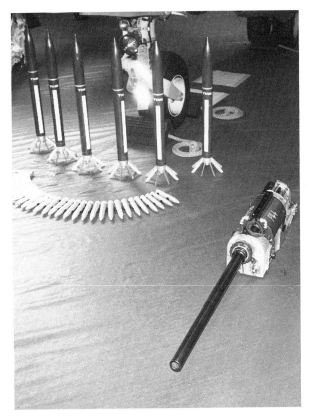

ALARM

Type: Medium-range anti-radar air-to-surface missile.
Length: 14ft 1¼in (4.3m).
Diameter: 8¾in (224mm).
Wing span: 2ft 4¼in (0.72m).
Launch weight: 584lb (265kg).
Warhead: HE.
Guidance: Passive radar.
Propulsion: Solid propellant.
Range: 28 miles (45km).

The ALARM (Air-Launched Anti-Radiation Missile) was developed as a replacement for the anti-radar Martel ASM (carried by Buccaneers and Nimrods) and AGM-45 Shrike (carried by Vulcans). Deliveries were scheduled to begin during 1987 but firing

Above: Two ALARM missiles attached to a Tornado GR.1. A BOZ-107 chaff dispenser is carried under the starboard wing, with a Sky Shadow ECM pod under the port wing. (BAe)
Right: Programme information is transferred to the ALARM anti-radiation missile whilst it is on the pylon. (RAF)

trials were not completed until 1990. The missile was rushed to the Middle East for operations against Iraq during the 1991 Gulf War, and existing stocks of the weapon were exhausted before the war ended, having being launched successfully against a variety of targets despite the fact that the missile's operating manual had yet to be drawn up. Guided by passive radar and capable of being programmed with likely target radar emission data, the missile climbs following launch and coasts towards the target area, diving directly on to a target once the target radar is acquired. If no emission is detected, the missile deploys a parachute and loiters until radar transmissions are resumed, at which stage the

parachute is jettisoned and the weapon dives towards the target.

Above left: A BL.755 cluster bomb under the wing of a Harrier GR.7.
Above right: AGM-84A Harpoons are assigned to the Nimrod MR.2P fleet.

BL.755 Cluster Bomb

Type: *Submunition-dispensing cluster bomb.*
Length: *(Body) 8ft 0½in (2.45m).*
Diameter: *1ft 4½in (419mm).*
Launch weight: *611lb (277kg).*
Warhead: *147 bomblets.*

Developed to destroy both soft- and hard-skinned targets whilst enabling the carrier aircraft to maintain a low-level attack profile, the BL.755 contains seven bays, each containing 21 submunitions. The body case opens after release from the carrier, allowing the first bomblet in each bay to deploy a spring leaf tail, followed by the second bomblet which is fitted with a retarding parachute (thus ensuring an increased angle of attack). The bomblets incorporate shaped charges capable of penetrating 250mm thick armour. The BL.755 can be carried by the Harrier, Jaguar and Tornado.

Mk 11 Depth Charge

Type: *Depth charge.*
Length: *4ft 6¾in (1.39m).*
Diameter: *11in (279mm).*
Launch weight: *320lb (145kg).*
Warhead: *176lb (80kg) HE.*

Developed for air delivery from the Nimrod, the Mk 11 depth charge features a cylindrical steel case with a tail section which detaches itself upon impact with the water, facilitating hydro-pneumatic arming and subsequent detonation. Training versions are also utilized, for carriage and release practice.

Hades

Type: *Area-denial weapon system.*
Length: *8ft 0½in (2.45m).*
Diameter: *1ft 4½in (419mm).*
Launch weight: *571lb (259kg).*
Warhead: *49 submunitions.*

Developed as a low-level, air-delivered weapon for attacking fixed targets and 'choke-points', the Hades system combines the BL.755 cluster bomb body with the area-denial submunition HB.876 carried by the JP.233 airfield attack weapon. Each Hades dispenser contains 49 submunitions which are parachute-retarded. The system entered RAF service in 1987 and can be carried by the Jaguar, Harrier and Tornado.

Harpoon

Type: *Long-range air-to-surface missile.*
Length: *12ft 7½in (3.85m).*
Diameter: *1ft 1½in (340mm).*
Wing span: *3ft 0in (0.91m).*
Launch weight: *1,151lb (522kg).*

Warhead: 485lb (220kg) HE blast penetration.
Guidance: Internal and active radar.
Propulsion: Turbofan.
Range: 75 miles (120km).

Entering service with the US Navy during 1977, the AGM-84 Harpoon anti-ship missile is cleared for carriage by the Nimrod MR.2P.

HB.876

Type: Area-denial munition.
Length: 6in (0.15m).
Diameter: 4in (100mm).
Weight: 5½lb (2.5kg).
Warhead: HE.

Developed as an area-denial submunition for the JP.233 airfield attack weapon, the HB.876 is ejected from its dispenser and a retarder is deployed in order to reduce impact velocity. The mine has an orientation facility, activated by sprung-steel legs, to ensure that it stands upright. Detonation can be achieved by time delay or by contact sensors.

JP.233

Type: Low-altitude airfield attack weapon.
Length: 21ft 6in (6.55m).
Width: 2ft 9in (840mm).
Depth: 1ft 11½in (600mm).
Weight: 5,149lb (2,335kg).
Warhead: 215 × HB.876 and 30 × SG.357 bomblets.

Developed for the Royal Air Force, the JP.233 is designed to damage airfield operating surfaces and inhibit their repair, effectively rendering the target airfield inoperative. Having been introduced into RAF service during the mid-1980s, the JP.233 was used operationally by Tornado GR.1 squadrons during the Gulf War, destroying significant portions of various Iraqi airfields. The system delivers two groups of submunitions simultaneously—a cratering bomblet to damage runways and taxiways and an area-denial bomblet to deter repair personnel and vehicles.

Matra 155 SNEB Rocket Pod

Type: Launcher pod for unguided rockets.
Length: 3ft 11in (1.2m).
Weight: 13.8lb (6.26kg).
Rate of fire: Salvo or single-launch facility.

The Matra rocket launcher is employed by the RAF's Harrier force. It normally carries nineteen TBA 68mm unguided, solid-propellant powered, high-explosive rockets. The pod is reusable.

Mauser 27mm Cannon

Type: Gas-operated automatic revolver cannon.
Length: 7ft 6½in (2.3m).
Weight: 220lb (100kg).
Rate of fire: 1,000rds/min.

The Mauser 27mm cannon was developed by Mauser in conjunction with Diehl and Dynamit Nobel as part of the MRCA (Multi-Role Combat Aircraft) programme. The Tornado IDS variant is fitted with two cannon, the F.3 carries one. German Alpha Jets and the Swedish Gripen are also equipped with Mauser cannon.

Left: A Matra rocket pod attached to a Harrier's port wing pylon. Rockets can be launched singly or *en masse*.
Right, upper: A Tornado GR.1 pictured at the beginning of a test flight, carrying a pair of JP.233 airfield attack pods. (BAe)
Right, lower: A Tornado GR.1 carrying a JP.233 airfield attack weapon, seen during a test drop with the submunitions falling to their target. (BAe)

MAUSER 27mm CANNON

Paveway

Type: Modular glide bomb with laser guidance (data for GBU-10E/B)
Length: 14ft 2in (4.32m).
Diameter: 1ft 6in (457mm).
Tail span: 3ft 10in (1,168mm).
Weight: 1,985lb (900kg).
Warhead: HE.

The Paveway family utilizes a common laser guidance and control assembly, with differing control fins to suit each particular bomb body. The laser kit directs the bomb towards the target, which is illuminated by laser energy from the delivery aircraft, a designator aircraft or a ground-based designator. With no electrical connection to the carrier aircraft necessary, the weapon is delivered in the same manner as a conventional bomb. It can be carried by the Harrier, Jaguar and Tornado.

Rapier

Type: Low-level surface-to-air missile.
Length: 7ft 4in (2.24m).
Diameter: 5¼in (133mm).
Wing span: 1ft 3in (381mm).
Launch weight: 94lb (42.6kg).
Warhead: 3.1lb (1.4kg) HE semi-armour-piercing.
Propulsion: Solid propellant.
Range: 23,000ft (7,000m).

Below: Rapier missile battery as used for airfield defence.

Above: A Paveway laser-guided 1,000lb bomb, with a TIALD (Thermal Imaging and Laser Designator) pod, under a Tornado GR.1's fuselage.

The Rapier low-level surface-to-air missile system was developed during the early 1960s in response to an Army and RAF Regiment requirement for a missile system to replace the Bofors air defence guns which were then in use. The first successful engagement (against a Meteor drone) took place in April 1967, and the first deliveries were made during 1970, initial operational capability being achieved with the RAF Regiment in 1973. The system, which continues to be regularly updated, is currently operated by Nos 26, 37, 15, 27, 48, 19, 20 and 66 Squadrons, Royal Air Force Regiment.

Sea Eagle

Type: Long-range air-to-surface missile.
Length: 13ft 7in (4.14m).
Diameter: 1ft 3¾in (400mm).
Wing span: 3ft 11¾in (1.2m).
Launch weight: 1,323lb (600kg).
Warhead: HE semi-armour-piercing.
Guidance: Internal and active radar.
Propulsion: Turbofan.
Range: 68 miles (110km).

The BAeD Sea Eagle was developed from 1977 as a replacement for the television-guided Martel anti-ship ASM. Although it can be carried by the Jaguar, Harrier and Sea King, it was originally utilized by the RAF's Buccaneer maritime strike squadrons; however, following the retirement of the Buccaneer two squadrons of Tornado GR.1Bs are now operational with the weapon. Based on the Martel airframe, the Sea Eagle incorporates an under-body air intake,

Above: Sea Eagle air-to-surface anti-shipping missiles, here attached to a Buccaneer, are now carried by the Tornado GR.1B fleet at Lossiemouth.

feeding a Microturbo turbofan engine. Mid-course guidance is internal, with terminal guidance provided by an active pulse radar terminal seeker. A radar altimeter provides sea-skimming height control, and a semi-armour-piercing warhead is fitted.

SG.357

Type: *Cratering munition.*
Length: *2ft 11in (0.89m).*
Diameter: *7in (180mm).*
Weight: *57lb (26kg).*
Warhead: *HE.*

Developed as an runway-cratering submunition for the JP.233 airfield attack weapon, the SG.357 is ejected from its dispenser and a retarder is deployed in order to reduce its impact velocity. The weapon detonates upon impact, the primary warhead detonating first, enabling the secondary warhead to detonate below the surface of the runway to produce a 'heave effect' crater.

AIM-9L Sidewinder

Type: *Short-range air-to-air missile.*
Length: *9ft 5in (2.87m).*
Diameter: *5in (127mm).*
Wing span: *2ft 1¼in (640mm).*
Launch weight: *192lb (87kg).*
Warhead: *21lb (9.5kg) HE blast.*
Guidance: *Infra-red.*
Propulsion: *Solid propellant.*
Range: *13 miles (8km).*

The famous Sidewinder dates back to 1953, when the first test flight was made. The missile entered USAF and USN service during 1956 and is now in its third generation. The AIM-9L was developed during 1970 as an all-aspect weapon—previous versions were restricted to tail-aspect only—with a long storage life. It has four control fins mounted towards the front of the missile body, with four fixed fins attached to the rear, featuring 'rollerons' on the trailing-edge tips. Sidewinders are used by both the Tornado F.3 and Hawk T.1A, and provide a self-defence capability for the Harrier, Jaguar, Tornado GR.1 and Nimrod.

Sky Flash

Type: *Medium-range air-to-air missile.*
Length: *12ft 0in (3.66m).*
Diameter: *8in (203mm).*

Below left: A Jaguar GR.1A carrying a Phimat chaff dispenser and an overwing-mounted AIM-9L Sidewinder.
Below right: Twin AIM-9L Sidewinders, here carried by a Hawk.

WEAPONS DIRECTORY

RAF were made during 1978. Later versions were fitted with a redesigned rocket motor. The missile features four centrally mounted control fins, with fixed stabilizing fins at the rear. The Sky Flash is now carried by Tornado F.3s.

Stingray

Type: Lightweight torpedo.
Length: 8ft 6¼in (2.6m).
Diameter: 1ft 0¾in (324mm).
Launch weight: 584lb (265kg).
Warhead: 88lb (40kg) HE, shaped charge.
Propulsion: Pump jet.

The Stingray torpedo was first delivered during 1981 (to the Royal Navy) and is currently one of the Nimrod MR.2's weapons options. An advanced lightweight torpedo, it has a multi-mode, multi-beam sonar and a quiet, high-speed propulsion system.

TIALD

Type: Laser designator.
Length: 9ft 6in (2.9m).
Diameter: 12in (305mm).
Weight: 463lb (210kg).
FLIR narrow FOV: 3.6° × 2.4°, 1.8° × 1.2° or 0.9° × 0.6°.
FLIR wide FOV: 3.2° × 2.4°, 1.6° × 1.2° or 0.8° × 0.6°.
Elevation: +30° to –150°.
Roll: Continuous rotation.

Top: BAeD Sky Flash missile, displayed here on a Hawk. (G. Ashley)
Above: A Sky Flash missile launch from a Tornado ADV. (BAeD)

Wing span: 3ft 4in (1.02m).
Launch weight: 430lb (195kg).
Warhead: 66lb (30kg) HE continuous rod.
Guidance: Semi-active radar.
Propulsion: Solid propellant.
Range: 25 miles (40km).

Development of the BAeD Sky Flash began during 1973 as a redesign of the AIM-7E Sparrow, incorporating a new semi-active radar seeker and a new fuze, autopilot and power supply unit. The missile was based on the Sparrow in order to allow RAF Phantoms to operate both types without the necessity for extensive alterations to the aircraft. Test flights began in 1976 and the first deliveries to the

One of the most advanced laser designators in the world today, TIALD (Thermal Imaging and Laser Designator) is easily integrated into any military aircraft possessing a modern avionics suite, combining accuracy and ease of use to devastating effect, as demonstrated during Operation 'Desert Storm'. It confers major benefits in the field of reconnaissance, including immediate battle damage assessment; the recording of imagery for post-sortie analysis; a lock-on facility so that a point of interest can be monitored while providing the aircraft with freedom of manoeuvre; low-, medium- or high-level employment; and the passive detection and recognition of airborne targets.

EQUIPMENT GALLERY

EQUIPMENT GALLERY

▲ 1

▲ 2

▲ 3

▲ 4

▲ 5

▲ 6

Previous page: Upper—Firefighting truck, 6 × 6 foam Mk 11 Scammell (Ken Marriott); lower left—Houchin ground power generator unit ; lower right—aircraft fuel servicing truck, 3,000-gallon, AEC Mammoth Major (Ken Marriott)
1. Bedford (left) and Leyland/DAF cargo trucks.
2. Range Rover with VIP security fit.
3. Massey-Ferguson Hallam tractors.
4. Thorneycroft firefighting truck.
5. TACR Mk 2 firefighting vehicle.
6. Fuel tanker truck, 22,500 litres, 16-ton Foden. (Ken Marriott)
7. Avia baggage loader. (Ken Marriott)

◀ 7

EQUIPMENT GALLERY

▲ 8

▲ 9

▲ 10

▲ 11

▲ 12

▲ 13

8. Main base loader, ground to aircraft level. (Ken Marriott)
9. Fork lift truck, 10.5K Henley. (Ken Marriott)
10. Snow removal trailer unit (runway clearance). (Ken Marriott)
11. Snow removal unit, self-propelled, ROLBA R400. (Ken Marriott)
12. Aircraft fuel dispensing truck unit, Leyland Road Runner. (Ken Marriott)
13. Aircraft towing tractor, wide-bodied, Reliance Mercury RM450. (Ken Marriott)
14. Aircraft towing tractor, heavy, Reliance Mercury RM350. (Ken Marriott)

◀ 14

EQUIPMENT GALLERY

▲ 15

▲ 16

▲ 17

▲ 18

▲ 19

▲ 20

15. Aircraft de-icing equipment truck, Dodge. (Ken Marriott)
16. Self-propelled rotary sweeper, Bedford/Lacre. (Ken Marriott)
17. In-flight catering truck, Bedford. (Ken Marriott)
18. Water replenishment truck, Dodge. (Ken Marriott)
19. An assortment of CBLS (Carrier, Bomb, Light Stores) units stacked on a transportation trailer.
20. Dodge coach.
21. Auxiliary power air starter unit

◀ 21

RAF TRADE GROUPS

RAF TRADE GROUPS

The RAF employs a huge number of officers and non-commissioned officers (NCOs) in support roles, ensuring that front-line flying operations are performed effectively and efficiently. The following listing, intended as a guide only, outlines the various trades which are available to airmen and airwomen.

Avionics

Aircraft Electrical Mechanic: Most Aircraft Electrical Mechanics are employed on operational flying stations. Their duties at the flight line concern the routine maintenance of aircraft electrical systems and general instrumentation, and their tasks include the rectification of minor faults and, perhaps, assisting with the flight servicing, ground handling and role preparation of the aircraft. Some Aircraft Electrical Mechanics may be employed alongside technicians in hangars and workshops, assisting with more extensive maintenance and repair work in respect of electrical installations, instrumentation and components.

Engineering Technician Aircraft Electrical: The Engineering Technician Aircraft Electrical is concerned with the maintenance and repair of the electrical generation and distribution systems, the weapon management systems and the general instruments fitted to aircraft. The electrical system provides the power for electronic equipment, instrument displays and controls necessary to the pilot and crew while flying and operating an aircraft. The weapon management system enables an aircraft's weapons to be selected, armed and released. The equipment maintained includes generators, alternators, voltage controllers, electric motors and actuators, air speed indicators and machmeters, electronic fuel control units and weapon computers, multiplexers, decoders and selectors.

Avionics Mechanic: Most Avionics Mechanics are employed on operational flying stations. Their duties at the flight line concern the routine maintenance of aircraft avionics systems and their tasks include the rectification of minor faults; they may also assist with the flight servicing, ground handling and role preparation of the aircraft. Some Avionics Mechanics may be employed alongside technicians in hangars and workshops, assisting with more extensive maintenance and repair work regarding avionics installations, equipment and components.

Engineering Technician Avionics: The Engineering Technician Avionics is concerned with the maintenance and repair of the complete range of air radar, air communications, airborne photographic, flight stability and control, air navigation and aircraft weapon aiming equipment used in the Royal Air Force. This includes weather radars, distance measuring equipment, radar altimeters, radio compasses, long- and short-range communications equipment, photographic reconnaissance and gun sight cameras, autopilots, instrument landing systems, auto-stabilizing systems, radio navigation aids, flight directors, inertial navigation systems, navigation/attack systems and weapon/missile control systems. Additional equipment, often specific to the role of an individual aircraft type, can be worked on after pre-employment training. Such equipment may include search and attack radars, terrain following radars and data processing and display systems.

Synthetic Trainer Specialization: Tradesmen in the synthetic trainer specialization are employed in the maintenance and repair of flight simulators and synthetic trainers of all types, including cockpit procedure trainers, crew trainers, systems trainers, instrument trainers, dynamic flight simulators and full mission simulators. Their range of duties is very broad, and they receive a grounding appropriate to trade in all aspects of synthetic trainer work and then pre-employment training on an installation.

Synthetic Trainer Mechanic: Synthetic Trainer Mechanics are involved in the routine maintenance of simulator and trainer installations. Their tasks include preparing simulators and trainers for use, after-use servicing, checking for signs of corrosion, damage or wear, functional testing and minor rectification. They may be required to load and unload operational and maintenance software.

Engineering Technician Synthetic Trainer: The Engineering Technician Synthetic Trainer is concerned with the maintenance and repair of simulator and trainer installations, systems and components. The equipment to be maintained includes computers, computer peripherals, interfaces and linkages, simulated aircraft systems, flight deck instrumentation and intercom systems, visual systems (including camera and projection systems and computer-generated imagery), cabin conditioning, breathing air systems, hydraulics/motion systems, anti-g simulation, power distribution equipment and fire detection systems.

Ground Electronic Engineering

Mechanics: The work of an Electronics Mechanic in the Royal Air Force concerns the maintenance and repair of a very wide range of ground based radar, radio and telecommunications equipment in the United Kingdom and overseas. After basic trade training, mechanics could be carrying out the tests and checks necessary to ensure that equipment is operating correctly, or they could use general-purpose and specialist test equipment to diagnose faults. They could also undertake repair, reconditioning, modification and installation tasks in accordance with written procedures. The work that a mechanic undertakes is at a lower level of skill than that of a technician, and most mechanics work as part of a team. All maintenance and repair work, whether by mechanics or technicians, is supervised and approved, where necessary, by NCOs in order to ensure that quality and safety standards are maintained.

Technicians: In the Engineering Technician Electronics trade, technicians of the Royal Air Force are, in general, concerned with the deeper levels of maintenance and repair that are beyond the capabilities of an Electronics Mechanic. The technician has a wide variety of employment in all areas of the trade group, and may be required to undergo additional specialist training for some tasks. The lowest rank in the trade is Junior Technician (Jnr Tech). With promotion, the technician may take on wider responsibilities, including supervision and instruction.

General Engineering

General Technician Ground Support Equipment: General Technician Ground Support Equipment tradesmen are employed at all RAF flying units and at Maintenance Units, on the maintenance of a wide range of aircraft ground support equipment, including diesel-, petrol- and mains-powered electrical generating trolleys for aircraft starting and servicing, diesel- and petrol-engine hydraulic system servicing rigs, compressors, air cooling and conditioning trolleys and low-pressure air starting trolleys. They also service aircraft jacking, lifting and haulage equipment, airfield arrester barriers and, after special training, maintain power supplies, air conditioning units and aerial turning gears of ground radar installations. The maintenance of ground support equipment is vital to the efficient operation of aircraft. The tasks vary from routine daily inspections to complete overhauls and fault diagnoses requiring training and mechanical knowledge.

General Mechanic Ground Support Equipment: General Mechanic Ground Support Equipment tradesmen are employed on various workshop tasks and the maintenance of ground support equipment. The range of equipment is immensely varied but includes such items as lifting jacks, aircraft arrester barriers and numerous types of test trolleys. In addition, there are Maintenance Units in the RAF which specialize in the overhaul, repair and manufacture of equipment, where General Mechanics may be employed to assist in major repairs or the development and production of prototype or specialized equipment.

General Technician Workshops: General Technician Workshops tradesmen are employed in Station Workshops at RAF units and in the larger workshops at Maintenance Units on a wide variety of tasks, using general engineering machinery and processes. The tasks, which are usually 'one-off' or concern small-batch runs, entail the use of centre lathes, drilling, grinding and other machine tools; welding, using oxy-acetylene, electric and inert gas processes; straightforward blacksmith work and the heat treatment of metal; and the manufacture of sheet metal parts involving development, bending, riveting and soldering.

General Mechanic Workshops: General Mechanic Workshops tradesmen are engaged in various engineering workshops tasks and on the repair and manufacture of a large variety of equipment essential to the support of RAF activities. Their duties will vary from day to day and from unit to unit but would normally involve employment in the metalworking workshop using power-operated drilling machines and turning, grinding and cutting machines, assembling and dismantling components for repair, and in soldering, brazing and oxy-acetylene cutting operations. In addition, there are Maintenance Units which specialize in the overhaul, repair and manufacture of equipment, where the General Mechanic can be employed to assist in major repairs and in the development and production of prototype or specialized equipment, such as particular tools or jigs. He also assists general technicians with more difficult tasks.

General Technician Electrical: General Technician Electrical tradesmen are concerned with the servicing and repair of all types of electrical equipment used in the support of aircraft servicing and ground operation, airfield lighting equipment, mechanical transport electrical systems, ground radar power supplies and certain domestic electrical equipment. He is usually employed in workshops equipped for carrying out extensive repair and servicing, in mechanical workshops or in battery charging rooms. In order to do this work he needs to possess a very wide knowledge of all aspects of the electrical trade, enabling him to deal with the varied range of equipment for which he is responsible. With promotion, the work is extended to include supervisory duties.

General Mechanic Electrical: The duties of the General Mechanic Electrical vary from station to station and are dependent upon the rank held. The vast majority of General Mechanics Electrical work in aircraft ground support electrical equipment servicing bays, on airfield portable electrical equipment and in station engineering workshops and can be equated to similar tradesmen employed in the maintenance of aircraft electrical support equipment by civilian airline operators. Work on this equipment involves the servicing and inspection of electrical equipment necessary for other trades in the servicing of aircraft and also the servicing of airfield, workshop and domestic electrical equipment. The duties of this trade, like those of the Gen Tech E, may involve working on platforms some ninety feet above the ground.

Aerial Erector: Aerial Erectors are responsible for the installation, servicing, modification and recovery of a wide range of large and complex aerial systems. Most of the work is, obviously, performed out of doors, and a climbing ability in addition to technical skill is essential to the trade. Much travel and hard work with a small team are required to achieve a high standard of the basic craft skill.

Mechanical Transport

MT Driver: Driving and operating the vehicles for which they are qualified, and undertaking servicing tasks such as wheel changes and oil replenishment, drivers normally operate on their own, often away from their unit, and are expected to show initiative in completing their tasks. As they gain experience and promotion they have opportunities to play their part in the running of their section, from the allocation of drivers and vehicles to, in the senior ranks, the overall management of an MT flight.

MT Mechanic, MT Technician: Mechanics work on the full range of MT vehicles, including fire and crash equipment. Their duties include regular servicing checks, the rectification of faults and the changing of major components. MT Technicians do the more specialized work on vehicles. On promotion they may supervise the work of mechanics and, as Senior NCOs, become involved in section management.

Air Traffic Control

AIRFIELDS

A number of Assistant Air Traffic Controllers work in air traffic control towers on RAF airfields, as described below.

Controller's Assistant: Keeps all displays of essential information up to date and relieves the Controller of many routine jobs, thereby allowing him to concentrate on his vital task. This assistant normally works for the Aerodrome Controller or the Radar Approach Controller and he is an important and valuable member of the ATC team.

ATC Driver: Drives an air traffic Land Rover equipped with a two-way radio. Frequently helps the control staff to co-ordinate work activities, both on the busy aircraft manoeuvring areas and elsewhere within the airfield boundaries. Positions portable airfield lighting and bad-ground markers, and may also be required to assist in the manoeuvring of aircraft and vehicles on the ground. Needs to be alert and know every inch of the airfield.

Movements Clerk: Records all movement details of aircraft flying to and from the airfield. Passes flight data to the Controllers' Assistants and other interested agencies. Processes and actions flight plans and signals messages concerning aircraft movements and their safety.

Switchboard Operator: Directs the many incoming and outgoing calls to and from the Air Traffic Control tower. Handles both administrative and operational calls, and the latter must be fed promptly and efficiently to the appropriate Controller or external control agency. This task often requires liaison with the Controller's Assistant, in the first instance, to avoid interrupting busy Controllers.

Bird Control Assistant: Carries out specialist bird control duties which aid flight safety by keeping the airfield clear of birds. This work reduces the risk of bird-strikes taking place in the vicinity of the airfield.

EN-ROUTE RADAR UNITS

Some Assistant Air Traffic Controllers are employed in the Air Traffic Control Area Radar Units which are manned jointly by civilian and RAF Controllers and their assistants. These radar units are equipped with longer-range radar than those at airfields, and they provide a radar safety and control service to civilian as well as military aircraft. Assistant Air Traffic Controllers form a vital part of the control team at these units, by listening to radio telephony (RT) messages between pilots and the Controller and keeping the computer-based flight data systems up to date with the latest information. They are also responsible for conducting handovers of aircraft between radar units, and for passing operational and management data on aircraft movements, both to airfields and other area radar units.

OPERATIONS CENTRES

Other Assistant Air Traffic Controllers are employed in Operations Rooms, which lie at the heart of the RAF's front line. They are responsible for assisting in the provision of flight and mission planning information, using the latest computer-based technology. The Assistant Air Traffic Controller could become an Operations Support Manager responsible for the effectiveness of the important assistant team, be employed within an operational flying squadron or work at one of the Combat Operations Centres, which are the 'nerve centres' of the RAF's flying stations. The Assistant Air Traffic Controller could also be based in one of the bigger Operations Rooms which serve the larger Headquarters.

Aerospace Systems

Aerospace Systems Operator: The ASop will normally work at an operational radar station as part of a team which will be required to obtain, process and pass on information regarding the air activity in the area for which the station is responsible. The network of radar stations and control centres which form the air defence system is manned 24 hours a day and maintains a continuous watch on the skies and out into space. ASops are employed in a wide variety of air defence associated tasks, often on shift work at many different locations, varying from large, air-conditioned underground operations complexes to small, independent reporting units or units which help air crew to improve their bombing accuracy. The ASop could also serve on one of the RAF's transportable air defence radar units, deployed in the United Kingdom or elsewhere. Specialized ASops may be selected to man a space tracking station, as part of the Ballistic Missile Early Warning System, or serve as Mission Crew on board the E-3D Sentry aircraft.

Senior NCO Fighter Controller: The SNCO FC will be trained to become an Interception Controller, using radio and radar to guide air defence aircraft to intercept their target. After promotion, SNCO FCs may work as a Controller in the Mission Crew of the E-3D Sentry.

Telecommunications

Telecommunications Operator: Members of this trade are required to send and receive signal messages and other data by visual display units, teleprinter, morse code, voice radio and facsimile equipment over a wide variety of communication networks and ground-to-air circuits of the RAF, allied and Commonwealth forces and civilian agencies; and to operate telephone switchboards. A limited number also operate morse equipment. The task involves the ability to operate a visual display unit or teleprinter keyboard at speeds up to 45 words per minute, send and receive morse at speeds up to 16 words per minute and decide the proper route for signal messages to reach their destination as quickly as possible. Telecommunications Operators are called upon to handle messages dealing with topics such as logistics, intelligence, administration, meteorology and operations. They may also be called upon to assist in the setting up, tuning and maintenance of radio and telegraph equipment.

Telecommunications Controller: Carrying out the responsibilities of supervising, controlling and managing RAF communications facilities, these personnel are given further training in computer-assisted signal message and data-handling techniques as well as the principles of planning and managing communications systems, including international networks, before promotion and entry to the trade. There are opportunities for Telecommunications Controllers to work on the development of new communications systems and techniques to meet the changing needs of the Royal Air Force.

Communications Systems Analyst: Members of this trade are specialists in many types of sophisticated telegraphic (as opposed to voice) communications systems and operating methods. They are trained to operate a wide variety of communications keyboard and modern automated data handling systems entering, or already in, service on a worldwide scale. They are also taught to recognize the many different international communications systems which are used throughout the world in order to provide the RAF with the sort of information necessary to carry out its operational missions. There are opportunities for the Communications Systems Analyst to train in and work on duties concerned with varied, highly complex non-communications systems, such as radar, and in the technical analysis of these systems. At the more senior ranks Communications Analysts may be employed on communications research projects and in producing authoritative reports on the findings of their research.

Communications Systems Analyst (Voice): Members of this trade are taught one modern foreign language and, as needs arise, may be taught one or more additional foreign languages. They are given the opportunity to attain good qualifying standards in both written and spoken aspects of their languages. Communications Systems Analysts (Voice) are specialists in modern voice communications systems and procedures, both national and international. In using the latest communications receiving and recording systems, including computers, data-processors and electronic keyboard equipment, they provide vital support to the RAF in fulfilling its national and NATO commitments, particularly the tactical exploitation of hostile communications used for electronic warfare purposes. Like the Communications Systems Analysts, members of the Communications Systems Analyst (Voice) trade in the more senior ranks may be trained and employed in communications research, and in producing reports.

Below: Education in aircraft engineering. (RAF)

Aircraft Engineering

Mechanic: The work of aircraft engineering mechanics in the RAF concerns the marshalling, towing, ground handling and flight line servicing of aircraft and the maintenance and repair of equipment, as appropriate to trade, to ensure that aircraft are safe and fit to fly and carry out their operational roles. On more involved maintenance activities, in hangars and workshops, mechanics may work as part of a team and will be under the supervision of technicians. All maintenance and repair work on aircraft, components, aero-engines and weapons, whether performed by mechanics or technicians, is supervised and approved where necessary by non-commissioned officers to ensure that safety for flight, operation, handling and storage is upheld.

Technician: In the field of aircraft engineering, the technicians of the RAF are, in general, concerned with the deeper levels of maintenance and repair of aircraft, components, aero-engines and weapons. At a flying station, technicians may work either in a hangar or on a flight line, where they will keep aircraft fit for immediate use. Alternatively, they may be employed in a hangar, undertaking more extensive inspection, diagnosis, repair and modification of aircraft and equipment. Furthermore, they may be employed in a specialist workshop comprehensively equipped to test, repair and modify equipment and components removed from aircraft.

Airframe Mechanic: Most Airframe Mechanics are employed on operational flying stations. Their duties at the flight line include the replenishment of hydraulic and gaseous systems, aircraft refuelling, routine maintenance—which includes examining for damage or wear—and the rectification of minor faults. Some Airframe Mechanics may be employed alongside technicians in hangars and workshops, assisting with more involved activities.

Engineering Technician Airframe: The Engineering Technician Airframe is concerned with the periodic examination of the aircraft's structure, flying controls and landing gear, the systems driving power-operated flying controls, flaps, air brakes, landing gear and other components, anti-icing systems, cabin air-conditioning and pressurizing systems and the storage and delivery of breathing oxygen. On helicopters, the Engineering Technician Airframe is concerned with checking rotor blades, rotor heads and transmission systems. Whenever faults are detected, he is the tradesman who changes, adjusts or repairs the faulty item. Specialist workshops of the airframe trade include landing gear, hydraulics and structure bays.

Propulsion Mechanic: Most Propulsion Mechanics are employed on operational flying stations. Their duties at the flight line include aircraft refuelling, the replenishment of oil systems, routine maintenance—which includes the examination of aero-engines for damage or wear—and the rectification of minor faults. Some Propulsion Mechanics may be employed alongside technicians in hangars and workshops, assisting with more extensive maintenance and repair of aero-engines and engine components.

Engineering Technician Propulsion: The Engineering Technician Propulsion is concerned with the maintenance and repair of all aircraft engines and propulsion equipment, ranging from the small types fitted to trainers and helicopters to the largest jet and propeller gas turbines fitted to multi-engine aircraft. The duties involve making regular checks of jet and piston engine installations and also encompass engine and propulsion unit overhauls. They range from examining for faults and component replacement at the flight line to the deep strip and testing of complete power units on test beds. In addition to the propulsion units of aircraft, the responsibilities extend to aircraft engine and propeller controls, jet pipes, propellers, engine-driven auxiliary gearboxes, auxiliary power units and fuel, oil and thrust augmentation systems.

Weapon Mechanic: There is a broad scope and variety to the duties of the Weapon Mechanic. Tasks on aircraft at the flight line include 'arming-up' with bombs, torpedoes, depth charges and guided weapons and the loading of rocket and gun installations. Tasks on armament installations include assisting in the scheduled maintenance, repair and replacement of such airborne armament equipment as gun pods, bomb carriers and rocket launchers. The work of the Weapon Mechanic also includes the storage, preparation, issue and receipt of weapons, assistance in the fusing of bombs, rockets and pyrotechnics and the assembling of such items with their associated fuses, tail units and other components. The Weapon Mechanic can also be involved with the maintenance and repair of rifles, automatic pistols, machine guns and heavier weapons such as mortars used by the RAF Regiment.

Engineering Technician Weapon: The Engineering Technician Weapon is concerned with the regular checking of aircraft armament installations, the scheduled maintenance, repair and replacement of airborne armament equipment and guided weapons, the control of storage, receipt and issue of weapons, the fusing of bombs, rockets and pyrotechnics for operational use, the maintenance of aircrew assisted-escape systems (including ejection seats), the maintenance, replenishment and repair of components and the rectification of faults in small arms and ground defence weapons. Some senior non-commissioned officers are trained in explosive ordnance disposal (EOD) techniques ('bomb disposal').

Photography

Air Photography Processor 2: The Air Photography Processor 2 is trained to operate high-speed air film processing and printing machines which are installed in either permanent or air-transportable photo laboratories on major reconnaissance units. The work is often carried out in field conditions in deployed sites or on survey operations in remote areas. Careful scientific control of quality is still maintained, even though speed of production is essential if intelligence is to be kept up to date. Some Air Photography Processors 2 are also employed on cine film processing on air defence aircraft units, or processing and printing work on strike or maritime reconnaissance aircraft bases, and duties involve the taking of photographs together with the associated processing, enlarging and finishing skills.

Air Photography Processor 1/Photographic Processing Analyst: Those Air Photography Processors 2 selected for promotion will undergo conversion training to the trade of Air Photography Processor 1. If subsequently selected for further promotion they will undergo a second conversion course to the trade of Photographic Processing Analyst. In these trades they will develop many skills associated with management of film processing, the construction of mosaics and the control of film libraries.

Photographic Interpreter (Assistant): After basic trade training, the Photographic Interpreter (Assistant) will be employed at the Joint Air Reconnaissance Intelligence Centre (JARIC), at a Tactical Reconnaissance Intelligence Centre in the United Kingdom or Germany, or in an intelligence support post. At JARIC he would be responsible for the plotting of reconnaissance imagery, supporting the Photographic Interpreter in his task of extracting intelligence information from imagery, recording, collating and issuing intelligence materials and, should he have a talent for technical drawing, illustrating intelligence reports and producing recognition material for the use of other intelligence personnel. In the tactical reconnaissance role at a RIC he would assist the Photographic Interpreters to prepare intelligence briefing materials, target folders and target/equipment recognition materials for photographic interpreter and aircrew training. He would also be responsible for maintaining an operations board during exercises and manning the communications systems for receipt of mission reports. The Photographic Interpreter (Assistant) may also be required to deploy away from base and operate overseas in support of tactical reconnaissance aircraft. Intelligence support duties vary greatly but could include the preparation of targeting materials, assisting intelligence officers to put events on situation maps or operating intelligence support computers.

Photographic Interpreter: Personnel selected for promotion will be offered conversion training to the advanced trade of Photographic Interpreter and will be employed at locations similar to those at which assistants work. At JARIC they might be expected to take charge of sections involving photography, intelligence and map libraries, or they might become experts in interpreting the photography of a subject of particular intelligence interest. They would also be expected to give presentations to high-ranking officers on specialist intelligence subjects. In the intelligence support role they could find themselves acting as deputy to the intelligence officer, examining reports, briefing and debriefing crews or running a small section.

Photographer Ground: Photographers Ground are employed at most major RAF stations, where they carry out a wide range of work which can include copying, technical and equipment photography, illustrative and architectural work and press and public relations photography. Airmen and airwomen in this trade also work in photo-lithography and may reproduce artwork and photography for printing or operate printing, collating and binding equipment. There are few RAF activities which do not require some form of photographic service and the Photographer Ground is trained not only to take photographs but also to become proficient in processing, enlarging and finishing techniques.

Air Cartographer: The primary role of Air Cartographers is the creation and maintenance of Flight Information Publications (FLIPS), which consist of aeronautical information maps, charts and books that provide the full, accurate and up-to-date information needed to facilitate the successful planning and completion of aircraft missions. The FLIPS will provide detailed information on such things as airfields, airways, navigation aids and air traffic rules and regulations. Most of the work is carried out by No 1 AIDU, although personnel are assigned to other units in the United Kingdom and Germany.

Accounting and Secretarial

Personnel Administrator: The Personnel Administrator is tasked with the provision of full administrative support to the personnel of the RAF. Training is provided for general service procedures together with administration, service writing, key-

Above: As in all large organizations, administration personnel work behind the scenes in the Royal Air Force to keep everything in order. (RAF)

board skills and typing to a minimum speed of 20 words per minute, registry procedures, the use of filing systems, the handling of correspondence and postal procedures and a wide variety of personnel management procedures. Personnel Administrators may be employed both in the United Kingdom and overseas, normally in unit administration offices, typing pools and registries, and the positions involve much contact with other personnel. Computer procedures are an increasingly important part of the trade.

Data Analyst: The Data Analyst undertakes general recording work, the consolidation of numerical data into tabular statements and the compilation of statistical returns. Other tasks include the coding of data for computer input and the use of a VDU to input data and to interrogate the computer as well as using specialized drawing and display equipment and materials to present data in chart and graph form. Employment will normally be at a United Kingdom or overseas air base, an RAF Headquarters, the Ministry of Defence or a NATO Head-

quarters where work with research teams or statistics departments may be undertaken.

Supply

Supplier: Both airmen and airwomen may be employed as Suppliers. As specialists, they use the very latest storage methods, material handling equipment and computerized accounting techniques. The Supplier tradesman handles almost every physical item needed to make the RAF an efficient fighting service; indeed, without Suppliers the RAF would not operate as such. Within the Supply trade there are opportunities for working out of doors on fuel installations, in storage areas or in the complex agencies that deliver urgently required priority spares to the operational scene. These jobs can be either on an RAF station or in the field, working alongside the Army or with the RAF's tactical Harrier and helicopter forces. There are also jobs available in Control and Accounting offices, at the nerve centre of a station supply organization. Other large supply depots are responsible for the distribution of equipment to RAF stations around the world. Tasks undertaken by the supply organization are interesting and varied, and personnel may serve both in the United Kingdom and overseas, with opportunities to use initiative and imagination.

Safety and Surface

Survival Equipment Fitter: Maintains the safety and survival equipment used by air crew and selected airborne forces. Duties include the examination of equipment, the rectification of defects and the incorporation of modifications to life rafts, air/sea rescue equipment, life preservers, parachutes, ejection seat components and air crew flying clothing (e.g. protective flying helmets, oxygen masks, anti-g suits and pressure jerkins).

Painter and Finisher: Responsible for the removal, replacement and routine maintenance of surface finishes on aircraft, ground support equipment, mechanical transport vehicles and associated equipment. Duties include paint removal using specialist methods, surface preparation and the application of paint by brush or by pneumatic or hydraulic spraying units and may require working from platforms up to 15m in height. This trade is also involved

RAF TRADE GROUPS

Above: The Royal Air Force Regiment is a crack fighting force which exists solely to defend aircraft and bases, and its mobility allows for rapid transfer to any RAF base worldwide. (RAF)

in the manufacture and repair of aircraft interior trim, fabric covers in aircraft, balloons, upholstery and other soft material furnishings which call for the use of light and heavy sewing machines and other fabric working tools.

RAF Police

RAF Policeman: In the early stages of this career, duties will include the carrying out of security patrols within specially controlled areas, manning security control or entry points, checking and searching personnel and vehicles, maintaining physical security on airfields, crowd control, attendance at ceremonies, assisting in air transport security and the initial investigation of minor crime and breaches of security. Later, following promotion, personnel may qualify for entry into the RAF Provost and Security Services, engaging in the prevention and investigation of crime, or in counter-intelligence duties, involving investigations, surveys and the close protection of VIPs.

Dog Handlers: Dog Handlers are given full training in this skill and may be selected for specialist training in connection with the detection of drugs or searches for firearms and explosives.

Kennel Assistants: Most Kennel Assistants are employed at the Dog Training Wing of the Defence Animal Centre, where they exercise, groom, feed and attend to RAF police dogs awaiting handlers. Each Kennel Assistant is responsible for a number of dogs and must possess basic veterinary knowledge so that signs and symptoms of illness may be recognized and good standards of animal hygiene maintained. Opportunities to serve abroad are also available. All personnel serving in the RAFP are qualified to drive light vehicles.

Gunner

Gunner: Members of the RAF Regiment, Gunners will normally serve with either a Field Squadron or a Rapier Air Defence Squadron. RAF Regiment Field Squadrons are designed for one of the most difficult combat roles—to counter an enemy attack against airfields and deployed sites such as dispersed helicopter sites and to counter a terrorist attack in peacetime. The Gunner is an expert in handling most infantry weapons such as rifles, machine guns, mortars and anti-tank rockets. The Field Squadron is equipped with Land Rovers and trucks in support. The Gunner will find himself in one of the most mobile and hard-hitting fighting units of the British armed forces. One squadron is also parachute trained. The RAF Regiment's air defence squadrons are equipped with one of the world's most advanced low-level air defence missile systems—the Rapier. On these squadrons, the Gunner's main responsibility is the effective control of a missile which, at over twice the speed of sound, can destroy the fastest and deadliest aircraft an enemy can send. Not only does the Gunner deploy the system, but he also has to operate it and defend it. Rapiers provide the last line of air defence for RAF airfields. Gunners are also employed on Chinook and Puma squadrons, and they man the Queen's Colour Squadron, representing the RAF at major ceremonial occasions.

Catering

Chef: Chefs are usually employed in the kitchen of an Officers', Sergeants' or Junior Ranks' Mess. Offic-

Above: A Rapier missile battery. (F4 Aviation Photobank)

ers' and Sergeants' Messes are equivalent to civilian hotels and clubs, the Junior Ranks' Mess being similar to a large refectory, providing multi-choice, self-service meals. Some chefs will be employed in hospitals or on flight catering duties. The RAF Chef's work, although similar to that of his civilian counterpart, may cover a larger field. Opportunities exist to work as an instructor and to cater in the field, using mobile equipment to provide meals during deployments of aircraft and supporting personnel.

Steward/Mess Manager: A Steward's duties vary from station to station, but the vast majority work in Officers' and Sergeants' Messes. Junior stewards are employed in the running of dining rooms, bars and reception offices. Stewards are also employed in RAF Transit Hotels, located at United Kingdom terminal airfields, providing restaurant, bar, reception and room service. Promoted personnel may be selected for tours as a members of the crew of a Strike Command aircraft, flying worldwide. Some stewards are employed on personal duties in senior officers' residences.

Clerk Catering: This trade is similar to that of Food and Beverage Controller in the civilian catering profession. Clerks Catering are employed within catering squadrons and flights at most RAF stations in the United Kingdom and abroad. The work involves the control and operation of computerized accounting for foodstuffs and commodities used in mess kitchens. Clerks Catering are also responsible for the ordering, storage and redistribution of these food-stuffs—thus they need a working knowledge of menu planning, butchery and the storage characteristics of the foodstuffs—and for their transportation. At some RAF stations they will be involved in the compilation and supply of special types of food for issue to passengers and crews of aircraft.

Medical Trades

Pharmacy Technician: Pharmacy Technicians (PH Techs) are normally employed at RAF hospitals and large medical centres. Their duties are to manufacture and compound medicinal products, read and translate prescriptions, check prescriptions for incompatibilities and dose irregularities and dispense medicines in accordance with the prescriber's instructions, complying with all laws and regulations in force at the time, and maintain a drug and preparation information service. In addition to their dispensing duties PH Techs are required to work in medical supply departments where they obtain, account for and issue medical equipment, materials, drugs and dressings.

Environmental Health Technician: The Environmental Health Technician (EH Tech) is concerned with the living and working environment and especially with the identification, measurement, evaluation and control of all physical, chemical and biological hazards which may affect the health and well-being of the community. He also deals with environmental stresses caused by noise, chemical pollution, micro-organisms in food and water, lighting, heating, ventilation, health education and pest control. Using chemical, physical and biological techniques, he monitors both the work and the working environment and is required to make recommendations on how the hazard or stress can be controlled and the environment made safe.

Operating Theatre Technician: Complex surgical operations are carried out in RAF hospitals and Operating Theatre Technicians (OT Techs) are important members of the surgical teams involved. The RAF trains OT Techs and upon the successful completion of his course a student will be posted to a hospital in the United Kingdom or abroad. A trained OT Tech's tasks will be many and varied and will include the preparation of instrument sets and sutures required for any surgical operation; the preparation of the anaesthetic room and all equipment used in modern anaesthesia; assisting the anaesthetist; assisting the surgeon at operations when required; the preparation and management of endoscopy clinics and assisting the doctor during investigations; applying plaster casts and cast bracings in orthopaedic clinics; and working in central sterile supply departments in the preparation of all packs and instrument sets required for hospital and medical centre use.

Electrophysiological Technician: Electrophysiological Technicians (EP Techs) are trained to use and maintain many of the electronic devices employed in the diagnosis of disease in modern medicine. These include the electroencephalograph, a machine used to measure the electrical activity of the brain; the electrocardiograph, to diagnose heart disease or malfunction; the electromyograph, for assisting in the diagnosis of muscular diseases; and audiometry equipment, for the testing of hearing acuity. They are concerned not only with the diagnosis of disease but also with the selection procedures necessary for aircrew. Trainees for this trade need both a technical and academic ability and are required to acquire a certain knowledge of electronics, anatomy, physiology and allied sciences. A trained EP Tech will not only need to understand the machines he operates but also have the ability to deal sympathetically with those patients who may display apprehension when confronted with complex machinery about which they may have little understanding.

Laboratory Technician: RAF Laboratory Technicians (Lab Techs) work in well-equipped pathology laboratories in the United Kingdom and overseas. The range of tests undertaken is comparable to that encountered in National Health Service laboratories. There is a requirement for RAF Lab Techs to have a good working knowledge of all disciplines of pathology. However, after completing their training Lab Techs are expected to specialize in only one discipline. The four main areas of specialization are clinical chemistry, haematology, histology and microbiology.

Radiographer: Radiography in the RAF is a speciality dealing with the taking of x-rays for diagnostic purposes; the personnel who take and process x-rays are Radiographers and the qualified medical officers who interpret them are the Radiologists. RAF Radiographers (Radiog) students are given an insight into ultra-sound x-ray techniques during training. Qualified Radiographers serve in RAF hospitals and other medical establishments both in the United Kingdom and abroad.

Physiotherapist: The Physiotherapist (Physio) assesses, systematically, musculoskeletal and neurological disorders of function, including pain and those of psychosomatic origin, and deals with or tries to prevent these problems by natural methods based essentially on movement, manual therapy and physical agencies. This speeds the recovery of the patient to full fitness and facilitates an early return to work—which is particularly important for the aircrew and technicians of a fighting service. The work of a Physio in the RAF requires a detailed knowledge of anatomy, kinesilogy (the study of movement), electro-therapy and other subjects such as physics, chemistry and biology.

Mental Nurse: The Mental Nurse (M Nurse) is, as the name implies, a specialist member of the nursing profession who holds the recognized civilian nursing qualification and works alongside highly qualified medical officers of the RAF, including psychiatrists in RAF hospitals. In the course of his duties the M Nurse will be conversant with the specialized diagnostic procedures and with modern treatments by drug therapy, social skills and individual psychotherapy. Depending on requirements, M Nurses may be trained to be Flight Mental Nurses, following which they may act as members of aeromedical teams whose task is the special care of mental patients on aeromedical flights from abroad, or sometimes within the United Kingdom.

Medical Assistant: Personnel in the trade of Medical Assistant (Med Asst) are trained in medical secretarial, nursing and advanced first-aid skills to enable them to carry out the full range of duties necessary for employment in station medical centres within the RAF. These skills include medical documentation, medical recording, the organization of appointments for doctors' consultations and the provision of drugs and medical supplies. Most medical centres provide care twenty-four hours a day, and Med Assts can expect to work a duty roster system. In addition to carrying out routine hospital ward work they will be responsible for providing immediate care for patients outside normal working hours and for aircraft crash and ambulance duties. Generally speaking, the role of the Med Asst is to support the medical officers in their important task of looking after the health of RAF personnel and, in certain cases, their families. Depending on RAF requirements, a Med Asst may be selected for training as a flight nursing attendant, following which he may act as a member of an aeromedical team, helping to care for patients on aeromedical flights from abroad or within the United Kingdom. There are also opportunities for training as a pressure chamber operator or electrocardiograph recorder and for field hygiene duties.

Staff Nurse: The Staff Nurse works alongside highly qualified service medical officers and civilian doctors and is a valued member of the team responsible for the care of patients within RAF hospitals and medical centres. Staff Nurses may also be selected for aeromedical training, qualifying as Flight Nurses, following which they may be in charge of an aeromedical team, caring for patients returning to the United Kingdom for specialist treatment on aeromedical flights from overseas.

Dental

Dental Technician: These personnel are required to construct all types of appliances in plastic materials as well as working in alloys of gold, silver and other metals. Gold inlays are required where the more conventional tooth fillings are inadequate and crowns of gold or porcelain may be needed to restore single teeth or to form parts of dental 'bridges' to replace missing teeth. Dental Technicians also assist dental consultants working at RAF hospitals where such appliances as metal splints for fractured jaws are required.

Dental Hygienist: The Dental Hygienist's task involves the motivation and education of patients in the techniques of preventive dentistry, which includes the use of a variety of aids to oral hygiene and toothbrushing techniques relevant to each individual patient. Hygienists also apply fluoride solutions and gels to the teeth which alter the surface structure, thus making it more resistant to acid attack, and seal the pits and fissures of decay-free teeth using plastic fissure sealant materials. They also talk to groups outside the surgery, such as new recruits to the RAF, children and pregnant and nursing women, on preventive dentistry methods, including advice on diet. Surgery work includes the removal of deposits from teeth, and the polishing of exposed surfaces together with the treatment of any disease process in the mouth as directed by the Dental Officer. They also take and develop radiographs and polish fillings and they play a full role as a member of the dental team.

Dental Surgery Assistant: Dental Surgery Assistants provide a second pair of hands for the dental surgeon. They are responsible for the care and maintenance of all instruments and equipment, maintaining an adequate stock of materials, preparing fillings, maintaining records, taking and developing x-rays and making models on which dentures are constructed. They are also responsible for the cleanliness of the surgery and making patients' appointments, and for after-treatment care.

Musician

Musician: Qualified Musicians are employed exclusively on musical duties. RAF bands are in great demand both in the United Kingdom and overseas, performing a wide variety of important public engagements such as state or Royal occasions and ceremonial and concert events. These performances require a variety of musical combinations ranging from salon orchestras to massed bands, dance bands and symphonic concert bands. The range of music requires the RAF Musicians to play their primary instruments to a very high professional standard.

Fireman

Fireman: In war, aircraft may return from their missions badly damaged. If they crash on return, their crews must be saved; if possible, the multi-million pound aircraft must also be saved. To do this, amidst the problems of burning fuel and ammunition, the RAF maintains a superbly trained crash and rescue force. RAF fire-fighters also watch over RAF interests in peacetime when rare but potentially disastrous aircraft crashes do take place and threaten life. The RAF fireman is trained for combat against fire, which he must face with calmness, determination, courage and fitness, so that he may save lives. He is also trained in fire prevention and in the whole range of fire-fighting activities which take place on RAF stations.

General Service

RAF Administrative: Members of this trade specialize in discipline, general administration, drill and ceremonial duties and the training of recruits. WRAF personnel will also have responsibilities for advising on matters affecting airwomen, and the supervision of airwomen's domestic accommodation.

RAF General Duties: These personnel are employed on a wide range of tasks of a general nature. Outdoor and manual work may be required, including heavy lifting.

RAF Physical Training Instructor: These personnel may be employed on basic trade duties or as specialists. Basic Trade Duties personnel supervise sports facilities, maintain sports equipment and organize, and officiate at, sports and games events. They may also instruct at physical education classes and at specialist survival courses required by aircrew, providing basic instruction in adventure training and leading expeditions. Trade Specialist personnel work at specialist training schools as parachute jumping, adventure training or remedial instructors.

Movements

Movements Operator: The Movements Operator is employed on basic duties associated with the RAF's air and surface transport work. At an Air Movements Squadron he will be required to handle, safely and efficiently, passengers and cargo for the three services. At a surface movements unit he will work at ports and RAF units as part of the Freight Distribution Service, and his duties will include the operation of a range of cargo-handling equipment and vehicles.

Movements Controller: These personnel are responsible for the planning of aircraft loads, ensuring that aircraft are correctly loaded and advising crews on the composition of these loads. Additionally, they might operate the RAF's computerized air booking system and communications network, or supervise the transportation of explosives by road, sea and air.